Sustainable Utopias

Sustainable Utopias

THE ART AND POLITICS OF HOPE IN GERMANY

Jennifer L. Allen

HARVARD UNIVERSITY PRESS

Cambridge, Massachusetts, and London, England · 2022

Printed in the United States of America

FIRST PRINTING

Library of Congress Cataloging-in-Publication Data

Names: Allen, Jennifer L., 1984– author.
Title: Sustainable utopias : the art and politics of hope in Germany / Jennifer L. Allen.
Description: Cambridge, Massachusetts : Harvard University Press, 2022. | Includes bibliographical references and index.
Identifiers: LCCN 2021034396 | ISBN 9780674249141 (cloth)
Subjects: LCSH: Grünen (Political party) | Berliner Geschichtswerkstatt. | Green movement—Germany—History—20th century. | Utopias—Political aspects—Germany—History—20th century. | Utopias in art. | Art—Political aspects—Germany—History—20th century. | Political participation—Germany—History—20th century. | Sustainability—Germany—History—20th century.
Classification: LCC HX806 .A6833 2022 | DDC 335/.020943–dc23
LC record available at https://lccn.loc.gov/2021034396

For my mother,
who surely would have had
something to say about all this

Contents

Sustainable Utopias

Introduction

In 2013, a new political party jumped into the spotlight in Germany. It branded itself *the* alternative to the political status quo. The Alternative for Germany (*Alternative für Deutschland,* AfD) cropped up, initially, as a response to growing skepticism toward the European Union and concerns about Germany's increasing political and economic responsibilities in the wake of the 2009 Eurozone crisis. The party stood at first on a fiscally conservative Euro-skeptical platform. But that platform gradually transformed as Germany struggled to decide what stance to take toward the wave of refugees driven to Europe's borders by the Syrian civil war and other international conflicts. Germans increasingly confronted ethnic and religious minorities or at least the specter of their heightened presence. Those refugees did not look German or speak German or subscribe to German traditions, but they nevertheless hoped to benefit from Germany's robust economy, job market, and welfare system, together with its promise of peace and personal safety. All this in a country that has repeatedly declared that it is not a land of immigration.[1] AfD drew on the anxiety the influx of foreigners provoked among many German citizens and began to inject a mix of xenophobia, Islamophobia, antisemitism, racism, and ethnic nationalism into its party program.

Only seven months old by the federal elections of September 2013, the young party clocked in at 4.7% of the total vote, only a fraction of a percentage point behind Germany's Free Democrats, a long-standing fixture in the Federal Republic's postwar political constellation. At just under 5%, AfD had failed to secure enough votes to win a place in Germany's federal parliament.

What the party did win, however, was attention. Having received more than two million votes, AfD demonstrated that it had its finger on the pulse of the German electorate. And that electorate had made clear it was not getting what it wanted from Germany's political establishment.

In a video message to the voters of the southwestern German state of Baden-Württemberg ahead of its 2016 state elections, AfD's spokesperson Jörg Meuthen argued that the rigidity of the German political system had left voters without a political home. And here, to convey the severity of their political alienation from the body politic, Meuthen used the historically loaded German term *Heimat.* A word without an easy English translation, it literally means "home" but connotes a place where one feels a unique and intimate sense of belonging and identity. Meuthen argued that Germany's established parties, with their career politicians and parliamentary clout, had completely lost touch with the real will of the German people. He lumped the Christian Democrats and their partners the Christian Socialists, the Social Democrats, and the classical liberals (the Free Democrats) together with two parties traditionally seen as offering a political alternative, namely the Greens and the one influential political remnant of the East German state, the Left Party (*Die Linke*). Despite providing a laundry list of options at the polls, the German political system presented only the illusion of choice, Meuthen explained. Behind its smoke and mirrors lay an indistinguishable politics of uniformity. Co-opting a critique of parliamentary democracy that was previously the reserve of the Left, Meuthen's video message claimed that contemporary German politics offered no real alternative to the status quo. Until, of course, the birth of AfD.[2]

The party was on to something. Over the next few years, AfD climbed in the polls and catapulted into parliaments around the country. It raked in more than two hundred seats in state parliaments and, by the end of 2019, managed to secure a place as the second- or third-largest party in seven of them: Baden-Württemberg, Brandenburg, Mecklenburg-Vorpommern, Rheinland-Palatinate, Saxony, Saxony-Anhalt, and Thuringia. When it made its debut into Germany's federal parliament in 2017, it did so explosively. Pulling constituents away from the parties that have historically enjoyed national leadership, and displacing several other established parties, AfD landed as the third-largest party in the federal parliament, with nearly one hundred seats. Elections to the European Parliament in May 2019, however, gave the party its strongest victory yet. The previous European parliamentary elections in 2014 had handed AfD only seven seats. The elections in 2019 resulted in eleven. More consequently, however, it placed as the top vote-winning party in two German states (Brandenburg and Saxony), while securing the second-highest ranking position in three others (Mecklenburg-Vorpommern, Saxony-Anhalt, and Thuringia). The 2019 European parliamentary elections signaled a dramatic victory for the young party seeking to deliver hope to disaffected voters on the right of the political spectrum.

Those hoping Germany's tango with the politics of xenophobia and extreme nationalism had long ago ended recoiled at such open support for policies that suggested Germany was becoming less tolerant of difference, not more. They began to draw worried parallels between AfD and that lingering historical shadow of far right extremism in Germany, National Socialism. And amid the increasing internationalism of a growing European Union, AfD's neo-splendid isolationism clashed conspicuously against optimism cautiously harbored for the fate of the European suprastate. Around the world, journalists wrung their hands over AfD's mounting successes. *The Atlantic* celebrated Germany as a defender of Europe's democratic infrastructures over the past three-quarters of a century but asked whether the Federal Republic would simply allow all that work to crumble by playing the wrong cards in response to the rise of the far right.[3] In a postmortem of Chancellor Angela Merkel's 2018 decision to step down as head of the Christian Democratic Union, which dominated early twenty-first-century German politics for sixteen years, *The Guardian* asked about the impact of her absence against the backdrop of a resurgent far right. Though objections to Merkel's control over European politics abounded, many simultaneously also treated her looming departure as equally threatening to the stability of the continent.[4] The newspaper *Die Zeit* went even further by asking whether Germany, by failing to keep its far right in check, might in fact be on the verge of unleashing onto the continent a new era of Nazism.[5]

Just as quickly as this apocalyptic thinking started to take hold, however, a counteroffensive gained steam. As AfD clinched an increasingly secure position within the German political landscape and stoked panic on the left, voters began to indicate where they saw a worthy opponent capable of providing a radical leftist alternative program for Germany's future. In nearly three-quarters of the next round of state elections held after AfD's 2017 success, voters handed the German Green Party a comfortable position in state parliaments: it was the third-largest party in Bremen, Lower Saxony, and Rhineland-Palatinate; the second-largest in Bavaria, Hessen, and Hamburg; and the largest in Baden-Württemberg. The Greens enjoyed an even more impressive showing in the May 2019 European parliamentary elections, in which they became the largest or second-largest party in nine of Germany's sixteen states. Along any metrics, these were successful returns. They stood out even more against the Greens' recent record. In the 2014 European elections, for example, the Greens never came in better than third anywhere in the Federal Republic, and their percentages of votes had declined almost across the board. And in Germany's 2017 federal elections, the party sank to a dispiriting sixth place with less than a tenth of the vote, which gave them the fewest seats of any party represented in the Bundestag. The year 2019 stood as an abrupt about-face for the Greens. *The Washington Post* dubbed them the new kingmakers in both Germany and Europe.[6]

At a moment of increasing attention to climate change and scrutiny of climate policy, these Green victories have invited an obvious explanation: the party has owed these successes to the urgency of mitigating climate change. The Greens have said as much themselves.[7] Without downplaying the gravity of looming environmental catastrophe, however, this rationale can only explain so much, especially when most major parties have already embraced environmentalism as a necessary component of their political programs, if perhaps without the same enthusiasm as the Greens. The commitment to fighting climate change also fails to explain the Greens' appeal in a Germany facing increasingly strong activism from the right. AfD has made no mystery of its skepticism toward climate science.[8] But combatting right extremism in Germany will require far more than implementing carbon taxes and increasing the use of renewable energy. So, what really explains this newfound affinity for Green politics?

As a vision for an ethno-nationalist utopia has come into focus on the right, the Greens have drawn on their history of championing programs for a superlative leftist future to supercharge their appeal. More than a one-dimensional environmentalist party, the Greens long counted among a school of new utopians in the late twentieth century intent on offering Germany radical alternatives to the present. This book is about those alternatives. It's about who conceived of them, when, and how. It's about the resilient and adaptable human capacity to imagine a superlative future, even when many insisted on its impossibility, and about the continued malleability of the concept of utopia itself.

The Melancholy of Anti-Utopianism

In some regards, a history of late twentieth-century utopianism fits neatly into histories of the twentieth century. Political theorist Susan Buck-Morss has argued that efforts to realize utopian projects on a mass scale enjoyed pride of place as the "dream of the twentieth century."[9] Though the content of this dream varied geographically and chronologically, twentieth-century Europe nevertheless shared a commitment to pursuing sweeping revisions to the structure and function of society. Europeans harbored both an optimism that the future could thoroughly improve the quality of human existence and a will to pursue that future. Their aspirations assumed as their object the totality of modern life—political, cultural, social, and economic. And they refused to relegate those aspirations to the realm of the conceptual. Instead, they endowed their ideas with the power to transform both the natural and the built world.

In other ways, however, a history of late twentieth-century utopianism appears incompatible with histories of the twentieth century, which proved as effective at destroying its dreamworlds as it did at initially conjuring them. Twentieth-century dreams became dangerous when the passions behind them were mobilized instrumentally and turned against precisely those masses they were originally intended to benefit. Even the century's most promising utopian projects—the elimination of political oppression through mass sovereignty, the elimination of material poverty through mass production, the cultivation of the creative capacities of society through mass culture—have had darker consequences. The pursuit of mass sovereignty led to bellicose nationalism; mass production to human and ecological exploitation; and mass culture to the anaesthetization of its consumers.[10]

By most accounts written after the collapse of the twentieth century's massive social engineering projects, utopia had become a hazardous idea with two equally bad faces. It stood for a naïve idealism represented in the golden chamber pots of Thomas More's imagined island of Utopia or the lemonade oceans and anti-lions of Charles Fourier's Harmony. But it also implied dangerous engineering of the sort that attracted Hitler and Stalin. Drawing momentum from a homophonic pun that links the Greek word for "no place" [*οὐ-τόπος*] with another meaning "good place" [*εὖ-τόπος*], utopian projects have typically prioritized this idealized place as a destination or an object of pursuit. So strong is the magnetism of the utopian object that it can subordinate the pursuit itself. The effect of this ends-oriented tunnel vision is the ability to use utopianism to legitimate horrific means like the concentration camps or gulags.

Utopia's Janus face led postwar intellectuals largely to abandon it. They participated in a protracted slash-and-burn campaign against the most ambitious visions proffered in the West, often yoking arguments for the end of utopia to arguments for the collapse of modernism, socialism, ideology, even history itself.[11] Already in the 1950s, American political theorist Judith Shklar augured this turn. She pointed to Romanticism's early nineteenth-century challenge to the optimism of the Enlightenment as the beginning of the downward spiral of Western political philosophy. Of the promises of Western liberal democracy, Shklar wrote cynically that "we know too little to feel justified in social despair," but "we know too much to fall into even the slightest utopianism."[12] Writing contemporaneously with Shklar, historian H. Stuart Hughes similarly assessed the mood of leftist European intellectuals, who realized to their shock that they preferred the pragmatism of capitalism to the idealism of communism.[13] Only a few years later, in 1960, sociologist Daniel Bell pronounced the end of ideology. The revolutionary impulses of Western radical intellectuals, which for a century and a half had transformed Western societies by propelling them to seek radical social and political alternatives, had reached, in Bell's words, "a dead end."[14]

With the collapse of state socialism in the East, the "bright hopes" invested in the century's major social and political projects—from national self-determination to internationalist socialism—disclosed themselves, in practice, as "dark tragedies."[15] The politically cataclysmic year of 1989 and the subsequent collapse of the Soviet Union appeared to confirm, according to historian Russell Jacoby, that "radicalism and the utopian spirit that sustains it . . . [had] ceased to be major political or even intellectual forces."[16] Western liberalism and advanced capitalism had prevailed over "really existing socialism." Their victory over the revolutionary potential of Marxism drove what seemed like the last nail into the coffin of ideological alternatives. The modern democratic project—that expansive social project that pursued political, personal, and material satisfaction for the whole of society—deflated when history reneged on the promises of socialism, and the oligarchies of advanced capitalism tightened their grip on both society and nature.

Writing as the dust settled from the fall of the Berlin Wall, the conservative German historian Joachim Fest declared a crisis of utopianism.[17] American political scientist Francis Fukuyama echoed Fest, arguing that the global victory of liberal democracy had finally punctuated the long sentence of humanity's political development.[18] Conservative British prime minister Margaret Thatcher bundled these ideas neatly in her pronouncement that "there is no alternative" to liberal democracy and free market capitalism. Though consumer culture continued to operate for some as a kind of personal utopia—it fulfilled the consumer's material if not intellectual, social, or emotional needs—it led to political cynicism, to disillusionment that it was "no longer thought necessary to guarantee to the collective that which [was] pursued by the individual."[19] Samuel Moyn has identified a last frontier of twentieth-century utopianism in the moral utopia of human rights. But the human rights movement has also faced the difficult challenge of defining "the good life" in a manner that transcended politics. "Ill-equipped by the fact of [its] suprapolitical birth," Moyn argues, it struggled to put forth a program for its realization.[20]

By the late twentieth century, then, what remained of political and social creativity appeared to give way to weariness, resignation, and withdrawal. A disgruntled coalition of Western scholars and public intellectuals had succumbed to a melancholy of anti-utopianism. They retreated into a conceptual paradigm that one Hungarian Marxist nearly seventy years earlier presciently called the romanticism of disillusionment.[21] Deep in the belly of liberal democracy and advanced capitalism, they gave themselves over to the allure of a myth of endings, believing they faced only the uninspiring choice "between the status quo or something worse. Other alternatives," Jacoby has argued flatly, "do not seem to exist." The politics of radical transformation showed itself to be a political illusion, having proved reliable only in running roughshod over Europe in the previous three quarters of a century. Anyone who still clings to utopian hopes today, per Jacoby, "is widely considered out to lunch or out to kill."[22] As the century drew to a close, utopian thinking appeared decidedly on the defensive, indeed, almost inconceivable.

Blueprints for a New Optimism: The 1960s

Writing at the same time as Fest and Fukuyama and at the tail end of Thatcher's reign, German historian Lutz Niethammer chronicled the Western obsession with the end of history in *Posthistoire.* He ended his book on a more sanguine note than his contemporaries, suggesting that the discourse of the end of history stood simply as a "disenchanted postscript to the nineteenth-century philosophy of history." He insisted on the possibility of a new paradigm capable of resisting the allure and melodrama of the ending myth. Niethammer conceived of a mode of historical writing capable of "[dispensing] with its ideal of greatness and power" and placing "the traditional hierarchy of historical tasks 'the right side up'" in a practice he and others called "history from below." According to Niethammer, this way of thinking about the past would allow its practitioners to "arrive at a realistic assessment of the space for action within and against existing social structures."[23] History from below was, in short, capable of realizing a radical ethical alternative. Niethammer published this argument in 1989. His optimism, though, likely stemmed from his socialization during the Student Movement of the 1960s. Though Niethammer himself was no left radical, he nevertheless learned about both the importance and the possibility of abolishing outdated systems while he was a university student and then a young professor in the Left scene of the 1960s and 1970s.[24]

Amid the twentieth century's powerful postwar anti-utopianism, the New Left and the revolutionary moment of the 1960s initiated an equally powerful effort to resist this pessimism. Activists and intellectuals in the West deemed the discourse of the end of ideology insufficiently critical and thus premature.[25] They were driven by a deep desire to build what historian Norbert Frei, channeling philosopher Ernst Bloch, has described as the "concrete utopia of a new society."[26] Though the precise features of that new society remained, to many, frustratingly vague, the investments of the alternative milieu of the 1960s and early 1970s tended to coalesce around a collection of themes. As historian Gerd-Rainer Horn has underscored in his study of the "Spirit of '68," activists devoted themselves to "the promotion of anti-hierarchical, anti-institutional, and anti-bureaucratic means and goals. Self-determination and self-management in all walks of life was their ultimate aim."[27] Embracing Herbert Marcuse's call for a "Great Refusal," the alternative milieu came to understand its brand of antiauthoritarianism as a challenge to autocracy and oppression as well as a way to emancipate the individual.[28]

Tony Judt has dubbed the 1960s "the great age of Theory."[29] But the activists of the 1960s and 1970s—let's call them "68ers" for the way their values congealed in 1968's "short summer of utopia"—paired their brains with brawn.[30] They tied their critique of society to an imperative of action, attempting not only to revive hope for utopian programs but also to put those hopes into practice. An early participant in the women's liberation movement, sociologist Wini Breines has emphasized that the central task of 1960s radicalism was "to create and sustain within the live practice of the movement, relationships and political forms that 'prefigured' and embodied the desired society." Breines called the 68ers' urge to live their values, rather than simply fight for them, "prefigurative politics."[31] Their efforts to rebuild a better world involved a kind of creative destruction, in which remaking the present involved, first, an act of dismantling it. Activists attempted to dismantle a technocratic political system by mobilizing a robust extraparliamentary opposition. They attempted to dismantle a global military-industrial complex together with what they understood as a kind of political imperialism by protesting the war in Vietnam. They attempted to dismantle an exclusive and rigid system of education by reenvisioning the way universities operate. They attempted to dismantle restrictive lifestyle expectations and sexual norms by creating communes. They attempted to dismantle the trappings of capitalism like private property by squatting.[32] In short, the alternative milieu pursued systems of critical self-management in nearly all areas of modern life that appeared, as one participant suggested, as a "working utopia."[33]

This embrace of the language of utopia by the 68ers was conscious and willful but also conceptually careful. In July 1967 at the Free University in Berlin, the intellectual beacon of the Student Movement, Herbert Marcuse, gave a lecture on "the end of utopia."[34] But as Wolfgang Kraushaar—both a participant in and, later, a distinguished historian of West Germany's Student Movement—has highlighted, Marcuse did not speak of an end "because he had abandoned his political hopes. Quite the opposite, he saw within the development of capitalism the existence of a social prerequisite for the concretization of utopia."[35] Here, however, Marcuse played with the meaning of utopia. He pointed to those projects of radical social transformation that society called "utopian" in order to discredit. With the language of the "end of utopia," Marcuse announced the collapse of "those ideas and theories that use the concept of utopia to denounce certain socio-historical possibilities."[36] He revisited an interpretation from sociologist Karl Mannheim, who understood utopias as a form of radical subversion. To those who rule, Mannheim argued in 1929, utopia appears as "all conceptions of existence which *from their point of view* can in principle never be realized." Utopia could be identified only retrospectively as its subversive practices overturned the worldview that proclaimed its impossibility.[37] Marcuse harbored considerable optimism for such subversive possibilities latent in the world the Student Movement inhabited. "All the material and intellectual forces which could be put to work for the realization of a free society," he argued, "are at hand." Blame for the failure to achieve such freedom lay with what Marcuse described as "the total mobilization of existing society against its own potential for liberation."[38] Reserving the term "utopia" for those proposals for social transformation that are not possible because they contradict established scientific laws—the pursuit of eternal youth, for example—Marcuse resisted applying the label to the 68ers' ambitions. "Precisely because the so-called utopian possibilities are not at all utopian," he explained,

> but rather the determinate socio-historical negation of what exists, a very real and very pragmatic opposition is required of us if we are to make ourselves and others conscious of these possibilities and the forces that hinder and deny them. An opposition is required that is free of all illusion but also of all defeatism, for through its mere existence defeatism betrays the possibility of freedom to the status quo.[39]

The term "utopia" had become a popular slur designed to do damage to efforts to effect radical social change, even when society already enjoyed the conditions of possibility necessary to bring about those changes. Rather than a rejection of the possibility of radical transformation itself, Marcuse's announcement of the "end of utopia" in fact signaled his refusal to tolerate society's resistance to that transformation.

Others used the concept of utopia with less compunction. Writing of her experience of the alternative milieu, Breines explained that "the 1960s changed our lives because movement politics promised utopia; we believed that we could achieve an egalitarian, free, and participatory society. And, immodestly, we thought that we glimpsed its beginnings in our own political activity."[40] The leftist journal and key mouthpiece of the 68ers, *Kursbuch*, made this belief in the achievability of utopian ambitions explicit when its editors opened the 1968 calendar year with an article titled "An Idea for the Future [*Ein Gedanke für die Zukunft*]," in which they offered a prize of DM 1000 for the best proposal for a "concrete utopia."[41] Kraushaar has identified the competition as a response to those who criticized the 68ers for their inability to put forth "a concrete program for a viable alternative" to existing society and for their preference to dwell at the level of abstraction.[42]

Such critics were plentiful, and the 68ers' methods made them easy targets. It often remained unclear, Kraushaar has noted, how the economy would operate in the newly liberated world activists aimed to create, for example. It remained unclear how that world could guarantee the freedom of the individual and avoid becoming a regime of injustice (*Unrechtsregime*). In their vagueness, 1960s activists had become adherents of a "political romanticism," charged the editor of the newspaper *Die Zeit* in 1968, one "that shoots for the moon in order to improve an always imperfect present [*Wirklichkeit*] and that fails to recognize how it ruins this actuality in the process. We've really had enough," she argued pointedly.[43]

Scholarship on the 68ers' ambitions has been more generous than many of their contemporary critics. Though historians frequently apply the label "utopian" to the projects of radical social transformation pursued by 1960s activists, it rarely appears as a slur in the manner Marcuse observed. Historian Martin Klimke, who has analyzed the transnational networks of the 1960s, together with linguist Joachim Scharloth stressed that "the late 1960s rocked the self-evident factualness of the traditional social order, transforming it into an object of reflection. The direct actions they employed created new ways of perceiving social inequality and power relationships and anticipated a new and utopian social order."[44] Historian of the global sixties Timothy Scott Brown has argued similarly by highlighting the "centrality of this utopian urge" to the culture of the sixties. Activists "insisted on the utopian possibility in the present" as a means of revealing "what had been lost in much of what remained of the so-called Old Left and what was central to the New Left: the possibility of a creative utopia free of hierarchy, bureaucracy, and lies."[45] Contrary to Marcuse's worry and Mannheim's analysis, in other words, most specialists on the 1960s have not used the language of utopia to diminish the ambitions or achievements of the decade's activists.[46] These readings of the radical promises of the 1960s and early 1970s also help to underscore the invaluable foundations for later utopian thought and practice that the activists of this period created, despite their failures.

But the flame of 1960s utopianism would not burn eternally. Historians have pinned the end of what they have dubbed the "Long 1960s" on the political, economic, social, and cultural crises that took root beginning in the 1970s: the end of the explosion of postwar economic growth, the correlate end of the expansion of the welfare state, and the rise of neoliberalism; the oil crisis of 1973, or even 1979, and the burgeoning environmental and energy anxieties that accompanied it; the transition between classical industrial and postindustrial society; the collapse of student radicalism and a floundering commitment to the participatory democracy trumpeted by 1960s activists; the arrival of a wave of homegrown terrorism; shifting patterns of consumption.[47] The precise historical hinges on which these analyses rest their weight vary, but each boils down to the claim that global circumstances foreclosed further pursuit of the possibilities born of 1960s optimism.[48]

In the context of this developing sense of crisis over the 1970s, Leftist utopian undertakings began to lose steam as they diverged along two troublesome paths. In some cases, the lodestars of 1960s led not to radical redesigns of society but to the violence of far left militancy. Academics and public intellectuals of the Left watched in frustration as the Red Army Faction replaced Rudi Dutschke, as teach-ins gave way to terror. In other cases, proposals from the 1960s merely revealed themselves as dissatisfyingly piecemeal reform, to use the language of Karl Popper, rather than as utopian blueprints for large-scale social transformation.[49] If the 1960s offered a kind of utopian revivalism, it was short-lived. Some have argued that radicalism after the Long 1960s came, at best, in quotation marks, or as what Pierre Bourdieu called "a cult of transgression without risk."[50] Others were content to write off utopias entirely after the floundering of 1960s radicalism. The success of the reform-oriented New Social Movements beginning in the 1970s helped this process along as the environmental movement, the women's movement, the peace movement, and the anti-nuclear movement, among others, achieved incremental successes. Though many considered these changes long overdue, few would label them utopian.

For others, however, the experiments of the 1960s only whet their appetites for the possibility of radical change occasioned from below. The West German state itself—and the Social Democratic Party (SPD) in particular—did its part, however inadvertently, to open up space for Germans to imagine alternatives. As the state tightened its grip over society amid the violence of the German Autumn, a sense of alienation from politics took hold. In an effort to combat this situation, historian Geoff Eley has argued, the Alternative Movement embraced many of "1968's countercultural values in a politicizing of everyday life."[51] They once again called out latent authoritarian tendencies in politics and society. They once again demanded participatory forms of democracy that challenged outmoded institutions. They once again pushed to build new subjectivities that inhabited the world guided by the leitmotif of "authenticity."[52] And they once again advocated for gender equity, this time via the elevation of women to positions of power. As Paul Berman has argued, the utopian experimentation of the 1960s stood as a rehearsal for the utopianism that would resurface two decades later at the end of the Cold War.[53]

A New Kind of Utopianism

The late twentieth century witnessed a growing faith in the possibility of overturning established institutions and implementing in their place superlative ones. At first muffled behind the din of an elegizing chorus that announced the end of ideology, history, and utopian ambitions, West Germans from a range of circumstances began to resist the temptation of ending myths and to speak out in support of radical new programs for Germany's future. These grassroots activists—generally participants in a left-liberal milieu—found themselves willing to consider that the concept of utopia might be capable of assuming a form different from that of the utopian ideas that had reigned in Europe since the nineteenth century. In this regard, they enjoyed good company. Europeans had fundamentally reconceptualized utopia once before, when they abandoned the tendency to think of utopias in spatial terms. Until the early nineteenth century, "utopia" had represented a place beyond the known world but still one capable of existing in the present. In the wake of the Enlightenment, however, Europeans increasingly ascribed a temporal, rather than a spatial, element to their utopias, such that a "utopia" became an idea not yet realized but capable of being realized at some point in the future under the right conditions.[54]

This temporal interpretation of utopia dominated until the late twentieth century, when a motley crew of academics, public intellectuals, and ordinary people began to pull back on the reins of anti-utopian melancholy by reimagining utopia's conceptual parameters once more. Beginning in the late 1970s, a scattered collection of unconventional approaches to utopian imagination developed into a wave of utopian revisionism. Although an affinity for this revisionism now spans the globe, it has important roots in West Germany. Initially via small countercultural circles, West Germans reassessed both the topography and temporality of utopianism. In contrast to the totalizing social engineering projects, whose bloody impossibility the twentieth century so thoroughly revealed, the utopian revisionists refused to take as their object society as a whole. Instead, they sought to enact modest but concrete instances of radical equality, peace, and justice in finite segments of society. They also began to imagine that utopia might have a different relationship to time. The exhaustion of grand utopias had discredited sweeping prescriptive visions for a static dream deferred—that is, utopias that did not exist in the present but that might exist someday in the future, absolutely and all at once. These new utopian revisionists adopted as their telos precisely the act of working toward. A superlative future, they argued, was realizable only through ongoing micro-attempts to approximate this superlative future in the present. At the heart of revisionist utopias thus lay a radical micro-practice. These new utopians engaged ordinary people in the act of collectively repeating a small behavior with a wildly ambitious aim. These micro-repetitions played out hundreds or thousands of times every day. Though small-scale, these programs were nonetheless utopian in that they proposed a normative agenda that would result in the best of all possible outcomes in their area of influence both in the present and for the future.

The notion of a modest, practical utopia would seem a paradox. A range of scholars writing in the first decade of the twenty-first century, however, have argued to the contrary. Among the vocal proponents of such an interpretive move is historian Jay Winter, who has written against the "very fashionable tendency" to treat any "notion of a different kind of international order, or an alternative vision of society . . . as the stuff of children or madmen." As a counterbalance to this trend, he has advocated investigating the "visionary temperament" of those who engage in the work of imagining viable alternatives for the world and whose work is illuminating, even should it fail. Winter separates from the "major utopias" of National Socialism and the Soviet Union, both of which left a mountain of victims in their wake, what he calls "minor utopias." Characteristic of minor utopias is their simultaneous use of a language of universalism in their efforts to transform society while also embracing "a particular ideology, the interests and outlook of discrete social and political formations." Minor utopian projects, Winter has suggested, "aim not at the total eradication of social conflict or the construction of an ideal city, but at partial transformations, steps on the way to a less violent and unjust society." He counts among these minor utopian projects the 1937 Paris Exposition (*Exposition Internationale des Arts et Techniques dans la Vie Moderne*), the creation of the Universal Declaration of Human Rights in 1948, and the vision of "globalization-from-below" after the collapse of the Soviet Union. These projects differ from the standard utopian exemplars of the twentieth century in that they could not be implemented through either "political thuggery or political compromise." In other words, they were neither totalitarian nor merely reformist.[55]

Sociologist Erik Olin Wright took a similar tack when he analyzed the possibility of what he termed "real utopias." Acknowledging the ostensible contradiction in terms, he notes that "nurturing clear-sighted understandings of what it would take to create social institutions free of oppression is part of creating a political will for radical social change to reduce oppression. A vital belief in a utopian ideal may be necessary to motivate people to set off on the journey from the status quo in the first place." Utopian abstractions risk leading an optimistic humanity into the lion's den of resignation. Instead, Wright suggests that society should set off in pursuit of "utopian ideals that are grounded in the real potentials of humanity, utopian destinations that have accessible way stations, utopian designs of institutions that can inform our practical tasks of navigating a world of imperfect conditions for social change." This is what he meant by the "realness" of real utopias. He admits that "the likely destination may fall short of the utopian ideal." Still, he argues that "the best we can do is treat the struggle to move forward on the pathways of social empowerment as an experimental process in which we continually test and retest the limits of possibility and try, as best we can, to create new institutions which will expand those limits themselves. In doing so we not only envision real utopias, but contribute to making utopias real."[56] As (quite disparate) examples of initiatives that engage in these kinds of practices, he volunteered the project of implementing a universal basic income, bottom-up or participatory municipal budgeting efforts, the worker-owned cooperatives of the Mondragon conglomerate in Spain, and the popularly sourced internet encyclopedia Wikipedia.

Others have taken up this mantle as well, with differences mostly in vocabulary. Sociologist Dennis Soron has highlighted the writing of journalist Daniel Singer, who rejected the "reactionary common sense of the 'post-socialist' era, whose gore-drenched images of misfired communist utopianism serve 'obvious political purposes—to frighten people, to warn them that any radical resistance, any serious search for change, is bound to end in a bloodbath.'"[57] Against this trend, Singer argued that intentional radical change remained a possibility, one he called a "realistic utopia," realistic in that

> it must manifest itself in present struggles, and must be tempered by an awareness of the necessarily slow and complicated nature of social transformation. At one level, this means that the utopian aspirations of the left must not ride on the impossible prospect of a total and instantaneous revolutionary transformation of existing society. At another level, it means that would-be revolutionaries cannot endlessly defer their own utopian goals, but must strive to realize them in their ongoing practices and social relationships, such that "the instrument of the present should somehow prefigure, foreshadow the future."[58]

Realistic utopias, Singer argued, must remain flexible, operating "as a draft, a provisional guide, which will be amended, improved, and broadened as the movement advances, drawing lessons from its struggles."[59] Another scholar has similarly advocated for the cultivation of a culture of contestation around alternative plans for the future and chose, instead, to call this social positioning a "critical utopia."[60] A group of anthropologists has called for projects that both aim for an ideal destination and designate a path toward it that traverses "real places, embodied by living people" who are informed by an actual past and whose interrelationship is maintained by quotidian interactions. They have dubbed these "grounded utopias."[61]

At the heart of many such revisionist utopias lies an immanent practical component. These are utopias not of ends but of means. Their programs do not deal with the construction of castles in the sky, static places that one builds once and for all time. Rather, they embrace as their telos ongoing action. As Geoff Eley has explained, these utopias possess an "impulse or kind of subjectivity, whose active presence is an essential ingredient for any reformism aspiring to popular resonance or staying-power—as a kind of longing, a dreaming of what might be, a necessary imagining, a credo of possibility, a willingness to think beyond."[62] Such projects operate as what one scholar described as "Utopia in the becoming" that understand themselves "not as a state to be realized but as a movement toward."[63]

Strange though an immanent practical utopia might sound, the logic that undergirds it had, by the late twentieth century, already begun to find expression in the concept of environmental sustainability. The idea of sustainability as we understand it contemporarily had come into vogue only in the 1980s.[64] Sustainability sets as its project for the world not a "fixed state of harmony, but rather a process of change in which the exploitation of resources, the direction of investments, the orientation of technological development, and institutional change are made consistent with future as well as present needs."[65] Sustainability is a program rooted simultaneously in both present and future practices, and its practices must be both enduring and adaptable. Despite the plethora of vocabulary already available to describe the late twentieth century's new utopianism, I prefer to call its products "sustainable utopias," given their practical affinities with the project of sustainability.

The Kohl Years: A Perfect Storm

This book charts the development of this concept of a "sustainable utopia" on the ground in West Germany from the moment of its conceptual possibility in the late 1970s through various—and varyingly fitful—attempts to realize it over the subsequent decades. Its narrative ramps up in the early 1980s, a decade that leading scholar of German contemporary history Andreas Wirsching has described as a "decade of social protest [*Dekade des gesellschaftlichen Protests*]," for the way West Germans once again found themselves dissatisfied with the status quo—political, social, cultural, and economic—and once again collectively pushed to refashion their world to address their concerns.[66] German historian Jenny Wüstenberg has called the 1980s "the pivotal decade," for its role in placing history and memory at the center of West German political consciousness.[67] One could also call the 1980s the decade of Helmut Kohl, who towered over German politics and society as chancellor of the Federal Republic from 1982 to 1998. Kohl's tenure as chancellor forms the rough backdrop to this book. He himself surfaces only infrequently in its chapters, but his profound influence over West German culture conditioned the very possibility of the vignettes the book examines.

Historians have filled library shelves with studies of Kohl's policies.[68] Those policies rested on Kohl's assessment that the prior thirteen years of Social Democratic governance had put the Federal Republic in a precarious economic, social, intellectual, and international position. He launched his chancellorship by insisting that the Federal Republic embark on a "spiritual-moral transformation [*geistig-moralische Wende*]" based on the recently adopted 1978 party program of the Christian Democratic Union (CDU). The CDU's "program of urgency [*Dringlichkeitsprogramm*]" aimed to walk back Social Democratic policies and substitute in their place a buttressed set of conservative values. "Out with more state, in with more market," Kohl demanded, "out with collective burdens, in with personal achievement; out with fossilized structures, in with greater movement, personal initiative, and strengthened competitiveness."[69] Historical sociologist Jeffrey Olick, however, has come down rather critically on the legacies of this aspect of Kohl's leadership, suggesting that Kohl's "neoconservative agenda ended up affecting few momentous changes in concrete policy areas." Instead, Olick joins a current in recent scholarship that argues that the beating heart of Kohl's *Wende* lay, in fact, in his cultural politics.[70]

Kohl intended that his new conservatism would inaugurate in the Federal Republic a process of renewal. Such an act of remaking made sense in the context of a growing consensus that West Germany had begun to depart from its status as a provisional state, which it had occupied since its 1949 Basic Law enshrined the anticipation of reunification in Article 146.[71] Kohl possessed a keen awareness that this shifting self-conception opened up space for Germans to think more seriously about the Federal Republic as a state with its own history. And in contrast to his predecessor, Helmut Schmidt, Kohl—a professionally trained historian—sought to prioritize government engagement with that history.[72] Already in October 1982 in a declaration of his government's policies and values (*Regierungserklärung*) delivered less than two weeks after assuming office, Kohl tied the CDU's "politics of renewal [*Politik der Erneuerung*]" to a new "reflection [*Besinnung*] on German history."[73]

Historians tend to stress the influence of Kohl's generational position on this stance.[74] Born in 1930, Kohl joined a generation of Germans too young to have participated actively in the Nazi regime but old enough to have strong memories of life under National Socialism and of the war that left them inclined to read everything in political terms.[75] They go by many names. The midcentury German sociologist Helmut Schelsky called them the "skeptical generation," for their tendency toward skepticism of political extremism.[76] Historian Dirk Moses has called them the "Forty-Fivers" on account of the radical remapping of their ideological system brought about by the collapse of National Socialism that year.[77] Kohl himself, speaking to the Israeli Knesset in 1984, described his generation as the first to have enjoyed the "blessing of a late birth [*Gnade der späten Geburt*, though *Gnade* could also be translated as "mercy"]."[78]

This generation occupied itself with the project of forging for West Germany a new, explicitly national postwar identity. Deeply influential in this project was the peculiarity among German intellectuals, Jan-Werner Müller has underscored, to insist upon "[changing] perceptions of the past if they seek to alter Germany's self-perception in the present." That tendency primed them to turn to history to legitimize that new national identity.[79] And in this context, Kohl set his sights on a particular version of German history. He sought to promote what Andreas Wirsching has described as a "historical balance [*Geschichtsbalance*]," refusing to allow the darkness of National Socialism to overshadow the richness of Germany's longer history.[80] Kohl aimed to give ample attention to Germany's historical "high points."[81]

The chancellor's pursuit of historical balance—and both the popular awareness and the controversies it helped generate—occasioned an explosion of historical engagement in the Federal Republic. Some of this work brought conspicuous and intentional changes to Germany's landscape of historical institutions. Already in the first year of his chancellorship, Kohl himself commissioned a central memorial (*Zentrale Gedenkstätte*) for the Federal Republic, originally planned for the West German capital of Bonn, and the construction of two new national historical museums. Kohl intended the museums—the German Historical Museum (*Deutsches Historisches Museum*, DHM) in Berlin and the House of History of the Federal Republic (*Haus der Geschichte der Bundesrepublik*) in Bonn—to assemble the most fascinating objects and stories from Germany's history. Both museums were to undertake an act of historical contextualization: they would situate the history of Nazism in terms of Germany's longer, richer past as well as the history of the Federal Republic in terms of German division.[82] Together, these two museums would fashion a new image for a new Germany by crafting a narrative that would help Germans understand who they were and where they were headed, both as Germans and as Europeans.[83]

The chancellor's investments did not shape only German institutions. Historian Jacob Eder has examined Kohl's heavy hand in shaping similar cultural-political projects internationally, especially in the United States. The chancellor played a key role, for example, in the founding of the German Historical Institute in Washington, DC, in 1987 and in the creation of the three Centers of Excellence for German Studies at Harvard University, the University of California Berkeley, and Georgetown University at the end of the decade. Each of these initiatives, Kohl believed, would advance an appreciation of German history that looked beyond its Nazi past. But the chancellor did not offer universal support for international projects that engaged German history. His abiding concern with West Germany's global image and his government's fear of initiatives that might threaten the Federal Republic's standing as a reliable player in a Western alliance guided Kohl's cultural interventions abroad. He strongly opposed the creation of the US Holocaust Memorial Museum in Washington, DC, for example, based on the worry that it would reduce German history, in American eyes, to the history of the Holocaust.[84]

With a history as weighty and complex as that of National Socialism, and the Federal Republic a hotbed of historical and commemorative activity, Kohl's administration was bound to stumble into cultural-political contention at some point. Some controversies were of his administration's own making. The commemorative debacle of President Ronald Reagan's proposed visit to West Germany in 1985 greased the wheels. Though both US and West German governments intended the visit to honor the fallen soldiers of World War II and to cement a strong relationship between the two countries, the Kohl administration's choice of Bitburg's Kolmeshöhe cemetery grew incendiary as revelations that the site held graves of Waffen-SS members made their way into the press. The choice of sites seemed to erase distinctions between Nazi war dead and victims of Nazi brutality. With no easy options to change course midstream, the two administrations went ahead with the event. Just six years after the extraordinarily popular television miniseries *Holocaust* brought conversations about the Holocaust into German living rooms, the Bitburg debacle upped the ante. It unleashed a public "debate over the hitherto undebatable," Charles Maier has argued.[85]

Such debates over the history and legacies of National Socialism became a conspicuous feature of the regime. Beginning in 1986, some of the Federal Republic's most prominent historians and public intellectuals took to the pages of major newspapers to engage in what Jan-Werner Müller has deemed "*the* major national self-interrogation about historical responsibility and national consciousness of the 1970s and 1980s." Those who participated in the Historians' Quarrel (*Historikerstreit*), which ran through 1989, tussled over fundamental interpretive questions concerning National Socialism: questions about the singularity of the Holocaust, about causality and the role of Stalin's political project, about German victimhood, and about the modernizing influence of the Third Reich.[86] At its core, it became a disagreement over whether ongoing discussions of the legacies of National Socialism had overstayed their welcome in Germany.[87] As such, Müller has argued that "what was at stake was not so much historical knowledge as the Federal Republic's present self-conceptualization."[88]

The later years of Kohl's chancellorship featured two additional historical quarrels. One brewed over a traveling exhibit coordinated by the Hamburg Institute for Social Research on the crimes of the German army—the *Wehrmacht*—between 1941 and 1944. The Wehrmacht exhibit, whose first installation ran from 1995 to 1999, challenged the "myth of a clean *Wehrmacht*" by displaying the ways members of Germany's ordinary military, not just the SS, engaged in criminal behavior in the East. Like the *Historikerstreit*, the debate about the Wehrmacht exhibit played out largely in the press and constituted what historian Christina Morina has called "one of the most important postunification historical debates in Germany."[89] A year after the launch of the Wehrmacht exhibit, another debate gained steam, this time over a book fresh off the presses by the young historian Daniel Goldhagen. *Hitler's Willing Executioners* made a splash in Germany.[90] Published in response to historian Christopher Browning's influential monograph *Ordinary Men,* which highlighted the confluence of circumstance and ideology that led the titular ordinary German men to become brutal killers in the East during the Second World War, Goldhagen took a different tack.[91] He argued that a deep-seated and abiding eliminationist antisemitism in German society convinced ordinary Germans of the necessity of annihilating the Jewish people.[92] Even before the translation appeared, it unleashed a virulent debate in the Federal Republic, carried out heavily in the press but complemented by public discussions and a book tour.[93] On one side stood a receptive audience of journalists and the German public, especially younger Germans. In a rebuttal of the notion that their late births should absolve them from confronting the dark legacies of the Holocaust, they were eager to address uncomfortable questions of origins and responsibility. On the other side stood leading historians of Germany and the Holocaust, who took issue with the book's tendency to caricature and oversimplify an immensely complex history, who worried about its tendency to reinforce popular myths about the Holocaust without substantiation, and whose own work had hardly ignored the influence of German antisemitism. Accompanying them were members of Kohl's administration and German diplomats, who worried the book would kindle anti-German sentiment abroad. In the end, the controversy functioned mostly as a mirror for Germany's ongoing confrontation with Holocaust history.[94]

Never before, historian Edgar Wolfrum has argued, "was the present so deeply oriented toward the past [*vergangenheitsbezogen*] in this way."[95] This flurry of historical and mnemonic activity, especially the Kohl administration's attention to historical politics, created a perfect storm. The perception of a conservative offensive directed toward German identity put already anxious left-wing activists on guard. Contrary to the conventional narrative that reads the 1980s as a decade of newfound stability, Frank Biess has emphasized that the 1980s, especially within the left-alternative milieu, seemed to nurture a heightening sense of fear about the future.[96] Sven Reichardt has gone so far as to deem this fear "apocalyptic."[97] Especially for activists operating amid what Jürgen Habermas described as the "exhaustion of utopian energies," their values seemed imperiled by a world ready to give up and give in to the status quo.[98] Safeguarding their investments became a key battle for the alternative milieu.[99] And here lies the irony of Kohl's administration. It proffered itself, as Uta Poiger has underscored, "emphatically, as a corrective to alleged leftist and alternative excesses."[100] But the effect of this self-presentation was that it, in fact, cleared the way for the formation of a strong left-liberal activist milieu.

The Making of Sustainable Utopias

This book offers a history of those activists and how they clawed back space for their ideas and the initiatives that advanced them. It follows three networks of intellectuals, politicians, and artists, each of which enjoyed popularity and a sustained impact on German society. The Berlin History Workshop (*Geschichtswerkstatt*), officially created in 1981, used historical methodology in an attempt to overturn undemocratic hierarchies of knowledge. This collection of amateur and professional historians argued that a direct line connected control over the archive and the power to narrate the past, on one hand, and social power, on the other. They fought to liberate historical research from the rigid confines of the university by bringing the historian's craft into local neighborhoods. By giving ordinary Germans both tools and opportunities to narrate their own histories seriously, these grassroots historians believed they could help broker a more ethical set of power relations. At the same time, Germany's newest political party, the Greens, implemented major changes to established political practices with the aim of cultivating a truly democratic society. Formally established in 1980, the party won its first federal representation just three years later. Its members brought politics out of the parliament building and into residential communities by making local plebiscitary politics central to their party program. With a great deal of momentum at both the local and the national level, the Greens immediately brought their grassroots political practices to numerous cultural projects. The creation of sites like museums and community centers became particularly important opportunities to put political agency in the hands of regular people. Such spaces promised to democratize Germany by turning the cultural encounters of its citizens into catechisms of radical democracy. A loose collection of artists of public space endorsed similarly ambitious objectives. They set out to change the way people thought and behaved in public space by using art to shift its contours. They installed ordinary objects in ordinary but unexpected places—along residential sidewalks, in empty lots, on streetlights. And they duplicated these installations often hundreds or thousands of times at different sites. The artists intended these unanticipated aesthetic encounters to grab the attention of passersby and, in that moment, to invite viewers to consider their stance toward a topic of contemporary relevance: racial discrimination or the threat of environmental catastrophe, for example. The works themselves were not passive. Each used the topography of the everyday to nudge viewers to embrace what philosopher Hans Jonas called an "ethics of responsibility" toward the artwork's subject. For the ways their work explored, overturned, and rewrote the boundaries of where art belonged and what it sought to do there—that is, for the ways their art intervened in public space—I call these artists "spatial interventionists."

These three groups are, admittedly, somewhat curious bedfellows. Though each has garnered scholarly attention, they are generally treated independently. The Berlin History Workshop has taken its place in the evolution of German historiography, for example. It contributed to the 1980s critique of the people-less structuralism of Bielefeld-era social history and illustrated the popularization of the subjects and methods of the history of everyday life.[101] The German Greens have offered a study in the transition from protest group to political establishment, a test case for Robert Michels's iron law of oligarchy, in which the exigencies of parliamentary power dismantle democratic ambition into political alienation.[102] The Greens have shaped the history of the postwar German Left, in which a set of unsatisfying reformist programs replaced revolutionary platforms in the late 1950s and left protesters and activists to seek a parliamentary voice in new arenas.[103] And they have served as a capstone in the history of an experimental politics of countercultural imagination, one that stretches from the radical hopes of the 1960s through the success, institutionalization, and mellowing of many of the New Social Movements of the 1970s and 1980s.[104] The artists of public space have played a role in the story of the democratization of museum access in the 1970s and 1980s and in a generational narrative about the overturning of centuries-old conventions of monument-making, challenged in the late 1980s by renewed debates about the status of Holocaust memory.[105]

Curious bedfellows though these three groups may be, together they offer a window onto the development of a new utopian milieu at the end of the twentieth century. These activists did not just traffic in ideas. Their work mattered because they created infrastructures in which ordinary Germans could test out and adopt new behaviors. They championed radical grassroots democracy by giving citizens agency over the creation of significant cultural products like museums and monuments. They decentralized that creative process, embedding it in the spaces and rhythms of everyday life in order to make it widely accessible. And they borrowed from the environmental movement's concept of sustainability the insistence that any alternative to existing society be both enduring and adaptable.

Through their efforts to resist an increasing sense of political disenfranchisement, social alienation, and cultural impotence in the late twentieth century, these groups reveal that German interest in radical alternatives to existing society had not, in fact, evaporated. Against the claim that the second half of the twentieth century spiraled into political and cultural apathy—that ending myths won—the history of these three groups demonstrates that West Germans rallied behind a collection of utopian cultural practices that pursued the radical and sustainable democratization of politics and culture in the topographies and temporalities of everyday life. Through these behaviors—what Michel de Certeau called "the practices of everyday life"—these activists put culture to work in an attempt to reconcile ideals with realities. They sought to realize a radically democratic, socially integrated, socially conscious, just, and peaceful Germany. Though they never mobilized the language of a sustainable utopia and used the language of both utopia and sustainability only occasionally, they not only envisioned a new German society but attempted to enact their vision in the manner of a sustainable utopia. In doing so, they reclaimed utopian hope from the dustbin of historical ideas.

This narrative unfolds over two parts, mirror images of one another that reveal the incremental process by which sustainable utopias became first imaginable, then practicable. It picks up in the late 1970s, after the 1973 oil crisis shook the world. Cold War anxieties had become institutionalized. In the West, most expected a Western triumph would bring relief from such apprehensions. Instead, it seemed to generate melancholy. A broadly Euro-American sense of crisis gained traction. With the victory of liberal democracy and capitalism over "really existing socialism," radical social and political alternatives appeared to many to have evaporated. With front row seats to the rise and fall of the Iron Curtain, West Germany seemed poised to embrace this sentiment. In this context, trumpeting utopian agendas still invited snickers or scowls. The concept of a sustainable utopia thus plays little role in the first half of the book. Nevertheless, viewed from the perspective of ordinary Germans, one finds that a commitment to the possibility of radical alternatives hardly disappeared in the late twentieth century.

Part I traces how each of the three groups came to embrace a set of foundational values that enabled them to begin thinking openly in utopian terms once again. Newly constituted or only weakly associated in the late 1970s and early 1980s, the three young groups cared deeply about the local communities in which they operated. They opposed the tendency of their respective societal spheres—intellectual life, political life, and aesthetic life—to operate in fundamentally hierarchical ways. To combat this predisposition, they each championed the pursuit of new, decentralized, more democratic geographies of cultural engagement, or "alternative public spheres." Each group, independently, came to understand radically new uses of local space in the execution of their cultural projects as the primary medium through which they could have the greatest impact on German society. The first three chapters trace the development of each of these groups individually as they coalesced around this shared goal.

Chapter 1 introduces this focus on localized, democratic engagement with public space through the work of two artists: Joseph Beuys and Gunter Demnig. Together, they represent the demographic diversity and shared investments of a loose group of artists critical of the passivity of art in public space. For them, traditional public artists had hitherto only *occupied* public space, in various ways. The point, however, was to *intervene* in it. Creating art that intervened in public space became their most urgent social, cultural, and political task. They understood their work to reconfigure the range of possible experiences of public space so as to generate a more democratic sense of investment in and agency over that space. Spatial interventionist art prioritized opportunities for dialogue about how ordinary people use space in their everyday lives, and its creators insisted that West Germany desperately needed more of these opportunities. By creating a new kind of public art that aimed to render mundane experiences of public space self-conscious, participatory, discursive, and even emancipatory, these artists created a foundation for more radical—indeed, utopian—demands on the aesthetics of public space.

Chapter 2 charts the birth of a grassroots historical movement that possessed a similar investment in local, democratic engagement with public space. The Berlin History Workshop counted among its most avid proponents. This hodgepodge group of aspiring historians took aim at traditional historical scholarship. They argued that it focused too much on the histories of social and political structures, famous men, and large-scale diplomatic conflicts. In place of top-down history, they advocated writing "history from below." The group drew inspiration from earlier efforts in England and Sweden to destabilize an exclusive, hierarchical historical profession. Their work employed the new historiographical turn toward the history of everyday life (*Alltagsgeschichte*). And it mobilized new theories that reassessed the social power of space and the production of authority. The group's members took a particular interest in West Germany's understanding of how National Socialism operated at the level of the mundane. Through a series of local historical research projects that engaged community residents in their own neighborhoods, the Berlin History Workshop attempted to tell German history through its local spaces. In doing so, it aimed to use history to advance a radically democratic intellectual project.

Chapter 3 traces the German Green Party's attempt to develop a cultural program. It argues that the young party, which positioned itself as *the* alternative to West Germany's political status quo, put culture at the heart of its early efforts to implement radical grassroots democracy and environmental politics in the Federal Republic. This argument runs contrary to conventional historiography as well as to charges from both within the party and without that the Greens had little concern for cultural issues. By analyzing the rambling and disorganized but passionate conceptual framework behind the Greens' first efforts to define a cultural program, this chapter demonstrates that the party's early conception of a rigorous environmental policy in fact hinged on art, aesthetics, and cultural institutions. Because they remained sheltered from the immediate exigencies of electoral politics, Green cultural programs offered a more flexible medium for working through some of the party's knottier agendas. Central to Green cultural investments was the placement of cultural institutions and practices into new local spaces. The party saw its plans for these spaces as pivotal to its efforts to create a Germany that was not only "Green," but also sustainably so.

The second part of the book runs from the mid-1980s through the mid-1990s, bookending the world-historical events of 1989–1991. The mid-1980s brought to all three groups a crisis of purpose that prompted them to reevaluate their priorities. Their focus on cultural environments made them particularly receptive to the idea of sustainability popularized after the convening of the World Commission on Environment and Development in the mid-1980s. These chapters trace how the three networks adapted the environmental idea of sustainability—with its utopian imperative—to the world of German culture. Their pursuit of a sustainable culture changed how the groups understood the timeline of their efforts to democratize local spaces. They came to believe they could not effect meaningful change through short-term, static goals. Rather, they viewed their efforts as ongoing processes, structured to be self-sufficient, self-sustaining, and adaptable: a renewable, future-oriented cultural movement in the present. This realization marked not only the continued vitality of both optimism and radicalism during this period but also a reconceptualization of the idea of utopia itself. Sustainable utopia had become imaginable for the first time.

Chapter 4 analyzes the Greens' sustainable utopian program. While major factional controversies pitted environmental fundamentalists against political realists within the party, other members asked what it meant to foster a "Green" culture now that they held seats in parliament. They tested their answers on a range of projects, but two represent these attempts particularly well. First, they participated in the creation of Berlin's Active Museum, intended as the key museum of the city's Nazi past. They refused to create a passive, didactic museum-going experience. Instead, they aimed to build a museum that would involve its visitors intimately in the ongoing construction of its form and content. Second, the Greens lobbied against Helmut Kohl's plan to establish the German Historical Museum, which proposed to bring the artifacts of Germany's long history under one roof. The Greens' work with both projects reveals the party's commitment to privileging the spaces, timeframes, and agents of everyday life. Only in this manner could they foster a self-sufficient, self-sustaining, and adaptable radical grassroots democratic culture in the Federal Republic.

Chapter 5 explores how the Berlin History Workshop echoed many of the Greens' investments when it created the "Mobile Museum." Housed in a double-decker bus, this transportable museum brought both historical discoveries and new research opportunities to Berlin's local neighborhoods. The History Workshop intended the museum as a serious challenge to the usual demographics of those writing Germany's history. By assisting ordinary residents in tracing clear causal connections between their past and their present, the History Workshop hoped to give them the skills to chart a path from the ideals of their present to the realities of their future. The museum also helped the group form a bridge to East Germany by bringing exhibits to the other side of the Berlin Wall. This partnership with the East was short-lived, however; the History Workshop favored autonomy over collaboration with eastern grassroots historical groups. The Mobile Museum's untimely demise amplified this discord. In the chaos after West Germany's 1990 World Cup victory, vandals destroyed the museum. In the aftermath, a combination of intransigence, misfortune, and interpersonal discontent would spell the end of the Berlin History Workshop's heyday and put a damper on its sustainable utopian cultural work.

The artists and their utopian aesthetic proved the most resilient of the three groups. Chapter 6 charts the explosion of spatial interventionist artwork in the late 1980s and early 1990s. These artists took advantage of the widespread conversation about Holocaust commemoration as a chance to rethink the potential of Holocaust monuments. Spatial interventionists began to create memorials that resisted traditional mnemonic styles. Instead of large, central, government-sponsored monuments, they crafted networks of small, inconspicuous mini-monuments scattered across large expanses. These memorial initiatives relied on the engagement of ordinary people for their popularization. Spatial interventionists used the novel spatiality of their artworks, ironically, to shift attention away from the fixed physical location of the work toward its discursive existence. The commemorative efficacy of these memorials stemmed from the conversations they generated among visitors and the way those conversations shaped visitors' relationships to the surrounding area. These memorials gained international attention and generated a series of spin-offs in places as distant as Buenos Aires and Moscow. Such international appeal has allowed the commemorative agenda of the spatial interventionists to survive for nearly three decades despite fundamental changes to German political, social, and cultural contexts.

The novel cultural practices of these three grassroots organizations, however, were never promised success simply on account of their modesty. The outcomes of their flirtations with utopia rarely measured up to the hopes invested in them. With major shifts in the international political landscape and the rapid expansion of their constituencies to include sixteen million East Germans alongside more pedestrian concerns like funding difficulties and interpersonal conflicts, these groups weathered the post–Cold War order with only varying success. The book ends with an account of the fate of their sustainable utopias into the twenty-first century. The Berlin History Workshop unraveled as it approached the new millennium. Having focused on newly narrating Germany's Nazi past, the group fell largely into irrelevance as engagement with Holocaust history became mainstream. It also struggled to integrate grassroots historians from the former East. After the Green Party's dismal results in reunified Germany's first Bundestag election, the party realized the path to success led through collaboration with the Social Democrats. Its realist faction won as the party initiated a major reform and rebranding effort. The institutionalization of the Greens and the practical limits of political power tempered their radical cultural program, though a more recent wave of Green successes suggests the party's ability to nurture hope still lingers. The artists, however, have managed to maintain their grasp on the emancipatory potential of space, and their contributions have proven more durable. They have generated international attention, which has further decentralized the management of these projects.

Though the rise of citizens' initiatives since the 1970s has leaned heavily toward the political left, the right also fueled its own grassroots activism. Far right activism has mobilized the methods—if not the substance—of sustainable utopianism, revealing the broad appeal of radically decentralized, democratized organization. The book's conclusion also points to the programmatic and methodological evolution of several prominent organizations on the far right that have peddled exclusionary, sometimes violent social and political platforms. Beginning in the 1980s, groups like the Citizens Initiative for a Moratorium on Foreigners (*Bürgerinitiative Ausländerstopp*) and the political party the Republicans (*Die Republikaner*) employed tactics similar to groups like the History Workshop, the Green Party, and the spatial interventionists in pursuit of their far right programs. And while many of the sustainable utopian projects on the left, ironically, proved not so sustainable after all, the right has demonstrated a persistent affinity for these methods. They continue to echo in more contemporary initiatives like the new but vibrant party—varyingly Euro-skeptic, xenophobic, racist, and antisemitic—Alternative for Germany as well as the far right youth movement the Identitarians. By highlighting the adoption of sustainable utopian methods by the far right, I test the limits of the concept itself. Together, these narratives from both sides of the political spectrum demonstrate the significance of this late twentieth-century conceptual shift by underscoring the enduring appeal of utopian thinking and practice among Germans. They suggest that one must be neither too sanguine nor too pessimistic about the resuscitation of utopian thought and practice.

PART I

New Geographies of Cultural Engagement

1

The Rise of the Spatial Interventionists

A gulf separated Joseph Beuys and Gunter Demnig in the early 1980s. The few hundred miles that lay between the two artists' studios accounted for perhaps the least of this expanse. By the 1980s, Beuys represented the artistic establishment, the "Old Guard" of the avant-garde in the West German art world, and was nearing the end of his life. Born in the early years of the Weimar Republic, Beuys had grown up under National Socialism and had both participated in the Hitler Youth and served in the Luftwaffe during World War II—most argue apathetically. After the war, he returned to a longtime passion and opted to pursue a career in art, enrolling in the program for the design of monumental sculpture at the Düsseldorf Academy of Fine Arts. To serve as his mentor Beuys selected Joseph Enseling, a sculptor who used art to represent the labor of industrial workers, though Beuys would later complete a master class taught by the artist Ewald Mataré, a sculptor whose stylized work the Nazis had dubbed "degenerate." After his training, Beuys's attempts to make a name for himself in traditional art media were met with only limited professional success. After working ten years as an instructor of monumental sculpture in Düsseldorf, he was removed from his post in 1972 on account of substantial disagreements with the school's administration and faculty. This institutional rejection, however, encouraged Beuys to push harder against what he saw as the limitations of the aesthetic status quo. His willingness to experiment with art's boundaries through sculptures, performance art, installations, and videos eventually won him international fame.[1] Remarkably protean, though, Beuys worked not only as an artist but also as a teacher, a sort of spiritual leader, and a political activist. Over the four decades he spent active in West German cultural and political arenas, Beuys articulated a fairly clear set of investments. A former student radical in the 1960s, he had professed his support for the New Left (earnest but conspicuous following his earlier affiliations with National Socialism[2]), and he continued his involvement in alternative political movements as a founding member of the German Green Party. The themes of democracy and democratic practices assumed a prominent role in Beuys's work.[3] By his death in 1986, he had received more invitations than any other artist to contribute to documenta, the world-renowned international contemporary art exposition held every five years in Kassel, Germany.[4]

In the early 1980s, Gunter Demnig stood as quite the contrast. Nearly thirty years Joseph Beuys's junior, Demnig had just emerged onto the art scene as Beuys was capping his career. A year before Beuys was removed from his post in Düsseldorf, a young Demnig enrolled 150 miles to the east in the University of Kassel, studying under the artist Harry Kramer, a proponent of kinetic art. Choosing at first to study art education and industrial design, Demnig later switched to monument construction and management. As the home of documenta, his location in Kassel gave him the opportunity to learn his craft in the presence of some of the world's most innovative artists, including Beuys. Perhaps it was this environment, conducive to bold creativity, that encouraged Demnig to push artistic boundaries. In his early thirties, holding a newly minted degree from art school, he got right to work making a place for himself in a crowded art scene. One of his earliest artworks included a representation of the American flag with skulls in place of stars. The painting, which protested the Vietnam War, resulted in a visit from the West German police. This would hardly be the last of such encounters for Demnig. Though he seemed to enjoy pushing the buttons of law enforcement, his style had yet to come into focus, and his broader agenda, however ostentatiously expressed, remained muddled.

Despite the generation that separated them, Beuys and Demnig together exemplify a coherent aesthetic opposition movement that developed in West Germany in the early 1980s. This movement responded to a long-term outcome of the aesthetic functionalism that reigned after the Second World War. Pragmatic rebuilding efforts, fueled by the "economic miracle" of the 1950s, dominated the aesthetic paradigms of the first two postwar decades. In a ruined German landscape, engagements with space had to focus on reclaiming space for everyday use. The need for rapid reconstruction rendered the pure purposelessness of *l'art pour l'art,* which had characterized nineteenth-century aesthetics, an unaffordable luxury and relegated aesthetic creativity to the realm of the functional. Art that appeared in public space after the war was often the product of efforts to install artistic adornments on public buildings, or *Kunst am Bau* initiatives. Many criticized them as aesthetically impotent and politically myopic.[5] Little improved in the first three decades after the war, and functionalism's exclusivity hit artists, particularly artists of public space, hard in light of the already limited opportunities for paid creative work. The aesthetic attitude that Beuys and Demnig represent took aim both at this stagnancy and at Germany's tacit permission of art that passively occupied public space. They engaged in a practical critique of art that merely occupied public space by creating an infrastructure through which art could *intervene* actively in public space. I refer to this aesthetic temperament as spatial interventionism.[6]

Social Sculpture

Joseph Beuys's greatest impact on the European art world was as a pioneer of what he called "social sculpture." The defining feature of this kind of artwork was that it invited its observers into the act of its very creation and that this act of collective art-making had the potential to alter what people think and do in the world. Beuys subscribed to the Romantic philosopher Novalis's prescription that every individual should lead an artistic existence.[7] He also endorsed the imperative that society should constitute itself as an artwork, a collage of its citizens' creative potentialities. Social and political "intentions need to be artistic," Beuys suggested, "that is, they need to originate out of human creativity, out of individual human freedom."[8] Of course, the notion of an aestheticized politics has a dark past in Germany.[9] But Beuys seemed not to fear the potential violence his artistic imperative might permit. Freedom, democratic practice, creative agency, and the ability to mold society to a set of collectively determined values, for Beuys, went hand in hand.

Beuys recognized, however, that the ability to live artistically as Novalis prescribed did not inhere in modern society. Its artists slumbered and had to be awoken if they were to engage in such a collective creative project. Social sculpture, as Beuys conceived it, served this function. As a participatory artwork, a social sculpture would activate the aesthetic power within society by mobilizing citizens to collaborate on artistic enterprises with social ramifications. Beuys aimed for nothing less in his social sculptures than to reweave the very fabric of society. Sculpture, after all, is only valuable to society, Beuys argued, "when it contributes to the advancement of human consciousness."[10]

Certainly in 1972 the democratic fabric of West German society appeared to have worn thin. Over the summer, the Palestinian terror organization Black September had used the first Olympic Games hosted in Germany since the Nazi era as an opportunity to murder a group of Israeli athletes. Terrorism further gripped West Germany as its own domestic terror organization, the Red Army Faction, bombed several high-profile sites, including the Axel Springer publishing house in Hamburg.[11] In this context, it made sense that Beuys would use his invitation to documenta 5 in the summer of 1972 to create a social sculpture that attempted to bolster German faith in democracy. And particularly because Beuys—much like his contemporary, Jürgen Habermas—acknowledged that the foundations for social and political change lay in rational dialogue, it also made sense that he would create a social sculpture that forged opportunities for social discourse. Beuys set up a small office at the art exhibition where he sat for one hundred days. During that period, he invited visitors to join him in conversation about the promises and challenges of direct democracy. Though the security of West Germany's democratic culture might have seemed threatened, exhibit visitors suffered from no shortage of ideas about how to fortify it. Participants in Beuys's installation raised environmental issues, women's issues, and educational and economic policy issues, and offered suggestions for improving parliamentary democracy through deliberate use of instruments like popular referenda.[12] Many of these issues, it bears noting, would not enter mainstream public discourse for another decade.

The *100 Days* project also highlighted Beuys's investment in creating social sculptures that occupied a liminal space between the museum or gallery and the extra-museological. Beuys's drive to test the limits of the gallery aligned with a contemporary impulse to challenge the function of the museum by challenging its form. It had taken nearly twenty-five years for Germany to liberate public art from the weight of National Socialism and its legacy of instrumental aesthetics. Even after the Nazi regime had been dismantled, the destruction it wrought on the German landscape continued to dictate how and where art could be produced, by whom, and for what purposes. By the 1970s, however, West Germany began to witness a reorientation of its cultural politics that permitted a reevaluation of the placement of its cultural products.[13] Willy Brandt's social democratic–liberal coalition brought with it a gradual dismantling of the cultural conservatism bolstered by West Germany's first chancellor, Konrad Adenauer. Mobilizing the succinct motto "Culture for Everyone [*Kultur für alle*]" popularized by the Social Democrat and Frankfurt city councilman for cultural affairs Hilmar Hoffmann, Brandt's coalition sought a radical expansion of access to cultural creations. *Kultur* would no longer solely connote privilege, in the specific sense of *high* culture. Like Beuys, proponents of this stance recognized that cultural products and experiences had the potential to operate in service of social democratic political, communicative, and aesthetic programs. They evaluated art and culture based on their capacity to make German society more humane (*menschlicher*) by challenging entrenched power structures and promoting the political and social emancipation of the individual.[14] (Presumably, however, they hoped to exempt their own claim on the entrenched power structures of the Federal Republic.)

This new demand for emancipatory democratic cultural access called attention to the kinds of spaces that permitted such access, namely public space. The 1970s helped cement the concept of "public art"—more literally, "art in public space [*Kunst im öffentlichen Raum*]"—as a coherent aesthetic category.[15] By heeding the imperative of equal access, art in public space could respond to contemporary cultural demands in ways the traditional museum—understood as exclusive and elitist—could not. Proponents of access positioned themselves against the modernist desire in the first half of the twentieth century to create works of art that were "more autonomous and self-referential, and thus transportable, placeless, and nomadic."[16] Instead, the German art world adopted a concern for the indivisible relationship between the artwork and the space it occupied—that is, for site specificity.[17] Artists began to recognize the site of an artwork as an actual, particular location, "a tangible reality . . . composed of a unique combination of constitutive physical elements" that included both natural and man-made topographical influences and limitations. These components—lighting and ventilation, for example—constituted an integral part of the artwork's meaning. To remove the work of art from its context was to destroy it.[18] The Irish sculptor and art critic Brian O'Doherty summarized this attitude in a series of influential and artfully written essays that critiqued the development of the art gallery since the early nineteenth century. The gallery, he argued, had gradually become a "white cube." This "white cube" operated according to a set of

> laws as rigorous as those for building a medieval church. The outside world must not come in, so windows are usually sealed off. Walls are painted white. The ceiling becomes the source of light. The wooden floor is polished so that you click along clinically, or carpeted so that you pad soundlessly, resting the feet while the eyes have at the wall. The art is free, as the saying used to go, "to take on its own life." . . . In this context, a standing ashtray becomes almost a sacred object, just as the firehose in a modern museum looks not like a firehose but an esthetic conundrum.[19]

Over the first half of the twentieth century, the gallery space had become megalomaniacal in its relationship toward the art spectator. The gallery, and particularly the wall on which pictorial art hung, dictated a stringent set of behavioral norms that shaped both engagement with the artwork and the interpretation of its meaning. The gallery, according to O'Doherty, does violence to art. He criticized the gallery for trying so hard to be "unshadowed, white, clean" and the artworks within it for the manner in which they "demand . . . *Lebensraum*," here using language reminiscent of the genocidal telos toward which the Nazis' social aesthetic propelled Germany. Artworks hang fully independent of one another and seemingly lifted outside of "time and its vicissitudes." Gallery art, per O'Doherty, "exists in a kind of eternity of display, and though there is lots of 'period' (late modern), there is no time." And as the conventional photograph of the gallery entirely emptied of spectators makes clear, "the presence of that odd piece of furniture, your own body, seems superfluous, an intrusion. The space offers the thought that while eyes and minds are welcome, space-occupying bodies are not."[20] Those who advocated experiencing art kinesthetically rejected this "Cartesian paradox" of the modern gallery. They argued that, by privileging the mind and eye as the only means of beholding and appreciating the idea of the artwork, one effectively eliminates the vehicle of that idea, the spectator. Instead, they demanded the physical presence of the viewer for the work's completion.[21] This hostility toward the traditional art gallery drove artists to seek out new spaces in their attempts to produce more accessible, more democratic art.

Beuys's next major project participated in this trend. The year 1982—a decade after *100 Days*—saw the inception of Beuys's final and perhaps most spectacular work: a five-year-long collaborative installation with the clever, alliterative, neological subtitle *Stadtverwaldung statt Stadtverwaltung*, which translates less gracefully as "urban forestation, not municipal administration."[22] For documenta 7 held that year, Beuys challenged the citizens of and visitors to Kassel to partake in a massive, decentralized tree-planting enterprise. Seven thousand trees, in all, were to be planted throughout the city. By spotlighting Kassel's many barren locations that could accommodate a sapling, the project aimed to draw attention to urban development undertaken at the expense of the environment. Beuys also aimed to begin a city-wide grassroots conversation about humanity's embeddedness in its natural environment. He viewed the environmental degradation caused by modern industrial society as a significant and imminent threat to both humans and nature. To reinforce this sense of urgency, Beuys installed seven thousand large basalt stones in the shape of a giant triangle on Friedrichsplatz in front of the Fridericianum, the central hub of documenta and one of the oldest public museums in Europe. Each time a tree was planted, Beuys removed one of the stones and placed it beside the sapling, creating a sort of stone clock, German art historian Götz Adriani and museum curator Ulrich Weisner have argued, that marked "the transposition of Joseph Beuys' idea into reality."[23] In addition to serving as a measure of the project's progress, the basalt stones also lent a certain permanence to the arboreal installation. In this way, *7000 Oaks* challenged the boundaries, temporality, and nature of authorship of traditional artworks. The Berlin-based art curator Heiner Bastian, in a multi-artist homage to Beuys's work, pointed to the project's spatial and temporal expansiveness. In its initial phases, the work was bound to a specific place and time, namely to Friedrichsplatz in the five years between documenta 7 and 8. But the totality of its existence transcends these bounds. It represents continuous temporal and spatial development. Beginning in 1982, the artwork slowly crept over the city of Kassel, unfurling as a leafy canopy with a basalt base. As the Friedrichsplatz triangle dwindled, the project gradually lost its most distinct landmark. But its imprint and impact remain. Beuys's trees cast

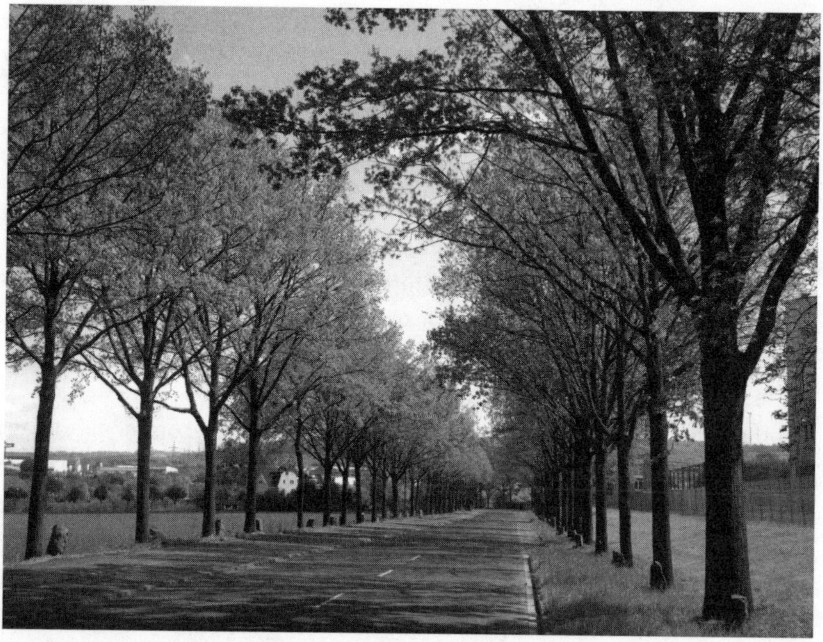

1.1 A stretch of trees planted as part of *7000 Oaks* along Dennhäuser Straße in Kassel, 2020. Baummapper / Wikimedia Commons / CC BY-SA 3.0 de.

a longer shadow over the city and root themselves deeper into its topography with each successive year.

Although there were actually forty-one different kinds of trees involved, Beuys titled the piece *7000 Oaks*.[24] The name nodded to the quintessential icon of Germanness and a long-standing symbol of strength and vitality: the oak, a tree that can live for more than eight hundred years under the right conditions.[25] While their geological markers represented endurance and fixity, Beuys's seven thousand trees themselves stood for evolution and change. Trees change seasonally and eventually die. Death, however, fuels rather than frustrates the project's imperative. Today, a publicly financed foundation committed to the project's preservation ensures that dead trees will be replaced. Though at any moment there may be fewer than seven thousand trees as aging, diseased, or dead trees are removed to make way for their successors, the project's concept provides a renewable goal whose repeated fulfillment demands both popular awareness and investment. Beuys provided the initial impulse, but *7000 Oaks* is an artwork made and continually remade by the thousands of people who have cared for it.

Upon the project's completion in 1987, the cultural spokesperson of the Green Party, Antje Vollmer, described *7000 Oaks* as responding to the most difficult questions facing contemporary Germany. Reflecting critically on the Alternative Movement in West Germany, Vollmer argued that previous emancipatory movements had articulated positive cultures of resistance. She lamented how the environmental movement—and, by extension, the larger Alternative Movement of the 1970s and 1980s—had not done the same. Instead, they contented themselves with sketching out depressing portraits of the status quo and bemoaning them. Beuys alone, she argued, offered a positive alternative. His installation showed art actively engaged in the work of survival (*Kunst als Arbeit des Überlebens*).[26] Beuys's *7000 Oaks* prompted a reconceptualization of the relationship between the human and natural environments.[27] It had accomplished the goals of social sculpture by using art to intervene in public space and demand democratic engagement with the aim of effecting social change. Its imperative was a process, not a finished product.

Leaving Traces

Beneath the canopy of *7000 Oaks*, a young Gunter Demnig had just made his first forays into the German art world after receiving his degree in the construction and management of monuments from the University of Kassel. While in Kassel, Demnig developed quite the reputation among his peers. Wolfgang Hahn, a sculptor and one of Demnig's former classmates, described him as a jack-of-all-trades who embraced the mentality that nothing is impossible. "The greater the challenge, the better," Hahn wrote of Demnig, claiming that his friend assumed working harder, longer, and more creatively would solve all his problems.[28]

By the early 1980s, like many of his artistic contemporaries, Demnig had already developed an interest in making art that rejected boundaries imposed by the traditional museum and the canvas. He decided that making good art must always involve working in and on public space.[29] Art should "operate centrifugally," he argued, bursting outward into "non-art spaces, non-art institutions, and non-art issues"—that is, into the spaces and subjects of ordinary people's everyday lives.[30] Here, Demnig's objectives echoed those of the "land art" movement, which originated in the United States and the UK in the 1960s and 1970s. Land art used the natural landscape as its canvas and natural materials—stones, wood, leaves, water, etc.—as its media. By redrawing the lines between nature and artifice, artifice and artwork, land art worked to dismantle the centuries-long tradition of displaying art in exclusive spaces that reinforced strict power hierarchies.[31]

The West German art community had proven particularly receptive to land art. German artist of public space Frieder Schnock, who would later gain international renown for his spatial interventionist Holocaust memorial installations, began his career, for example, with a dissertation on Richard Long, a British sculptor and pioneer of land art.[32] Long's works explored how the passage of time changes spaces and how movement can link discrete, otherwise unrelated spaces via a temporal bridge. Transformations became his overriding focus. His first major artwork, *A Line Made by Walking* (1967), for example, featured the young artist pacing back and forth in a line in an English country meadow until he had trampled a path, which he then photographed. But the photograph was not the artwork. By combining art object with art performance, Long's sculpture was essentially a documentation of time. It existed in the tension between the photograph, which confirmed that Long had in fact created the line, and the knowledge that the subsequent passage of time would eliminate his line as the grass grew back.[33] The appeal of land art to artists like Schnock or Demnig lay in its ability to link experiences of space, experiences of time, and the appreciation of aesthetic meaning in this way.

But land art's appeal also stemmed from the manner in which it protested the strictures of the art gallery and commercial art market. Land art was generally too large and too site-bound to be accommodated in the gallery space. Often, it could not be moved. Sometimes its existence was ephemeral. And it resisted sale. By placing "an unprecedented strain on established patterns of (re)producing, exhibiting, borrowing / lending, purchasing / selling, and commissioning / executing art works in general," alternative art practices that rejected the gallery destabilized the art community from within, curator and art critic Miwon Kwon has observed.[34] The spatial interventionists carried this torch.

Demnig's earliest projects wrenched art out of frame and gallery. In his own kind of "conquest of nature," his large-scale but temporary installations inserted art instead into natural landscapes.[35] In 1977, for example, Demnig traveled with his adviser and another classmate to Quebec to carve a men's restroom, complete with three standing urinals, out of a large snow bank. They titled the piece *Sculpture out of Snow: An Homage to Duchamp* in a nod toward Marcel Duchamp's famous ready-made artwork, *Fountain,* which had unsettled the global art world when it debuted sixty years earlier in 1917. Like Duchamp, Demnig explored the way the placement of an artwork shapes its meaning. Instead of conceiving of landscape as something art should merely represent—a likeness as in classical painting—Demnig regarded landscape as a "field for direct artistic action," a space to be worked in and upon, an essential medium between artist and spectator.[36]

Demnig's pursuit of new fields for aesthetic action won him the reputation of a wanderer. One classmate explained that when Demnig made art, "he walked everywhere."[37] But as Karlheinz Schmid, the publisher and lead editor of the art journal *Kunstzeitung,* carefully added, Demnig was less an aimless itinerant than an artist without a place—or more accurately, an aesthetic medium—to call "home." More tellingly, Demnig was seen as a rebel who tirelessly sought out new boundaries just so he could overstep them.[38] His search for new forms and frontiers for art became a work of art in itself as he attempted to capture, in material form, his quest for an emancipatory artistic space. As one of his colleagues once clarified, "the creative process, the production, is also the result, the work itself."[39]

It was only a short leap from Demnig's earlier intention of leaving his mark on and through the landscape to his more specific interest in creating artworks that would leave "traces" (*Spuren*).[40] Among his peers, this style would earn Demnig the moniker *Spurenleger,* or "Leaver of Traces." This work, in some ways, drew on his training in the maintenance of traditional monuments. Both monuments and traces could fit German photographer and author Rolf Sachsse's description as remnants of the past in the present or "legacies" (*Hinterlassenschaften*). But the list of shared features largely stopped there. Monuments are generally constructed intentionally with fixity in mind. One presumes that they will continue to do work in society. Traces, by contrast, exist as residue or debris (*Überbleibsel, Abfälle*) whose incidental remainders lack the intentionality of monuments. Traces string a thread between past and present almost accidentally. Demnig's novelty lay in allowing these two modes—intentionality and accident, fixity and movement—to coexist.[41] The tensions between them appeared prominently in Demnig's early work. After completing his dissertation in 1979, a thirty-three-year-old Demnig initiated his first major independent artwork: *Duftmarken Kassel-Paris Demnig 80.* Over the next three years, he would complete two additional projects—*Blutspur Kassel-London* (1981) and *Ariadne-Faden Kassel-Venedig* (1982). Together, these pieces became a public stage on which Demnig worked through his ideas about the aesthetic trace.

His first project was driven by frustration. Demnig took issue with the relative lack of attention paid to the placement and purpose of artworks within major centers of aesthetic appreciation.[42] For his first major work, he chose two: the Academy of Fine Arts in Kassel and the Centre Pompidou in Paris. Using a handmade bicycle-like printing wheel, he inked a short text in gesso onto the roads between them. Though the literal connection he drew between them would last only until the paint wore away, the work also signified a more permanent figurative connection. He titled the piece *Scent Marks* (*Duftmarken*), even though it involved no odors. Rather, the project referred metaphorically to the way that animals mark their territory. Demnig's "territory" was the potential spaces for art in the topography of the mundane that lay between these two sites. Like a scent, however, his artwork began to dissipate as soon as it was deposited. Well before he reached his destination in Paris, the first traces of the project had already started to disappear. Though temporary, the project nevertheless amounted to a massive undertaking: a total of 508 miles, which Demnig walked with his ink wheel over twenty-one days. It marked the completion of one of his adviser's most radical assignments. On the grounds that "every artist should be the world champion of something," Harry Kramer challenged his students to try to log a record in the *Guinness Book of World Records.*[43] Presumably to Kramer's great pleasure, *Duftmarken* (1980) won Demnig an entry in 1982 as the world's longest work of art.[44]

Fueled by the positive reception *Duftmarken* received, Demnig undertook a similar project the following year. He would print another short text on the roads between Kassel and the Tate Modern in London. Instead of a trail of gesso, however, he chose to use a more provocative medium. Demnig had worked closely with a friend to develop a chemical solution that could initially be printed colorlessly. Only later, after Demnig had moved on with his printing wheel, would a deep red color appear, suggestive of blood. The project, titled *Blutspur* or *Trail of Blood,* was ready for installation when the chemist upended all their preparatory work by suggesting they use actual blood. Ever the provocateur, Demnig liked the proposal. So, they did. Sticky, stinky, and foamy, the pig's blood disgusted viewers, especially the members of the press tasked with reporting on the piece.[45] Gradually, though, Demnig's foul print wore away. "As an artist, one works with symbols," Demnig explained. In this case, he opted for blood for its symbolic reference to life.[46] *Blutspur* marked a moment of vitality: the vitality of the many spectators he attracted, puzzled, and disgusted; the vitality of the art communities in each town through which he walked, roused to reaction by his installation; and the vitality of the artist himself, whose youthful persistence (and impertinence) made the project possible. But the artwork also symbolized death: not only of the countless pigs who enabled its creation but also of the artwork itself, whose life cycle began to draw to a close the moment it was printed on the ground. The project allowed Demnig to explore the fading away of a work's imprint on society, literal and figurative—that is, the process by which artworks die. And he examined art's afterlife by testing the limits of its resurrection through only dim and scattered memories.

The last in Demnig's trilogy of artistic treks materialized in 1982. The year was a significant one in the art world. For the first time, two of the most important international exhibitions of contemporary art—Kassel's documenta and Venice's Biennale—would take place simultaneously. To mark this occasion, Demnig walked for thirty-six days in a straight line from Kassel to Venice, leaving behind him 1,000 kilometers of red thread connecting these two beacons in the global art world.[47] Sachsse called the piece the most concise expression of Demnig's trace-laying: "downright unspectacular, made out of a material whose remnant can still be found years down the road."[48] Demnig named the installation *Ariadne's Thread* after the Greek myth of Ariadne, who gave her beloved Theseus a thread to help him escape the Labyrinth after slaying the Minotaur. Just as Ariadne's thread led Theseus from one end of the maze to the other, Demnig's thread allowed the spectator to connect the alpha and omega of the international art community. Here, as with the other two projects, however, "only conceptually do beginning and end ever meet."[49]

Demnig stressed that "this kind of art does not give any answers. It only spells out the questions."[50] He saw it as his task to leave signs (*Zeichen*), a roadmap that points the way to an answer that only the beholder could travel.[51] In 1988, Sachsse noted presciently that *Ariadne's Thread* marked a stylistic transformation for Demnig. Thereafter Demnig would place at the heart of his projects a conscious working-through of the tense relationship between the artist's process of crafting and the artwork's own process of becoming permanent in the world.[52] Demnig's greatest work, the *Stumbling Stones* (1992–present), would embody this tension and, through the collaboration of hundreds of thousands of people, take on a life of its own.

Territorial Transgressions as Dialogic Transgressions

Joseph Beuys's magnum opus *7000 Oaks* met with general acclaim, while Demnig's three exploratory works drew a mixed response. Popular and professional assessments of all four works agreed, however, on the novelty of their effects. Critics spoke of the way these projects set in motion more than just dynamic artworks. They unleashed a new way of thinking about art in public space. This new aesthetic mentality unsettled the usual parameters of art production, the temporality of the artwork, the rules of the canvas and the frame, and the very nature of the creative process. According to one account, it prioritized individual creativity, inventiveness, innovation, and absolute freedom of thought.[53] Another pamphlet argued that it radically democratized the production of art, vindicating Novalis's mantra that every person should be an artist.[54] What set works like *7000 Oaks* and Demnig's trace trilogy apart from more traditional public art was the manner in which they challenged conventional modes of understanding and engaging with public space. Beuys and Demnig would have agreed with Heidegger that one could never escape one's spatial situatedness in the world.[55] But they saw space as more than just a physical condition of the possibility of human experience. They placed great weight on those moments in which one's reason renders meaningful the "empty and innocent spatial spread" of one's physical environment.[56] These were pregnant moments. Encounters with space had the power to shape political, cultural, and social action, and the spatial interventionists sought to harness this power.[57] Instead of simply critiquing art in public space, these artists offered critiques that simultaneously initiated a new kind of aesthetic practice designed to reconfigure that public space, the meaning people gave to it, and the ways they thought and behaved within it.

Spatial interventionists, of course, had models aplenty for how to put art to radical uses. Already in the 1950s and 1960s, postwar neo-avant-garde artists had set out to craft art appropriate to the wounded but recovering world they now inhabited. They wanted to dismantle art's bourgeois claim to autonomy in order to craft a new, more intimate link between art and the lived world. Revisiting the media, methods, and ambitions of the avant-garde of the 1910s and 1920s, neo-avant-gardists made art that challenged the conventions of the art world: scale, temporality, site, and authorship.[58] But remaking traditional art categories to occasion a revolution if not of society writ large then at least of cultural production is a tall order. And the neo-avant-gardists' failure to do so—especially given the derivative nature of their approach—won them the disfavor of many prominent art critics, who saw the neo-avant-gardist effort as "a simulacral world of failed repetitions and pathetic pastiches."[59] Still, after the violence of the first half of the century, the possibility that art might serve as a more successful tool to effect meaningful political and social change held immeasurable appeal to weary but determined artists.

As the neo-avant-gardists worked with ready-mades and collages, other artists rejected avant-garde and neo-avant-garde art for what they saw as its inability to work upon the world. Out of this cloud of criticism emerged new groupings of artists who thought they could get the work of radical transformation right this time. The late 1950s brought the formation of the Situationist International (SI) and SPUR. They shared some aesthetic ambitions with their radical forebears, namely that they wanted to create art whose primary task was to dismantle capitalism and to effect "a revolution of the whole life of society."[60] But they approached these ambitions differently. They placed aesthetic alienation at the core of their enterprise. Their works attempted to "hijack and re-function" a particular aspect of society in order to alienate the audience from it, defamiliarize it, and create space for the construction of a new social imaginary. Their work was anti-hierarchical, ephemeral, disruptive, and collaborative.[61] SI believed that only "the collective takeover of the world," art historian Frances Stracey has argued, "would enable active, autonomous and politically engaged agents to emerge." And their art—"situations"—would operate "as incendiary devices heralding an unpredictable eruption of an alternative, non-capitalist and poetic life."[62] They played a key role in fueling the revolutionary activism of 1968. But SI's principled commitment to radical social and political transformation rendered the group rigid and combative. It was notorious for expelling subgroups it interpreted as uncommitted to its goals. And although the list of artistic and activist organizations indebted in some way to SI is extensive, this influence was not sufficient to prevent SI from dissolving in 1972 amid Europe's shifting political terrain.

The subversive, spectacular, provocative, participatory, and revolutionary elements of Situationist International's work possessed considerable magnetism in the postwar art world. For their embrace of approaches like performance art, kinetic art, and Happenings, the late 1950s and early 1960s signaled "a radical temporalization of the arts."[63] The collision of these investments generated a stream of new movements in the 1960s and 1970s. Some radicalized SI's principles. In the early 1960s, West Germany watched as the provocative, often violent group Subversive Aktion coalesced behind disgruntled former SPUR member Dieter Kunzelmann. Kunzelmann took aim at the oppression of consumption-oriented industrial society. But he took no consolation in criticism. Kunzelmann argued that overturning capitalism required action, not the naval-gazing creation of new theories. In work that bridged art, political activism, and anarchism, Subversive Aktion pushed for direct action against the state in the form of micro-rebellions.[64]

This rejection of conventional art forms on account of their vulnerability to capitalist consumerism found other expressions in the 1960s as well—among them, the practice of auto-destructive art. Coined by the artist Gustav Metzger and fueled by similar anti-capitalism and anti-consumerism, auto-destructive art tied the creation of an artwork to its destruction, which curtailed (but often did not entirely eliminate) the possibility of its participation in the market.[65] Equally critical of the capitalist order but less cynical than auto-destructive art, the rise of Fluxus in the 1960s and 1970s brought an embrace of nonsense and play. Proponents turned to the "dross of everyday life" as their media and the techniques of experimental music and theater as their method to create artworks that could undermine the social order and bridge the gap between life and work. In contrast to auto-destructive art, which produced works that were, in a sense, dead on arrival, Fluxus created pieces designed to evolve continually, never to reach completion. The artwork-in-flux, art historian Natilee Harren has argued, "reconfigured not only the artwork as a material entity, but also artistic authorship, labor, and the systems of art's distribution in ways that have been carried forth by later generations of artists." Despite this bequest, though, precisely its radicality doomed the movement. Its creation of intentionally trashy objects and lengthy, confusing performances, its embrace of uselessness and boredom "practically ensured Fluxus's marginalization."[66]

The spatial interventionists absorbed much from these neo-avant-garde and neo-dadaist forebears. They shared with the neo-avant-garde an appreciation of the urgency of overturning the priorities of the gallery and the canvas. They echoed the Situationist International's demand for participatory, collaborative artworks that challenged the nature of authorship. They played with the temporality of their pieces and, like Fluxus, refused to create art that could easily be pronounced complete. But the spatial interventionists also worked to distinguish themselves from the movements on whose shoulders they stood. Though they were generally of the left, they never took up capitalism itself as their explicit target and never danced to the beat of a single theory like Marxism. Nor were they satisfied with the project of land art. Its remove from everyday life and embeddedness in the individual creative experience of the artist rendered its full meaning nontransferable to the spectator and thus an inadequate vehicle for addressing broad social concerns. Even site-specific art lacked something. Though it "gave itself up to its environmental context" and rejected a Cartesian mode of appreciating the world in favor of one that emphasized lived, bodily experience—or, in the deeply critical language of the art historian Michael Fried, "theatricality"—it never enabled a radically democratic form of power.[67] The spatial interventionists refused to content themselves with creating "mere" public art.

The spatial interventionists were, in other words, dissatisfied with their options. Whether art whose creation implied its own destruction or the "event scores" of Fluxus or the "situations" of the Situationist International or the micro-rebellions of Subversive Aktion, the most promising art forms they had at their disposal had hitherto only *occupied* public space in various ways. The point, for Demnig and Beuys, however, was to *intervene* in it. Spatial intervention rejected bureaucratized forms of power routinized in the sites of public art. It aimed to overturn the priorities that governed the construction of, interaction with, and behavior within these sites. It regarded public space as an articulation of social values. And it generated opportunities for ordinary people to engage regularly in contesting and thus fabricating those values. Society, they argued, had accepted as a mundane reality a lack of control over the creation of meaning in the spaces of daily life. Against this current, the spatial interventionists sought to generate opportunities for ordinary people to engage regularly and consciously in contesting the meaning embedded in their quotidian environments. The people, they argued, should reappropriate every street, sidewalk, and façade.

As their art gradually occupied more prominent spaces outside of the gallery, spatial interventionists began to think more critically about what it meant to liberate art from the "white cube." They had started, as O'Doherty demanded, to "see not the art but the *space* first."[68] Artists in West Germany began to acknowledge that the site possessed a constellation of social influences that worked upon the viewing subject. Increasingly, they interpreted site not only in physical and spatial terms but "as a *cultural* framework." Whereas aesthetic minimalism had challenged "the idealist hermeticism of the autonomous art object by deflecting its meaning to the space of its presentation," this new group of artists criticized the hermeticism that operated in the presentation itself. The asceticism of the modern gallery and museum spaces increasingly appeared, in Miwon Kwon's words,

> as an institutional disguise, a normative exhibition convention serving an ideological function. The seemingly benign architectural features of a gallery / museum, in other words, were deemed to be coded mechanisms that actively disassociate the space of art from the outer world, furthering the institution's idealist imperative of rendering itself and its hierarchization of values "objective," "disinterested," and "true."[69]

To intervene in spaces beyond the traditional gallery or museum did not imply an attempt to escape norms entirely. These artists did not seek a tabula rasa upon which they could rewrite a set of self-consciously postmodern values to govern interaction with their art. Instead, they wanted to create a new cultural constellation that would lend their art new life. They paid attention to the "socioeconomic relations within which art and its institutional programming find their possibilities of being." And they rejected spaces tied to what Miwon Kwon has described as "the ideologically suspect if not morally corrupt power elite."[70] Instead, they prioritized sites with less-restrictive rules for use that would give the viewer more agency. But simply moving art beyond the gallery's walls would not address the problem of passivity. Art that passively occupied public space risked becoming mere ornament intended only to beautify the spaces of everyday life, or in the blunter words of one art historian, serving as "a form of decorative atonement for the sins of certain town planners, architects and landscape gardeners."[71] One curator of alternative art installations argued "that the majority of works in public space are mediocre, if not actually bad." The spatial interventionists viewed these kinds of works as an aesthetic Band-Aid. Through "artful camouflage" they patched up the aesthetic wounds that the self-abnegating functionalist art culture of the postwar era had inflicted upon itself. But such artworks, the curator suggested, "lead nowhere."[72] If acceptance of the gallery's hermeticism and static nature counted among the defining features of art inside the white cube, art beyond the white cube had to exhibit a perpetual discontentedness with the nature, the bounds, and the visitors to its site.

The object of these artists' discontent began to crystallize in their demand that artists replace the traditional primacy of visual perception with a kind of embodied aesthetic engagement. Spatial interventionist art prioritizes the body, rather than just the eye or the mind, as the epicenter aesthetic appreciation. The philosopher Michel de Certeau made such corporeal activity central to his definition of site. Site, or "space" for Certeau, was place "practiced"—that is, "composed of intersections of mobile elements" and "actuated by the ensemble of movements deployed within it." Space emerged as a product of action, not as a precondition for it. It remained "situated as the act of a present (or of a time), and modified by the transformations caused by successive contexts."[73] In this respect, space, according to Certeau, lacks stability or fixity. Its existence depends, precariously, on practice, on the act of intervention.

The stakes of aesthetic interventions in public space were high. We might understand the commitments of the spatial interventionists through the gravity philosopher Hannah Arendt attributed to spatial action. It formed the nucleus of her understanding of freedom. Arendt predicated the idea of freedom on the space in which that freedom is exercised, or what she called "the living space of freedom."[74] By rooting political freedom in humans' creative capacity to act and speak freely in concert with one another—what she dubbed the "web of human relationships"—Arendt offered a definition of freedom constituted intersubjectively and in the world.[75] Totalitarianism, she famously argued in 1951, originates in the conscious or unconscious limitation of the space of political action, in a withering away of the "public." Such a "fundamental deprivation of human rights," she claimed, appears "above all in the deprivation of a place in the world which makes opinions significant and actions effective."[76] By eliminating spaces for free action, or as Arendt suggested, by

> pressing men against each other, total terror destroys the space between them; compared to the condition within its iron band, even the desert of tyranny, insofar as it is still some kind of space, appears like a guarantee of freedom. Totalitarian government does not just curtail liberties or abolish essential freedoms; nor does it, at least to our limited knowledge, succeed in eradicating the love for freedom from the hearts of man. It destroys the one essential prerequisite of all freedom which is simply the capacity of motion which cannot exist without space.[77]

To limit public spaces for political action was to curtail one of the most essential elements of human life: freedom as the physical and discursive space between men.

The problem, as one American installation artist noticed, was that the most obvious spaces in which to enable such action had already been put to other use:

> The vertical is allotted to architecture, the horizontal to landscape architecture, and the network of lines between and through them to engineering. The city has all the design it needs. . . . Public art has to squeeze in and fit under and fall over what already exists in the city. Its mode of behavior is to perform operations—what appear to be unnecessary operations—upon the built environment: it adds to the vertical, subtracts from the horizontal, multiplies and divides the network of in-between lines.[78]

This crowded topographical canvas posed a challenge that would continue to preoccupy artists of public space into the twenty-first century. But the spatial interventionists began to see these limits as an opportunity. Fueled by a nagging uncertainty about West Germany's political program, spatial interventionists sought to use their art to radically expand such pivotal spaces for action. To seek new places for art did not mean the mere relocation of existing artistic expressions. It demanded the development of new, generative art concepts capable of creating new sites within an ostensibly limited topography. O'Doherty claimed that "space now is not just where things happen; things make space happen."[79] The American artist Vito Acconci made the same point when he argued that the "function of public art is to de-design." Public art had to deconstruct established norms of aesthetic engagement with public space by first making those norms visible. Then it had to give its viewers the opportunity to overturn those norms by fashioning a different relationship to that space.[80] As Miwon Kwon explained a few years before Acconci, the task was to

> decode and / or recode the institutional conventions so as to expose their hidden yet motivated operations—to reveal the ways in which institutions mold art's meaning to modulate its cultural and economic value, and to undercut the fallacy of art and its institutions' "autonomy" by making apparent their imbricated relationship to the broader socioeconomic and political processes of the day.[81]

Art's site "evolves away from its coincidence with the literal space of art, and the physical condition of a specific location recedes as the primary element in the conception of a site." Instead, it is the "*techniques* and *effects* of the art institution as they circumscribe the definition, production, presentation, and dissemination of art that become the sites of critical intervention." For the spatial interventionists, the nature of the work of art shifted from a static existence to an active enterprise. As Kwon has theorized, "the 'work' no longer seeks to be a noun / object but a verb / process, provoking the viewers' *critical* (not just physical) acuity regarding the ideological conditions of that viewing."[82] Here, the original object of critique, the disembodied Cartesian thinker-viewer, is reintegrated dialectically into a process of art production and reception. The spatial interventionists placed this act of uniting production and reception at the heart of their efforts.

Practically speaking, the process of renegotiating the politics of power in public space most often revolved around the official permission required to alter these sites. Among the first questions the spatial interventionists confronted was whether they were actually allowed to do anything with the spaces in question beyond those uses already sanctioned by the city or state.[83] Because the administration of cultural matters in West Germany rested in the hands of regional authorities rather than with the central government, municipal idiosyncrasies in cultural policy tended to put these artists at the mercy of local administrators. While creating *Duftmarken,* for example, Demnig had not officially registered his project and was consequently arrested in France because, as he discovered, "you are not allowed just to go about printing things on the streets."[84] Such an observation may seem banal, but it indicated that the spatial interventionists had encroached upon spaces that had hitherto been closed to artistic manipulation.

Their artworks challenged what was commonly understood as art's "territory." They made central to their work the project of exploring, overturning, and rewriting the boundaries of where art belonged and what it sought to do there.[85] The boundaries that most concerned the spatial interventionists were not obvious physical boundaries—the walls of the gallery, the edge of the frame, or the perimeter of public space. They were, instead, figurative boundaries imagined and maintained through social consensus and dialogue. Demnig wanted to expand what he understood as art's "communicative contexts" in order to tie it to a larger community of interlocutors: academics, scientists, community leaders, and, most importantly, the broad category of "the public."[86]

This relatively straightforward objective of spatial interventionist art was what made it both so powerful and so confusing. These artists used the spatiality of their artworks, ironically, to shift attention away from the fixed physical location of the work toward its fluid, virtual, discursive existence.[87] Here, the spatial interventionists absorbed a facet of philosopher Jürgen Habermas's thought. For Habermas, the bourgeois public sphere had constituted itself not in a particular physical space but in the diffuse, anonymous "space" of public conversation.[88] Drawing from Arendt's understanding of human action as linguistically conditioned, or as understandable "for what it is only through a narrative account," Habermas identified the rise of a form of publicity during the Enlightenment in which a predominantly visual public became an auditory one. In Habermas's work, the "space" of the public sphere shifts away from Arendt's topographical and spatial understanding of the space of action toward one in which spoken words and printed media play a leading role.[89] Similar to what Benedict Anderson would later call an "imagined community" constituted by the "homogeneous, empty time" of a collective, simultaneous readership of mass media, Habermas identified a publicness or "public sphere" (*Öffentlichkeit*) formed through the depersonalized communicative medium of print capitalism: citizen-readers engaged with a marketed text rather than immediately face-to-face with its author.[90] Though their medium took the form of art rather than print capitalism, the spatial interventionists assimilated their own version of Habermas's claims. Citizens would engage one another in a dialogue provoked by the spatial medium of spatial interventionist artworks. The space of the artwork thus became more capacious. It could incorporate sites as diverse as "different cultural debates, a theoretical concept, a social issue, a political problem, an institutional framework (not necessarily an art institution), a community or seasonal event, a historical condition, even particular formations of desire."[91]

The transgression of spatial interventionist art, although mediated by physical space, was thus actually an intervention in public dialogue. Their work foregrounded the site as a discursive "field of knowledge, intellectual exchange, or cultural debate." That is, the site did not exist *a priori* but was produced by the artwork itself. Kwon has argued that "unlike previous models, this site is not defined as a *pre*condition. Rather, it is *generated* by the work (often as 'content'), and then *verified* by its convergence with an existing discursive formation."[92] The art historian James Meyer has echoed Kwon's argument by referring to these artworks as occupying a "functional site" rather than the "literal site" of more traditional art. The literal site indicates "an actual location, a singular place," a work "*in situ.*" The capacity of art embedded in this literal site to generate discourse or meaning is determined by that specific physical location.[93] The functional site, by contrast, operates dynamically within and upon the work. This site lets go of its physical space and becomes, instead, "a process, an operation occurring between sites, a mapping of institutional and discursive filiations and the bodies that move between them. . . . It is a temporary thing, a movement, a chain of meanings and imbricated histories: a place marked and swiftly abandoned. The mobile site thus courts its destruction; it is willfully temporary; its nature is not to endure but to *come down.*"[94] The effect of the functional site is to orient the artwork discursively rather than phenomenologically. It "textualizes spaces . . . and spatializes discourses," Kwon argues, similar to the way one can "surf" the internet. The ability to conceive of the site of an artwork as something more than a particular place requires a major conceptual leap as well as a redefinition of the "public" role of art and artists.[95]

The discursive nature of the functional space helps make sense of the power of Beuys's and Demnig's work. The permanence of their artworks as intentional and recognizable works—that is, the significance of their literal site—faded with time. Demnig's physical traces dissipated. Beuys's trees have gradually become routinized as trees rather than as art installations. But the discursive trace remained, repeatedly reconstituted in public memory and dialogue.[96] Johannes Stüttgen, an artist as well as a student and friend of Joseph Beuys, noted how the gradual replacement of place by dialogue, the literal site by the functional, the phenomenological by the discursive, marked dialectical moment in these spatial interventionist artworks. This moment signaled both an end and a beginning—an end to the obsession with the physicality of the artwork and the beginning of the work's afterlife, like a grain of sand in an oyster, an irritant that provoked society to smooth out its edges and incorporate the pearl into its conceptual framework. This process of social reckoning with art was collective and dialogic, undertaken repeatedly and voluntarily by independent artists and citizen-viewers. For that reason, Stüttgen understood these artworks to "stand for a kind of internal democracy." Both the individual and the collective willingness to engage with the artwork's concept "cannot be delegated, abdicated, [or] relinquished because it is rooted in the individual and in that individual's personal creative capacity as an artist" to remake art continually as a fixture on the gallery wall of society.[97]

2

A Workshop of "History from Below"

In an obituary published in 1997, German historian Peter Schöttler drew a particularly poignant picture of the deceased, a British academic, whom he described at once as a heretic, a pathbreaker, and an ideas-man. With the tenderness of a student charged with representing a cherished mentor's legacy, Schöttler mused about the scholar's lecture style. He arrived with a large shopping bag overflowing with sheets of paper that he would spread across the lectern. Out of this jumbled mess of citations, images, embryonic ideas, and unanswered questions, he "assembled his lecture right before his audience's very eyes." Though many of his colleagues saw his ad hoc pedagogical style as a sign of deficient professionalism, he understood every lecture as a workshop. By showing his cards and by inviting from the audience interruption, questioning, corrections, and elaborations, he believed that, together, they could create the lecture's content.[1]

The obituary honored Raphael Samuel, British Marxist historian and father of Britain's hub for alternative social history, the History Workshop. Schöttler's vignette appeared just four months after Samuel's death in *Werkstatt-Geschichte,* a German-language journal that emerged out of Germany's own History Workshop movement.[2] Schöttler admired Samuel's methods. An exponent of "history from below," Samuel championed historical inquiry that featured the working class, whose daily lives capitalism's bourgeois ideology had excluded from the historical record. Samuel demanded those histories be written, and written from the perspective of those who had lived them. He regarded social history and the history of everyday life as an "open text."[3] In Samuel's lecture style, Schöttler saw the epitome of such open, interactive historical inquiry. It also represented the objectives of a popular trend in West Germany that the German magazine *Der Spiegel,* in 1983, dubbed Germany's "new history movement."[4]

Nearly four decades after the collapse of National Socialism, four decades of politics and society full steam ahead, West Germany finally stopped to catch its breath. After almost forty years "hectically in pursuit of 'getting on with things [*Vorwärtskommen*],' a whole generation was struck with a retrospective impulse," a young historian named Ulrich Herbert claimed. Stuttgart history professor Axel Kuhn argued, abstractly, that a generation of students had begun "to grasp that its history was being taken away [*weggenommen worden ist*]." A hodge-podge collection of German academics, social workers, teachers, librarians, and interested local citizens agreed.[5] For some, the culprit was only the turning of calendar pages. Others positioned themselves against what they labeled, pejoratively, the "Historians' Guild (*Historikerzunft*)," by which they designated professionally trained historians in secure and hard-to-come-by university chairs.[6] Though these historians claimed neutrality in their work, many saw them as reinforcing a power dynamic that excluded from historical inquiry the voices of ordinary people, or what they called "*kleine Leute.*"

With a rhetoric mirroring Raphael Samuel's British history collective, partisans of Germany's New History Movement aimed to "work through history from the bottom up, from the perspective of and, when possible, with the participation of those who lived through it."[7] The movement ramified quickly. It generated new museums, historical walking tours, student research competitions, and a kind of historical forensics (*Spurensicherer;* literally, trace-savers) that tried to preserve the remaining physical residue of Germany's past. The most concise crystallization of its agenda, however, was the formation of German History Workshops.

Founded as a national organization in Göttingen in 1982, the German History Workshop or *Geschichtswerkstatt* (henceforth in German to distinguish it from the British example; plural, *Geschichtswerkstätten*) engaged individuals committed to building a "Left-pluralistic forum for alternative historical research."[8] From Oldenburg to Konstanz, Berlin to Solingen, Schöttler explained in 1984, these grassroots historians ramped up their efforts to explore new modes of nonhierarchical historical inquiry.[9] They wanted to use this historical knowledge to advance a radically democratic worldview.[10] This chapter follows the development of the particularly active Berlin branch of the *Geschichtswerkstatt*.[11]

The Berlin *Geschichtswerkstatt* (BGW) organized historical exhibits, installations, tours, and lectures based on three principles. First, it sought to facilitate grassroots democratic historical inquiry. Members insisted history should be narrated by everyday people as well as told from their perspective. The Berlin *Geschichtswerkstatt*'s projects thus became a community effort. Second, it stressed decentralization. Rather than hosting events at convenient high-traffic sites in the heart of the city, the group chose to locate its projects "*vor Ort*"—that is, at the places where historical events actually happened. These were often residential streets, quiet alleyways, or underdeveloped open spaces. Finally, the Berlin *Geschichtswerkstatt* attempted to endow its projects with an internal motor. Its members resisted presenting their research findings as final theses. Instead, they intended their work to generate ongoing debate and continually evolve as participants uncovered more information. Like Raphael Samuel's lectures, the *Geschichtswerkstatt* created a forum to facilitate interactive, discursive, bottom-up historical analysis.

A collection of recent scholarship has newly underscored the historical significance of the *Geschichtswerkstätten*. In her detailed study based heavily on interviews with former participants, Jenny Wüstenberg has contextualized the group in a diverse grassroots activist milieu, whose interventions shaped postwar German memory politics.[12] Ian Gwinn's comparative analysis of the British and West German History Workshops also relied on oral histories. Gwinn has revealed the groups' aim to dismantle undemocratic hierarchies of knowledge by building solidarities across gender and class.[13] This chapter builds on this important work. By tracing the formation, conceptual influences, and first major projects of the Berlin *Geschichtswerkstatt*, it demonstrates how the organization used the study of history to advance not just a democratic mode of historical research, but a radically democratic spatial project.

The Emancipatory Potential of History

Many of the BGW's founders remember the group's origins only vaguely, as an "atmosphere." Dates and names have faded. What remains from the first meeting, a brainstorming session on 19 November 1980, is its imperative. The twenty-five attendees made a poster to hang in student centers and elsewhere around Berlin, demanding "COME BUILD A BERLIN GESCHICHTSWERKSTATT." It summoned guests to a second meeting two months later. To the group's organizers, the stakes of attendance were high. "It was obvious," one participant wrote, that they "considered the various movements and battles of the Left to have waned, and they worried that their stories might perish in the great underworld of historical scholarship." The first members of the *Geschichtswerkstatt* appealed to those who wanted to oppose "the state-sponsored historical narrative . . . with alternative histories 'from below.'" Their call-to-arms extended to "all who [wished] to prevent (this) history from going to the dogs and being forgotten." As would later become evident, however, the message was much clearer than the means to advance it.[14]

For its reputation as an epicenter of grassroots organization and alternative culture in Berlin, the neighborhood of Kreuzberg served as the group's gathering point for its first official meeting on 23 January 1981. The eighty individuals who participated met in the Mehringhof, the first of Berlin's apartment buildings to have been occupied in the 1970s during the city's housing crisis. With such a large turnout, disagreement reigned as participants tried to establish a set of objectives. One faculty member from Berlin's Technical University gained traction when he charged the group with pursuing three pillars: it should promote the communication of historical experiences, develop an archive of materials in short supply in established archival institutions, and mediate contact between similar organizations. But these pillars offered little help in narrowing down the group's concrete interests. Participants proposed research projects as diverse as the worker's movement during the Weimar Republic and the House Occupation Movement in the 1970s.[15]

Participants did, however, share a set of social circumstances that aligned their basic commitments.[16] Many were academic transplants to Berlin, drawn to the city's reputation for alternative thinking. The study of everyday life in Berlin offered a detailed roadmap to acquaint them with their new environment. Many wanted to engage politically but found opportunities to exercise political influence mostly beyond their reach. Stories of historic resistance efforts became an antidote to their sense of disenfranchisement. Many nurtured a fascination with the legends of the so-called Red Wedding, a militant Communist district in the central part of the city whose violent struggles against the Nazis in the 1920s made it an enduring icon of the struggle against fascism. A study of Wedding's response to the renter protest movement that had begun the previous decade was a natural choice for one of the BGW's first activities.[17]

That at least a third of those present at the initial meeting were female would later influence the group's agenda. At the time, however, these gender demographics mostly generated friction over what to call their organization. Theo Pinkus—a Swiss publisher and bookseller who would become a key mentor for the organization—suggested the Franz Mehring Society in honor of one of the leaders of Weimar's radical leftist Spartacus League and the namesake of their meeting site. Though his suggestion met with considerable approval, its reception was chillier among the women in attendance. They pointed out that naming it after Clara Zetkin—a Spartacist and women's rights activist—could accomplish the same goal. One of the women present, Ursula Schröter, settled the disagreement by stressing that the group should communicate openness rather than a narrow political agenda. She suggested they simply call it the History Workshop or *Geschichtswerkstatt,* as in the original advertisement. Her suggestion stuck, and four months later, on 25 May 1981, the Berlin *Geschichtswerkstatt* was officially founded.[18]

BGW members likened the spirit that motivated them to that of the generation of 1968. They saw themselves as participating in a broad social and political movement invested in critiquing Germany's dominant institutions.[19] The organization advanced what its participants understood as a "novel kind of historical analysis," one that approached history as a collective, non-elitist, public activity. By bringing the practice of historical research out of the confines of the university and by prioritizing the study of everyday life, they believed they could enable more democratic engagement with history. They described their methods—which combined archival work, oral interviews, lectures, and neighborhood walks—as stretching from "traditional and academic" to "unconventional and experimental."[20] And they distinguished their products both from a top-down understanding of history oriented around the nation-state and from narrower folk histories.

The Berlin *Geschichtswerkstatt* was not alone in its concern about the university's proprietary relationship to the practice of history or its interest in using history to stimulate popular political engagement. In 1983, the German magazine *Der Spiegel* published an article that described a "new history movement [*neue Geschichtsbewegung*]" sweeping West Germany.[21] A motley and interdisciplinary crew of professional historians, other social scientists, and educational administrators had begun to join ranks with laypeople to form regional working groups dedicated to using history to intervene in the politics of their communities. They generated interest among adherents of the New Social Movements of the 1970s and 1980s, the newly formed German Green Party, and students whose initial interest in history had been piqued by West German president Gustav Heinemann's national Student Research Contest in History, held annually since 1973.[22] The professional academic half of the History Movement included ethnographers like Hans Medick and Alf Lüdtke in Göttingen; members of Dieter Groh's Marxist group in Constance; oral historians like Lutz Niethammer, Franz-Josef Brüggemeier, and Ulrich Herbert; German feminists like Regina Schulte, Dorothee Wierling, Annette Kuhn, Ursula Nienhaus, and Karin Hausen; and quantitative historians. On occasion, they also received support from older established historians like Martin Broszat.[23] Through their resistance to the conservative cultural milieu created by the Kohl administration, they were set to become, Jenny Wüstenberg has argued, "amongst the most important actors in German memory politics" of the late twentieth century.[24]

In November 1982, a year and a half after the founding of the Berlin *Geschichtswerkstatt*, many of these historians gathered in Göttingen to bring to life a national *Geschichtswerkstatt*. They wanted to create an umbrella association to coordinate the regional historical groups that had begun to form throughout the Federal Republic. One hundred people gathered again in May 1983 in Bochum, where they formally registered the organization and drafted the group's charter. Its research priorities included the histories of gender, power, repression, resistance, everyday life, and the local. Members remained open to using traditional archival sources like government and press documents, but they stressed the need for more conscious use of the objects and records of everyday life together with eyewitness testimonies.[25] They envisioned this research as "cooperative" and "solidarity-generating" and believed that, by revealing the relevance of the past to the challenges of the present, it would fuel greater interest in history and greater civic participation. By the end of the decade, the national *Geschichtswerkstatt* grew to more than three hundred members and at least forty local affiliate groups.[26]

Within Germany, the phenomenon of the History Movement was unique. Writing in retrospect, two professional historians explained that "history, which used . . . to be such a solemn social science" in Germany, "is now the only discipline in the humanities that can boast a grass-roots movement."[27] Being identified as a movement, however, did not simultaneously imply its internal coherence.[28] Those *Geschichtswerkstatt* members also employed in universities hoped to use the group to advance the academic discipline of history.[29] Political activists pushed to use history as a medium for popular political education. Critics of the increasingly reformist and middle-class Social Democratic Party saw the *Geschichtswerkstatt* as an opportunity to advertise the history of the Left.[30] Former contributors to the Student Movement held on to their disappointments over failed revolutionary projects and sought to put the *Geschichtswerkstatt* to work identifying the deeper causes of their failure.[31] Women's groups wanted to write history's female agents back into the historical record.[32] Teachers called for an exploration of new historical pedagogy. Locals wanted to cultivate a "sense of belonging," or *Heimat*, by learning the history of their own communities. But public representations of the *Geschichtswerkstätten*, both self-generated and in the press, often swept these differences under the rug. Before they "could catch their breath to discuss who they were and what they were all about," the media hype gave them a sense of "false unity."[33] Only in 1991 did the national *Geschichtswerkstatt* publish on the challenges of its internal fragmentation.[34] Still, *Geschichtswerkstatt* members found themselves drawn together by their self-conception as "memory workers." They recognized that ordinary people often leave behind few traces and thus set out to reconstruct and catalogue their lives as few others had.[35]

Despite its peculiarity in Germany, precedent for this kind of a grassroots historical organization existed beyond German borders, namely in Britain. Two decades prior, during a postwar crisis in the British Left, a peculiar "unorthodox and critical Marxism" birthed an intellectual movement in England that abandoned the economism of orthodox Marxism and Stalinism as well as Leninist vanguardism and instead took as its subject the autonomy of culture in social life. Less a political movement than the catalyst in the creation of a "space for cultural politics and theory in Britain," the British New Left distinguished itself from the traditional Left by rejecting the historical inevitability of socialist transformation. At the same time, its proponents attempted to reclaim an "appreciation of historical traditions of popular resistance."[36] The British History Workshop emerged from within this climate. Members took on the two-part project of telling the histories of ordinary people and of democratizing efforts to write this history from below.[37] In the manner of Marxist historian and intellectual luminary E. P. Thompson, they sought to "rescue" ordinary historical actors "from the enormous condescension of posterity" by treating them not as "passive victims of historical circumstances but active makers and creators of their own history."[38] On account of its breadth, culture could not be mastered by a small group. It was, thus, an "intrinsically democratic" subject matter.[39] Accessing "culture from below" required that members of the History Workshop tap into new kinds of primary sources and assemble them into a narrative using plain language to make their content accessible to a broad audience. Because they understood history as an inroad to contemporary political engagement, the stakes of this fight for accessibility were high.

Basic affinities between the British and German History Workshops were obvious. The German *Geschichtswerkstatt* is, for one, a literal translation of the English "History Workshop," and both groups formed as a challenge to dominant historiographical cultures. But the *Geschichtswerkstatt*'s indebtedness to its British predecessor, some fifteen years its elder, remained at best a specter in the 1980s. German speakers attentive to historical issues would have had at least a perfunctory awareness that a group of socialist historians and laypeople with an interest in history had assembled in the mid-1970s in Oxford, England. They might have known that this historically minded collective had gathered oral testimonies about the beginning of the workers' and women's movements. The 1983 *Spiegel* article devoted three paragraphs to the international models that inspired this new German interest in the past, including the British example.[40] Those with more specialized historical investments might have picked up the 1985 collection of essays devoted to this "new history movement," where they would have encountered the German-language essay by British historian and student of British Marxism's greats, Richard Evans. Evans's contribution introduced German readers to a more nuanced story about the origins and content of the History Workshop.[41] But attention to British influence on Germany's History Movement was ultimately slight.

Among publications released by the national *Geschichtswerkstatt*, a 1984 special issue of its (short-lived) journal *Modern Times* (*Moderne Zeiten*, or *MOZ*) gave Raphael Samuel just three pages to explain "the British model" and its goals.[42] Otherwise, this issue of *MOZ*—released just before the largest gathering of *Geschichtswerkstatt* members and supporters, the 1984 "HistoryFest" (*Geschichtsfest*) in Berlin—reserved a scant thirty words for the History Workshop.[43] Berliners proved slightly more generous in their citations. The Berlin *Geschichtswerkstatt*'s engagement with the theories and methods of the history of everyday life in their self-published book *Alltagskultur, Subjektivität und Geschichte: Zur Theorie und Praxis von Alltagsgeschichte* (Everyday culture, subjectivity, and history: On the theory and practice of the history of everyday life) (1994) devoted two pages to "people's history," oral history, and the background of England's History Workshop movement.[44] A subsequent chapter also gave a hat tip to the scholarly developments abroad, particularly the work of Thompson.[45] The *Geschichtswerkstatt*'s founding newsletter—both less formal and likely more widely read—however, made no references to England. Nor did its first stab in 1984 at a programmatic leaflet printed for broad distribution or its twenty-year retrospective published in 2001.[46] Even in an English-language write-up on history workshops in Germany published by the British History Workshop itself, German historian and *Geschichtswerkstatt* participant Michael Wildt noted the nominal similarities between the two groups, but otherwise used their substantive differences as a springboard for discussing the German example, absent any comparative analysis.[47]

The *Geschichtswerkstatt*'s stunted appreciation for the History Workshop may have been a product of limited materials available in translation. As of 1997, only two essays of Raphael Samuel's had been translated into German.[48] Works from the British Marxist historians who operated to varying degrees in tandem with the History Workshop were more numerous, however. German translations for select texts by E. P. Thomson, Christopher Hill, Eric Hobsbawm, George Rudé, and R. H. Hilton were available as early as 1977.[49] If Schöttler's flattering obituary for Samuel offers any indication, the impact of the British History Workshop on the German iteration may have become clearer only in hindsight.

The reasons people chose to participate in the *Geschichtswerkstatt* were as individual as the histories they narrated. Two motivating factors, however, frequently surfaced. Many were drawn in by the new wave of interest in Holocaust history that swelled in the late 1970s and 1980s. The year 1979 saw the West German release of the four-part American television series *Holocaust,* and 1984 brought the first season of the German series *Heimat.* These series invited Germans to reconsider the violence of National Socialism and their post-Holocaust national identity.[50] The power of round numbers also helped. The year 1983 marked the fiftieth anniversary of—sometimes referred to, more coolly, as the fifty-year "distance" (*Distanz*) from—Hitler's ascension to power on 30 January 1933. The date not only occasioned the creation of many *Geschichtswerkstätten.* It also generated popular curiosity about the role ordinary people played in the Nazi state.[51]

Also bolstering interest in the *Geschichtswerkstatt* was the broad "crisis of identity" that many West Germans confronted during the Kohl years. The historian Klaus Tenfelde argued that German society stood before a turning point. "The exhaustion of modernism, the aridity of the communist *Dasein,* the tedium of the unchained individual, the substance-less nature [*Wesenlosigkeit*] of monolithic political slogans—all of this signals that a long era is gradually coming to an end," he claimed.[52] Many began to subscribe to the idea that modern life had not only destroyed social connections but also the social spaces in which those connections were made.[53] Even Secretary of the Department of the Interior Horst Waffenschmidt suggested that West Germans had begun to recognize social alienation and disorientation as the high price for economic progress.[54] Some claimed that West Germans had lost their ability to locate themselves as part of a historical narrative.[55] The task, executive committee member Alfred Georg Frei argued, was to side with Marxist philosopher Ernst Bloch, who understood the "root of history" as "the working, creating person, the person who revises and refashions reality. Once he has grasped himself," Bloch argued in his book *The Principle of Hope,* "and established what is his, without expropriation and alienation, in real democracy, there arises in the world something . . . in which no one has yet been: Home." The *Geschichtswerkstatt,* Frei claimed, gave people tools to search for "home" in a country that seemed to lack it.[56] This renewed desire to locate oneself socially and spatially generated an attentiveness to the physical places people inhabit. *Geschichtswerkstatt* members tended to gravitate in their research toward the mundane spaces where everyday life takes place even in the most radical of historical moments, or what they described as historical work *vor Ort*. This concern for a diversity of local sites, the Berlin *Geschichtswerkstatt*'s 1983 organizational program explained, led group members to prioritize narrating history in the plural, rather than trying to articulate *the* history.[57]

They likened their mode of historical inquiry to a kind of localized excavation. Undertaking historical work *vor Ort* required that you "dig where you stand." With this phrase, they gestured to an important source of inspiration in the Swedish nonfiction writer Sven Lindqvist. Frustrated with his inability to find information on the history of Sweden's ordinary citizens, particularly its industrial working class, Lindqvist embarked on a project in the late 1970s to write these workers into Sweden's historical narratives.[58] Lindqvist argued that the workers themselves should be the ones to write these histories.[59] They lacked only competence in the basic methodologies of sound historical research. To facilitate their efforts, Lindqvist wrote a practical handbook for worker-cum-historians interested in researching their trades. In 1978, he completed *Dig Where You Stand* (*Gräv där du står*).[60] The attraction of what became known as the Dig-Where-You-Stand Movement, Lindqvist explained, lay in its ability to reveal the ways history "lives on in the bodies of living people" and still pays dividends by conferring power on some people but not on others.[61]

It took several years for Lindqvist's works to appear in German translation, but he managed to maneuver his way into German conversations earlier. The 1983 *Spiegel* article pointed to Lindqvist and the hundreds of local research circles in the Swedish Dig-Where-You-Stand Movement as a template for Germans.[62] Not all press on Lindqvist's influence was uncritical. In 1989, the historian of everyday life Alf Lüdtke argued that the imperative to dig where one stood was "necessary but . . . not sufficient" for the Germans who, he claimed, needed "to delve deeper while [also] extending one's own diggings horizontally."[63] But German practitioners of "history from below" generally welcomed Lindqvist's insights. Admittedly, the discussion of his lessons consisted more of hype than substance. Terms like "history from below" and "history of everyday life" remained largely "euphoric key words, without much theoretical or methodological consideration," noted one Berlin *Geschichtswerkstatt* member. Nevertheless, the BGW turned to Lindqvist for guidance on democratizing the project of writing history, enabling citizens to research their own histories, and connecting these histories to current political dialogue.[64]

Performing New Power Relationships

Germany's receptivity to historical analysis that took local history and the history of everyday life as points of departure was conditioned by the rise of the New Left over the prior two decades. It offered a model of bottom-up historical consciousness in the service of the present and future. If intellectual luminary Herbert Marcuse was the New Left's "*Stichwortgeber*"—literally, the one who provides keywords but also the one who prompts others to articulate themselves—among his key contributions was his notion of "practice." Practice (*Praxis*) and its relationship to theory had been fraught for decades within the German Left, as had the question of whether Germany's contemporary political situation called for a new form of political practice.[65] But as the New Left jettisoned rigid theoretical allegiances, it tended to side with those who privileged action over theoretical rigor. As American sociologist C. Wright Mills explained, being a Leftist meant consciously linking cultural and political criticism with concrete programs.[66] This combination of disillusionment with existing politics and a demand for action gave the New Left occasion not only to envision but also to attempt to realize an alternative political practice. Its proponents embraced informal popular politics, the expressions of which "grew out of imagination, necessity, and a desire to be heard."[67]

After the fire of the New Left, the Student Movement, and the promises of 1968 began to dim, two programmatic points retained their spark. The first was the politicization—specifically, the democratization—of everyday life. Amid the excitement of the late 1960s, young Leftists had startled the increasingly reformist Social Democratic establishment by advocating not for moderate, modernized socialist policy but for radically transformative systemic reforms (*systemüberwindende Reformen*). Intent on "democratizing all realms of life," they encouraged a grassroots politics of everyday life (*Alltagspolitik*) and tapped the whole of society to lead this initiative.[68] This demand prompted the creation of a new political habitat. The New Left had occasioned a reevaluation of spaces for its activism. Sometimes, in the process, it also discovered new spaces for public engagement. Historian Hanno Hochmuth has described these as "counterpublics [*Gegenöffentlichkeiten*]."[69] Historian Belinda Davis has called them "alternate public spheres."[70] As the Student Movement dissipated at the turn of the decade, the university lost some of its centrality in the effort to galvanize political organization.[71] The work of alternative politics increasingly moved "behind the scenes," Davis has suggested, into these alternate public spheres the New Left had nurtured. This shift played an active role in "creating new spaces for communication, affording alternative modes of living, working, and interacting, and sometimes offering protection from repression."[72]

The *Geschichtswerkstatt* developed as one of these extracurricular, extraparliamentary attempts to defend the radical democratization of everyday life. According to one founding member, it was the offspring of a generation of students "still wooed to West Berlin by the myth of the Student Movement but who found no more connection to 'the movement' there."[73] Drawing on the work of the leftist sociologist and former member of the Socialist German Student League (*Sozialistische Deutsche Studentenbund,* or SDS) Helmut Dahmer, *Geschichtswerkstatt* members argued that society's ability to "master" its present hinged on the individual's ability to grasp one's situation as historically determined.[74] Seeing themselves as the torchbearers of the spirit of the Student Movement and the New Left, *Geschichtswerkstatt* members pushed progressive historical work as a means of social and political emancipation.

When *Geschichtswerkstatt* members wanted to drive home the liberating potential of the practice of history, however, they evoked the language not of the New Left but of the Enlightenment. One leader of the national *Geschichtswerkstatt* argued that progressive (*aufklärerisch*) historical work must be used as a weapon against immaturity or *Unmündigkeit.* Here, he cited the historical theorist Jörn Rüsen. But Rüsen's phrasing immediately calls to mind Immanuel Kant's 1784 essay on the question "What is Enlightenment?" For Kant, Enlightenment demanded "mankind's exit from its self-incurred immaturity" and the ability "to make use of one's own understanding without the guidance of another." For Rüsen, "history as Enlightenment" meant giving individuals the capacity to write their own histories. The *Geschichtswerkstatt* interpreted this demand as a call to detach the practice of writing history from the university's exclusionary spaces and rituals. Three principles guided such historical work. First, *Geschichtswerkstatt* members rejected a Rankean pursuit of history "as it actually was." Even the best researcher, they argued, could not *construct* history. History is always a reconstruction that reflects how the researcher imagines the past. They understood these reconstructions, second, as shaped by the problems of the present. Third, they insisted that researchers approach their work as goal-oriented (*ziel-gelenkte Geschichtsarbeit*). Channeling sociologist Max Weber, they insisted history should call into question dominant socioeconomic structures and challenge the purposive or instrumental (*zweckrationaler*) form of reason that they understood to structure contemporary life. *Geschichtswerkstatt* members wanted their work to override (*aufheben;* here, they also channeled Hegel) contemporary modes of rationality in favor of an ethical rationality organized around the pursuit of a "democratic, peaceful, and human global society."[75]

What made history such a fruitful means for the *Geschichtswerkstatt* to pursue a more democratic, more peaceful, less disaggregated society lay in the group's understanding of the practices of history as practices in the democratization of space. They wanted their work to change their physical environment, and they wanted these changes to enable new kinds of social interactions. These desires made *Geschichtswerkstatt* members particularly receptive to the new conceptual and methodological developments in the field of history that studied these spaces and interactions, namely the history of everyday life (*Alltagsgeschichte*). Arguably the most important development in West German historiography in the 1980s, *Alltagsgeschichte* found one of its clearest manifestations in the work of the *Geschichtswerkstatt*.[76]

Alltagsgeschichte first gained traction when history students of the 1960s and 1970s graduated only to find themselves jobless. From its inception, it thus developed as a largely extracurricular phenomenon. It drew support from some scholars employed within the academy. The historians Lutz Niethammer and Alexander von Plato among others at the University of Hagen proved particularly invested. But its primary momentum came from individuals working outside of the university system.[77] This new fascination with the everyday attracted practitioners from museums, local cultural institutions, the media, and film. They brought with them a combination of "zeal, anti-academism, and populist politics."[78]

These historians-against-the-grain understood formal historiographical traditions to have excised the world of ordinary life from their purview.[79]

Because their "discovery" of the alternative world (*Gegenwelt*) of everydayness coincided with the rise of the German Green Party and its grassroots democratic ambitions, some have regarded the popularization of *Alltagsgeschichte* as a "greening" of the social history pioneered in the 1960s by the Bielefeld School.[80] Bielefeld practitioners had used the methods of social science to reveal the structures that guided society's operations. Among Berlin *Geschichtswerkstatt* members, however, some understood themselves as "[declaring] war on modern social history with its valorization of objective categories and its suppression of the significance of categories of human subjectivity."[81] A key figure in the rise of *Alltagsgeschichte,* Alf Lüdtke concurred, arguing that "the history of everyday life demands the *systematic decentering* of analysis and interpretation. . . . The classification of individual phenomena and their systematization no longer occupy center stage. At issue now," he claimed, was "the very act of 'conceptualizing, idea formation [*Vorstellen*].'"[82] Proponents of *Alltagsgeschichte* opposed Bielefeld's tendency to hold individual actors as the "mere bearers of the potential for modernization" and to regard long trade cycles, population mobility, development of a rational state, bureaucracy, and political parties as the agents of their histories.[83]

Practitioners of *Alltagsgeschichte,* by contrast, wanted to treat the farmer, the artisan, the factory worker as the agents of history. Through these kinds of historical actors, they demanded to see "the 'insides' of the society's structures, processes, and models analyzed" by the historical social science of the Bielefeld School: the totality of values, orientation, models of behavior, and interpretive frameworks.[84] *Alltagsgeschichte* sought to measure historical change by its "internal costs" to the "informal domain of the everyday," not in terms of the "alienated world of formal political engagement."[85] Historians of everyday life looked to Friedrich Engels, for whom "the dynamism and contradictory character of radical historical change are linked with the 'production and reproduction of real life.'" *Kleine Leute* became "simultaneously both the objects of history and its subjects."[86]

These historians wanted to pursue history "from below" without the mythical, often racist connotations given to the earthly by National Socialism.[87] It was the doubly suggestive association of "from below" that made it particularly suitable for describing *Alltagsgeschichte.* The phrase, first, suggests "the history of those who were and are 'below.' Its goal is the dialectical consideration of the 'other side,' that is, the contradictory relationship between power and accommodation [*Anpassung*], between oppression and resistance," Peter Schöttler explained. "Second, however, it also expresses sympathy for the difficulties of the lower classes [*Unterschichten*]."[88]

While practitioners of *Alltagsgeschichte* prioritized the experiences of the lower classes, Marxist theory—or theory in general—provided their ideas no real infrastructure (unlike the History Workshop in England). They conceived of class, at best, broadly. From the French Marxist Henri Lefebvre they learned to remain wary of the strong arm of consumer culture, the fetish character of money, and the experience of psychological and moral alienation.[89] Still, the working class was never their emancipatory subject. *Alltagsgeschichte* challenged historians of the Left by showing patterns of self-organization based on different modes of life within classes as well as revealing the limits of organization in terms of class.[90]

This approach did not sit well with some important members of the academic establishment. What Alf Lüdtke described as "[decentering] entrenched ways of seeing historiography" Bielefelder Jürgen Kocka called "new irrationalism." Kocka qualified *Alltagsgeschichte*'s practices as "fundamentally unscientific" and thus "hostile to Enlightenment values." Shortly after the *Historikerstreit,* he lumped practitioners of *Alltagsgeschichte* together with historians Ernst Nolte and Andreas Hillgruber, whose comparison of Nazi Germany's totalitarianism with Soviet Russia's won them the wrath of many leftist intellectuals. Kocka chastised the lot for failing to adopt the "rigorous method" and "argumentative . . . presentation" of history. These, he argued, were the field's bulwarks against a blind embrace of myth. Bielefeld behemoth Hans-Ulrich Wehler agreed. He suggested that practitioners of *Alltagsgeschichte* engaged in "dangerously sentimental" intellectual pursuits when they dismissed the norms of critical scholarship.[91] Wehler reprimanded them for embracing "romantic, glorifying pseudo-realism" that dwelled "lovingly-blinkered, in the antiquarian details of proletarian existence." In so doing, *Alltagsgeschichte* "fritters away unsharply, unsystematically, on the hunt for excerpts."[92] He distinguished them from "scientifically educated" scholars with the nasty epithet "barefoot historians [*Barfußhistoriker*]."[93]

Even sympathetic historians like Lutz Niethammer warned historians of everyday life against "romanticized simple solutions," which sloppily equate the "unexplored everydayness of the present" with the "unreconstructable everydayness of yesterday."[94] *Alltagsgeschichte* often faced the charge of confusing the imperative to take its historical subjects seriously with an imperative to treat them with boundless sympathy. For this tendency, *Alltagsgeschichte* earned from some critics the unfavorable sobriquet of "affect history" (*Betroffenheitsgeschichte*).[95] Even the professional historians who participated actively in the *Geschichtswerkstatt*'s projects recognized that the group sometimes exploited emotion in order to turn *Alltagsgeschichte* into "a kind of sugar-coating for the pill of political education." Michael Wildt, for example, argued that the organization's project "[ran] the risk of using the search for identity to project one's own values onto people in the past."[96] History "is not the place for the production of identities," Wildt argued in a separate article with fellow *Geschichtswerkstatt* member and historian Thomas Lindenberger. "History cannot make good the loss of identities." History cannot serve as a substitute for one's family, career, or sexuality. And it cannot "function as a kind of compensation for a loss of meaning."[97]

What some condemned as the dangerously "uncritical obsession with details" that resulted from *Alltagsgeschichte*'s "relentless pursuit of the individual," Lüdtke tried to vindicate.[98] He described *Alltagsgeschichte* as "[attempting] to bring subjectivity and engagement into the process of research as a creative force, without falling into the trap of blurring what Gadamer called the 'different levels of meaning.'" All the while, it also sought to avoid "narrow-minded 'empirical social research.'"[99]

The attraction of everydayness broke down, by and large, along generational lines. Historians of everyday life were chastised by their elders as a "generation without history" and accused of being ignorant of both the methods and content of two generations of postwar history. Practitioners of *Alltagsgeschichte* awarded themselves a more sympathetic epithet. Dubbing themselves the "generation of alienation," they nodded to the effects of the political, economic, and social transformations in Germany since the end of the war.[100] Among the most conspicuous features of this generation of young, historically inclined West Germans was that it consisted largely of unemployed academics.[101] One participant in the Berlin *Geschichtswerkstatt* recalled the dearth of opportunities for academic work when he finished his studies at the Free University in the early 1980s. One stood a greater chance at employment in a museum or government office than at a university. That over six hundred eager participants showed up in 1984 for a Berlin gathering of lay historians demonstrated just what a substantial accumulation of intellectual drifters West Germany's unfavorable academic job market had generated.[102]

For many, scholarly work was "synonymous with the rat race for jobs and limited funding, coupled with the personal battle to establish and maintain a reputation," Lüdtke argued. To make matters worse, the fight for success in the academy "played out behind a constructed impression of busyness and untiring diligence."[103] In their war against historical myth, historians of the academy had allowed a new myth to dominate their practices: the myth of professionalism. By employing the diligent gatekeepers of suffocating jargon and hierarchy, the ivory tower convinced itself that it held a "monopoly on historical truth finding."[104] According to one historian at the time tenuously employed as an affiliate researcher at the University of Bremen, it was no coincidence that support for the *Geschichtswerkstätten* swelled among "free-floating," professionally trained, either unemployed or precariously employed historians. Intended from the outset as a venue for historical researchers to exchange and discuss their work, the *Geschichtswerkstätten* offered ideal shelters to jobless historians, occasionally (though infrequently) with pay.[105] They wanted to create a new kind of discussion forum that would free their members from the highly competitive environment of university engagement and generate an ersatz source of intellectual solidarity.[106] The BGW insisted, for example, that everyone should have a chance to speak at membership meetings, even at the gatherings of its quasi-executive board, the "Monday Group." And it worked to implement a rotation principle for leadership roles, which divided both the burdens of labor as well as the privileges of administrative authority. In attempting to disaggregate power, one member argued, "we frequently succeeded."[107]

In an attempt to challenge the dichotomies between professional academic and grassroots historical practices and to bolster the *Geschichtswerkstatt*'s investment in creating opportunities for lay historians, some group members turned to the ideas of Italian Marxist Antonio Gramsci. Employing Gramsci's concept of the "organic intellectual," the national *Geschichtswerkstatt* stressed that "every person is a potential intellectual." At the same time, it recognized that time and finances limited its work and thus rendered it "only an attempt to implement such lofty goals."[108] To scholars outside of the *Geschichtswerkstätten*, this appeal to Gramsci's work would have appeared anomalous. On account of their resistance to the labels, rhetoric, institutional affiliations, and theoretical frameworks so readily used by official history, practitioners of history from below often received the indictment of "theorylessness" (*Theorielosigkeit*).[109] This assessment stemmed from a misinterpretation of their lack of a coherent conceptual system. Though they were not philosophers, their university training left them well placed to be able to piece together the theoretical odds and ends they had at their disposal.[110] They worked, in other words, as intellectual *bricoleurs*.

Their mode of theorizing bore the imprint of their own precarious situations. Their interest in working through their own experiences of powerlessness occasioned an interest in the historical performance of power relationships and the voices those relationships had silenced. Michel Foucault's claim that power in modern society had become radically diffused provided a foundation for understanding its dynamics. *Geschichtswerkstatt* participants took an interest in what Foucault understood as the "micro-physics" of the state, in which "power no longer belongs to the 'repression apparatus,' to coercive measures, or to public institutions in general; it is much more a component of the smallest and most intimate human relationships."[111] The experiences of workers, artisans, women, children, and outsiders—that is, those whose voices had been omitted from the historical record—took the fore in their projects.[112]

To make sense of Foucault, they turned again to Gramsci. Writing for the Berlin *Geschichtswerkstatt,* the historian Geoff Eley argued that Gramsci's concept of hegemony "allows us to see how various sources and places of power can be organized to function in tandem."[113] The decentralization of power relationships appeared to the *Geschichtswerkstatt* not only as the problem but also as its solution. If the "most powerful bastions" of hegemony reinforced these power relationships in the spaces and temporalities of daily life, then "that is where the struggle against it [hegemony] needs to go on," one member argued.[114] But theirs was not to be a wholesale revolution in power politics. After the frustrated revolutionary hopes of the Student Movement and the subsequent reform-oriented politics of the social-liberal governments of Willy Brandt and Helmut Schmidt, anyone hoping the political Left would be the emissaries of a radically different Germany had reason to look elsewhere. Gramsci offered *Geschichtswerkstatt* participants a method for their struggle. They turned to his notion of the incremental radical change of society, or what Gramsci called "molecular transition [*molekularer Übergang*]."[115] While Gramsci had criticized the idea of small victories by associating it with the passive revolutionary practices of bourgeois politics, practitioners of history from below, by contrast, praised the idea of incremental radical change by emphasizing the importance of localized, individual contributions to that process, or what Gramsci called the practice of "civil hegemony."[116]

These historians understood their craft as a part of both the quotidian construction of social power relationships and their reconstruction. Historiography generates authority, Lindenberger and Wildt argued, quoting from Michel de Certeau's last major work, *Histoire et psychoanalyse entre science et fiction* (1987). Insofar as history

> presents itself as a representation of a past reality, every narrative that deals with a what-is-happening (or what-has-happened) institutes the real. It derives its authority from the fact that it passes itself off as witness of what is, or what has been. It seduces and imposes itself in the name of events which it supposedly interprets. . . . Indeed, every authority is based on the real that it is supposed to signify. It is always in the name of the real that believers are produced and "made to function." The discipline of history gains this power by presenting and interpreting "facts."

That act of presentation and interpretation operates as a performance. "It makes what it says 'believable,'" Certeau continued, "and as a consequence, it leads to action. Producing believers, it ultimately produces actors. The solemn voice of narration transforms, displaces and regulates social space. It exercises an immense power which evades control, since it presents itself as the true representation of what happens or what happened."[117] History narrated from above, Lindenberger and Wildt claimed, makes "credible a vision of the social as centralized, and of society as hierarchically and functionally structured." If narrated from below, however, these histories could present what German philosopher Wolfgang Welsch termed the "radical plurality" of the past.[118] Historians would lose their place as the sole narrators. The hierarchy of knowledge that they substantiated would dissipate. These transitions would make way, Certeau argued, for an "interdependent differentiation of subjects."[119] In the eyes of the historians of everyday life, radical plurality had the power to decenter unrepresentative narratives. These historians saw this process as an essential "precondition for political and cultural self-determination" and, thus, understood themselves to possess a powerful tool in the refashioning of social power relationships.[120] Their work offered a "critique of knowledge [*Wissenschaftskritik*] . . . carried out on the political and cultural terrain of the practice of history itself."[121]

Having rejected the university as the traditional site of historiographical authority, these historians turned their attention to the physical spaces of everyday life and their associated histories as the stage on which to articulate new power dynamics.[122] They understood local or micro-history to give access to the "terrain, where the actual content of the abstractions of power and exploitation can be found and worked through" and where a "healthier" organization of individual and social life could be brokered.[123] They also recognized that their critique of knowledge could not stand beyond criticism. Inspired by Marx's "Theses on Feuerbach," which demanded that "the educator must become educated himself," they intended that their work would implicate them in a process of self-criticism, self-transformation, and "radical-democratic self-understanding."[124] In this manner, the *Geschichtswerkstätten—history* workshops—earned from some the label of *Zukunftswerkstätten,* or "*future* workshops." They refused to understand the work of the historian as impotent, despite its orientation toward the past. Rather, historiography in service of radical plurality, they claimed, would contribute to the construction of the present and the future.[125]

Geschichtswerkstatt participants thus saw their work not only as retrospective but also as prescriptive and normative. "'History from below' is not just a method for us," wrote founding member of the Berlin *Geschichtswerkstatt* Andreas Ludwig. "It is a political practice."[126] This capacious interpretation of politics rejected the subordination of the environments of everyday life as "unpolitical." Instead, it recognized them as spaces of political contestation, power, and resistance. *Geschichtswerkstatt* participants understood hegemonic politics to play out "on the border of public and personal life" and recognized that this "terrain" harbors the "democratic politics of opposition and of emancipation."[127] The politicization of history from below, in other words, rendered it an essentially spatial project.

The space of historical experience, Berlin *Geschichtswerkstatt* member Udo Gößwald explained, existed as a site of a construction (*Ort einer Konstruktion*), "an in-between space [*Zwischenraum*] in which the set pieces of the past and present meet." Writing specifically about historical exhibits, Gößwald argued that the visitor "composes himself mentally into its space," such that historical experiences negotiate between personal historical meaning and sensual experience.[128] Not a "contemplative sensuality [*betrachtende Sinnlichkeit*]," in which one's mind takes one "where one's feet no longer can and where the ground itself remains inaccessible," Gößwald explained. He rejected this kind of historical sensuality because it required no movement, only reflection and the "comfortable enjoyment" of the past. He understood historical sensuality, instead, through Ernst Bloch, for whom sensuality meant awareness (*Kenntnis*). For Bloch and Gößwald alike, it promised to serve as "the actual basis of understanding." As engineered relationships between proximity and distance, historical exhibition spaces attempt to make history "experienceable" (*erlebbar*).[129] As "sites of reconstructed sensuality [*rekonstruktuierter Sinnlichkeit*]," Gößwald argued, these spaces generate "a critical encounter with one's own history." But they not only direct their visitors toward the past; quoting Walter Benjamin, Gößwald suggested that they also "point us toward the invisible stranger—the future—which left them behind with us."[130] The past, in short, works upon the future.

In order for history to work on the future and to remake the power politics of German society, the *Geschichtswerkstatt* had to take the mundane objects and topographies of everyday life that enabled an undemocratic system of political, social, and cultural agency and make them widely popularly accessible.[131] Historians of the *Geschichtswerkstatt* wanted to present their research "in places where they would reach their intended audience . . . in the most direct way." Locally relevant exhibitions and walking tours offered to their public a "rare opportunity to experience history where it happened, as something almost tangible."[132] By understanding the histories of these spaces and objects and by making their histories "comprehensible [*nachvollziehbar*]," "inhabitable [*als für sich besetzbar*]," and "available to be experienced [*erlebbar*]," the historians of everyday life thought they stood a better chance of altering the systems those objects and spaces empowered.[133]

Berlin as a History Workshop

The Berlin *Geschichtswerkstatt* changed considerably in the first decade of its existence. One of its founding members bracketed the years from 1981 to 1984 as a period of "productive chaos," tone-setting, and putting down roots.[134]

During this short stretch, the BGW pursued three primary tasks, based on the three pillars proposed at the organization's initial meeting. First, the group worked to generate a forum for research projects on Berlin's local histories. Second, it undertook to create an archive that would serve as a repository for the results of this research. Third, it regarded its work as public outreach (*Öffentlichkeitsarbeit*). Members attempted to mediate between other small local history groups in Berlin and to facilitate interactions with Berlin's public via meetings, exhibits, and publications.[135] In the group's first three years, the BGW resisted the tendency to censor projects in their earliest phases. Its members associated this gatekeeping practice with the guild mentality of academic life, which they opposed. Instead, the organization preferred to see where evolving projects would lead. They believed that "democratic, self-directed activities" would themselves dictate a project's success or failure.[136]

The BGW held its first event in early February 1981, even before the group officially registered with the city. A film screening on the history of Berlin's massive steam engine manufacturer, Borsig, brought out over one hundred participants and boosted early interest in the BGW.[137] Participants drawn from this gathering divided into several subgroups based on their interests. The Peace Group hoped to engage with the history of war and the rise of the peace movement in Berlin. The intensifying debate over the stationing of American nuclear missiles in Germany became the locus of their interventions.[138] The Theater Group aimed to use Berlin's cultural history to uncover new details in the histories of violence, resistance, and assimilation in Germany. Its first project involved creating a multimedia theater piece, *The Way through a Herd of Cows* (*Gang durch die Kuhherde*), which documented the life of Berlin's political cabaret group, the Catacombs, from 1933 to 1935. The Postwar Group set out to chronicle the survival mechanisms of those living amid the ruins of postwar Berlin. Its first exhibit, "Myths of Postwar History," took place in 1982 at Berlin's alternative educational consortium, the VolksUni.[139] The real excitement within the BGW, however, clustered around the history of National Socialism in Berlin. "In the beginning . . . was National Socialism," quipped one BGW member, riffing not only on the Book of John but also on a famous opening line from establishment historian Thomas Nipperdey.[140] "I remember a sort of gold rush atmosphere [*Goldgräberstimmung*]," another member explained, describing the enthusiasm around the fiftieth anniversary of Hitler's ascension to power on 30 January 1933. That date became the primary historical signpost orienting the group's earliest work.[141] Two 1983 projects led the way: "Saving Traces: Everyday Life and Resistance in Berlin in the 1930s" and the "33-Project."

"Saving Traces" aimed to record and present the experiences of those who experienced the transformations of National Socialism directly.[142] Too young to have participated in the regime themselves, BGW members benefited from a decoupling of *interest* in totalitarianism-at-work from *implication* in it. Project participants set out to document the roles ordinary people played in bolstering National Socialism and how the spaces for action (*Handlungsspielräume*) in everyday life enabled the Nazis to generate mass political consensus.[143] The group chose to focus on two neighborhoods: Charlottenburg, a bourgeois area in the western part of the city that fell along the primary artery in Hitler's plans for his World Capital Germania; and Schöneberg, an area southeast of the city's center, which housed both a relatively affluent Jewish community as well as one of Berlin's hubs of Left activism during the Weimar and Nazi years. They received the support of eyewitnesses like one who justified his participation in the BGW's research on the premises that he "[did] not want to be a nostalgic relic." Instead, he insisted, "I want to try to contribute a path into our future."[144]

As the BGW began to conceptualize the "Saving Traces" project, it had to decide how to mediate "history from below" to a broader public. The group concluded that it opposed static representations: "No monuments," one member insisted—"instead, a center that works actively to save the traces of the past."[145] Communicating history's dynamism became a key ambition. The project's organizers presented their findings via a surprisingly conventional exhibit in the former shopping center–turned–cultural center Kaufhaus Kato, adjacent to the Schlesisches Tor subway station. But they also pursued alternative ways to mediate their work. They took a particular interest in the challenge of appealing to younger Berliners and, with financial support from the Berlin Senate, they began to organize walking tours of both neighborhoods that focused on alternative culture and resistance efforts during the Nazi era.[146] The task of crafting these tours generated such interest among both BGW members and locals that a separate BGW working group formed to manage their creation.[147]

"Saving Traces" lit a fire in the BGW and resulted in the creation of a new effort, the "33-Project." In June 1982, Ursula Schröter announced with some

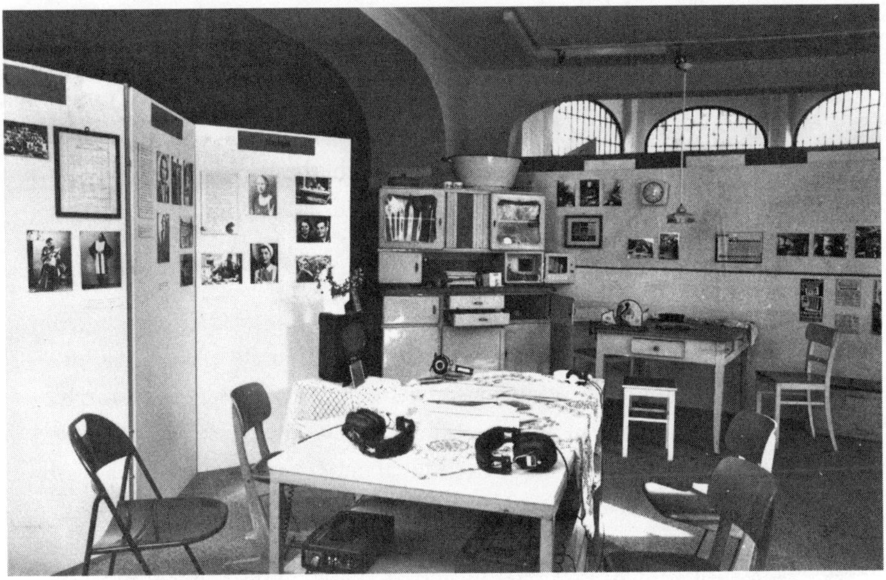

2.1 "Saving Traces" exhibit in Kato, Kulturbahnhof Kreuzberg, June 1983. Regina Cohn, Berliner Geschichtswerkstatt e. V., Signatur AUS-6-SPU.

surprise that the Berlin Senate had granted the BGW 90,000 DM (around $35,000) for her proposal to document the Nazi rise to power in everyday Berlin. The "33-Project" set out to examine how ordinary spaces without political associations—garden plots or the representation of the family in photographs, for example—changed after Hitler came to power. She wanted to explore, specifically, how Berliners encountered propaganda and were acculturated into National Socialism through film and theater. Given relative autonomy by the BGW's quasi-executive board, the Monday Group, the project's three leaders found themselves with the freedom to realize their vision for an alternative historical initiative.[148]

As the "33-Project" gained steam, it became clear that the BGW's meeting site in the Mehringhof could no longer accommodate its growing numbers. In June 1982, the BGW relocated to what would become its permanent home in the heart of Schöneberg. In addition to serving as a meeting space, these new headquarters on Schöneberg's Goltzstraße operated as an information center in service of the "33-Project" and an archive.[149] The center managed the mass of materials the "33-Project" assembled: oral interviews, family photographs, letters, diaries, and other memorabilia left in the hands of the group after it assumed responsibility for several personal archival collections. (Incidentally, "33-Project" members were not let off the hook for the exciting new burden they created for the BGW. They were tasked with staffing the group's new headquarters.)[150] Those who brought the center to life envisioned an archive of the "world of experience [*Erlebniswelt*]" of everyday life, particularly private encounters.[151] With assistance from Berlin's State Center for Political Education, the information center also began to assemble a small library that emphasized the theories and practices of historical research "from below."[152] Though its purview remained modest, this archival work played an important role in the BGW's efforts to dismantle undemocratic hierarchies of knowledge. It belonged to a wave of alternative archives that had popped up around Europe by the late 1980s and that understood their work as emancipatory.[153] If one accepts scholar of memory Aleida Assmann's claim that the archive legitimates power structures by serving, per Michel Foucault, as the "law of what can be said," however, the capacity of the Goltzstraße center to forge new claims on and for historical knowledge was, in fact, less modest than it at first may seem.[154]

The BGW also intended the Goltzstraße headquarters as a gathering space and resource for grassroots activists with similar investments: not only historical initiatives but also the city's renters' associations, Antifa groups, participants in the women's movement, foreigners, and youth organizations.[155] They intended this kind of broad networking to impact the city's contemporary political dialogues. Though the administrative responsibilities of managing the Goltzstraße site soon began to weigh on its coordinators, it nevertheless offered proof of the lengths BGW members were willing to go in the name of studying the people, objects, and spaces of everyday life during the Nazi era.[156]

The "33-Project" generated three additional historical initiatives, each of which underscore the BGW's spatial approach toward historical work. The first was the study of the cooperatively organized living community in the south of Schöneberg, the Lindenhof. Built during the Weimar Republic by the ambitious modernist architects Bruno Taut and Martin Wagner, the Lindenhof housing development aimed to fulfill not only the structural but also the social needs of the working class. Located in the middle of an industrial area, the development remained relatively isolated from both the heart of

Berlin and the center of Schöneberg. As a result, the Lindenhof provided its own services to its residents: schools, businesses, social organizations, etc. It also provided a set of political values. With community leadership consisting of Social Democrats, the Lindenhof leaned left. As a relatively closed architectural unit, the Lindenhof developed its own identity, and inhabitants came to see the "little fortified town" as "theirs."[157] This sense of community, invested solidly with leftist values, made the Lindenhof an ideal site for researching how National Socialist ideology worked its way into less-receptive environments.

In the summer of 1982, motivated by the city's sluggishness in planning for the fiftieth anniversary of 1933, a small working group proposed four thematic vectors along which to study the evolution of the Lindenhof community, from its construction in 1918 through the mid-1930s. Its members wanted to trace changes in Lindenhofers' experiences of childhood. They wanted to examine the development of neighborly relationships through associations, festivals, gardening culture, and other expressions of community solidarity. They wanted to chronicle social changes immediately after 30 January 1933 and chart opportunities for reaction in the wake of 1933. By studying how the Nazis penetrated the social fabric of the Lindenhof and fractured its sense of community, the project's organizers planned to chart the limits of resistance and the slippery path into acquiescence, collaboration, and organized support. They began to conduct oral interviews with present and former residents and to collect historical Lindenhof paraphernalia like photos, posters, announcements, receipts, and minutes from meetings of the community's leadership.[158]

As with many of the BGW's ambitious early undertakings, the Lindenhof project began to overwhelm its organizers, who responded by pulling in more volunteers. In this context, the decision to bring on three trained biographers in the lead-up to the city's 750th anniversary celebration in 1987 was unsurprising. They brought a great deal of momentum to the project in its last years. Their work conducting intensive interviews with Lindenhof residents reinforced the BGW's witness-oriented, oral history approach to research.[159] The project's successes, however, were insufficient to offset fully the tensions that had developed within the group between those receiving a stipend from the state for their work and those expending time and energy without compensation. These tensions point to the BGW's difficulty reworking established hierarchies of the historical profession, despite the organization's professed distance from them.

Presentations of Lindenhof research appeared soon after the project's initiation. Starting in 1984, the Lindenhof Working Group prepared an exhibit and a short brochure.[160] As the project evolved, so did the exhibit, which the BGW installed not only in the Lindenhof itself but also in other sites throughout the city. Working with the Schöneberg branch of *Die Falken*, the youth organization of the SPD, the BGW displayed twenty-four biographies over eleven open-air exhibits. These installations narrated the evolution of the Lindenhof over four generations, from its founding to its physical and social reconstruction after the Second World War. After the exhibit's conclusion, the BGW collected their materials in the Goltzstraße archive and later used them to offer courses on conducting oral history interviews.[161] They also published a volume on the project in 1987.[162]

Out of the work for the "33-Project" emerged another Schöneberg-oriented research project. It focused on an "island" in Schöneberg created by three intersecting train lines. Dubbed the "Red Island" (*Rote Insel*) after one precocious SPD resident hung a red flag from his window to protest implementation of Bismarck's Anti-Socialist Laws in the late nineteenth century, this small community won for itself a reputation. Over the past century, a storied group of residents had called the Red Island home. The German entertainer Marlene Dietrich was born there at the turn of the century, as was Alfred Lion, a Jew who, in exile in the United States, cofounded Blue Note Records, the jazz label that recorded greats like John Coltrane and Miles Davis. The "island" also boasted its share of political heavyweights. The socialist leader August Bebel lived on the island from the late nineteenth century until his death just before the First World War, while Social Democrat and Nazi resister Julius Leber worked along the area's southernmost perimeter. The first postwar president of West Germany, Theodor Heuss, made a home in the Red Island for some years, as did the second president of the West German Bundestag, Hermann Ehlers. The East German prime minister Willi Stoph spent his childhood in the community, which overwhelmingly voted socialist until the rise of the Green Party in the 1980s.[163]

In comparison to Berlin's other, more violent hubs of Nazi resistance, the Red Island offered a tempered example of resistance efforts. But its small, finite geography made it easy to research, and its strong self-conception offered a compelling case study in the construction of "resistance myths."[164] The BGW never intended the project would focus solely on Nazi dictatorship, however. Rather, researchers aimed to trace the Red Island's evolution from a late nineteenth-century epicenter of railway construction, through the destruction of workers' solidarity during fascism, to its process of rebuilding in the postwar period.[165]

The Red Island Group's methods mirrored those of the Lindenhof project. Its members wanted to uncover the area's history in a joint effort with its residents. They planned to conduct oral history interviews with older residents and to display their findings in interactive audio-visual installations throughout the island. But they ran into snags along the way. As outsiders, they often had trouble winning the trust of longtime residents, and they struggled to spark interest among younger or newer residents. Over the project's four-year existence, however, it gradually generated participation from initially skeptical locals.[166]

The connection between space and history crystallized most clearly in a third BGW project, enabled by a serendipitous collision of agendas in June 1982. Just as the BGW was considering how to expand its historical city tours beyond Berlin's streets, the Berlin boat tour company, Riedel, expressed interest in the BGW's research on the city. Historical city tours by boat suddenly became a possibility.[167] Despite "friendly disinterest" among BGW members toward the idea of using the River Spree and Berlin's network of canals as tour venues, the relative autonomy the BGW awarded to the nascent project allowed this experiment to proceed.[168] When the BGW's Steamship Group (*Dampfergruppe*) began hosting regular tours of Berlin's historic architecture, residential neighborhoods, and industrial districts from river cruise boats in April 1984, the project met with immediate success among guests of all sorts.[169]

The popularity of the BGW's boat tours, which have run continuously since they first began, derived at least in part from their vantage point. "The urban waterways of Berlin," the BGW suggested, "mediate the unexpected." They give access to "places that one would otherwise never visit. Everywhere you look, you encounter hard evidence of the past." Berlin's Westhafen, the city's largest inland harbor, for example, highlights the importance of inland shipping to Berlin's history as an industrial metropolis. The Landwehr Canal reveals Germany's long revolutionary history. One of its

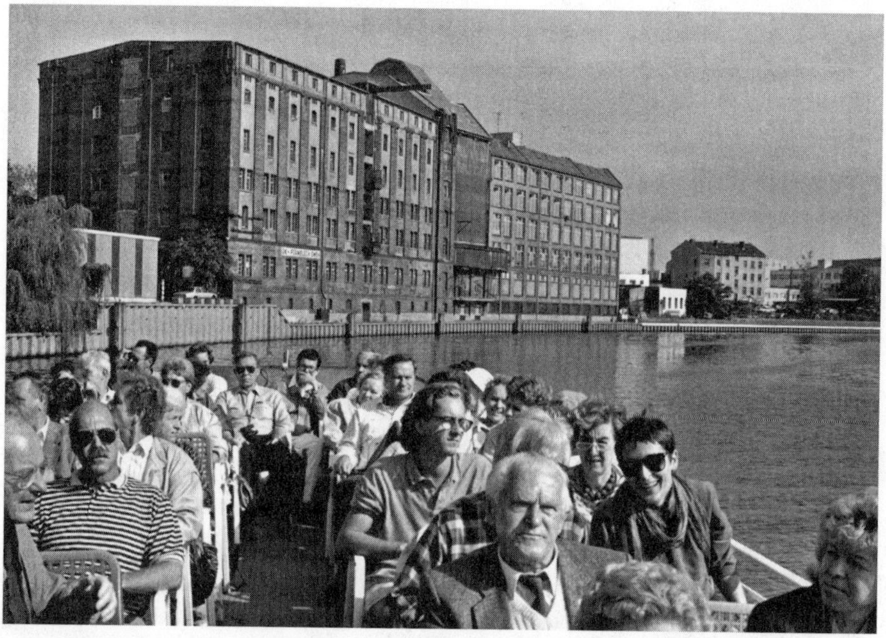

2.2 A boat trip on the River Spree in the neighborhood of Moabit, Berlin, 17 September 1989. Detlev Davids, Berliner Geschichtswerkstatt e. V., Signatur SOK-Dampf-35-21.

embankments—named after Max Reichpietsch, a socialist leader of the 1918 sailors' mutiny in Kiel—allows the BGW to explain the toppling of the German monarchy, the rise of the Weimar Republic, and the hopes for a socialist revolution that accompanied these events. The tour offers a topographical metaphor for the brevity of the German Revolution's more radical phases by highlighting that, shortly after the Kiel Mutiny, Freikorps members disposed of the body of murdered communist activist and symbol of revolutionary hope, Rosa Luxemburg, near the Reichpietsch Embankment. As much as ambitions for a revolution in German politics survived the assassination of communist leaders, so too did hopes for an alternative survive National Socialism. This same area along the Landwehr Canal served as the headquarters for the planning of the failed 1944 attempt on Hitler's life. By yoking together events like these, the boat tours did more than merely present history, the BGW argued. They "make history vivid [*anschaulich*]. We want to see where history happened," they insisted, and "we want to make [that history] more accessible."[170] Berlin's waterways allowed the BGW to transform the city into a historical "classroom" (*Lernort*), whose physical spaces, members argued, helped explain complex historical connections better than even the best lecture could.[171]

The first phase of the BGW's existence culminated in the appropriation of the group's name and purpose by a broader public. By the middle of the 1980s, alternative groups and ordinary citizens alike had begun to embrace the idea that the topography of Berlin operated as a "history workshop." Much as Beuys argued that every person could be an artist, the BGW stressed that all citizens, by engaging with this topography, could become historians. This language appeared prominently in response to the public frustration that had developed toward the treatment of one of Berlin's most infamous sites. By the 1980s, Wilhelmstraße 102–106 had stood for decades as an empty lot. Beginning in 1934, however, the Rococo-style Prinz-Albrecht-Palais that called the address home served as the headquarters of the Third Reich's security apparatus—SD, SS, and Gestapo—under Reinhard Heydrich. Destroyed in the Battle of Berlin, the site remained empty after its rubble was cleared in the mid-1950s. With the rise of the History Movement, however, murmurings of popular interest in turning the site into an open-air monument began to gain traction. Efforts to reckon with the role the grounds played in the atrocities of National Socialism were "long overdue," activists argued.[172]

When a group of concerned citizens took on this mantle, they planted the first seeds of the Active Museum (*Aktives Museum*, AM). The project's early advocates included members of nearly a score of various organizations from around the city. They imagined creating a museum that would offer a space for visitors to use the site to learn about the history of fascism, from preconditions to effects, from top to bottom. They refused to allow the site to serve as a static, authoritative presentation of National Socialist history. Instead, they wanted to fashion a site of historical "encounters" (*Begegnungsstätte*). They envisioned visitors engaging not only with the site's history but also with other visitors and with their own personal relationships to Germany's complex past. The site would become a forum for facilitating controversial discussions among museumgoers. Much like the BGW, AM activists believed a truly democratic German history had to be written with the active participation of Germany's citizens, hence the project's name.[173] They hoped such a history would emerge from the debates the museum generated.

The Active Museum appealed to the young BGW. In 1984, the BGW joined efforts to develop a conceptual foundation for the museum. In this work it saw an opportunity to advance its promotion of grassroots historical work *vor Ort.* Though the AM drew participants from a wide range of organizations, members of the BGW occupied a special place in the early planning.[174] (A willingness to host AM meetings at their Goltzstraße headquarters may have played a role.)[175] Coordinators of the AM agreed to put two BGW members, Udo Gößwald and Andreas Ludwig, in charge of overseeing this formal conceptualization process, and the Active Museum's first official chairs, Gerhard Schoenberner and Heinz-Dieter Schilling, continued a lively collaboration with the BGW.[176]

The goodwill between the BGW and AM eventually dissipated as the museum transitioned from the realm of the conceptual to the space of the real. The multitude of BGW working group meetings meant that AM meetings often conflicted with events on the BGW's calendar.[177] More importantly, however, the BGW soon discovered that the museum would not actually realize the BGW's spatial approach to history. In the first plans for the museum, drafted in September 1983, organizers foregrounded the museum's "affirmation of radical intent [*Bekenntnis zur Radikalität*]." This aim aligned with the BGW's goal of constructing a dynamic (*veränderbar*) museum whose visitors were given sufficient power to constitute its character and make the museum "their own." Over the next seven months, however, these plans were watered down.[178] The BGW criticized the consensus-winning version of the AM's conceptualization as "thin," "weakly articulated," and insufficiently distinct from existing historical institutions.[179] Summarizing the group's disappointment with the trajectory of the museum's development, Andreas Ludwig explained that "we wanted an active museum, not activities for a new museum."[180]

Though plans for the AM followed a different path than the BGW had hoped, the project still managed to underscore the group's impact. The broad uptake of the BGW's historical objectives was evident in the public response to the evolution of the AM. In 1984, Kreuzberg's local Green Party, *Alternative Liste,* argued that the grounds of the former Prinz-Albrecht-Palais should occasion "the immediate creation of [a] living history workshop."[181] On 5 May 1985, members of the BGW joined members of the Active Museum to do just that when they started a symbolic excavation at the site, this time lit-

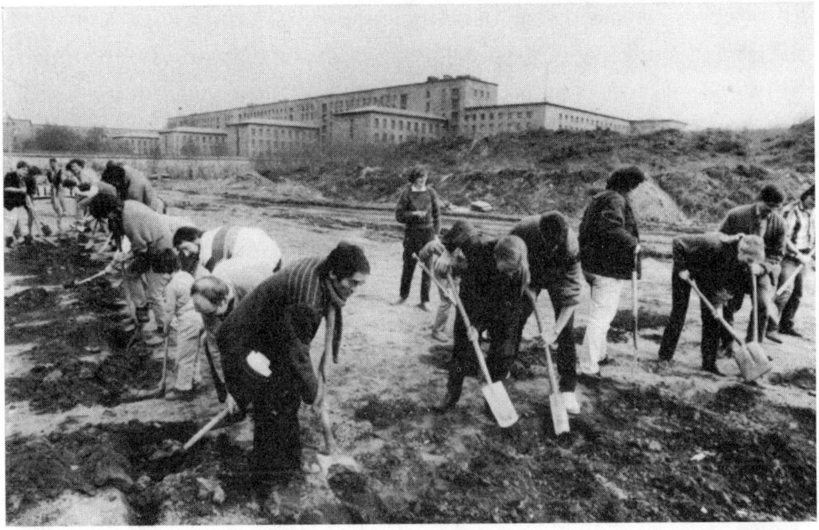

2.3 Symbolic Dig at Wilhelmstraße 102–106, 5 May 1985. Hans-Peter Stiebing, Berliner Geschichtswerkstatt e. V.

erally digging where they stood. (The dig, however, was purely symbolic. Though participants followed the presumed floor plan of the Gestapo building, they only dug about a foot deep. Had they dug deeper, they would have uncovered the Gestapo cellar, which had remained buried beneath the rubble of Wilhelmstraße 102–106 for forty years. But their effort was sufficient to get the attention of city officials. Afterward, more serious archaeological work, given its gravity, was left to the professionals.)[182] Excavation participants followed it with a public statement. Anyone concerned with understanding the origins of National Socialism and Germany's process of coming to terms with that history, they argued, needed to pay attention to Berlin's topography. Indeed, topography continued to lie at the heart of the effort to transform the former Gestapo grounds into a collaborative mnemonic space. After two and a half decades of planning, several memorial installations, three design competitions, and considerable squabbling over the results that left the space of the former Gestapo building in limbo for long stretches of time, the Topography of Terror Documentation Center (*Dokumentationszentrum Topographie des Terrors,* TT) finally opened to the public in May 2010. In addition to an open-air installation that both displays historical information about Nazi violence as well as preserves remnants of the original building, the site includes a museum, a library and research facility, and space and support for a series of multilingual workshops. The TT, in its final form, is admittedly a far cry from the grassroots democratic vision proposed by its earliest supporters. But their ambition to create an interactive, dynamic museum closely connected to the space it occupies and the communities that surround it lives on, if imperfectly.[183]

Several years after the 1985 symbolic dig, in response to Chancellor Helmut Kohl's proposal to create a national German historical museum in Berlin, the Alternative Liste argued that

> Berlin is, itself, already a great historical museum of recent German history. If this project is really about making history visible and tangible, then the millions of Marks from Bonn should go first to already-existing sites where history actually happened, like the Wannsee Villa, the site of the former synagogue on Levetzow Street in Tiergarten, or that of the former headquarters of the security apparatus of the Third Reich on Koch Street. These sites should be made visible, tangible, and available to the public to be experienced once again. *Let's make West Berlin into a history workshop.*[184]

This rhetoric, German historian Axel Schildt has emphasized, drew attention to the "artisanal [*handwerklichen*] character" of the New History Movement and stressed its grassroots nature.[185] With the popular uptake of the language and logic of the Berlin *Geschichtswerkstatt,* the group took its first real step toward realizing its radical spatial project for history.

Berlin found itself in the spotlight as both a space of history and a space for historians. It offered the *Geschichtswerkstätten* clay for molding a form of their idealized historical practice. It gave physical substance to their arguments that the project of narrating history should be undertaken in spaces where history happened. It allowed them to stress the dynamism of history as a social construct and to ground that constructive process in grassroots democratic participation, where possible with the participation of eyewitnesses.[186] And it helped them show how grasping history could facilitate contemporary political and social engagement. The city of Berlin itself became a history workshop and, as such, something of a pilgrimage site for Germany's hundreds of free-floating grassroots historians.

As the BGW faced several looming "round numbers," its work grew more challenging. The most important of these—Berlin's 750th anniversary—was slated for celebration in 1987. Although the city dragged its feet in preparing for the fiftieth anniversary of Hitler's rise to power, there would be no similar delay with this occasion. Already in 1984, debates had started over how to do justice to the city's complex history. The BGW joined planning efforts, and they did so under the "warm shower of [state] money" that fell on Berlin's cultural scene in the lead-up to its jubilee.[187] As the BGW filled its coffers, it increasingly had to negotiate large amounts of state funding, corresponding pressure from above, and strong popular demands. This constellation made it more difficult for the group to continue to work autonomously as it had thus far. Its response to these pressures in the second half of the decade would determine the fate of both the BGW and its radical spatial historical practice.

3

Green Culture

The most significant changes to Germany's political map have emerged out of moments of upheaval. Catholics formed the Center Party in 1870 as a unified front opposite Bismarck's cultural offensive waged over their allegiance to the Vatican over the nation. In demonstration of resilience against monarchist Bismarck's anti-socialist legislation, which outlawed both the forums and mouthpieces of socialist organization, the Social Democratic Party (SPD) reconstituted itself in 1890 out of a coalition of workers' parties that had crystalized over the preceding three decades. The Communist Party of Germany assembled in the wake of the First World War out of disagreements within the SPD over the war, the Bolshevik model, and the trajectory of socialism. The National Socialists likewise emerged out of the traumas of World War I, militantly opposing the armistice and advocating nationalist, racist, and violently expansionist domestic and foreign policies. The Christian Democratic Union (CDU)—an inter-confessional party with a platform of social and fiscal conservatism—and the Free Democratic Party (FDP), which advocates classical economic liberalism, materialized from the ashes of the Second World War. No such fanfare, however, preceded the Greens' entrance onto the German political stage.

More than thirty-five years after the end of the Second World War, well into the Cold War, two decades after the political commotion of the mid-1950s, and more than a decade after the most incendiary events of 1960s activism, the founding of the German Green Party occurred during a moment that can, at best, be called a "soft turning point" or "silent revolution"—that is, a turning point not imposed by war, revolution, or a breakdown of an empire. Certainly, the end of the Long 1960s precipitated change. The year 1971 brought the collapse of Bretton Woods, which destabilized the international monetary system. OPEC's oil embargo of 1973–1974 sent the West into a period of great inflation and inflamed international political relations. And 1975 halted the nineteen-year-long Vietnam War. During this decade, Germany experienced the end of the *Wirtschaftswunder*—the wave of unprecedented prosperity that crested over the postwar years—and the beginning of a period of increased unemployment and economic stagnation. These years also saw the decline of manufacturing, the beginning of deindustrialization efforts, and the reorganization of labor markets. Together, these effectively replaced industrial society with its new, postindustrial offspring. Finally, the 1970s arguably also brought the first sustained challenges to the patriarchy and paternalism of Western Europe both at home and abroad. The activism surrounding feminism and decolonization alongside the developing discourse of human rights began to dismantle centuries-old practices of injustice.[1] But, at least in comparison to the global destruction of the first half of the twentieth century, these were decidedly non-cataclysmic transitions. If they were to be lights at the end of the twentieth century's tunnel of political, diplomatic, and economic trauma, they were dim, at best.

Domestically, a period of relative political rigidity compounded these uninspiring international circumstances. Characterizing the political topography that the Greens would unsettle was the growing inflexibility of Germany's three-party political system. In 1957, when federal election returns for the All-German Bloc / League of Expellees and Deprived of Rights (GB / BHE) fell to 4.6 percent, German politics entered an election pattern in which only the SPD, the CDU together with its Bavarian sister party, the Christian Social Union (CSU), and the FDP attracted a constituency sufficiently large to cross the 5 percent voting threshold required to win representation in the Bundestag. Though after half a century of political chaos this stability had its appeal, the increasing entrenchment of this new party trifecta was hard to ignore. Between 1949 and 1980, Germany shifted from a system in which these three parties won 72 percent of the vote to one in which they won 98 percent.[2] Their security served as an apparent endorsement of the status quo. This was not, in other words, a situation conducive to political innovation. It was nothing short of groundbreaking, then, when an ostensibly single-issue party barely three years old managed to clear the 5 percent hurdle with an extra .6 percent to spare in the federal elections of March 1983. With their robust environmentalist platform, the German Green Party became the first fourth party to enter the Bundestag in over a quarter of a century.

It is easy to interpret the significance of the Green Party in terms of its most obvious legacy: it put ecology on the political agenda as well as at the heart of the New Left. Some have even claimed that one "simply cannot be a leftist in Europe today and disregard . . . ecology." Everyone, in other words, "has become a Green on this issue."[3] Arguably, however, the more important of the Greens' legacies was also a subtler one. Their enduring success broke a long-standing German political malaise. In doing so, the party inspired a new optimism about the potential not only for political change in Germany but also for environmental, social, and cultural change.

The Greens' debut on the political stage was, admittedly, far from flawless. Shortly after the party's first victory in the federal elections, critics jumped to highlight several of its most embarrassing failures. Designed to deter the rise of career politicians, its innovative two-year rotation system for its elected officials, for example, simply pulled Green representatives out of office just when they had begun to learn the ins and outs of parliament. And its adherence to an "imperative mandate" curtailed representatives' individual discretion. These policies had done little to prompt changes in the behaviors of West German parties or parliaments. The Greens in fact failed, one political scientist argued, to call into question any of West Germany's less desirable parliamentary practices in any significant or sustained way.[4] The very fact of the Greens' entry into parliament, both in Bonn and regionally, however, overshadowed their underachievement. In their first seven years, the Greens crossed the 5 percent threshold in eight of West Germany's eleven states: Bremen in 1979; Baden-Württemberg in 1980; Berlin in 1981; Lower Saxony, Hamburg, and Hesse in 1982; Bavaria in 1986; and Rheinland-Palatinate in 1987.[5] These local victories quickly earned the party a widespread and diverse constituency and gave it strong local roots that would allow it to weather early factionalism at the national level. One of the party's major accomplishments was disproving the long-standing assumption that it was not possible for new parties to overcome the hurdles of West Germany's electoral system. Still, public and party confidence remained tenuous. With each new election, the 5 percent hurdle loomed, and narrow margins meant that the vicissitudes of voting preferences always threatened the Greens' privilege of parliamentary presence. But optimism also persisted. To West Germans in an uninspiring economic, political, and social context, the Greens offered evidence that powerful, stagnant traditions were no match for the force of active voters. They signaled that something important in West Germany had begun to change.[6]

This chapter examines how the German Green Party understood itself as offering an alternative to West Germany's political status quo. Though the party's ecological agenda won it attention, the significance of its political alternative extended well beyond environmental policy. Contrary to conventional depictions of the party—both historical and contemporary—which narrate its impact using the language of ecology, the Greens' success should be measured against an even more sweeping legacy, namely that it occasioned a paradigm shift in cultural politics. Prevailing accounts of the Greens' agenda have regarded culture as irrelevant to the party. It is ostensibly absent from the party's four governing pillars—grassroots democracy, social responsibility, ecology, and nonviolence. The Greens, however, not only cared about cultural issues but also regarded them as an essential framework within which they could reconcile otherwise conflicting values. It is worth distinguishing between investment in an issue and the publication of formal statements about it. The Greens' cultural philosophy was, admittedly, disorganized and more diffuse than the traditional understanding of German *Kultur*. And their accompanying programmatic demands of culture were abstract and sometimes contradictory. It would be shortsighted, however, to claim simply on these grounds that culture played a subordinate role in the society the Greens envisioned for Germany. In fact, the Greens engaged early and vigorously with cultural questions, even if many of their contemporaries failed to take note.

The early Greens' conception of a rigorous, effective environmental policy hinged on their concept and support of culture: in order to be a good environmentalist, one had to engage in cultural projects. The Green alternative took the form of an "aesthetic state," a notion whose origins date to the emergence of Hellenism in ancient Greece, but which possesses a German heritage of considerable substance.[7] From Friedrich Schiller to Richard Wagner to Herbert Marcuse, the idea that aesthetics could be used to create and sustain a democratic polis has resonated among German intellectuals at key points in the development of the modern German state. The Greens, however, initiated the first sustained effort by a political party committed to participatory democracy to render Germany what one might call an "aesthetic state in practice." They put at the heart of their political program a commitment to cultivating the creative, artistic impulses of the German people. Theirs was not the "aestheticization of politics" embraced by fascism and National Socialism in the 1930s and 1940s, whose neo-Renaissance treatment of the state as a work of art that could be beautified catalyzed violently racist nationalisms.[8] The Green aesthetic state, rather, combined radical participatory democracy and an intellectual agenda inherited from the German Alternative Movement that stressed individual creativity practiced on a daily basis. Nurturing such aesthetic capacities hinged on the space they were given to flourish. The Greens thus put at the core of their program a commitment to undertaking cultural projects that mobilized space—particularly local spaces—in new ways. This component of "Green" culture would later become central to the party's efforts to create a Germany that was not only "Green," but also sustainably so.

Good Politicians as Good Environmentalists

Using the momentum that propelled the movement against the use of nuclear weapons and energy in the early 1970s, a group of citizens' initiatives with a shared commitment to an antinuclear program banded together in 1972. They formed the Federal Association of Citizens' Initiatives for the Protection of the Environment (BBU). The BBU served first as an umbrella organization for groups mobilizing against the construction of nuclear plants in Germany. Soon, however, it became a mouthpiece for wider-ranging ecological concerns. Partially as a result, the last two years of the decade saw the appearance of a rash of groups that blurred the lines between oppositional movement and political party. Uniting them was their investment in the environment. The year 1978 initiated an extended period of electoral victories for what, just two years later, would officially become Germany's Green Party. Beginning with the Green List for Environmental Protection (GLU) in Lower Saxony and Hamburg, the Multicolored List or *Bunte Liste* (BuLi) in Hamburg, and the Green Campaign for the Future (GAZ) in Bonn, political groups with an environmental bent took root in most West German states.[9] In 1979,

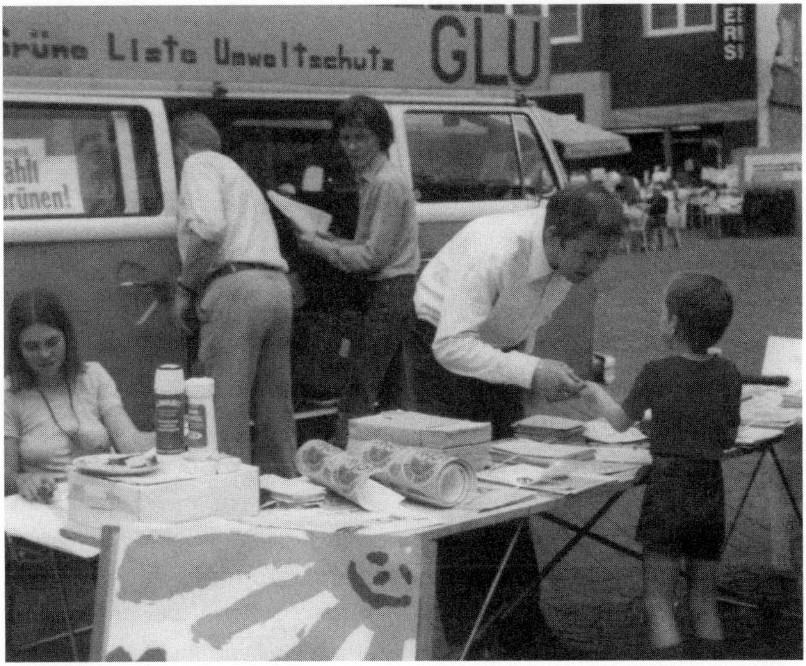

3.1 The GLU campaigns for the 1979 elections to the European Parliament in Meppen, Lower Saxony, 29 May 1979. Archiv Grünes Gedächtnis der Heinrich-Böll-Stiftung e. V., Signatur FO-01651-06-cp.

Bremen's Green List was the first of these groups to gain seats in a state parliament.

The early platforms of these groups were frequently broad and impressionistic. The GLU, for example, put "the maintenance and improvement of the basis of life" at the heart of its agenda. The GAZ advocated for a "simple, less materialistic lifestyle." Often, they disagreed with other Green-alternative groups on fundamental questions of governance. Hamburg incubated what would later become the "eco-socialist" branch of the Greens. It understood environmental problems as an epiphenomenon of the crisis of capitalism. Unlike Marxist-Leninist groups, however, the eco-socialists never went so far as to advocate overturning the established political order entirely. The GAZ, by contrast, rejected any attempt to substitute radical democratic or socialist institutions for the status quo and instead advocated reform in the direction of traditional values. Fissures like those between the GLU and GAZ motivated these political newcomers to run separate tickets early in their existence. This move cost the Green-alternative bloc critical votes, which all but assured its inability to win at least 5 percent of the vote and thus seats in parliament.[10] Even after the Greens gained momentum on a national level, however, this principled reluctance to compromise would continue to haunt the party.

Elections to the European Parliament in 1979 provided an opportunity for these groups to overlook their antagonisms. Under the name *Die Grünen* (the Greens), the GLU and GAZ, together with the Green List of Schleswig-Holstein and the Action Group for Independent Germans, formed an official political alliance. This new collaboration gave them occasion to draft a common program. Though their election returns of 3.21 percent were insufficient to win them seats, they were more than enough to put them in the international spotlight. Equally important, European parliamentary elections prompted them to consolidate in time to contend for the West German federal election of 1980. In the southwestern city of Karlsruhe on 13 January 1980, the Green Party was formally established on the basis of four "pillars"—grassroots democracy, social responsibility, ecological consciousness, and nonviolence. Members intended that these principles, if pursued in tandem, would shake up Germany's stagnant political system. In its federal program of 1980, the newly constituted Green Party presented itself as the alternative to traditional parties. It marketed this alternative not only with blueprints for a different kind of policy but also, more capaciously, with pledges of a new way of living. The party called for the replacement of impenetrable centralized bureaucracy with decentralized grassroots-democratic political and social institutions. That process began with the direct election of the delegates tasked with managing these institutions. They would be numerous and their tenure short. And they would follow to the letter the mandate of their constituents. These first steps would begin to combat the sense of political impotence and social alienation the Greens argued had come to characterize West Germany.[11]

The young party's soaring ambitions did not, however, yield similarly elevated voter returns. The federal elections of 1980 brought dismal results. With only 1.5 percent, the party was far from winning a place in parliament. Its pie-in-the-sky program provoked the ridicule of critics far and wide. Some barbs were more measured. An editor for the newspaper *Die Zeit* suggested that perhaps the Greens had bitten off more than they could actually chew. "To warn of the decline of the industrial West is one matter," he argued. "To offer an alternative is another; and to carry it through, still another." The Greens were most successful as harbingers of doom because they could highlight tangible, recognizable, exigent problems, he claimed. As real agents of radical social transformation, however, he suggested simply that they were condemned to failure.[12] Other critics resorted to ad hominem attacks and name-calling. Romantic utopians, Nietzschean nihilists, flipped-out anarcho-Communists, flighty *Wandervogel* types, and court jesters appeared among the many popular epithets.[13] (It bears noting, however, that court jesters possessed the uncommon power to speak the truth to authorities in medieval courts.)

Within a few years, popular reception of the Greens changed considerably. Broadening their focus beyond environmental concerns, the party put Germany's high level of unemployment and generally uninspiring economic situation at the heart of its national campaign platform. Organizing its long-term plan around quality-of-life issues, its members advocated, for example, for the development of small technology to create jobs locally. And their foreign and defense policies set them apart from the center-right by rejecting the use of Pershing II and cruise missiles, a hot-button issue in the early 1980s. The 1983 federal election marked a watershed moment not just for the Greens but for the German political system at large. The nascent party had engaged issues of national importance to the satisfaction of an ambivalent constituency and, with a return of 5.6 percent, it became the first new party to cross the 5 percent parliamentary threshold in twenty-six years. "It was the first time anywhere in the Western world," one historian underscored, "that a party of this kind (i.e. embodying the legacy of the 1960s and representing a coalition of various alternative movements) . . . entered the most important locus of legislative power on a federal level."[14] That same scholar, writing only two years after the Greens' national victory, discouraged unchecked optimism in the face of this benchmark. He warned that the party owed this success to its oppositional stance rather than the substance of its proposed alternatives and that its balloon would deflate quickly when its hot air ran out. But the German electorate did not share his skepticism and increasingly accepted the Greens as a serious political player. By the end of 1983, as environmental concerns rose to the top of political agendas across party lines, members both of the general population and the political arena could no longer criticize the Greens as "merely a band of 'sunshine soldiers' pushing a sometime thing."[15]

Seats in parliament represented an opportunity to effect real change in Germany. The year 1983 thus began a crucial transition for the Greens as they attempted to put their ideas—many of which had, until then, remained either abstract or untested—into practice at the national level. But the task of adapting to conventional parliamentary politics posed a significant challenge to the party. Insofar as decisions surrounding political coalitioning and compromise might need to be made without an opportunity for plebiscites, yielding control to federal parliamentary representatives stood at odds with the Greens' grassroots-democratic agenda. On this issue, the Greens remained divided. With one hand, they held fast to their commitment to *Basisanbindung*—the grassroots communicative network through which the party's direction takes shape from the bottom up. And they reiterated the importance of the imperative mandate, which bound them to that locally determined agenda. But these principles collided with the need for flexibility and pragmatism in the Bundestag.[16] Party members found themselves scattered across a spectrum with principle at one end and reform at the other. The tensions between these poles drove a deep, long-lasting wedge into the party.

Factionalism fractured the Greens quickly, as two major camps formed.[17] On one side stood the realists, who stressed cooperation with the SPD with an eye toward real parliamentary victory. On the other stood the fundamentalists, who clung to principled extraparliamentary politics over compromise. These two groups earned the Swiftian-sounding nicknames the Realos and the Fundis. The fundamentalists, or radical ecologists, emerged in the early 1980s around Jutta Ditfurth, a sociologist, founding party member, and committed proponent of radical naturalist policies. She heavily criticized capitalism and called instead for the establishment of a deindustrialized, grassroots democratic society. Alongside Ditfurth worked Rudolf Bahro, an East German dissident deported to West Germany in 1979 over the publication of his dissertation, which lambasted "real existing socialism." Like Ditfurth, Bahro argued that industrial-urban civilization was unsustainable. As the alternative, he advocated social reform through the formation of small, close-knit communities. In contrast to the established political parties as well as to several other factions within the Greens, however, Bahro called for a biocentric worldview instead of an anthropocentric one. He espoused a kind of environmentalism fueled by a vision of looming ecological catastrophe. His preference for privileging nature over humanity made many uncomfortable.

Despite the best-laid plans of the Fundis, the Green ideal of radical grassroots democracy began to fall victim to what the German sociologist Robert Michels described in the 1920s as the "iron law" of party politics. The practical responsibilities of governing bodies eventually render oligarchical even those parties with the most democratic of intentions.[18] Electorally successful local and regional branches of the Greens found themselves increasingly confronted with the mundane and often overwhelming exigencies of political power. They began to privilege parliamentary efficacy over principled plebiscitary democratic practices.[19] These realists—radical-outsiders-cum-reformist-insiders—rallied around the former Student Movement activist Joschka Fischer. At the heart of the realist agenda lay political feasibility. Its proponents abandoned a politics of protest for parliamentary pragmatism. They stressed a reform-based project for the ecological and social restructuring of industrial society at the expense of constructing a rigorous ideological profile.

Dissatisfied with the agendas of either the Realos or the Fundis, two additional camps arose. Drawing on the party's early and considerable support from the Left—the Greens were sometimes called "watermelons" (that is, green on the outside but red, or socialist, on the inside)—a group of "eco-socialists" banded together to emphasize the historic importance of the workers' movement and its desire to create a socialist society. They understood the crisis of ecology as a side effect of the battle between workers and capitalists. Many of these members would leave the party after the fall of the Berlin Wall when it became apparent that the project of using Green means toward communist ends had failed definitively.

That the Greens, under the eco-socialists, risked veering away from a Green agenda toward an expressly Social Democratic one was lost on few—Wolf-Dieter Hasenclever in particular, a politician with inconsistent allegiances, who first left the SPD to found the Greens but later left the Greens for the FDP at the turn of the millennium. Hasenclever opposed what he saw as the cavalier instrumentalization of parliamentary democracy among other Green factions. He understood his fellow party members as engaged in dismantling the representative parliamentary scaffolding that had made the party and democracy itself possible in the first place. In its place, he argued, they sought to implement a naïve experiment in large-scale direct democracy. Though this stance won Hasenclever a following, the "eco-libertarians" that gathered around him never gained a large percentage of the party's delegates.

Unsettled by the distracting extremism they saw taking root in their party, several influential centrist groups cropped up in the late 1980s. These included Grüner Aufbruch '88, which formed around the leadership of Antje Vollmer and Ralf Fücks. These two figures would play pivotal roles in the development of the Greens after reunification.

Despite these cleavages, an important commonality united most of the early Greens. Beginning with their first federal party program, the Greens explicitly rejected what they saw as the traditional parties' dependence on passive citizenship.[20] In its place, they committed themselves to instituting a new politics of the self. The Greens shared classical liberalism's commitment to the freedom of the individual. Unlike the self-interested individualism of Smithian liberalism in which the fulfillment of the self drives the actualization of a free market economy, however, the Greens' valuation of the self was neither market-oriented nor egocentric. As an antidote to the problems previous generations of leftist German intellectuals had identified in modern society—deep social alienation disguised by the superficial distractions of mass culture—the Greens advocated for a conception of the self whose essential mode of being in the world involved empathic engagement in community.[21] The party understood the practice of democracy "in collective terms as a participatory versus a mere representative model of politics."[22] Against recriminations that the Greens lacked a coherent master plan, Manon Maren-Grisebach—a founding member, early party spokesperson, and one of the engines driving efforts to develop a party philosophy—argued that the party's objective was nothing short of a fundamentally different way of life.[23] "Green," she argued, "is the color of living differently [*die Farbe des sich ändernden Lebens*]."[24] Their bête noire was the social milieu of advanced capitalism in which the individual lived disaggregated from an empathic community, one's social needs sustained only by one's vague knowledge of participating anonymously in a network of mass consumption. Individuality had gotten lost in the abstraction of the mass ornament. The Greens, Maren-Grisebach argued, supported more robust expressions of selfhood amid the commotion of modern life.[25]

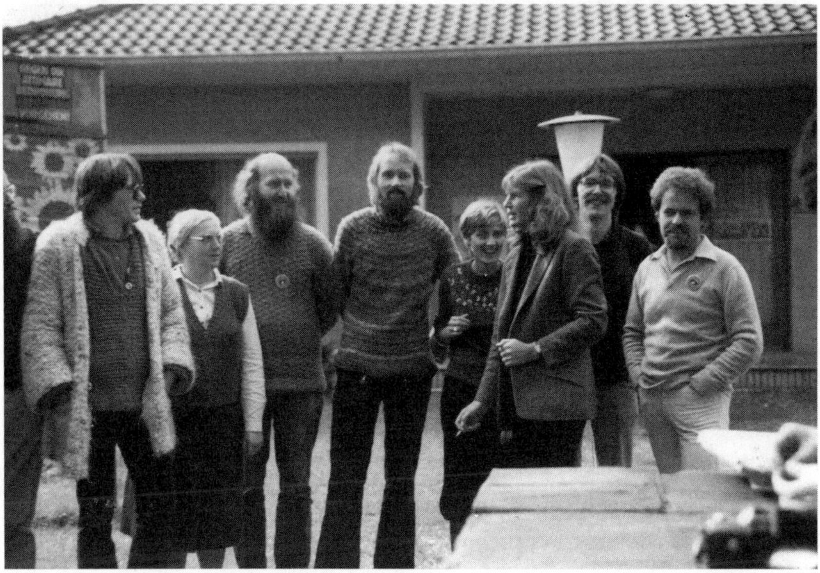

3.2 Federal executive board of the Greens, 1982. Manon Maren-Grisebach third from right. Archiv Grünes Gedächtnis der Heinrich-Böll-Stiftung e. V., Signatur FO-03473-01-cp.

The emphasis Maren-Grisebach placed on empathic community, belonging, self-expression, and quality of life over economic and physical security planted the Greens squarely on one side of a paradigm shift in values. The political scientist Ronald Inglehart has called such political programs "postmaterialist." Absent the economic crises of the first half of the twentieth century, German values were freed to drift away from material concerns.[26] If values are dictated in part by scarcity, the generation of 1968 and their countercultural successors—including the Greens—clarified that interpretations of scarcity alongside socially acceptable standards of subsistence had transformed with time.[27] The scarcity that defined this new generation was one of opportunities for self-expression in politics and society. Socialized into conditions of peace and relative prosperity, Germany's ascendant educated middle class, by the late 1970s, expressed greater concern for the rights of political and cultural participation and agency than had their parents, the war generation. In this regard, the early Green agenda can also be read as the product of a generational conflict, part of a cyclical rebellion of young against old, a crisis of identity and authority.[28]

Their origins aside, Green politics leaned decidedly toward a transformational individualism. The party understood its task as nurturing hope. And that hope was, first, to be directed inwardly: hope for self-actualization, for a sense of belonging in and to nature, for equality (*Gleichrangigkeit*) but not sameness (*Gleichheit*). Maren-Grisebach understood this kind of individualized hope as a precondition of political engagement. Without it, constituents with little time or money to spare would be hard-pressed to participate in the political process. Sufficient hope, however, would provide fuel enough for them to pursue a new life-sensibility (*Lebens-Sinn*). In short, Maren-Grisebach argued, "the Greens are building a party based upon the hope for life [*Hoffnung auf Leben*]."[29] The party represented this drive toward political and cultural transformation with the imperative to "concretize utopia." As two specialists on Green politics have explained, "this phrase combines the romantic and idealistic inclination to take utopian designs seriously with the exhortation of the Enlightenment tradition that humans' reason and obligation to civic action encourage them to implement their ideals. This new tradition moves beyond both the Kantian admonition to think critically but obey superiors and the German romantic inclination to seek private development over civic action."[30] The self-centered focus of postmaterialism might appear at odds with an environmental or ecological program, which would seem, de facto, to possess an outward, external orientation. The Greens, however, understood postmaterialist individualism and the collectivism of environmental politics as coterminous and mutually dependent.

Good Environmentalists as Good Artists

The unexpected link that coupled the Greens' collective, collaborative large-scale environmental agenda with its inward, individualistic postmaterialist values was the understanding of the concept of "environment" that the Greens gradually adopted. They conceived of "environment" expansively. It consisted not only of the natural world but also of the built and social worlds. The Greens expressed this totality through the language of "culture." Anyone plugged in to established cultural networks in 1980s West Germany, however, would have encountered the argument that the Greens had a "culture problem." Often this indictment appeared in the broadest terms from critics who charged the Greens with anti-intellectualism and theorylessness. They could not talk meaningfully about the concept of culture because they lacked a coherent theoretical framing for it.

In some ways this assessment was overblown. Party members had been socialized into the era of student rebellion and educational expansion, whose engagement with theory, while messy, was nevertheless conceptually rigorous. A patient reader could identify in the rhetoric of some radical ecologists vague recitations of Theodor Adorno and Max Horkheimer's touchstone critique of humanity's dangerous domination of nature. But these echoed only faintly. Early pamphlets hinted that the Greens had an affinity for other thinkers, too. Kant, Schiller, Nietzsche, and Freud all appeared sporadically, though their ideas were cherry-picked, decontextualized, and instrumentalized. More their contemporary, Hans Jonas offered an appealing eco-ethical conceptual framework in his 1979 advocacy of "the imperative of responsibility" in technologically sophisticated societies.[31] Marxist philosopher Ernst Bloch was a particular favorite for his emphasis on hope and the liberation of humanity from the oppression of modern civilization. The party, however, remained generally wary of rigid philosophical systems. They wished to avoid becoming the handmaidens of what they often saw as backward-looking intellectualism. Not without some irony, they mobilized Bloch's writings to make this point. Citing his book, *The Principle of Hope,* the Greens argued that the "dream"—that is, their political and social goal—"is only directed forward when it anticipates the future." They refused to recapitulate old ideas and called instead for the pursuit of the "not-yet-known [*Noch-nicht-Bewußte*]," the novel, the creative, and as Bloch instructed, the utopian.[32] In contrast to the generation of 1968, whose genuine investment in revising Marxism often won them the respect of the intellectual community, the Green-Alternative Movement had no interest in establishing intellectual continuities. Participants championed instinct over contemplation and demanded a "new politics of the gut [*die aus dem Bauch herauskommt*]."[33] The strength of a line of reasoning, the brilliance of its formulation, or its critical force took a backseat. They judged arguments as captivating, rather, based on their ability to mediate "life-historical authenticity [*lebensgeschichtlicher Authentizität*]."[34]

As a result, the Greens' command of conceptual systems was often described as insufficient, incomplete, and unsatisfactory. Some softened the blow of unfavorable analyses by suggesting that the Greens and their critics simply talked past one another.[35] Others qualified their criticisms by suggesting that the Greens were in fact intellectuals insofar as intellectuals are "specialists in general concerns." They produce *Zeitdiagnosen,* or evaluations of their times, by engaging discursively with diverse fields. But *Zeitdiagnosen* are always destined to be insufficient and thus disappointing.[36] Prominent West German public intellectuals often chided the party for its lack of a theoretically rigorous politics and argued that it provided only eagerness as a substitute. Social systems theorist Niklas Luhmann, for example, dismissed the Greens on the grounds that they "[camouflaged] their lack of theoretical clarity by moralistic fervor."[37] Like Luhmann, most intellectuals tended to keep the Greens at arm's length.

On other occasions, critics presented the Greens' problem with culture in specifically aesthetic terms. One musician called the Greens philistines (*Kunstbanausen*), described their attention to aesthetics as "deficient," and admonished them for their negligible public discussion of art.[38] Historian Sabine von Dirke found this reticence curious for two reasons. First, the Greens' constituency was largely middle class, a group traditionally supportive of the arts in Germany. Second, the Greens received considerable endorsement from artists, Joseph Beuys of course among the most famous. Von Dirke suggested that nature may have been the greatest obstacle to Green aesthetics, insofar as nature, by definition, opposes artifice. By privileging nature as the ultimate point of reference, the Greens seemed to relegate art to mimesis.[39]

Anyone looking to chide the Greens for a weak cultural platform needed to look no further than their first federal program. It devoted little attention to cultural initiatives, calling only for their decentralization in the form of traveling exhibitions and the creation of community-oriented cultural centers. The Greens themselves agreed that they had directed their attention elsewhere. In a retrospective written two years after Berlin's Alternative List for Democracy and the Protection of the Environment (AL) entered the state parliament in 1981, AL's assistant for cultural affairs, Hajo Cornel, confirmed that culture and cultural policy played almost no role in the AL's election program. AL representatives often required the party's Cultural Committee to justify its existence. Though this branch of the Greens unexpectedly received a position on the Senate Cultural Committee upon winning seats in the Berlin Senate, it was only because more coveted committee seats had already been claimed.[40] Speaking on behalf of the Greens' Federal Working Group for Culture (BAG-Kultur), Klaus Becker dismissed criticism of the Greens' engagement with cultural issues by deflecting responsibility onto the general German political system.[41] In a 1985 position paper for the party titled "A Vote for Culture," he explained that Green cultural politics had not yet fully gelled. It was "no disgrace" to the party that they needed further tweaking. After all, he pointed out, none of the other political parties took *Kultur* seriously either. Nevertheless, he urged the party to get to work. The development of a radically new cultural program, he argued, offered an opportunity for the Greens to be "truly alternative."[42] Other party members valued culture as a point of access to the electorate. Annemarie Borgmann, a Green member of the Bundestag, stressed that, while the dense rhetoric of policy could alienate constituents, the average person found culture approachable. But the Greens, she lamented, wanted "damned little [*verdammt wenig*]" to do with culture. Reflecting on her first two years in the Bundestag, she noted tellingly that there were "always more important things to do!" Even a cultural consultant appointed by the party threw up his hands after several months of work. If the Greens had any hopes of amplifying their investment in cultural issues, he argued, they had best make *Kultur* another pillar of the party.[43]

Part of the Greens' trouble with *Kultur* came down to its definition. What they meant by "culture" was hardly obvious. To those who drew on the term's storied and weighty history in Germany, *Kultur* implied exclusivity, elitism, *high* culture.[44] To appreciate the accomplishments of high culture indicated a level of personal cultivation that distinguished one from the uneducated masses, Norbert Elias stressed in his 1939 analysis of European social attitudes, *The Civilizing Process*. Cultural appreciation offered a source of pride and a sense of legitimacy, a holdover from the bourgeois mores of the eighteenth and nineteenth centuries. Its absence could invite shame. *Kultur* encapsulated the long history of creative expression—artistic and intellectual—that has since become a stereotype of Germanness: literature, philosophy, opera, art, classical music. Their understanding required deep, thorough education (*Bildung*). Their appreciation was a quasi-spiritual affair.[45]

But German culture had other faces as well, including a thriving alternative side that enjoyed a perhaps equally storied past. The Weimar era's legendary art world, for example, pushed the boundaries not only of the aesthetically pleasing but, even more dramatically, of what constituted art itself. It cultivated the Dadaism of the Cabaret Voltaire and the epic theater of

Bertolt Brecht. It welcomed the fresh jazz styles of Black America and the expressionist film of Fritz Lang. It became an incubator for radical aesthetic innovation.[46] The 1960s and 1970s took the torch from Weimar and engaged broadly with questions of oppositional aesthetics.[47] Painter Gerhard Richter's inconsistent oeuvre joined photo-realism and abstract neo-expressionism as a rejection of the need for coherent artistic styles. Sculptor Joseph Beuys pioneered the social sculpture, whose participatory nature evolved the old Wagnerian idea of the *Gesamtkunstwerk.* Artistic creation, Beuys believed, should not be solely the purview of the artist. These same years, however, also saw the tidal wave of that "irresistible" empire of American consumer culture sweep through Europe. Coca-Cola and Elvis Presley represented the success of a global cultural conformism.[48] It remained unclear to the Greens what, precisely, they should include under the rubric of culture.

In a presentation to the Greens of Marburg in 1984, party member from Baden-Württemberg and expert in cultural politics Eckard Holler advised, first, that a Green alternative cultural policy must offer a self-critical program for engaging with bourgeois cultural products. But it must also support and develop traditional popular culture (*Volkskultur*) and oppositional culture. Second, Holler advocated understanding culture not simply as art (*Kunst*) but as the aggregate expression of human creativity.[49] Though Holler's talk was likely heard by few members of the party, by the time it was printed eight months later in the journal for philosophy and the social sciences, *Das Argument,* the question of the boundaries of the Greens' concept of culture—their *Kulturbegriff*—had become a topic of considerable contestation.

Many party members embraced a capacious notion of culture. Sabine Weißler, a member of Berlin's Alternative List and curator of the city's New Society for the Visual Arts (NGBK), for example, argued in 1984 that essentially everything had the potential to become the subject of cultural politics.[50] At that time, to follow Holler's and Weißler's line of reasoning meant aligning with a cultural politician of a different party affiliation: Frankfurt's well-known Social Democrat, Hilmar Hoffmann. Within cultural-political circles in West Germany, Hoffmann's name usually accompanied the motto he popularized in 1979: *Kultur für alle,* "Culture for everyone."[51] Praised for the way it put art and cultural institutions more broadly in the service of urban renewal and development in Frankfurt, Hoffmann's motto also won him his fair share of enemies.[52] In 1985 Christoph Schröder, a member of the cultural group of Hamburg's Green-Alternative List (GAL), published a polemic against fellow party members who had allied—imprudently, he argued—with Hoffmann and other Social Democratic cultural advisors. Instead of Hoffmann's motto, Schröder preferred the formulation drawn up at the international congress of Green and Alternative Movements in Liverpool in November 1984: *Kultur von und mit Allen und gegen Wenige*, "Culture from and with everyone and against few." This phrasing allowed him to allude directly to the Hamburg GAL's socialist inclinations: the "few," here, meant "the ruling class," which rendered culture a key battleground in the trajectory of class conflict. It also allowed him to avoid the unpalatable economic instrumentalization of culture he read in Hoffmann's approach. Schröder disliked that Hoffmann was in the pocket of conservatives and that his cultural policies aimed not at generating social consciousness but at stimulating the economy. This stance, Schröder argued, threatened to render aesthetic production uncritical, instrumentalized, mechanical, "depraved [*verkommen*]." Instead, he called the Greens to conceive of culture as a rebellion against the status quo. Through this culture of opposition, society could begin to realize a new value system and world orientation.[53]

Out of the problem of culture in practice grew the problem of the concept, or *Begriff*, of culture. The Berlin AL, for example, hosted a long and controversial debate about their *Kulturbegriff* in the summer of 1983. They managed to agree that Berlin cultural politics should always leave space for both alternative and established cultural institutions. But they could come to no further consensus about the content of their notion of culture. In the run-up to the 1985 elections, they justified their slow progress on the clichéd grounds that "good things come to those who wait" and resigned themselves to a cultural program that addressed only short-term issues. It offered little direction on the long-term trajectory of Berlin's cultural landscape.[54]

The desire to articulate a well-defined *Kulturbegriff* remained a concern through the mid-1980s. In October 1985, the Greens organized a cultural political debate at the federal level. First up on the agenda was to determine the status of the Greens' *Kulturbegriff*. The BAG-Kultur had already spent its previous two meetings debating this theme. But the result—a blurry catch-all definition—disappointed many. When it came to culture, Annemarie Borgmann reported somewhat awkwardly, "green" would remain a "multicolored color." That is, the Greens were willing to engage with the full spectrum of political perspectives. The Greens, she claimed, had had enough of boundaries and exclusivity.[55]

Not all representatives took so kindly, however, to this curious obsession with definitions. Christoph Schröder denounced it as nothing more than a distraction. Taking a swipe at intellectuals and academics, he argued that no hearty declarations or sophisticated philosophical guiding principles could ever matter as much as political practice. He challenged the BAG-Kultur to prompt action among both representatives as well as regular party members, rather than serving as armchair intellectuals.[56] Noting that their constituents were disappointed with the party's flagging engagement with culture, other representatives joined Schröder in his calls to revive it.[57]

Despite what the great *Begriff*-distraction and the unmet expectations of crisp programmatic statements might suggest, the Greens engaged a great deal with practical cultural matters. Between January and October 1984, the party organized three cultural congresses.[58] Anticipating accusations like Schröder's, the first of these congresses, held in Hamburg, focused exclusively on cultural practice. It postponed categorical, definitional debates to future meetings.[59] After the dust had settled from the first congress, the journal *Alternative Kommunalpolitik* released an issue devoted entirely to alternative cultural politics. In preparation for the second congress, to be held in Frankfurt that June, this mouthpiece for local Green and alternative political issues consolidated the resolutions arrived at in Hamburg in January. Two points of accord stood out. First, the Greens had little patience with established cultural institutions that they believed had become outmoded and whose innovative inclinations had stagnated. They concluded, for example, that high theater and opera had grown too comfortable with their substantial state subsidies. The elitism and exclusivity of these arenas undermined their ability to carry out their project of the cultural enrichment of the German people as a whole. Second, the Greens were particularly sympathetic with new, struggling cultural initiatives forced to fight for recognition and support.[60]

In a landmark move, shortly after the Greens concluded the third cultural congress, the Bundestag opted to host West Germany's first federal debate on cultural policy in November of 1984.[61] On behalf of the Greens, Hubert Kleinert, a Bundestag representative from Marburg, rose to speak in opposition to the *Wirtschaftswunder*-generated blinders that he understood many politicians to wear when adjudicating the value of cultural products and institutions. He underscored that the Greens advocated a cultural orientation that established cultural value on grounds other than economics. "It's inconvenient to many of you," he quipped, "that many of us have realized that there are things besides earning and producing, besides growth and increasing standards of living, that make life meaningful." He argued that the Greens rejected an economically grounded cultural framework because of its capacity to stifle, even suffocate, artistic creativity.[62]

Though Kleinert's brief speech largely failed to animate his party, the young scholar of the New Social Movements Roland Schmidt marshaled Kleinert's sentiments when he called for party members to remember that Green aesthetics were also Green politics. Channeling political sociologist and second-generation Frankfurt School member Claus Offe, Schmidt criticized the separation of politics from aesthetics, practice from perception, as objectionably bourgeois. To Schmidt, these "false dichotomies," which he saw represented in the work of prominent political scientist Wolfgang Kraushaar, merely reinforced the disjuncture between action (*Handeln*) and desire (*Wollen*). Offe identified this incompatibility as the structuring principle of bourgeois democracy.[63] By Schmidt's understanding, the nature of alternative movements meant that their politics could never be separated from the culture they inhabited. Alternative culture grew both in reaction to and as a solution for societal crisis. It aspired to generate a collective oppositional identity out of an otherwise undifferentiated political culture and to combat the tendency of an overzealous economic life to "colonize the life-world."[64]

Hajo Cornel took this argument one step further than Schmidt. To his mind, the objective of any cultural political program should be to enable more democratic access to cultural education, the means of cultural production, and cultural products themselves. Insofar as support for all stages of cultural production involves a process of adjudicating cultural value, Cornel also demanded radical transparency of aesthetic judgment. German citizens should not only know who determines the cultural offerings to which they are given access and by what standards access is granted. They should also play a central role in both the negotiation of those standards and the process of adjudication itself. Only by retaining grassroots democratic control over the arts could Germans preserve art's power to register dissent (*Widerspruch*).

Culture, Cornel argued, should stand as a "permanent moment of opposition [*permanentes Widerspruchsmoment*]."[65]

Berlin's Sabine Weißler saw the same argument from the opposite vantage point. She predicated the politics of opposition on a politics of creativity and potentiality. Drawing on the Bremen Greens' more capacious *Kulturbegriff*, Weißler suggested that alternative culture, which emerges out of the friction between competing visions for society, is simply the preservation of the possibility of something different. It makes no distinction between its producers. Contrary to bourgeois cultural understanding, Weißler argued, every individual—not just artists or scholars—possesses the capacity to contribute new visions for society. With a Green vernacular, she echoed the argument made by both the spatial interventionists—channeling Josef Beuys—as well as the *Geschichtswerkstatt* members. In other words, culture is essentially democratic. Weißler urged the Greens to advance cultural policies that would cultivate this radically democratic potential for creativity.[66]

Like Weißler, Manon Maren-Grisebach understood bourgeois cultural and social expectations as outdated. The Greens faced a great opportunity to revise them. Just two years after the Greens' founding, Maren-Grisebach published a book that attempted to articulate the new party's philosophy. Though far shorter than other chapters and appearing at the end of the book, her pithy statement on Green aesthetic philosophy was hardly an afterthought. At the heart of the party's ethical demands for the environment, society, and the life-world, Maren-Grisebach placed aesthetics, or more specifically, what she called "play" (*Spiel*). Not the kind of play accompanying games with rules, *Regelspiel;* rather, play without purpose (*Spiel der Zwecklosigkeit*). This kind of play, she argued, nurtures the pursuit of fantasies and dreams. The Greens' appreciation of the non-utility (*Un-Nutzen*) of play worked to their advantage. If general social, political, and environmental renewal (*Rundumerneuerung*) required first upsetting capitalism's means-end rationality (*Zweckrationalität*), the Greens possessed a powerful weapon in the form of their playful orientation to the world.[67] Aesthetics and creativity, as a medium of play without purpose, formed a bridge between the practices of every life and the ethical imperative of the Greens' ecological program.

The emphasis Weißler and Maren-Grisebach placed on creativity makes sense against the Greens' early embrace of postmaterialist politics. Creativity and cultural production affirmed the self. Weißler drew inspiration from

Elsbeth Mordo, a member of Baden-Württemberg's state parliament, who stressed that *Selbermachen*—meaning do-it-yourself as well as, more abstractly, the experience of one's own aesthetic creativity—was central to the Greens' understanding of culture. *Selbermachen,* Mordo claimed, fosters self-affirmation.[68] The Greens had endorsed this assertion since the party's earliest days, when founding party member, president of the Foundation of Political Ecology, and former chair of the German Writers Association Carl Amery published an article in 1980 on the philosophical foundations and consequences of the Alternative Movement. His point of departure was what he interpreted as the essential problem of modern society. The article responded to the pessimism of Sigmund Freud who, fifty years prior, famously lamented that "the greatest impediment to civilization" rested in society's own internal enmity and human antagonisms. This was the death drive, *Thanatos,* in action.[69] Amery argued that society could foster a life-affirming world opposed to this drive toward self-destruction if it could first create a new culture to support it.[70] Culture functioned not as an epiphenomenal component of historical materialism, but rather as an essential means of Being in relation to the physical world. As a corporeal phenomenon, it emanates from the body and engages the senses. By reinventing West Germany's technical and political establishment to celebrate humanity's creative capacity, Amery argued that West Germany could begin to eliminate its culture of domination, possession, and global annihilation. These ideas would stay with Amery, who delivered them in a lecture at Oldenburg University seven years later. In his talk, he argued that the task of solving the ecological problems facing the modern world, in fact, amounted to a massive cultural undertaking.[71]

Through different rhetorical means but with the same objective as Amery, another founding party member, Wolf-Dieter Hasenclever, critiqued the destructive tendencies in modern society. Hasenclever had been driven into the arms of the Greens by his opposition to the SPD's tacit acceptance of nuclear weapons under NATO's Double-Track Decision. His solution drew on the Baden-Württemburg Greens' party program, which endorsed ecological humanism as the guiding principle of the Green movement. Hasenclever understood ecology as the science of life's interconnections (*Lebenszusammenhänge*). He argued that a political system guided by a humanistic ethic would permit both humanity's social freedom as well as its harmonious coexistence in and with nature. Hasenclever acknowledged Ernst Bloch's imprint on his thinking.[72] To Hasenclever, ecological humanism meant recognizing the sacrosanct dignity (*unantastbare Würde*) of humanity. He argued that this dignity derives from the human capacity to live creatively in a kind of symbiotic coexistence with the natural world, the social world, and the future world. Modifying slightly the theologian, philosopher, and physician Albert Schweitzer's concept of "reverence for life" (*Ehrfurcht vor dem Leben*), Hasenclever challenged the Greens to embrace reverence for living creatively and to make it the foundation of all human activity. Such veneration of humanity's capacity to transform its world creatively, Hasenclever argued, had the potential to forestall the otherwise catastrophic trajectory of contemporary society.[73]

Such emphasis on the creative enterprises of individuals carried risks, though. Individual creativity, at its most extreme, slips into an abyss of social and cultural isolation. Where that boundary lay was by no means obvious. As the Green Party's membership grew, some lost the sense that they belonged to a community. By 1985, Bundestag member Annemarie Borgmann could argue that the party's annual federal conventions lacked a sense of cohesiveness and that members were reluctant to speak of fellow party members using "we." In the absence of opportunities to foster a sense of belonging and collective identity, she lamented, the Greens "have become strangers to themselves."[74]

Others disagreed. They argued that immersion in self-directed aesthetic activities need not lead to social alienation. Mordo suggested that individual acts of aesthetic creation possess an inherently communal quality. These acts generate communicative experiences in which individuals enter into relationships with others by re-envisioning their shared way of life (*Lebensgestaltung*).[75] Manon Maren-Grisebach drew on Ernst Bloch to make the same point. Bloch, she noted, spoke of a solidarity constituted by a polyphonic multitude (*personenreichen, höchst vielstimmigen*), which resembled the Green saying "Unity in Diversity." Strong egos (*Iche*), Bloch suggested, make for strong voices that, together, build strong solidarity. Maren-Grisebach referred to that which emerges from this solidarity as the "products of the 'we.'" Through their interactions, significant and mundane, people leave traces on one another, such that no idea and no encounter is ever radically one's own.[76] Roland Schmidt concurred. He suggested that alternative movements build for themselves a collective identity by acting on their shared set of concerns

(*Betroffenheit*) about contemporary society. He used the research of Thomas Ziehe, a scholar of education and specialist in processes of cultural modernization, to argue that the centralizing structures, means-end rationality, and technocracy of social activity in modern society dominated—in his words, "colonized"—even the most personal of social spaces. As an antidote, Ziehe and Schmidt called for the localization of cultural activities. This local collaboration promised to facilitate expressions of belonging and shared *Betroffenheit* rather than experiences of social fragmentation.[77]

The historian of German countercultural movements Sabine von Dirke has argued that the facilitation of individual creative capacity lay at the very core of the Greens pillar of social responsibility. Beyond social responsibility conceived in terms of welfare programs and aid to developing countries, the Greens also understood *sozial* to mean

> a vague notion of a better, nonalienated life, in which the human being will be restored to his or her full creative powers. Green politics strove for a society in which the subject is not reduced to a passive recipient either of food stamps and unemployment checks or of the commodities that the market economy provides. In contrast, the Greens advocated a model of a society in which everybody has a chance for self-actualization and political, social, and cultural participation.[78]

Broad participation of this sort, von Dirke noted, conflicted with a political system based on representation. Political representation required political centralization and consolidation. And these needs stood at odds with the "braid of relationships" that defined the Green-Alternative Movement's vision for a better society. The braid had knots of varying sizes, but its real strength, Roland Schmidt argued, was that it lacked a center.[79] As a result, access to the politics and content of alternative culture would always remain fragmentary, heterogeneous, and dynamic. Schmidt understood the Green-Alternative Movement as employing a new collective "politics of the first person."[80] This kind of politics played out not in parliament but locally, on the ground, or, using the popular catchphrase of the Alternative Movement, *vor Ort,* in places it saw as dissociated from the existing political process.

Christiane Zieseke, a member of the Greens and of Berlin's Cultural Council (*Kulturrat*) as well as a founding member of Berlin's Active Museum, argued that citizens deserved locally accessible opportunities to develop their cultural sensibilities and realize their individual creativity, rather than simply being towed along by the state.[81] The party proved quite sympathetic to this view. Moreover, the Greens believed themselves to possess a particular aptitude for rooting out or creating these new spaces of free expression that slipped the colonizing impulses of modern society. Sabine Weißler and Elsbeth Mordo thus tasked their party with creating and supporting sites where ideas about art and culture could be discussed together, where laypeople would be encouraged to exercise their aesthetic creativity, and where artists of all sorts could interact directly with their publics. In other words, the party should nurture, Weißler suggested, the "completely quotidian character that engagement with art, history and all the manifestations of culture should have."[82]

The New Local

The Greens' failure to articulate an official party-wide understanding of culture hardly stood in the way of their local efforts to add Green dimensions to cultural ventures still in planning phases. Throughout West Germany, local Green constituencies pushed to inject everyday life with more culture. They attempted to create and sustain conditions in which art and culture could serve as a medium of resistance to the less desirable qualities of modern life. And they used these cultural projects to advocate for transformations in the ways everyday Germans interacted with their world.[83] In the wake of their first major electoral successes, the Green-Alternative Movement began to make a name for itself in Berlin's cultural scene, for example. Only a month after its 7.2 percent election return in 1981 won it nine seats in the Berlin Senate (two more than the FDP), Berlin's Alternative List released a parliamentary interpellation (*große Anfrage*) on an art exhibit featuring the work of artist Arno Breker, whose sculptures won acclaim during National Socialism. Fueled by considerable popular protest, the AL's inquiry unleashed a heated parliamentary debate about whether the celebration of art with such a shadowy past should be tolerated in Berlin.[84] The positive reception their early critical cultural engagement received fueled further efforts.[85] The party undertook to consolidate, organize, and intensify its cultural policy work by naming an official cultural assistant (*Bereichsassistent für Medien und Kulturpolitik*, later *Fraktionsassistent*). They tasked this assistant with ensuring the party's continuous engagement in Berlin's cultural community. He or she would help the party establish contacts, mediate between those contacts and party leadership, and fill in the gaps in the party's cultural program. Chosen as AL's first cultural assistant, Hajo Cornel would later criticize the structure of the party itself as the primary obstacle to the advancement of its cultural ambitions. The Greens' small number of parliamentary seats as well as the policy mandating a two-year rotation period for representatives meant a quick turnover in leadership.[86] The first three representatives tasked with managing the party's cultural issues also had to split their investments with other more pressing political concerns. This divided attention meant that they often gave cultural issues short shrift. Cornel lobbied the Greens to choose instead a designated cultural politician with knowledge of Berlin's diverse cultural topography, reminding them pointedly that grassroots democratic political participation need not imply that "anyone can do anything."[87]

The Greens' participation in cultural policy debates and their efforts to put cultural policies into practice increased quickly in the first few years they occupied offices at the federal, state, and local levels. Though the pursuit of a Green cultural agenda involved work via a number of different media, the most important of these was space. The Green cultural program, in practice, involved the deliberate attempt to find the best spaces for culture in contemporary German society. The Greens' concerns about the site of culture had its roots in what Geoff Eley calls the "new radicalisms of sixty-eight," which changed the landscape where politics could occur. Greater disposable incomes in the 1960s brought new opportunities to engage in capitalist consumerism. These shifts altered both how and where one participated in the economy. The Student Movement brought political, social, cultural, and economic battles into the spaces in which Germany's younger generation lived, worked, and played.[88] Both on the streets and in the classroom, the Student Movement called on young Germans to challenge traditional authorities of space. New negotiations of spatialized power shaped the 1970s, too. The Alternative Movement embraced cooperative living, squatted apartment buildings to protest their demolition during housing shortages, and advocated the inviolability of the space of the body through liberated sexual and gender politics as well as drug use.

Anxieties about agency over space filtered into the 1980s and became a particular concern of the Greens. In 1985, for example, Berlin's Alternative List insisted that the Greens needed to lobby on behalf of public spaces in which they could nurture their oppositional culture and grassroots democratic practices. And where the Greens could not repurpose existing spaces for this task, they needed to create new ones. The AL understood the provision of sufficient space as essential to fostering self-expression and self-administration within German society. Admittedly, even the AL recognized that such support had some limits. Its cultural assistant acknowledged that not everyone who organizes an alternative group should automatically receive financing. Still, the AL argued that "there should be space to conceptualize a product and to determine whether there is an audience for it."[89]

For a party still gaining its political footing, administering space meant first winning allies among those with louder voices and greater influence. In Berlin, the party's first victory on this front involved earning the trust of the Berlin Cultural Council. Influenced by the unflattering media portrayals of the Greens, the council initially regarded with skepticism the Alternative List's investment in cultural issues. The council assumed the Greens' interests were narrow and instrumentalized and expected few returns from collaborative work with the young party.[90] In spite of their reputation, however, the Greens insisted on meeting with the Cultural Council in early 1982. The AL expressed its support for the Cultural Council's old, repeatedly dismissed plan to repurpose an underutilized building designed in the late nineteenth century by Martin Gropius, the great uncle of Bauhaus founder Walter Gropius. Restorations of the Martin Gropius Building, partially destroyed by the Second World War, had begun only in the 1970s. The Cultural Council, however, had long since recognized the building's potential. Its members had lobbied for the site to house a center for the visual arts, but until the Greens' involvement, these petitions fell largely on deaf ears.

The AL also supported the Cultural Council in its bid to host a major art exhibition and event series in observance of the fiftieth anniversary of Hitler's ascension to power. The anniversary project, called "Destroying Democracy—the Seizure of Power and Resistance, 1933," appealed to the Greens' commitment to the sanctity of democracy. And its attempts to make art and history more accessible to everyday Germans aligned with the early formulations of the Berlin Greens' cultural concept.[91] The AL's enthusiastic support for the "Destroying Democracy" project, both within the Berlin Senate and via public media outlets, became a breakthrough moment for the party.[92] It elevated the AL to the status of a serious player in Berlin's cultural politics.

In September of 1982, the Berlin Cultural Council wrote to thank the AL expressly for its parliamentary backing. Acknowledging its initial pessimism, the Cultural Council was pleased to find the AL "unconditionally supportive" and willing to collaborate with other parties to win the city's approval. The party's performance went a long way, the council suggested, toward changing popular and parliamentary attitudes toward the AL and its investment in cultural affairs.[93] In fact, the Cultural Council's signatory on these correspondences, Christiane Zieseke, would become so persuaded by the Greens' agenda that she later not only joined the party but also rose to office, serving as an AL representative in the Berlin Senate. The AL continued to maintain its alliance with the Berlin Cultural Council and provided support as the council lobbied against the conservative Senate majority to reformulate the city's plan for its 750th anniversary celebration.

But such momentum was hard to sustain. The party faltered at the end of 1982. The AL had gotten caught up with the SPD in a sluggish battle against the CDU and FDP over the laws governing the number of state representatives who served on the board of Berlin's public radio and television service. Introducing no new initiatives for several months, the party drifted into what one member called a "cultural political wasteland [*kulturpolitische Brachzeit*]."[94] But over the next year, Berlin's AL nevertheless managed to win another major ally in the newly constituted but vocal, visible, and tenacious Active Museum.[95] The organization boasted an impressive membership roster from among the city's most prominent alternative social, cultural, and political groups. In response to Active Museum's first press release, the Greens issued one of their own. It expressed the party's approval of the organization, its goals for the anniversary of 1933, and its grassroots democratic methods in pursuit of collective, collaborative, communal memory work. AL celebrated Active Museum as further evidence that it was "possible to make cultural-political initiatives from below an important part of Berlin culture, even if the force behind them must be great in order to maintain the attention of a disinterested senate."[96] The AL committed to providing Active Museum with support—personal, parliamentary, and financial—and not much later, succeeded in placing several active AL affiliates among the group's membership.[97]

In 1981 Jost Hermand, a German émigré, literary critic, and cultural historian working in the United States, elaborated on this theme of cultural-political issues from below. He argued that a true democracy should extend into all arenas of life and demand radically democratic access to all expressions of culture, including those of the past. In cultural politics, Hermand called for the use of the past—that is, of cultural heritage—in the present in the name of building a better future.[98] This question of how to regard cultural heritage, however, proved a sticky point for the Greens. Abstractly, the appropriation of cultural heritage could harmonize with Green ideology. Maren-Grisebach argued that cultural renewal need not necessitate washing heritage away. The objects and sites of cultural heritage prompt an experience of "sentimental nostalgia," she suggested. By cushioning these experiences in a sufficiently critical grassroots democratic framework—that is, in local rather than top-down initiatives—she believed citizens could reconcile open, creative self-discovery with the closed cultural inheritances of the past.[99]

In practice, however, traditional spaces of cultural heritage carried for the Greens troublesome baggage. They threatened to eliminate individual experiences of culture and to substitute hegemonic narratives in their place. This Green perspective occupied a prominent position in the barrage of criticism leveled against Chancellor Helmut Kohl, for example, after he commissioned the German Historical Museum in Berlin and House of History in Bonn.[100] From the Greens' point of view, the space of the traditional museum already commanded authority. They saw Kohl as unfairly mobilizing that authority to push a streamlined, state-sponsored national historical narrative that would patch over Germany's history of conflict and diversity. They feared that the version of "culture" articulated in such a national museum would turn citizens into passive cultural consumers rather than active agents of cultural critique. The concurrent plan to build a large central national monument in Bonn "to the victims of war and violence" met with equal disapproval from the Greens.[101] They criticized the use of traditional, imposing memorial forms in locations that did nothing to change the ways people remember—here, the heart of Bonn's government area. The monument, they claimed, instrumentalized memory for questionable international diplomatic aims. German architect and Green Bundestag representative Walter Sauermilch argued that Germany did "not need a mammoth monument the size of four football fields merely as a receptacle for wreaths." Such a monument would enable the pomp of commemoration without prompting critical reflection on history in order to promote peace.[102] Against what one Green member referred to derisively as the plans for a "Walhalla in Bonn," the federal Greens chastised the Bundestag for attempting to build a new national consciousness by constructing monumental forms grounded in forgetfulness.[103] They argued that West Germany had no need for a national monument, in Bonn or elsewhere. Any visiting foreign dignitary who wished to lay a wreath in honor of the dead had an unfortunate wealth of pre-existing sites from which to choose. In any case, in the absence of a national monument, visitors would surely understand that erecting a national monument in Germany was no simple matter. Some more pessimistic party members even suggested that such a project was doomed to failure because it tried to commemorate victims and perpetrators in a single space.[104] The Greens tasked the Bundestag, instead, with supporting regional and local initiatives to erect memorials "where history actually happened" in order to make evidence of that history apparent and available for everyday experiences.

The Greens also had mixed feelings about repurposing existing spaces. Although they supported the Berlin Cultural Council's plans for the Martin Gropius Building and requested to rent the space for a rotating exhibit of the visual arts, they nevertheless remained critical of its use.[105] They rejected, for example, the Berlin Senate's plans to transform the Gropius Building into a massive exhibition site with art and historical installations in honor of the 750th anniversary of Berlin's founding. In the Senate's plans to assemble an exhibition in which one could simply "stroll through history [*Geschichte vorbeiflanieren*]," the Greens saw an attempt to extract cultural-historical engagement from the everyday environments of ordinary people's lives and to centralize it in a more convenient, more controllable space.[106]

The Greens preferred to make use of new, often local spaces whose novelty as sites of cultural production and experience meant that visitors were not locked into established norms of engagement. They also expected local citizens, rather than the state, to share the primary responsibility for their development. In this respect, the Greens were symptomatic of a general shift in local political agendas in Germany during the 1980s. In addition to opposing centralized, bureaucratized political oligarchies at the state level, the Greens at the local level offered an alternative to the tradition of local political engagement that dated from the decades immediately following the Second World War. Certain hotspots like Berlin in the wake of the blockade of 1948–1949 had wrestled with deeply contentious local politics; the project of dividing local utilities and other infrastructural systems, for example, left few with neutral feelings.[107] Outside of these spotlights, however, the "old local politics" of the early postwar decades were, by and large, characterized by nonconfrontational decision-making processes acceptable to the occupying forces. The combination, first, of highly educated local officials invested in the juridical components of governance rather than the political and, second, their jurisdiction over issues that were largely unpolitical at best (the administration of kindergartens, for example) or downright boring at worst (drainage management) made for underinvested leadership. Restrictions on confrontational engagement with politics imposed by the occupying powers further dampened public interest in local issues.[108] The rise of the New Social Movements in the 1970s and 1980s, however, generated heightened expectations of local authorities and the affairs they governed. With the concurrent implementation of administrative reforms that made local organization easier, a new local political style gradually emerged.

To the Greens, these new local politics meant that local political actors should dictate local political structures. In the 1984 Bundestag debate on cultural politics, Green representative Sauermilch criticized the exclusivity of contemporary conservative cultural politics on the grounds that they had lost sight of where real cultural meaning was generated, namely regionally and locally. "The government limits its cultural engagement," he claimed, "to . . . the advancement of particularly important institutions, events, or other activities through which the dignity of the German nation and state finds expression." That is, state-commissioned, state-administered institutes, events, and activities received the most attention. This kind of cultural understanding, he argued, threatened to destroy culture from below by eliminating its opportunities to exercise agency.[109] As a corrective to this problem, the Greens demanded the establishment of locally and democratically administered regional cultural centers. Their physical proximity to the homes and workplaces of average citizens would bring conversations about cultural issues into their everyday lives, thereby reintegrating politics, including cultural politics, into social practice.[110]

Empowering local cultural agents meant, first, giving them space in which they could exercise that agency. Insofar as the success of cultural initiatives from below was predicated on self-organization and decentralization, argued Peter Finger, a member of the Berlin AL's cultural committee, the availability of inexpensive spaces in which to assemble was an essential precondition for cultivating democratic culture and cultural democracy. In a budgetary meeting for cultural political issues, Finger demanded that the state create conditions—fiscal and physical—in which it was possible to allocate sufficient free space to these groups.[111] Using the language of postmaterialism, Sabine Weißler put the same objective in different terms. The Greens recognized the importance of cultural self-determination (*Selbstbestimmung*) as the foundation of all *Kultur.* But they also recognized that they could not simply campaign on behalf of cultural self-determination. They had to carve out, fight for, and secure physical spaces where it could occur, Weißler argued.[112] As an example, she highlighted sociocultural centers—sites that offered opportunities to engage with local social and cultural affairs like youth outreach to the elderly, for example, or community theater productions.[113] The Greens had repeatedly pursued the creation and support of these kinds of centers, though with mixed success.[114]

The Greens also lobbied against attempts to consolidate small grassroots groups. Practices like subsuming them under umbrella organizations, coordinating their activities, or physically relocating them threatened to curtail their ability to shape their cultural products autonomously. In 1984, for example, Jürgen Kunze of the Berlin AL opposed the creation of the Cultural Foundation of the German States (*Kulturstiftung der Länder*). What was intended as a source of funding and a hub for preservation efforts for the artifacts of German cultural heritage Kunze understood as a potential instrument for the mass reproduction and celebration of state-sanctioned forms of cultural expression. He feared the foundation would overshadow and slowly stamp out the cultural creativity and agency of individual artists and their supporters.[115]

Yet the Greens also recognized the potential pitfalls of programs that emphasized decentralization but that did not have the funding or personnel to ensure its full realization. On one hand, careless advocacy of decentralized cultural forms and sites could result in their trivialization. Axel Stozenwaldt, a Green representative from the town of Hofheim near Frankfurt, reported to the BAG-Kultur that uncritical advocacy of grassroots culture had inadvertently eclipsed interesting and innovative cultural projects in his administrative region by privileging only the simplest expressions of local culture: popular and folkloric culture.[116] Stozenwaldt also lamented the centripetal force of metropolitan culture, which drew cultural agents away from smaller cities and towns like his. From the opposite side of the country, in Lower Saxony, Heidemarie Dann also spoke on behalf of those inconvenienced by an inconsistent politics of cultural decentralization. In her 1985 "Theses on Cultural Politics," Dann noted that residents outside of Germany's major metropolitan areas had been culturally disadvantaged. She called upon cultural institutions to attend to the cultural needs of all citizens, not just urban ones.[117]

The Greens, however, made no attempt to disguise their uneven application of cultural programs. In their 1985 campaign brochure, the Berlin AL acknowledged explicitly the problem of "cultural deserts" and pledged, in the next governance cycle, to invest greater energy in spreading cultural opportunities more uniformly beyond the heart of the city.[118] Some, like Stozenwaldt, openly displayed their distaste for metropolitan culture. They called on their fellow party members to set aside their investments in urban areas and to work, instead, for the benefit of cultural projects in rural and suburban locations. A true grassroots cultural program, Stozenwaldt suggested, would focus on celebrating the individual cultures and histories of all Germany's regions. In doing so, it would eliminate the dangers of cultural alienation that accompany the cultural offerings of a cosmopolitan urban space.[119] Maren-Grisebach was more tempered in her treatment of urban culture. Decentralization, she argued, need not mean ignoring art and culture in urban areas. Instead, she rejected the concentration of cultural centers and projects in cities and called for a broad dispersal of culture throughout both city and countryside. While early Green programs took steps in the right direction, she noted vaguely that the material preconditions for such an undertaking were still lacking.[120] Dann's solution was to kill two birds with one stone by servicing both urban and nonurban cultural needs simultaneously: she advocated for greater investment in mobile cultural sites.[121]

Some have argued, more cynically, that the Greens' focus on decentralized cultural space and action "on the ground" was pragmatic. The slogan "think globally, act locally" had become a rallying point for Green politicians and their constituents alike, as had the attempt to show that the national, even the international, was deeply connected to the regional and local.[122] Some claimed that beneath this decentralization, however, simply lay a practical measure to lessen the imposing amount of bureaucratic paperwork confronting a small, inexperienced political party.[123] Nevertheless, decentralized cultural work was hardly the path of least resistance. Despite their efforts, the Greens frequently met failure. In late 1982, their attempts to ramp up community cultural projects stagnated, as did subsequent efforts to encourage local, alternative cultural leaders to work together with the leaders of established cultural institutions.[124] Perhaps postmaterialism had gotten the best of them. German political scientist Hans-Joachim Veen, who argued for understanding the Greens as a milieu party, criticized the early Green milieu for the way it had "become increasingly inward-looking."[125] Demands "for a radical change of the system," he argued, had been displaced by a growing "apathy towards anything that [occurred] outside of their own personal environment."[126] Political scientists and specialists on the Greens, E. Gene Frankland and Donald Schoonmaker agreed. They suggested that Green programs should have helped to "integrate the demands and identities of heterogeneous activists," but because of the Greens' navel-gazing self-interest, they only led to efforts that reflected "the evolving balance of power among ideological subgroups more than the outcome of creative efforts to grapple with real world problems."[127]

Despite these failures as well as the party's internal antagonism, the party nevertheless understood culture as the way forward. It recognized that capitalism and its associated culture industry stifled human creativity. As a solution, BAG-Kultur member Klaus Becker pointed to the party's common desire to occupy the world in a new way through reimagined, revitalized social and political institutions.[128] A free culture—which none of the Green cultural factions opposed—would expose society to the diversity of human creativity and initiate the creation of institutions to support it. They understood a commitment to nurturing that creativity, whatever disagreements might accompany it, as preserving for the party a common rallying point. Cultural politics, however fraught, offered one of the few good chances to work against the fracturing and collapse of the party and to reinvigorate the optimism of the Green constituency.[129]

PART II

The Pursuit of a Sustainable Alternative

4

A Sustainable Cultural Politics

By the mid-1980s, the Greens had solidly crossed the 5 percent voting threshold. This victory sent the group into a tailspin, though, as its mode of existence shifted from protest to power politics. A distracting factionalism grew out of the battle between an all-or-nothing environmental dogmatism, on one hand, and the flexibility, coalitioning, and collaboration required for success in parliament, on the other. Already weakened from within by this factionalism, the Greens lost their *raison d'être* as they watched the rapid normalization of their environmental agenda. Environmentalism became a buzzword in the platforms of every major West German political party. Seen from one angle as the unequivocal success of the Green Party, from another this broad embrace of ecological consciousness seemed to indicate the party's obsolescence. Its original motivation—the absence of meaningful environmental policies in Germany—had dissipated. At the same moment they began to become prominent players on the German political stage, in other words, the Greens confronted an obstacle that eliminated straightforward ecological activism as a sufficiently robust platform for retaining the attention of their constituency. It plunged the party into a crisis of purpose. What else was left for a party seen colloquially as a single-issue lobby group?

In order to retain their still precarious position in parliament, some Green party members began to focus on carving a new space for themselves in Germany's political landscape. Though the party of course continued to engage with stricter, more conspicuous environmental policies, its search for a new mouthpiece through which to articulate what it meant to be "Green" led away from this spotlight. Building on the ad hoc, disorganized, but passionate engagement with culture of their earliest years, the Greens reimagined a sustainable practice of radical local grassroots democracy by reimagining the methods and media of grassroots cultural expression. They formulated more clearly what it meant to marshal a "Green" culture in the wake of both party-wide and Bundestag debates on the status of culture and cultural politics in Germany.

This chapter identifies the content and methodology of this newly defined Green cultural idea in practice. Unlike the party's approach to many other items on its agenda, the Greens pushed for relatively modest changes in the arena of culture.[1] Though modest, these demands appeared relatively consistently. The party called into question, first, the topography of traditional cultural practices in Germany. The Greens moved cultural projects into different physical spaces within German society, pulling them away from the city center and placing them instead *in situ,* amid the pulse of everyday German life. They also wanted to alter the times when Germans participated in these projects. The Greens challenged the temporality of cultural practices by bringing them into the timeframe of daily life. Green culture took on a mundane, ongoing quality in place of cultural experiences bracketed from everydayness as finite, exceptional moments. Finally, the Greens criticized hierarchies of cultural agency. In place of state and municipal authorities, the party wanted to make average citizens the principal mediators of culture.

Though these modifications were unostentatious, the Greens saw them as essential preconditions for creating a radical grassroots democratic culture. This "Green" culture—and, by extension, a "Green" Germany—they determined, was not a static product that simply did or did not exist. *Being* "Green" involved the commitment to engaging in a continual process of *becoming* "Green." These three challenges to the West German status quo helped the party sketch out "a democratic future beyond 'the capitalist horizon'" that would "make hope practical"—that is, something one practices.[2] They were concerned with means as much as with ends. Being Green required occupying the environment—conceived capaciously as the composite of natural, built, and social spaces—in a way that facilitated a *sustainable* practice of radical grassroots democracy. These transformations, in other words, formed the foundation of a new German culture that would be self-sufficient, self-sustaining, and adaptable. In short, it was utopian.

Though the Greens left an imprint on cultural projects large and small during the second half of the 1980s, two stand out for the sustained critical engagement they saw from the party. The Greens supported the founding of the Active Museum and, by contrast, vehemently rejected the establishment of the German Historical Museum (DHM), both in Berlin. Their contributions to these projects highlight the three central tendencies of this new Green culture.

A Utopia of Sustainability

In 1983, German political scientist Joachim Raschke published an article describing the prevalent sentiment that the Federal Republic's established political parties—at that time, the CDU / CSU, the SPD, and the FDP—had lost touch with the times.[3] Capitalizing on this weakness, the young Green Party marketed itself as an antidote: the Greens, unlike their competitors, had their finger on the pulse of the German electorate. It was high time, they believed, to challenge both the structure and content of the conventional German party apparatus. The Greens' two-year rotation principle, their adherence to the imperative mandate, their calls for a shortened thirty-five-hour workweek amid uncomfortably high unemployment rates, their stringent rules designed to correct long-standing parliamentary gender imbalances, and their eagerness to disregard parliamentary codes of dress and behavior won the party the reputation of being unruly newcomers.[4] The Greens found their strength in exploiting the traditional parties' conviction that it was not possible "radically to tackle new problems without undermining the gains of the past."[5] The Greens appeared ready to destabilize the postwar order that had otherwise successfully pulled Germany out of the shadows of National Socialism, economic insolvency, and physical ruin onto the well-lit international diplomatic stage of the Western power bloc. Balanced between protest movement and political party, the Green experiment quickly attracted sympathizers. This growing support contributed to one of the worst defeats their closest competitors—the SPD—had seen in the postwar period.[6] Only a few years since their official formation, the Greens rode atop a wave of success.

That success derived not only from their ability to rework political practice. It also stemmed from the motor that drove those changes. The party offered not only the promise of difference but also the promise of better. The Greens trafficked in optimism, in hope. In the latter years of the Cold War, it seemed one came by hope only with some difficulty. Historian Samuel Moyn has argued that the global rallying cry of the human rights movement, beginning in the 1970s, offered "the most inspiring mass utopianism Westerners have had before them in recent decades."[7] It straddles catastrophe prevention and utopian construction. It aims to advance a minimalist ethics that would end the large-scale human tragedies that have featured reliably in human history. At the same time, it seeks to implement a maximalist political program that would "[give] people the freedom and capacity to develop their lives and the world."[8] But when Moyn dubbed human rights the "last utopia" of the twentieth century, he overlooked another major utopian enterprise that won global favor concurrently: the project of sustainability.

This utopia of sustainability became the fulcrum of the German Green Party's political program as it attempted to revitalize political radicalism. Despite some disagreement over the precise meaning of sustainability, Israeli architectural scholar Yosef Jabareen has stressed that it privileges a vision for society in which "people live and flourish in harmony with nature."[9] Based on the definition in the 1987 report by the United Nations World Commission on Environment and Development—often called the Brundtland Commission after its Norwegian chairperson, Gro Harlem Brundtland—sustainability clearly shares foundational similarities with previous utopian projects. The Brundtland Commission called for the implementation of social, political, economic, and environmental practices that would sustain "human progress not just in a few places for a few years, but for the entire planet into the distant future." It zeroed in on humanity's ability "to ensure that it meets the needs of the present without compromising the ability of future generations to meet their own needs." The commission rejected the inevitability of widespread poverty and called for more effective management of and improvements to "technology and social organization . . . to make way for a new era of economic growth." Commission participants set ambitious goals for this growth. It must meet the basic needs of all humanity, they argued, and "[extend] to all the opportunity to fulfill their aspirations for a better life." As such, they stressed the importance of equitable resource distribution, down to the poorest in developing nations. They understood such adjustments to require "political systems that secure effective citizen participation in decision-making," both domestically and internationally.[10]

One final feature of the project of sustainability, however, stood out in the context of the Greens' work. Above all, the commission grounded its ambitions in hope, a word that appears no fewer that twenty-six times in its report. It conjured an idealized memory of the 1960s as defined by "hope for a braver new world, and for progressive international ideas," and it lamented society's departure from this optimism. The world stood at the edge of the grave it had dug for hope over the previous fifty years, the report suggested. It quoted Cacilda Lanuza of the Brazilian Ecological Movement, who, in 1985, claimed that society's "greatest crime" would be to permit the death of hope, the death of a generation's faith in the future, and the death of that generation's chance to realize its ideal future to the fullest of its abilities.[11] Fortunately, the commission noted, hope had not yet been extinguished.[12] Commission members called for a "new era of international cooperation based on the premise that every human being," present and future, "has the right to life, and to a decent life." The flame of hope for the future, in short, need only be rekindled. And the commission expressed its confidence in the capacity of the international community to "rise . . . to the challenge of securing sustainable human progress."[13]

An international body of scholarship has recognized the utopian resonance of this global project of sustainable development. British political scientist and Green Party candidate Andrew Dobson, for example, has analyzed the reliance of the environmental movement on utopian anticipations of a radically different world.[14] Dutch political scientist Marius de Geus has stressed that a "utopian ecological imagination" fuels the pursuit of an ecologically responsible society.[15] Jabareen, the Israeli architect, has argued that the ecological utopia of sustainability does not limit its focus to environmental concerns. It also readily incorporates "political and social concepts such as solidarity, spirituality, and the equal allocation of resources."[16] Though the Belgian geographer Marc Antrop sees in sustainability a new framework for increasing quality of life on a global scale, he rejects qualifying it as utopian largely on account of utopia's conventional associations with the foolish, the naïve, and the unrealizable. He argues that the project of global sustainability is, by contrast, quite viable.[17] To correct for utopia's bad associations, the Swedish environmental philosophers Patrik Baard and Karin Edvardsson Björnberg have offered new terminology to describe sustainable development: it is "cautiously utopian." That it aims for long-term desirable environmental, economic, and social consequences makes it utopian. It is also cautious, however, in that its goals "are believed, but not certain, to be achievable" and to remain desirable while also remaining "open to future adjustments due to changes in desires" or other circumstances.[18] It was precisely this utopian element of sustainability that made it such a valuable aspect of the Green platform. The Greens offered West Germans a package deal: a commitment to environmental sustainability bundled with a commitment to supplying hope.

By the mid-1980s, though, the sun had begun to set on the party's easy glory days. Soon, the Federal Republic's established parties began to develop their own politics of sustainability. Environmental responsiveness had been creeping into the programs of the Federal Republic's major political parties since the late 1970s.[19] The Social Democrats, for example, adopted the Greens' antinuclear stance by joining them in rejecting NATO's Double-Track Decision, which threatened to introduce more nuclear weapons into Western Europe.[20] The SPD also embraced a program for strengthening business and lowering unemployment that emphasized a small, manageable, decentralized, and ecologically sensitive economy.[21] And the SPD's 1986 move to heighten "quality of life" via increased attention to environmental degradation, overcentralization, nuclear energy, the use of technology, and equal representation of women in the Bundestag brought them even nearer the Greens. By the latter half of the 1980s, organized labor largely embraced the compatibility of economic development and environmentalism. Historians Andrei Markovits and Philip Gorski have noted that "German industry joined the country's very costly recycling system not because it was compelled to do so by legislation, but because it [was] operating in a social environment with a fundamentally changed public consciousness which demands ecological vigilance."[22] The CDU / CSU's position in the political minority during the thirteen-year social-liberal coalition government from 1969 to 1982 prompted it to recast its openness to many of these programs as well, though some have interpreted the political right's engagement with these "new politics" as "image engineering," rhetorical, and merely symbolic.[23] By the late 1980s, crucial components of the Green platform had been appropriated by all of West Germany's major parties.[24] The meeting of the World Commission on Environment and Development in the middle of the decade symbolized this gradual institutionalization of the Green ecological program—the "greening" of the German political system.[25] The commission's only delegate from the Federal Republic was Volker Hauff, a Social Democrat, not a Green.[26]

Insofar as they became a model for other parties—both domestically and internationally, both Green and not—the Greens clearly saw considerable success over the 1980s. But these victories were bittersweet. Despite the great irony that the Greens might take umbrage when the rest of Germany joined them in recognizing the exigency of environmentalism, they nevertheless criticized other parties when they greened their own platforms. They referred to this practice derisively as "issue theft [*Themenklau*]."[27] Many Greens alleged that their party had become "stinking normal."[28] The challenging predicament of the party's increasing irrelevance following the broad normalization of the Greens' environmental agenda threatened to cripple the party. Its loss of uniqueness meant a correlate loss of much of the Greens' modest political upper hand as well as its chance to implement radical changes in West Germany. This situation forced the Greens to redefine their relationship to sustainability in order to maintain their distinctive appeal.

As their utopia of environmental sustainability lost its political singularity, the Greens began to reinvest their energies in German culture for its ability to facilitate the radicalism they championed. After all, Susan Buck-Morss explains, the products of cultural expression "provide a sensual, cognitive experience that is capable of resisting abusive power's self-justification."[29] This capacity appealed to the party as an alternative medium for articulating a distinctly Green catechism of a sustainable society, particularly one able to resist the internalized hegemony of postindustrial capitalist society.[30] Convenience also played a role in this stance. Cultural politics occupied something of a political safe zone in West Germany in the 1980s. Cultural projects tended not to receive the same scrutiny as policymaking in other fields. In 1984, CDU / CSU party chair Alfred Dregger called for artists and other cultural producers to "respect the boundaries between art and politics" and promised that politicians would do likewise.[31] With the CDU / CSU occupying nearly half of the Bundestag, Dregger's demand spoke volumes about the Bundestag's general posture toward cultural politics. Parliament was a place to deal with weighty political issues. Cultural concerns, by and large, did not count among them. When they did, they were handled on an ad hoc basis rather than as part of a coherent ongoing effort. And often these debates proved susceptible to the kinds of euphemisms that disguised and thus enabled the impulses of capitalism. The commercialization of culture promoted its consumption among a wider audience but failed to actually democratize it.[32]

Precisely because they took a backseat to more exigent political issues like the elimination of nuclear energy, participation in NATO, and the relationship of West to East Germany, cultural politics became a crucial experimental space in which the Greens could work out the content and long-term methodology of the "Green" way of being in the world. Unlike the remainder of their political agenda, which revolved around the party's four content-based conceptual pillars of ecological responsibility, social justice, grassroots democracy, and nonviolence, Green culture found its direction in three different, unspoken methodological pillars: spatial decentralization, quotidian temporalities, and radical democratic agency.

The Greens made a topography of decentralization the spatial foundation of their cultural program. Space provides the foundation for "ordered, harmonious societies," cultural geographer David Pinder has noted. As the "concrete visual field" of society's imagination, space often plays a central role in radical social renewal.[33] "In the will to transformation, issues of space are privileged in the assumption that if these are sorted out then social matters will follow."[34] For a party whose values privileged the space of the natural world, it is no surprise that a Green cultural program also emphasized physical space. And a politics of localization promised to temper the constraints that accompany centralized administrative oversight and thus to make room for the kind of playful creativity (*Spielraum*) that these postmaterialist politicians celebrated.[35]

Successfully decentralizing culture, however, was no small task.[36] The Greens understood culture to saturate all aspects of life and rejected the tendency to make cultural engagement an exceptional experience. Rather, it should occupy an integral position in one's everyday world. This attitude led the Greens to prioritize spaces of democratic access, those whose topographies did not limit participation by, say, charging an access fee, for example. Mobilizing a concept that had structured the left-alternative milieu since the 1960s—a concept used, Sven Reichardt argues, to stake a claim to political power—they also privileged what they described as spaces of "authenticity."[37] They had in mind spaces that possessed meaning for real communities, past or present, rather than spaces whose meaning derived from a forced reproduction of historical importance.[38] The Greens generally, though not dogmatically, preferred to keep their cultural projects away from the city center. Instead, they brought them to the heart of ordinary local neighborhoods.

They understood these spaces to permit a kind of "emotional access" that played a crucial role in the internalization of the cultural messages they mediated.[39]

Topography, however, was not the Greens' only concern. They recognized that the timing of cultural projects mattered just as much as the spaces they occupied. Locating cultural production in the mundane moments of everyday life, rather than in a temporality of exceptionalism, thus became a second aim.[40] In Kassel, home to the art exhibition documenta, for example, the city's Green representatives saw the exhibition as an opportunity to query visitors about how to use art to bridge "utopian agendas and everyday realities [*Utopien und die alltägliche Wirklichkeit*]."[41] But this investment in the temporalities of the mundane, while necessary, was not sufficient. Mobilizing the lessons they had learned from their commitment to environmental sustainability, the Greens oriented their efforts not just toward building a cultural utopia, but rather toward building a cultural utopia that could sustain itself. The Greens did not conceive of their modest utopia as offering the kind of static, final condition that critics of utopian projects tend to find both so unrealistic and so dangerous.[42] It was not object-oriented. Aligning with the Brundtland Commission, the Greens saw their project instead as process-oriented.[43] Their utopian objective was accessible via a series of ongoing radical micro-actions practiced every day. Claudia Siede of the Greens' Federal Cultural Bureau captured this ambition when she described the party as working to "connect reality with concrete utopias via 'transgressive practices' [*konkrete Utopien in einer 'grenzüberschreitenden Praxis' mit der Realität zu verbinden*]."[44] Prioritizing practice, however imperfect, over conceptualization allowed the Green utopia of cultural sustainability to aim for self-propulsion. It would envision, pursue, and continually revise its destination in an ongoing dialectic of creation.[45]

Of course, the practices of a Green democracy could not exist without its demos. Antje Vollmer, Green Party cultural spokesperson and leader of the party's moderate wing, was fond of arguing that democracy without popular participation is like ecology without nature. Green culture needed to counteract the paradoxical reality that political regimes intent on empowering the masses tend to implement power structures that operate outside of popular control. The Greens had resolved to wrest political agency from the centralized bureaucratic oligarchy of the German Federal Parliament, where it had been carefully rehabilitated since the fall of Hitler, and place it in the hands of the German masses in the form of functional grassroots democratic practices (*Basisdemokratie*). The mechanisms for popular cultural participation that Vollmer envisioned included, among others, extensive decision-making opportunities for German citizens. The power to decide, she argued, would both cultivate among citizens the courage to confront the hegemony of parliamentary oligarchy and delegate administrative responsibilities in radically democratic ways.[46] Public intellectual and early Green Party member Micha Brumlik echoed Vollmer, arguing that

> the task of a democratic art and cultural-political program must be to weave together general political debate and the discourse of artistic experts. Ideally, all citizens of a community should be in a position to decide, according to aesthetic criteria, how to advance the production, reception, and communication of public art. The best way to generate thoughtful and aesthetically-cultivated citizens is for those citizens to participate directly in political and aesthetic debates that deal with the development of their communities and environments.[47]

Cultural engagement thus became a catechism for "Green" living. It aimed to locate and sustain opportunities for radical grassroots democratic practices across ordinary space, at ordinary moments, and among ordinary people.

Over the second half of the 1980s, the Greens became increasingly conscious of the utopian quality of their demands of culture, sometimes using the language of "utopia" explicitly. What Green culture demanded was a continuous succession of micro-attempts to approximate a superlative future in finite segments of society. The modesty of the Greens' utopian agenda, though, did not relegate it to timidity or depoliticization. Their cultural program aimed for nothing less than a full-scale transformation of these circumscribed political, social, and cultural spheres. It demanded from its proponents one trait above all: imagination. Long a motor of radical plans for the future, imagination had guided twentieth-century visionaries from André Breton to Herbert Marcuse. While Breton argued that imagination "offers . . . some intimation of what *can be*," Marcuse stressed its liberating potential and drew on the Student Movement's rallying cry, "All power to the imagination [*Phan-*

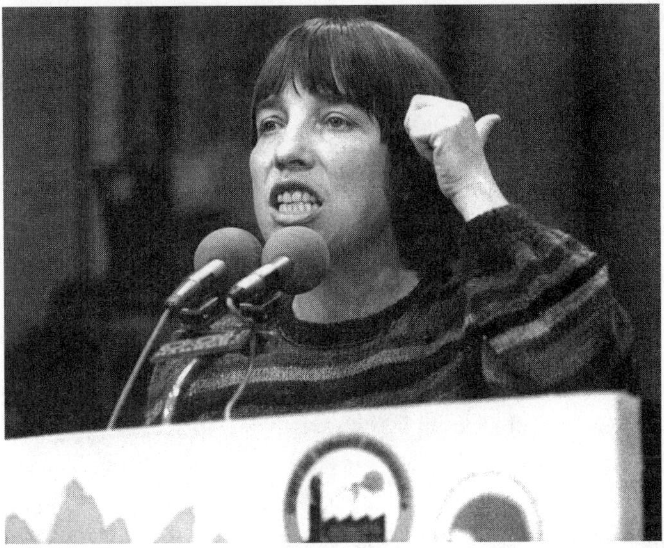

4.1 Antje Vollmer speaking at the Green Party Federal Convention in Hamburg, December 1984. Ralph Rieth.

tasie an die Macht]!" After the dramatic collapse of the dreams of the interwar period and the fizzling out of the revolutionary ambitions of the Student Movement and the New Left, imagination cropped up once more in the early 1980s as an essential point of access to utopia.[48]

Being Green

The Greens put their utopian imaginations on display through their involvement in a broad range of cultural projects, from the establishment of local operas to the creation of centers in which the elderly could interact with young people.[49] The tensions between two related initiatives in the mid-1980s—the founding of the German Historical Museum in Berlin and the efforts to establish Berlin's Active Museum—bring the characteristics of the Green utopia into relief.

Chancellor Kohl billed the German Historical Museum as a "gift" to the city of Berlin in honor of its 750th anniversary. Together with the conservative Berlin Senate, Kohl envisioned the museum as a "place of reflection and awareness driven by historical memory." He intended it to initiate critical engagement among its visitors and generate for them both "historical questions and official answers." Its purpose was to facilitate understanding (*Verstehen*) about German history and identity.[50] These political origins left many activists from Germany's alternative scene—among them the Greens—deeply skeptical of the museum. The Active Museum, by contrast, developed independently as an initiative propelled by grassroots and leftist organizations.[51] Green Party members counted among the Active Museum's founders, administrative board, and active members.[52] Among those party members not directly involved in the planning of the museum, one could nevertheless also find considerable support for the project. In 1983, Hajo Cornel, on behalf of the Berlin Greens, for example, congratulated the Active Museum on its founding. He stressed that the Greens not only welcomed the organization's proposal but that they were also prepared to participate in and support it vigorously. The party, he promised, was ready to use its leverage—parliamentary and extraparliamentary—to the benefit of the project.[53] The need to respond to these two initiatives gave the Greens an express opportunity to articulate their conception of their responsibilities to others, to their communities, and to their environment—in short, what it meant to be "Green."

A Green way of being necessarily concerned the environment. Green politics of space addressed land use issues such as the expansion of harbors and airports; urban renewal; topics related to public and private transportation; and nuclear power, including the placement of power sites. That these issues often laid competing, even irreconcilable, claims for urban space, meant that they also tended to generate factionalism within the party. Ecosocialists and radical ecologists—particularly in Hamburg, Bremen, and West Berlin—privileged the natural environment. Realists, pragmatists, and ecolibertarians—especially in more rural states like Baden-Württemberg and Lower Saxony—prioritized a more pliable politics of space.[54] Beyond the confines of strict environmental policy, however, the Greens defined the environment capaciously. They refused to build their normative rubric around a prelapsarian vision of land, sea, and sky. Instead, they made room for spaces shaped by human artifice.[55] In a major parliamentary interpellation, Walter Sauermilch, a Green Bundestag representative from the northern state of Schleswig-Holstein, registered this capacious definition. He lamented how existing policies endangered not only Germany's natural environment but also its built environment (*gebaute Umwelt*). Sauermilch celebrated the built environment as a composite of historical residue that peeked through the sediments of time into the present. The built environment also offered a glimpse of durable cultural meaning in a society characterized by anomie and alienation. The hazards of environmental destruction threatened constructed environments differently than natural ones. Society could regrow forests, for example, to promote better air quality. It could not regenerate the built environment in the same way. "Houses," Sauermilch argued, "don't grow back again." He proposed that the party endorse a social "obligation to preserve [*Erhaltungspflicht*]" that would apply not only to the natural environment but also to the environment Germans had fashioned for themselves.[56]

In parliament, the Greens were not alone in endowing space with great significance. Both the former president of West Germany—the Free Democrat Walter Scheel—and the conservative German historian whose writing would later help stoke the flame of the *Historikerstreit,* Michael Stürmer, stressed the connection between space, history, and meaning. They charged that Germany was in danger of becoming a land without a history. Such vacancy of meaning would leave German politics and identity vulnerable to suppression, even subjugation.[57] Though Scheel and Stürmer shared with the Greens a commitment to the layers of social significance nestled within the environment, the manifestations of their commitment differed considerably.[58] The investments of the Bundestag's conservative CDU / CSU–FDP coalition appeared in the proposal it presented for the German Historical Museum. An impressive undertaking, the museum was slated for a tract of land in the eastern part of Berlin's Tiergarten near the Reichstag totaling 55,000 square meters (over 13.5 acres), of which the museum itself would occupy 36,300 square meters (nearly 9 acres). By contrast, the most important building in the vicinity, the Reichstag, occupied a modest 11,200 square meters.[59] As a repository for artifacts and narratives from the *longue durée* of Germany's history, the museum was to serve as a structural testament to the richness and diversity of the German past and as ballast for national identity.

For this reason, the DHM proposal troubled the Greens. The party was eager to live "with history," but it worried about what particular historical narrative this space would license the museum to promote. After all, Hitler and his architect Albert Speer had elevated it as the heart of the "Capital City of the Eternal Empire of the German People." The Greens feared that pride of place might embed in the museum's structure or contents a similarly dangerous kind of nationalism. They also bristled when the museum's supporters described this location as the "heart" of Berlin. Certainly, it represented the historic center of prewar Berlin. But only a few meters to the east ran the Berlin Wall. Treating this area as Berlin's hub endorsed the fiction of a Germany and a Berlin that no longer existed by ignoring the amputation of one half of the city from the other. And to make matters worse, the Greens argued, the museum reinforced "the dangerous dream of the imminent reunification of Berlin."[60] Here, the Greens joined ranks with the Social Democrats in questioning the cultural work the DHM required Berlin's landscape to perform. Must West Berlin, a former capital, half of whose expanse had been amputated, be responsible for the past while Bonn addressed the present and the future? Should West Berlin focus on presenting a national history, or should it consider its place in the common history of Eastern Europe, Western Europe, and the world?[61] These questions yielded no easy answers. The Greens worried the museum would resort to authoritarianism in an attempt to circumvent harder conversations.[62]

The party harbored a particularly pointed concern that plans for the museum would forcefully streamline historical narratives from above. The choice to locate the museum at such a remove from everyday life lay at the heart of this anxiety. The Greens worried the DHM would evolve independently from precisely those Germans whose collective past it was tasked with representing. In the absence of popular oversight, the museum could quietly sanction a leveling of the layers of historical meaning that coexisted both on the site itself and within German society at large.[63] Such an artificial flattening of German history conflicted with the Greens' *Erhaltungspflicht,* which demanded they preserve the palimpsest of historical narratives embedded in local spaces. Rather than leading the Greens to fixate on the literal space the museum would occupy, these apprehensions directed Green attention toward the museum's symbolic spaces for popular participation, debate, and contestation. DHM plans, however, earmarked little space—literal or figurative—"for democratic public discussion" of the themes the museum took up.[64] As a spatial representation of power, the museum seemed to stand for hegemony, not democracy.[65] It provided insufficient opportunities, the Greens argued, for visitors "to engage with and question the possibilities and boundaries of the museum." This criticism followed the lead of Lutz Niethammer, a leftist historian and an intellectual inspiration for grassroots activists in the 1980s. Niethammer championed spaces whose meaning remained open to discussion. Rather than positioning their contents in a prescribed interpretative framework, what Niethammer called "sites of affect [*Orte der Betroffenheit*]" encouraged visitors to participate in an act of collective interpretation.[66] This stance appealed to the Greens, who similarly insisted on creating spaces in which individuals could exercise "all imaginable forms of expression and perception." German citizens, they suggested, needed room to explore their world playfully, enjoyably, free from oppression, and motivated by fantasy. They regarded this objective as a goal both "for individuals and for groups, both for society at present and society as utopia."[67]

Berlin had no need to fabricate new sites for free and creative engagement with history, the Greens claimed. Echoing their contemporaries in the *Geschichtswerkstatt,* they insisted that the city already operated as a giant living historical museum. Mobilizing an argument that similarly drove the spatial interventionists and the grassroots historians, they suggested that a worthier initiative would focus on making visible, accessible, and tangible the ample history already present in the city. Instead of earmarking millions of Marks for the DHM, the state should direct them to existing sites of historical significance in order to improve both preservation efforts and general public access. That included the (generally neglected) monuments to German history already present in the Tiergarten. Rather than sealing off nearly fourteen acres of public green space to create a superfluous museum, the Greens demanded the government commit those grounds to the promotion of recreation of various kinds. West Berliners, they argued, preferred that option. Conveniently, a green recreation space would also help foster the kind of social play the party supported.[68]

In practice, this preference took the form of supporting History Workshops, creating information centers, and building memorials throughout the Federal Republic in places "where history actually happened [*wo Geschichte stattgefunden hat*]."[69] For the ways it promised to provide opportunities for visitors to think critically about the legacy of National Socialism, the Active Museum became the Greens' preferred alternative to the German Historical Museum.[70] Slated for construction on the site of the former Gestapo headquarters and with a design that wove aspects of the original site into its blueprints, it proposed to amplify rather than mute the significance of its site.[71] As chair of the Active Museum Gerhard Schoenberner explained, the museum aimed "not to hide behind the partial history of the concentration camps." Instead, it intended to give its visitors access to "the heart of all the Treblinkas, Lidices, and Dachaus" located right in Berlin's center. The Active Museum proposed to use the site that fueled the Gestapo's violence as a medium through which Berliners and others could work through the history of that violence.[72]

The task of consciously re-embedding historical meaning into everyday life required more than just attention to space, though. Green activists also addressed the temporalities of cultural projects. They believed that a Green culture needed ample time to grow in order to thrive. It would not suffice to work according to the punctuated timelines of sensationalist projects that could capture attention easily but lose it just as quickly. They traded initiatives that promised to engage citizens only in fits and starts for projects that would develop via the slow but steady mundane time of everyday life. When the Greens opposed the German Historical Museum on the grounds that Berlin already served as a massive decentralized history workshop and had no need for a redundant centralized historical museum, they relied on the blurry boundaries between cultural topography and cultural temporality.

In 1985, Christiane Zieseke—Green representative in the Berlin Senate and member of Berlin's Cultural Council—participated in a public panel discussion titled "Why Do Kohl, Hassemer, Momper, Momsen, Fichter, and Hoffman-Axthelm Want to Lock History inside a German Historical Museum?" Zieseke put herself on record as arguing that the "Central Zone" slated to house the DHM was hardly "central" to ordinary West Berliners. It was sufficiently out of the way such that a visit to the museum would have to be intentional and planned.[73] The museum's pursuit of topographical centrality landed it in a temporal prison. It was guilty of robbing citizens of opportunities for historical encounters in the mundane, nonexceptional moments of their everyday lives.[74] Zieseke's objection was not anomalous among the Greens. Claudia Siede similarly chided the museum's planners for occasioning not only the spatial but also the "temporal . . . exclusion of historical experience" from everyday life. By rounding up under one roof such an extensive collection of historical artifacts, the DHM created a boundary that unnecessarily restricted when people could engage with the pasts whose narratives they helped communicate.[75]

The Greens believed it was possible to create a museum that operated according to different temporal parameters. During its earliest years, the evolving Active Museum became something of a canvas on which the Greens could sketch out their vision of a different kind of museological time. When the Active Museum's founders announced the winner of the competition to design its grounds—selected by a seventeen-person jury from among 194 proposals—a group of Green Party members from Berlin wrote to the museum board to offer their congratulations.[76] Though the competition had ended, they noted, an important conversation about the methods and content of the museum had only just begun. The Greens endorsed the immediate creation of "this living history workshop."[77]

Green praise for the project stopped there, however. The rest of the letter criticized its design. Sculptor Jürgen Wenzel and architect Nikolaus Lang had proposed to "seal off" the Gestapo headquarters' original 62,000-square-meter footprint with a relief sculpture made of cast iron plates. Out of this iron base would grow five hundred chestnut trees, whose canopy would shroud the entire site. This dark grove confounded the Greens. Though each of the iron plates would bear the text of a different "document of terror" drawn from around Europe, it otherwise offered scant insight into the history it commemorated, including Germany's postwar engagement with the legacy of National Socialism.[78] Party members worried that the site would become purely ornamental after debates about the museum faded from public consciousness. Such routinization risked obscuring the ongoing nature of Germany's efforts to reckon with its past, the Greens argued, particularly since many other important sites of fascist oppression had been allowed to evade popular attention entirely.[79]

The winning design failed, in short, to realize the concept of an *active* museum. And it failed because it disregarded the museum's temporal ambitions. The museum's original supporters had used the descriptor "active" to connote self-conscious, self-critical, and open to continual popular revision. They saw Wenzel and Lang's design, however, as little more than a static sightseeing destination. To the design's harshest critics, it seemed set on burying both the history it marked and further opportunities for the public to interpret its legacies. The original objectives of the Active Museum's founders had gotten lost in the shuffle, the Greens claimed. The only solution they could envision was to scrap the existing plans and reframe the project in a way that foregrounded its open-ended, discovery-oriented essence. Any new design needed to make museum visitors paramount and prioritize a gradual, bottom-up, collaborative process of working through the historical residue embedded both in the site itself and in Berlin's topography at large.[80] In response to a barrage of criticism, the city quietly abandoned the museum's initial design.

Though the Active Museum's first iteration fizzed unspectacularly, it nevertheless motivated the Greens to define more clearly the parameters of a Green cultural temporality. Over the next five years, as debates over the Active Museum's form continued, the Greens periodically revisited the question of how to mirror the Active Museum's temporal goals in their own cultural platform. Green time, they determined, demanded three things.

First, cultural exploration needed to take place in the midst of the rhythms of everyday life, not set apart from them as something different, special, or otherwise exceptional.[81] The Greens agreed with the art historian Diethard Kerbs, who argued that Germans were owed the right to encounter "traces of history in [their] field of vision." Remnants of the past trapped in museum display cases could hardly meet this need.[82] Instead, the Greens advocated leaving history's remnants—and the cultural projects that grew up around them—scattered. Cultural preservation and engagement should not come at the expense of decentralization. Vacant buildings in less trafficked neighborhoods, for example, could be used to house exhibits and cultural meetings. The Active Museum's ambitions to organize community outreach projects that would bring its work beyond its walls possessed a similar appeal. Such decentralization would make opportunities for cultural engagement more accessible to all citizens. One need not reorganize one's life schedule to accommodate them.[83]

Second, the Greens embraced a kinesthetic understanding of grassroots cultural learning. Cultural lessons required active and protracted participation.[84] The party was drawn to the Active Museum's earliest conceptual program, which argued that the museum could not be made *for* its visitors. An *active* museum could only emerge *with* or *through* its visitors. Its workshop character blurred the boundary between the museum's management and its guests, who would play an essential role in determining the museum's evolving content.[85] The Active Museum's early program demanded that its installations, events, research work, and resources be determined by open, even controversial discussions initiated by all who passed through its doors. Its coordinators hoped the same visitors would also engage in self-directed research.[86] The diverse perspectives of the museum's visitors would help ensure an ongoing dialogue and would prevent the museum from simply reacting passively to trends.[87] In short, sociologist Matthias Greffrath argued that Germany needed a historical cultural laboratory in which German citizens could observe, measure, test, and evaluate their country's history. Their work would determine what of that content society could keep, what required repair, and what it must discard. The Greens agreed: Germany needed a forum in which the accomplishments, hopes, disappointments, and perversions of modernity could be not only displayed but also worked through over time, critically and democratically.[88]

Finally, the Greens treated this kind of exploration not as a destination but as a pathway (*Weg dorthin*).[89] In a 1989 speech to the Bundestag just before the fall of the Berlin Wall, Green Party cultural speaker Antje Vollmer argued that an effective cultural institution needed to be dynamic across time, continually revisable (*wiederum korrigierbar*), and re-interpretable (*umdeutbar*). Vollmer here echoed a much older prescription for the Active Museum that it must be a "museum in flux [*Museum im Wandel*]."[90] Cultural sites retained their value to the German people only insofar as they remained in a constant state of becoming. Their content, management, methodology, and meaning must remain permanently on the table for revision.

Figuring out how to preserve and display Berlin as an evolving, living city occupied a central place on the Greens' agenda. They sought ways to invite citizens to balance the wounds of the past with their dreams for the future. The political scientist Otto Kallscheuer called the consciousness of occupying such a state of constant negotiation between the fragments of past, present, and future a "*Bruchbewußtsein*." The cultivation of this kind of awareness of fragmentation, the Greens argued, would transform cultural experiences into moments of dynamic self-determination.[91]

The Greens' final revision to German cultural sensibility was their reevaluation of cultural agency. Efforts to challenge the distribution of power in West German life were hardly new in the postwar period.[92] The activists of the Student Movement in 1968 rejected the perceived autocracy of German political leadership.[93] In the 1970s, the Red Army Faction used terror to target the fascist elements allegedly embedded in the West German government.[94]

Despite their diverse investments, West Germany's New Social Movements of the 1970s and early 1980s grew out of a shared commitment to strengthening grassroots social and political organization.[95] By the time the Greens targeted the question of popular agency in West Germany, they were recycling a well-worn theme. What they believed set them apart from their predecessors was their attention to the infrastructures that would sustain the possibility of such agency over time. Not only did they advocate for the exercise of power "from below." They simultaneously aimed to establish a system that would ensure its practice in the future.[96]

Like many on the Left, some Greens pinned the constriction of democratic agency, abstractly, on the bourgeois character of modern society. In Frankfurt, for example, party members tended to blame bourgeois-industrial consumer culture for the sense of social alienation of which many of their constituents complained. It fostered a society in which individuals could satisfy their superficial material needs by replicating each other's consumption patterns without needing to engage in any real neighborly relations. This kind of lifestyle deadens the will to live differently, they argued.[97] Other Greens were quick to find fault in the agendas of their political opponents. Those in power, some party members noted, eagerly awarded agency to individuals and institutions whose ideologies reinforced existing power structures.[98]

The source of the Greens' angst over restricted cultural agency might not have been readily apparent just listening to Chancellor Helmut Kohl. In reviewing the merits of the German Historical Museum, Kohl suggested that it enabled meaningful popular engagement with Germany's rich but complicated past. In doing so, the museum would also favorably condition efforts to formulate a meaningful plan for Germany's future. He envisioned the DHM as emphasizing the common cultural heritage of both sides of the Berlin Wall, though he also viewed the museum as a chance to demonstrate Germany's long-standing commitment to the politics and ethics of the West.[99]

Kohl's remarks irritated the Greens. They took particular umbrage at his description of the museum's impact, namely its promotion of historical, cultural, and intellectual "maturity" among the German population. Meant as praise, Kohl's account sounded patronizing instead. He used the words *mündig* (mature) and *Mündigkeit* (maturity), which denote not only the capacity for intellectual discrimination that comes with age but also the transition to an age of legal majority—that is, from childhood to adulthood.

Mündigkeit, of course, occupied a central role in Immanuel Kant's 1784 essay defining the concept of "Enlightenment." By the Greens' interpretation, Kohl was no Kant calling on his country to have the courage to use its own reason. Rather, his comments suggested Germany was a country of personally, socially, and politically immature children in need of administration.[100] Kohl's claim that Germans, lacking both home and roots (*heimatlos und wurzellos*), would flounder without the museum added fuel to the fire.[101]

The Greens also found much to criticize in the museum itself. Though Kohl intended to give the museum as a "gift" to the city of Berlin, the act lost its aura of benevolence when seen through the eyes of the tax-paying constituents who would ultimately fund it.[102] Party members also cringed at the undemocratic history the site represented. Berlin Green representative Christian Ströbele protested that the museum was slated to be built at the site of "Speer's Walhalla of German imperialism and fascism, the burning Reichstag, and Göring's crimes." Not an insuperable obstacle, the site nevertheless created an additional challenge for those wishing to reassert the importance of democratic agency. And the initial designs hardly seemed up to this task. Green delegate Christiane Zieseke argued that the conservative bloc behind the museum's planning ironically disguised autocratic governing mechanisms behind the rhetoric of showcasing the rise of republican traditions. That the state had handed the museum to the German people via a unilateral decision from above signaled this hypocrisy.[103] "It's as if we are still living in an absolutist regime," one Green member complained of the decision-making monopoly (*Entscheidungsmonopol*) in Bonn.[104] Others found their cause in the monopoly on interpretation that the museum's creators claimed over its content. The Greens understood the museum as an instrument of exclusion, comparable to the Berlin Wall. They feared it would communicate a one-sided historical account told from the perspective of the political leadership of West Germany.[105] As the historian Michael Wildt argued, this was a fight against cultural hegemony.[106] The stakes were no less than the constitution of the Federal Republic, whose clauses protect the autonomy of its states to administer cultural projects. Cultural pluralism was built into Germany's legal foundation. By dismissing the rights of Berlin's citizenry to shape its own cultural landscape, the Greens understood the German Historical Museum to threaten this license.[107] Historian Lutz Niethammer summarized these concerns by posing a rhetorical question. He asked how the German Historical Museum, with its "totalizing history," would make space for opposition? His unspoken answer was that it would not. The museum served as a case study in the increasingly dire relationship between democratic politics and disagreeable power in West Germany.[108]

But proponents of this view resisted succumbing to an unqualified pessimism. Instead, many nurtured the conviction that a thoroughgoing reconceptualization of politics might still be possible. They listened to proposals like those of the artist and education scholar Rainer Zech, who asked what it might look like for society to forge a new kind of politics. He was particularly interested in how it might foster viable grassroots political practices without simply copying traditional party politics. The answer, he argued, required that society understand politics as a cultural project at the intersection of ethics, subjectivity, and aesthetics. In this trifecta, Zech awarded aesthetics the real weight. He zeroed in on art's ability to prompt rethinking by creating moments of irritation, curiosity, confusion, or doubt about expectations. These moments, he suggested, prompt viewers to call their expectations into question and to recognize new possibilities for knowledge. Zech wanted to bring these kinds of artistic experiences to politics and believed that the creativity they facilitated could have an especially powerful impact if they involved a large audience.[109]

The Greens translated Zech's ambitions into their own vernacular by endorsing projects that engaged a participatory audience. They prioritized giving citizens the opportunity to shape their cultural landscapes via debate, discussion, and plebiscitary decision-making. This priority recast the contentious debates surrounding the DHM. Much in the manner of the philosopher Jürgen Habermas, Antje Vollmer understood democratic communicative engagement as emancipatory. Although they could not redeem the initial museum plans themselves, these debates thus represented an important opportunity for German citizens to articulate how they understood their history, to determine how to document it, and to express what they hoped to gain through its documentation. Vollmer suggested that, in fact, the ultimate bone of contention was not between "museum" and "no museum." The real concern surrounded the methods the museum and its organizers used to promote (or incapacitate) a fundamentally democratic engagement with the past.[110]

The Active Museum provided the Greens with a model for a more constructive form of cultural agency. Party members admired the Active Museum's rejection of what its executive board described as a monotonous array of curio cabinets and accompanying informational plaques. In place of passively consuming museum content, visitors should find a space to "[participate] actively in the work of the museum," including identifying its weaknesses and collaborating to strengthen them. The effect of this rather modest goal was to explode the traditional boundaries between public access areas and private administrative spaces, between visitor and associate. To be an *active* museum, the board claimed, was not to work *with* guests but rather *through* them. Without their involvement, it could not function.[111]

In this spirit, the Greens rejected "cultural spectacles": events planned *for* citizens rather than *by* them or *with* them, particularly events that capitalized on the purchasing power of tourists and risked subordinating the content and method of cultural politics to their bottom line. (Here, the party took aim at events like Berlin's 750th anniversary celebration.) The effect of such events was the "draining" of substance (*Entleerung*) from cultural politics.[112] As grassroots historian Andreas Ludwig suggested, democracy only functions when its population participates actively in its sovereignty. Only collaborative negotiation among ordinary Germans themselves could restore substance to Germany's cultural program.[113] Using projects like the Active Museum as a template, the Greens called for initiatives that invited broad, direct participation. Through these scaled-down cultural initiatives—they called them "workshops"—the Greens attempted to place radical democratic sovereignty at the heart of their cultural program.[114]

Even the Dead Will Not Be Safe

In the wake of the party's earliest electoral victories, the Greens' trajectory was hardly without complications. Growing factionalism weakened the party's internal coherence, and these tensions made it more difficult to determine what agendas it actually supported. For a party intent on marking itself as a compelling political alternative, ambiguities of this sort created a serious obstacle. Ironically, one major point of consensus would become the party's Achilles' heel in the first election after the fall of the Berlin Wall. As the Wall opened to chants that the Germans were "one people" and reunification began to seem inevitable, the Greens rejected the idea of such a union. Their aversion stemmed in part from a desire to curtail the perceived imperialism of the West and in part from a desire to avoid creating a distraction from issues they considered more pressing. In the company of citizens' movements like East Germany's New Forum, the Greens lobbied instead for the Federal Republic to foster a more open diplomatic relationship with the German Democratic Republic as a separate state, based on a more humane and more democratized socialism.[115]

What sympathy this posture initially enjoyed faded in the lead-up to the elections of December 1990 as public sentiment shifted in favor of rapid reunification. Out of sync with the West German consensus, the party bled both dissatisfied constituents and dissatisfied representatives to its political opponents. Its dismal performance, which nearly ousted the party from the Bundestag, became a loud wake-up call.[116] The Greens' Realist faction registered a clear victory as the party initiated a series of reforms that allowed it to remain an active player in the German political arena. These changes brought the Greens a new string of victories beginning in 1991 and culminating in the successful 1998 coalition with the Social Democrats under Gerhard Schröder's leadership. This relationship won the party a new seat at the head of the political table. But the exigencies of political power that accompanied it required the Greens to curtail some of their more radical and innovative impulses.

The party's ambition to create a radically democratic cultural milieu, however, managed to survive this transition period, sheltered in the gap created after the postwar SPD lost its monopoly on utopian politics.[117] The Greens attempted to put hope back on the political map by rethinking the spaces, timeframes, and agents of political change. And they reinforced this political project by championing opportunities in which this "process of rethinking will be brought into motion and accelerated." The party anticipated that the impact of this work would be broad. But it imagined its catalyst more narrowly: What, the party asked rhetorically, "will realize the Green utopian blueprint if not art and culture?"[118]

In a critique of the German Historical Museum, one Green representative wielded the words of Walter Benjamin on hope and cultural creation. He drew from Benjamin's "On the Concept of History" to argued that "only that historian will have the gift of fanning the spark of hope in the past who is firmly convinced that not even the dead will be safe from the enemy if he wins. And this enemy has not ceased to be victorious."[119] Hope, in other words, stood on perilous ground. In the battle between status quo and radical innovation, hope would serve as the trophy for the victorious. And as so many scholars have argued, the persistence of an anti-utopian milieu had left the modern Western world uncertain that hope might ever again fall into hands that would put it to good use. A sense that hope was withering had begun to gain traction. Its rescue was urgent. Both the necessity of a fight against West Germany's status quo and the reward of victory—the reclamation of hope—shaped the Greens' cultural agenda in the second half of the 1980s. The party understood itself as the torchbearer of a new democratic cultural society. The utopia of the Alternative Movement, one Green wrote, rested on its hopes, aspirations, and intentions. This utopian program assumed the mantle of changing society's forms of cultural expression and engagement and, with them, the materials and structures of governance.[120] But, perhaps melodramatically, the Greens also understood themselves as standing on a monumental precipice. If they traversed it successfully, they could bring world-historical change to German society by creating an infrastructure that would invigorate an optimism for the future. If they failed, they would fail not only the present German electorate but their country's past and its future.

5

A Sustainable Historical Practice

If the Greens heeded the lessons of Benjamin only metaphorically, the Berlin *Geschichtswerkstatt* interpreted them more literally. Where the Greens saw themselves as emissaries of a utopian democratic political culture, the BGW understood itself as the mediator of a utopian relationship to history. The work of the *Geschichtswerkstätten* involved rendering historical knowledge and methodology accessible to anyone who wished to use them. The *Geschichtswerkstätten* aimed to facilitate the project of Enlightenment by inciting people "to use their minds and rational capacity freely and to apply those things to the exploration of their own history."[1] To *Geschichtswerkstätten* participants, the stakes of historical research were far too high simply to lock it in the ivory tower or relegate it to the triviality of a Sunday afternoon hobby. They demanded support for popular historical study because they believed its lessons could prompt ordinary people to reassess their beliefs about society and how they behave within it. Historical research thus carried the seeds of radical social change.

This commitment positioned BGW members in a genealogy that included the utopian ambitions of the 1960s. With activists of the 1960s and 1970s they shared a drive to confirm Germany's status as a truly democratic society and an inclination to do so by making sense of the motors of National Socialism. They asked, rhetorically, whether the history of a nation whose last phase of national unity ended in genocide could ever again generate a positive national identity. Though they seemed uncertain how to answer their question, they were adamant that the answer could not be handed down from above. The BGW's aversion to historical initiatives from the top down grew apace with the strengthening of Kohl's conservative cultural agenda. Members joined the Greens, spatial interventionists, and others to chip away at the cultural politics of Kohl's *Wende*.[2]

Geschichtswerkstatt historians recognized that the activism of the 1960s and 1970s had failed to improve society in radical ways. These failures prompted BGW members to reassess the theories and practices that drove New Left and Student Movement participants. The most effective way to combat conservative attempts to force a new postwar national identity and to generate comprehensive solutions to "the problems of the present," they decided, was to champion the political potential of history and promote decentralized, democratic historical work.[3] Over the course of the 1980s, the *Geschichtswerkstätten* established themselves as serious players in the field of German historical studies. From this position, they faced vocal critics, who opposed efforts to bring history to the masses. Intellectual heavyweights like Bielefeld historian Hans-Ulrich Wehler argued that the grassroots historians had adulterated historical method and thus backtracked on Enlightenment ideas.[4] But the *Geschichtswerkstätten* had a response for such critics. They insisted that their grassroots historical work *vor Ort*—particularly on National Socialism—generated such controversy precisely because of its timeliness. Their contributions mattered because they "hit home [*machen betroffen*]."[5]

In Berlin, early projects like "Red Island" and "Lindenhof" successfully brought historical inquiry out of the university and the city center and deposited it instead into the local spaces to which it directly pertained. But precisely this prioritization of the local created an obstacle for the BGW. Localization risked provincialization. And provincialization threatened to defang the BGW's frontal attack on West Germany's status quo. The group began to test new techniques to broaden its reach without compromising its values or methods. Experimentation with mobility won particular favor.

The early success of its boat tours offered evidence of the promise of mobile history lessons. They allowed the BGW to penetrate the city's ordinary spaces while also overcoming constraints posed by the group's site-bound exhibits. But the project also encountered impediments. Bad weather, ticket fees, and limited availability of boats stood in the way of the BGW's plans to practice radical historical study from below. When the BGW stumbled upon an opportunity to purchase a retired double-decker bus from the Berlin

Transport Company (*Berliner Verkehrsbetriebe*), they immediately recognized a way to control for many of these problems. The BGW transformed the bus into a flexible event and installation space and, in honor of what they saw as its greatest strength, dubbed it the "Mobile Museum." Over its short three-year-long existence, the museum offered the clearest expression of the BGW's sustainable utopian historical agenda: it allowed the group to bring its historical projects to many different communities; it created more opportunities for locals to get involved in the BGW's work; and it facilitated collaborative work with other grassroots organizations, including on the other side of the Berlin Wall.

But just as hopes rise, they also fall. Soon the BGW discovered it was just as fallible as the visionaries on whose shoulders it stood. Disagreements over how to realize its ambitions fueled major interpersonal conflicts. The desire for intellectual autonomy led to financial instability. And an inadvertent process of bureaucratization slowly transformed the BGW into the kind of organization from which it had once worked hard to distinguish itself. Its real heyday ended as the dust cleared from the opening of the Berlin Wall.[6] Facing the most significant historical event to unfold during the group's existence, this vocal community of historians responded to the end of the Cold War with surprising silence. Their first sustained engagement with the world historical events of 1989 came a full decade later.[7] Though the Berlin *Geschichtswerkstatt* played an important role in challenging the demographics and sites of intellectual work in Germany, and though the group remains active today, the great irony is that its sustainable utopia proved not terribly sustainable in the end, as the group slowly collapsed beneath budgetary problems and irreconcilable infighting. And yet, much like the Greens, perhaps the greatest driver of its decline was its success. Remarkable, given the group's short life span and unspectacular decline, is the quiet but powerful legacy the Berlin *Geschichtswerkstatt* left for both German cultural projects and the field of historical practice.

The Life and Death of the Mobile Museum

The momentum to create the Mobile Museum came from opposition to Berlin administrators' plans to stage a massive series of events to celebrate the city's (largely fabricated) 750th birthday in 1987.[8] Many feared that the official anniversary spectacle would skirt over the city's difficult past. Given that extensive rebuilding and renewal efforts since 1945 had stripped the city of many clear indicators of where the Nazis had organized and executed their crimes, the lingering aesthetics of trauma tended to be subtle. Such an act of erasure would not have been hard. The BGW took a stand against this possibility. If anniversary planners understood themselves as undertaking "truly worthy historical work," one BGW member insisted, they must strive to "lay bare the sites of Berlin's forgotten or repressed past."[9] In its insistence that the city engage with the history of National Socialism, the BGW enjoyed the company of the Active Museum, Alternative List, Humanistische Union, the Internationale Liga für Menschenrechte, Aktion Sühnezeichen, and the Vereinigung der Verfolgten des Naziregimes (VVN).[10] These organizations banded together to develop an alternative to the city's plans that would more fully represent the complexities of Berlin's past.

The prevailing proposal came from a member of the VVN, who suggested the groups collectively purchase one of the city's retired buses and outfit it as a traveling exhibit and event space.[11] The museum featured a modest but flexible interior that shared some features with more conventional museums. It could house installations, films, slideshows, audio displays, and lectures. But commonalities largely stopped there. The Mobile Museum's mobility allowed it to avoid being "bracketed [*abgeschirmt*]" from everyday life, a criticism the BGW lobbed at many of Berlin's other museums.[12] Rather than putting down roots at one location, the bus could "show up with small-scale historical exhibits anywhere in the city where it is necessary to oppose historical forgetfulness."[13] The Mobile Museum's coordinators intended their historical work to engage actively with the sites where the bus parked "and, in doing so, make a specific part of Berlin's history accessible" to those who inhabited those spaces. BGW members claimed that the Mobile Museum's ability to bring historical knowledge production to ordinary people in their everyday environments would be "better suited than all previous presentation forms" to "laying bare the traces of Berlin's history."[14]

Over the museum's life, it would host exhibits on a wide range of subjects, many of which departed from its initial emphasis on forgotten sites of Nazi trauma. The first and perhaps most successful, however, dealt with the "opening act of Nazi genocide," National Socialism's euthanasia program.[15] The program's headquarters gave the medical experiment its code name:

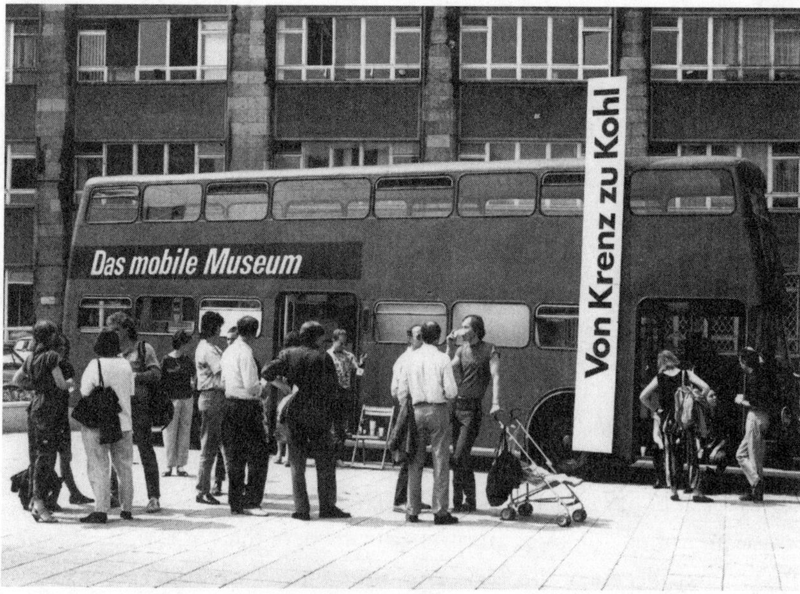

5.1 Opening of the Mobile Museum exhibit "From Krenz to Kohl" at the Fernsehturm, 18 June 1990. Detlev Davids, Berliner Geschichtswerkstatt e. V., MM DOK-KK 56-30.

Action T-4, for its location at Tiergartenstraße 4. It also gave the bus a clear destination. By 1987, the site lay somewhere in the middle of the parking lot of Berlin's legendary Philharmonic. As one BGW member complained, "One finds only a pavement desert, a final stop on a bus route with no sign of the past." To undo this act of historical erasure—a literal act of paving over the past—the Mobile Museum's organizers proposed to use the bus to commemorate Action T-4's 200,000 victims. Under the guidance of the journalist and Holocaust historian Götz Aly, they initiated a project to bring scholars and doctors together to discuss this history. Their proposal won the backing of two major institutions in Berlin's medical community, the Berlin Medical Association (*Ärztekammer Berlin*) and the Karl Bonhoeffer Psychiatric Hospital.[16]

Plans for the exhibit started small. The bus would feature twelve posters documenting the euthanasia program's structure, personnel, research, and murderous techniques as well as the public reaction it provoked, both acceptance and resistance.[17] Gradually, however, the exhibit grew more sophisticated. Launched by a press conference in front of the Philharmonic and fol-

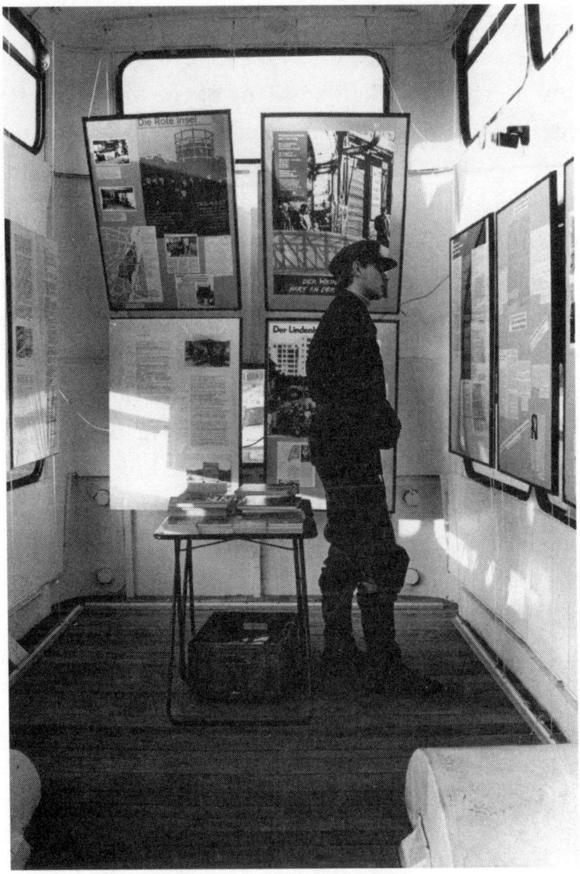

5.2 Interior of the Mobile Museum, c. 1989. Detlev Davids, Berliner Geschichtswerkstatt e. V., Signatur D 100/28.

lowed by commentary from the president of the Berlin Medical Association, a representative from the Cripple Initiative (*Krüppelinitiative*) in Hamburg, and a medical historian from Leipzig, it ran the entire month of September 1987 under the title "Forgotten History? Tiergartenstraße 4 Euthanasia Campaigns, 1939–1945." Exhibit coordinators screened the 1941 euthanasia propaganda film *Ich klage an* (*I Accuse*) at the prestigious independent film institute Arsenal. In the nearby Saint Matthäus Church, the group sponsored a lecture on euthanasia's impact on the field of psychiatry in Germany, delivered by the prominent psychiatrist Klaus Dörner. A subsequent lecture explored whether Berlin's Karl Bonhoeffer Psychiatric

Hospital pursued an analogous euthanasia program between 1933 and 1945. The monthlong exhibit wrapped up with a lecture by an immunologist and medical historian from East Berlin.[18] Many of the Mobile Museum's sponsoring organizations developed concurrent event series of their own. Active Museum member Sabine Weißler, for example, proposed a lecture series in the nearby Gropius Building on the question of autonomy in managing one's health during the Weimar Republic.[19]

In conjunction with the exhibit and event series, the Mobile Museum's coordinators proposed to install a plaque commemorating T-4's victims at the same site. It would accompany an abstract sculpture the city had recently installed. The American artist Richard Serra's *Berlin Junction* had originally been intended for another site, however, and thus made no reference to the gruesome history of Tiergartenstraße 4.[20] The text of the proposed plaque would correct for this commemorative silence. It would implore viewers to "Honor the forgotten victims / Remember the politics of killing."[21] Additional text would highlight the history of the T-4 campaign, whose victims died at the hands of their ostensible caretakers, and close with a warning about the danger of an overzealous state. Since Serra had already contributed a piece to the site, the Mobile Museum group requested he design their plaque as well. Although he initially agreed, he missed an important planning meeting in May 1988, and the Mobile Museum group never heard anything further from him. Left hanging, the memorial's planners appealed to Berlin's senator for cultural affairs, Volker Hassemer, for help creating a commemoration "worthy" of T-4's victims. "To those who were murdered or tortured, to those who were never offered redress, including their relatives," they explained to Hassemer, "we are all responsible."[22] With the city's assistance, they installed their memorial in front of Serra's sculpture in September 1989, on the fiftieth anniversary of Germany's invasion of Poland.

Public responses to the Mobile Museum's first efforts were generally positive. In a letter to the "Friends of the Mobile Museum," the BGW's Bernhard Müller invited his colleagues to congratulate themselves on the public engagement they generated.[23] Visitors, often drawn from among the Philharmonic's audiences, came in surprising abundance.[24] They "reacted with great concern" toward the exhibit's historical content and expressed their "considerable approval" of the Mobile Museum generally.[25] But the novice museum-makers also encountered obstacles. These originated less from museum patrons than among the organizers themselves. The museum's academic director, Götz Aly, provided one catalyst. The source of the conflict was small: Aly had omitted the Active Museum from the list of supporters of the T-4 exhibit that he acknowledged in his book on the history of the euthanasia headquarters.[26] The Active Museum, however, took umbrage at the slight. The creation of the Mobile Museum had hinged, after all, on the solidarity and collaboration of many small, local initiatives. Those groups may have lacked the gravitas of more prestigious donors like the Berlin Medical Association, but they provided the bulk of time and labor that made the museum possible.[27]

Relations with Aly quickly deteriorated. He claimed the Mobile Museum never aspired to longevity and that the museum's coordinating organizations had agreed at the outset to dissolve the initiative at the end of the exhibit. They would then donate the bus to whoever wished to continue its use. Regardless of the bus's fate, however, Aly dictated in no uncertain terms that the T-4 exhibit would never leave the lot of the Philharmonic. He had provided the bulk of the exhibit's content and was not prepared simply to hand over its posters to the Mobile Museum. He forbade their subsequent use after the conclusion of the exhibit and further prohibited the Mobile Museum's organizers from giving away or selling any of the exhibit's brochures. "They neither belong to you," Aly wrote tersely, "nor are they available for your use." Failure to comply, he argued, would openly threaten his intellectual property rights.[28] In light of Aly's wish to resolve the conflict amicably (that is, without a lawsuit), the Mobile Museum group agreed that he would end his work with the project upon the conclusion of the T-4 exhibit and that all texts would be destroyed to prevent their distribution. The Mobile Museum's coordinating groups would assume the cost of the posters and the printed texts, and they would abstain from pursuing legal action.[29] An awkward and unpleasant end to an otherwise successful project.

The T-4 exhibit, however, was hardly the Mobile Museum's last. One exhibit series that kept the bus on the move was the BGW's street-renaming initiative. The Berlin *Geschichtswerkstatt* had taken an interest in the names given to Berlin's everyday spaces. The group recognized that governments tend to inscribe their political agendas into the physical landscape. Urban topography often operates as a shrine to their aspirations of enduring power, or what Bernhard Müller—a participant in the BGW's street names working group and a member of the Mobile Museum initiative—dubbed an *Ewigkeitstempel.* Müller noted how dramatically Berlin's national and global standing had changed since 1945. "But the problem of street names," he argued, had "not followed suit." Architecture, urban layouts, even the enamel on street signs bore evidence of bygone political systems. "To this very day, we see manifest Hohenzollern domination, imperial and colonial behaviors, but also racist, antisemitic, misogynistic elements." In the so-called African Quarter in Berlin's Wedding neighborhood, for example, names like African Street, Cameroon Street, Togo Street, and Swakopmund Street (named after the Namibian coastal city and former German colonial holding) absentmindedly recalled nineteenth-century German imperialism. In a BGW newsletter, Müller clarified that researching historic street names had nothing to do with "nostalgic representations" destined for "anecdote-rich biographies about [the streets'] namesakes or harmless, idyllic neighborhood descriptions." Publications of that sort already existed, often with sanction from the state. For the BGW, researching street names was not an expression of sentimentality but a response to a political problem "like hardly any other." Street names "impact everyone directly in their everyday lives and living spaces," Müller reminded group members. The problem of inappropriate street names, he argued, fueled "insurmountable conservatism," political myopia that inhibits change.[30]

The BGW recognized that precisely these obstacles had hampered previous renaming initiatives. Undeterred, however, the BGW launched three related projects in the Mobile Museum in May 1988. First, participants created an exhibit on the history of street names. Second, they organized a research workshop to continue studying such histories. That same year, they published a book chronicling their discoveries.[31] They intended these initiatives as the first step in informing an uninformed public. By positioning the bus "quasi in-the-way" on the streets in question, the BGW hoped to prevent residents—quite literally—from sidestepping the problem. Whether as a curiosity or as an irritant, the bus was designed to prompt residents to consider the meaning of something so routinized as the names of the streets they walked daily.[32] Ultimately, however, the historians wanted the Mobile Museum installations to catalyze popular action. The third project was, thus, to renew lobbying efforts to change offending street names. Though the BGW, like its predecessors, made little headway, the group remained dogged in its efforts.[33] The

Mobile Museum circulated widely and, to broaden its reach, the BGW solicited participation from regional groups, including the SPD, the AL, the Young Socialists, the Peace Initiative, and several school groups.[34]

The wheels of the Mobile Museum kept turning. In late 1987, the bus parked in front of Berlin's Japanese-German Center to showcase an exhibit on antimilitarism, which the BGW had organized together with the German-Japanese Peace Forum.[35] For the fiftieth anniversary of the 1938 November Pogrom, the Mobile Museum hosted an exhibit on how the district of Wedding—sometimes called Red Wedding, for its strong socialist political inclinations—experienced the antisemitic outburst. The exhibit detailed the integration of Jewish lives and businesses into the traditionally working-class neighborhood. The BGW hoped to awaken among Wedding residents a greater curiosity about the history of their neighborhood.[36] In conjunction with the Wedding exhibit, the BGW organized another for Berlin's famous commercial artery, Kurfürstendamm. Foreshadowing a more permanent exhibit that the neighborhood of Schöneberg would install five years later, the BGW affixed to light posts texts and images detailing the lives of Jewish community members and organizations that once operated nearby.[37] Spatial interventionists would later highlight that the museum's decentralization stood in conscious opposition to the idea of a "new centrality" in West Germany's relationship to its past that had governed Berlin's postwar development.[38]

After the fiftieth anniversary of the November Pogrom, the Mobile Museum shifted its focus to a more contemporary subject: the AIDS epidemic and the history of discrimination against those infected. In conjunction with a program at Berlin's New Society for the Visual Arts, the museum brought an exhibit to the neighborhoods of Schöneberg and Charlottenburg. Titled "Contagious Measures," it aimed to combat "the stifling taboo" surrounding public discussion about AIDS that contributed to its spread. The exhibit stressed the ways existing attitudes toward AIDS—both official and popular—isolated victims, catalogued them, punished them, and enabled their persecution. "Bold headlines and strong political language stand opposed to real education about AIDS, changes in sexual behavior, and a change in the interactions with those infected with AIDS," members of the BGW's AIDS Project Group argued. Social exclusion and discrimination permitted uninfected individuals to relinquish any sense of responsibility, "a self-deception," they suggested, "that only facilitates the spread of the virus." For these reasons, the BGW stressed the importance of offering AIDS education to groups beyond prostitutes, drug addicts, and the gay community. Embracing widespread AIDS education, the exhibit advertisement claimed boldly, "will make history."[39] Its organizers hoped to jump-start this historical social change by fostering a dialogue that would challenge Berliners to rethink their relationship to AIDS.

The AIDS exhibit embodied the Mobile Museum's utopian ambitions as it transformed into something of a "trademark" of the BGW.[40] To many of its coordinating members, the Mobile Museum offered a chance to correct for the failures of previous projects. The Active Museum, for example, had also demanded that its own museum be "variable and mobile" such that "its concept could be realized both within the grounds of the former Gestapo headquarters and outside of them."[41] Its final form, however, proved not terribly different from conventional institutions like the German Historical Museum. As a truly decentralized historical educational enterprise, the Mobile Museum, however, could use its mobility to accomplish what other initiatives had struggled to. It could reach a diverse audience. It could to call into question visitors' relationships to the city, their neighborhoods, and the spaces of their daily lives. And it could challenge the thoughts and behaviors that those relationships bolstered in order to direct them to better ends.

Greater public recognition also meant more attention from less thoughtful museum visitors. The museum became a target for vandals. Though its organizers committed in June 1990 to a complete refurbishing, their efforts were cut short later that summer. As part of a collaborative project with a local museum from former East Berlin, the BGW organized a summer exhibit on allotment gardening. It parked the bus in the district of Treptow, in an annex of one of Berlin's many such gardening communities. The exhibit happened to coincide with the 1990 FIFA World Cup, in which West Germany beat Argentina to win their third world championship—the first since 1974. Perhaps in a fit of celebration, vandals destroyed the bus beyond repair.[42] That November, the Mobile Museum group decided to scrap the bus entirely rather than attempt to repair it. Though the BGW quickly assembled a new bus group in an attempt to initiate Mobile Museum II, the project never gained real traction. Bogged down in bureaucratic details—long-term parking, financing for advertisements, sponsorships, insurance, and arrangements for necessary repairs—the effort stalled before it could get a new museum up and running. Less than five years after the T-4 exhibition opened, the Mobile Museum and the hopes invested in it remained little more than a memory.[43]

Perestroika in Action

One of the Mobile Museum's greatest gifts to the BGW during its short life span was its ability to bring installations to the other side of the Berlin Wall. The BGW had, for some time, nurtured an interest in the East. The group's research on Wedding—a neighborhood on the edge of the British and Soviet sectors of the city—had piqued members' curiosity about life in other border neighborhoods.[44] The BGW even rented a storefront in Wedding to facilitate their study of *Alltagsgeschichte* along this periphery.[45] And through their study of the working class "Red Island," they began to ask analogous questions about the histories of the "workers' and peasants' state." They found themselves drawn to comparative studies of the Left across the Iron Curtain and started to cultivate relationships with archivists and historians from the German Democratic Republic (*Deutsche Demokratische Republik,* or DDR).[46]

The seeds of substantive exchange had been planted in the summer of 1988, when the BGW ran a successful month-long Mobile Museum exhibit in West Berlin titled "Pictures of Russians: Berlin 1945." It featured photographs of Russian soldiers after German capitulation. That the photos portrayed the soldiers as young and confused rather than confident and victorious made it that much more surprising when the BGW negotiated a six-week-long stay for the exhibit at the Soviet Museum in the East Berlin neighborhood of Karlshorst. In November and December of 1988, the exhibit ran adjacent to the site of Germany's capitulation.[47]

The BGW introduced several small alterations to make the exhibit more appropriate for an East German audience. It included new introductions to the exhibit in both German and Russian, an explanation of the project's intentions, an overview of the West German discussion about German capitulation in 1945, and a description of the BGW itself. It also reformulated some of the images' captions and replaced some photos with text only, as with one image that dealt obliquely with the threat of rape from Russian soldiers (see fig. 5.3).[48] Otherwise, the BGW presented effectively the same exhibit it had shown in West Berlin. Members were also allowed to distribute BGW

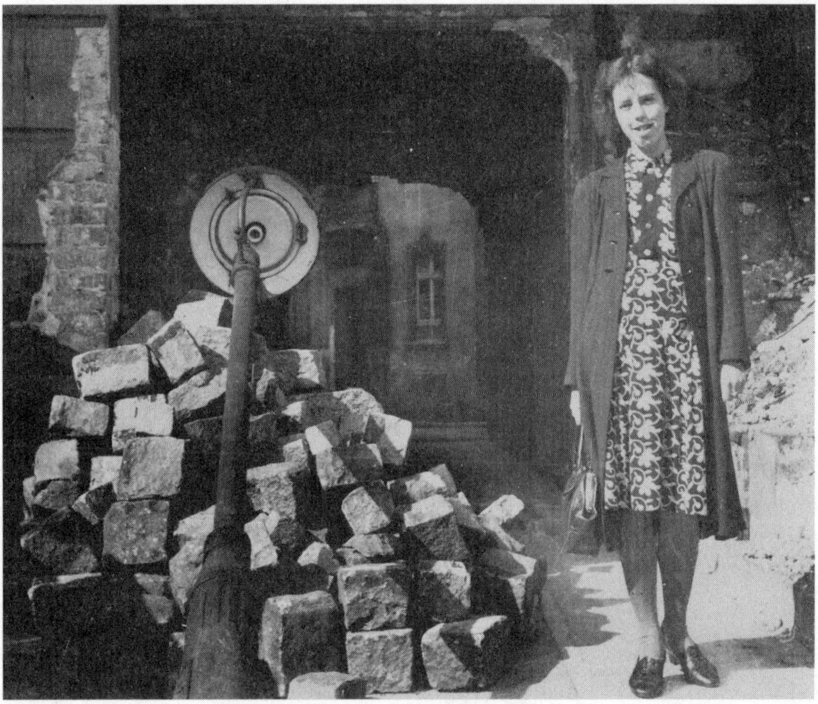

5.3 A young German woman stands before the entrance to her apartment building, which had been barricaded to prevent Soviet soldiers from setting up camp in the courtyard, from which they could more easily access the building's female residents, 1945. Berliner Geschichtswerkstatt e. V., Signatur RiB-9-24.

pamphlets and sell the group's publications. Two historians later praised the initiative as "perestroika in action."[49]

"Pictures of Russians" was hardly an intuitive choice for an East-West cultural exchange. But it broke the ice sufficiently that the BGW's next excursion to East Berlin came at the invitation of DDR officials. This time, they brought over the Red Island project.[50] Though it had met considerable success in the West, its focus on a left-leaning, working-class, political vanguard neighborhood made it well suited to an eastern audience as well. As with "Pictures of Russians," the BGW was given relatively free license to determine the content of the exhibit. Its alterations focused only on making the exhibit more comprehensible to its new public. In 1989, on the occasion of the

DDR's first of May holiday, the "Red Island" exhibit went on display at the East German Museum of Workers' Life in East Berlin's Prenzlauer Berg neighborhood.[51]

Although the BGW originally agreed to run the exhibit until the end of the summer, it received such a warm welcome that the Prenzlauer Berg museum extended it for four additional weeks. Over its run, the exhibit averaged one hundred visitors per day, more than the original 1987 exhibit in the Red Island itself. Laudable statistics appeared in other areas, too. The BGW recorded more than five hundred exhibition catalogue sales, and the twice-monthly lecture series organized jointly with the Museum of Workers' Life, "Museum on Wednesday," regularly brought in a full house. Guest speakers came from both East and West. Discussion subjects ranged from media relations in the workers' movement to the biography of communist political activist Willi Münzenberg to more contemporary issues. Particularly for visitors from the West, these conversations offered an eye-opening view to the East. They found themselves "taken aback by the openness with which current issues and grievances were thematized and pilloried in the discussion."[52] These experiences challenged Western assumptions about the nature of public discourse in the DDR.

To augment the Red Island exhibit in the Museum of Workers' Life, the BGW parked the Mobile Museum in front of the brick-and-mortar museum. They used it to inform visitors about the *Geschichtswerkstatt*'s other work, especially its boat tours around Berlin's waterways. The Mobile Museum also became a vehicle for distributing the group's publications to a new East German readership. And at least once per week, BGW members opened the bus for a public discussion forum. Though these events regularly drew an audience, the exchanges they generated among visitors were not always enthusiastic. Younger visitors in particular often seemed uninspired. Balancing their relative disinterest, however, was the animated engagement of older East Germans who had once lived in the Red Island neighborhood. Their reflections on their experiences gave the BGW fodder to expand the content of the exhibit.[53]

These productive exchanges cut both ways. Their East German hosts treated BGW members to a historical tour around East Berlin that featured local monuments and regional museums. The BGW also benefited from opportunities to interact with East German academics. In June 1989, many BGW members participated in a professional conference on working-class cultural history, which informed West German BGW members about analogous East German work on history from below. They took a particular interest in the research groups that had cropped up around the East German historian at Humboldt University, specialist in *Alltagsgeschichte,* and ethnographer of working-class life, Dietrich Mühlberg, and the methods these historians employed.[54]

The BGW's work in East Berlin also generated a buzz about the group in DDR media outlets. East German journalist and architectural critic Wolfgang Kil published a full-page report on the BGW's other work in the weekly newspaper *Sonntag,* issued by the official cultural association (*Kulturbund*) of the DDR.[55] The East Berlin radio station Berliner Rundfunk featured a forty-five-minute segment on the group in its cultural program. And shorter reports appeared in *Abendschau, Zitty, Neues Deutschland,* and *BZ.* Although a visit by West Berlin's Cultural Committee to the exhibit in the Museum of Workers' Life rattled the BGW's East German hosts and cast a shadow over an otherwise positive cultural exchange, BGW members took it in stride as evidence of the gulf between East and West at a diplomatic level. And they saw it as a gulf that practical cultural collaborations like their own could begin to bridge.[56]

In late 1989, however, the context in which the BGW operated changed. The opening of the Berlin Wall on 9 November 1989 and German reunification just shy of one year later on 3 October 1990 freed the BGW to study the former East Germany to a degree not previously possible. The City Tours by Boat working group took immediate advantage of the changes. Having already requested special permission to travel East Berlin's waterways in 1985, its members jumped at the chance to incorporate eastern sites into their tours freely.[57] As early as 1990, the group began to offer a three-hour tour of the Spree River and Landwehr Canal.[58] For the two-year anniversary of reunification, the group hosted a special thematic tour titled "Hurray, We're Reunified" that aimed to chart the development of reunified Berlin with a touch of humor.[59] But a bit of apprehension accompanied their levity. Group members noted that traces of the DDR were "slowly getting blurry. Many things have been repressed or blown out of proportion." The history of the DDR "does not consist just of Trabis and the Stasi," they emphasized. "Sixteen million people lived in this country." The 1992 tour through the heart of East Berlin, "40 Years DDR—Over With and Forgotten," aimed to tell some of their stories.[60] In 1998, the group added another tour, "Rebellious Berlin," that explored Germany's major revolutionary moments.[61] By putting 1989 in a chronology with 1848, 1918, and 1968, the BGW narrated reunification as part of a longer, shared German history of revolution.

Reunification kindled a lively discussion over Berlin street names. Efforts to reconsider the city's street names in terms of a common German history enabled the BGW to expand its ongoing street-naming research eastward. Although the 1988 Mobile Museum exhibit on street naming had focused primarily on the history of West Berlin, the group had initiated research on the East and began to build networks there that would facilitate a more robust eastern orientation later. By reunification, the BGW had already begun researching street names in the East Berlin neighborhood of Mitte and had plans to tackle the Prenzlauer Berg neighborhood next. Their own assessments frankly overstated the importance of this work. They described the project of uncovering the history of street names in East Berlin since 1945 as "a huge effort with inestimable value for the DDR itself." (Admittedly, they may have based their appraisal on an expression of interest from the DDR's *Kulturbund.*)[62] The results of their post-reunification efforts, however, were mixed at best. Many instances of successful lobbying to change street names in the former East simply resulted in reversions to more traditional names. The city did demonstrate an interest in bringing women's names more prominently into the urban landscape. And the BGW successfully lobbied the city to append quotes from women to some relevant street signs.[63] But the group ultimately made little headway in its attempts to rename streets after women.

New projects that dealt with history from below in reunified Berlin appeared on the BGW's roster as well. In the fall of 1991, it took up research on the Oberbaum Bridge, the checkpoint that connected West Berlin's Kreuzberg neighborhood with East Berlin's Friedrichshain. After reunification, BGW members explained, the bridge awoke "from a Sleeping Beauty–like slumber, transforming from a hardly used border crossing into one of the most important hinges between the two halves of the city." During the Cold War, however, the bridge had occupied a mythic position as "the end of the world" for residents on both sides of the Wall. The BGW aimed to develop an exhibit on the bridge as a site of tension. It was both a space of division and a space of unity, both a boundary and a bridge—literal and metaphorical. It stood as the border between two cities and then as a key artery within a single city. The River Spree beneath it operated as a divided site of industry, and its banks formed the backdrops for two versions of everyday life.[64] The BGW intended to bring these tensions into relief.

In 1998, the BGW took up another project as the 150th anniversary of the 1848 democratic revolutions approached. Its members were puzzled by the Berlin Senate's relative lack of attention to this round number anniversary and turned to a historical comparison to make sense of this seeming indifference. Against the backdrop of a nascent Cold War, the 100th anniversary of 1848 had loomed much larger in occupied Germany. Anniversary celebrations became a political laboratory in which to test the agendas of the occupying forces. Rallies organized in the western parts of Berlin drew more than seventy thousand people to the Reichstag's ruins despite pouring rain. The Western Allies made 1848 a symbol of Germany's "overwhelming commitment to freedom." Anniversary activities, the BGW argued, thus became an expression of anticommunist sentiment. Meanwhile, the future president of the DDR, Wilhelm Pieck, presented the failures of 1848 as the product of bourgeois betrayal and argued the time was ripe "to conclude the battle for Germany's national unity and the wellbeing of the German people." The Socialist Unity Party (*Sozialistische Einheitspartei Deutschlands,* SED) put its anniversary celebrations in service of the People's Congress Movement (*Volkskongreßbewegung*), which sought to fight German division and implement in the Western zones social-political programs more favorable to the SED.[65] In March 1948, unity was still on the lips of German leaders in all occupation zones. But considerable opposition had already kindled between east and west, foreshadowing the next forty years. Through this lens, the BGW interpreted the lackluster response to the 150th anniversary as an attempt to avoid disinterring memories of discord in a young, reunified state that desperately needed consensus and solidarity, not renewed enmity.

Reunification thus spurred the BGW to ask new questions of Germany's past and to employ newly accessible sources in answering them. One major omission from this line of inquiry, however, spoke volumes about the outlook for the group in reunified Germany. That omission was the Berlin Wall itself. Writing twelve years after the fall of the Berlin Wall, BGW member Martin Düspohl described 1989–1990 as a "moment of awakening" in Germany. Instead of hovering over the past, "everyone and everything suddenly began to look forward."[66] BGW members found themselves just as surprised and unsettled by the opening of the Wall as other Germans. It was arguably "the most important political event in the history of the organization." It also proved their "greatest challenge." BGW members seemed to have real difficulty engaging with German reunification as a historiographical paradigm shift. They met the world historical event unfolding before their eyes with surprising silence.[67] In the immediate wake of the global, European, and German sea change of 1989–1991, the BGW hosted no major conference, published no major materials, and ran no major exhibits that took up the theme of German reunification.[68] Their reticence may have stemmed from the challenges reunification posed to the projects of local history and *Alltagsgeschichte.* The "rush to German unity" touched all areas of life—not only political, but also economic, social, and cultural—such that "world history and everyday history were intimately intertwined with each other [*ganz dicht aufeinander und ineinander*]," one member explained.[69] Certainly, reunification generated some enthusiasm for the pursuit of history from below. From a Western perspective, Germany had just absorbed forty years of East German history. And in the East, the state played such a prominent role in the fabric of everyday life that working through the history of the former involved working through the history of the latter. Nevertheless, the Federal Republic's novel circumstances tended to generate popular interest in the newly constituted national and to eclipse the idiosyncrasies of the mundane. The bread and butter of the BGW, in other words, had suddenly fallen out of favor.

Not until a decade after 1989 did the BGW finally publish reflections at length on the moment's historical importance. In 1997 several members issued a call in the *Berliner Zeitung* to both Berliners and non-Berliners to share their experiences of the days surrounding the ninth of November. They wanted to record the accounts and emotions of ordinary people during what was, for many, the most decisive event in their lives: "feelings of chaos, fraternization, fear for the future, above all limitless nearly-impossible-to-describe happiness and amazement at the sudden world historical event." The untimeliness of their work was evident in the weak response their call for submissions received. Two years later, in 1999, they revisited the project, republishing the advertisement in *Tagesspiegel* and the weekly newspaper of the evangelical church. Perhaps driven by the approaching round-number anniversary, the second ad generated more enthusiasm. They gathered seventy submissions, including contributions from professional writers like Heinz

Knobloch, Freya Klier, and Peter Schneider. Still, the project struggled to gain traction. After failing to find a press willing to publish the book, their only option was to publish it themselves.[70]

The BGW's surprisingly delayed engagement with the watershed of 1989–1990 augured its difficulties establishing its relevance in post-Wall Germany. As the Germanys sped toward reunification, the BGW decided, for example, that it would be unrealistic to expect a positive outcome from its annual application for government funding and chose not to submit one at all. The group reinforced its precarious financial situation when it declined to submit a joint application for emergency funding with East Berlin's Museum of Workers' Life. Many, including the Berlin Senate, saw the groups as similar. Rather than competing for funding from the same pot, a common application would have increased the likelihood of funding for both organizations. The opportunity generated among BGW members a lengthy discussion of the group's self-conception. Preferring instead to remain financially, methodologically, and substantively independent, both organizations opted out of a shared application. This obstinacy put a damper on their relationship only shortly after they had initiated two projects together: a photodocumentation project titled "From Krenz to Kohl" and a chronicle of the DDR's last year called "No Man's Land." Neither drew substantial audiences. The choice by both East and West to limit joint work to assistance with specific projects meant that, beyond these two initiatives, collaboration never really blossomed.[71] The reluctance of the Museum of Workers' Life to adopt the practices and research projects of the BGW represented a larger skepticism toward the *Geschichtswerkstatt* movement in former East Germany.[72] "People in the East want consumer goods, not history," explained one disappointed western historian.[73]

The BGW simultaneously began to work with the East Berlin *Geschichtswerkstatt* (OBGW), which had formed in December 1989. The BGW expected smoother relations here. The OBGW's research agenda certainly passed muster with its western counterpart. In its first years, the organization explored the history of forced ethnic immigration from the nineteenth-century diamond-mining area in Germany's Namibian colonial holding; the history of women's contributions to the economy of the former Soviet Zone; everyday life on the German-German border; street food in the Second Reich; East Berlin Social Democrats and the Social Democratic milieu of the 1950s; and efforts to preserve historical traces (*Spurensicherung*) in Prenzlauer Berg.[74]

Despite shared investments, however, neither contact nor collaboration between the BGW and OBGW proved particularly strong.[75] The OBGW's demographics did not cut an impressive figure in the eyes of the western group. All of its members—just over a dozen—were professionally trained, most held academic positions, and only a few were bone fide East Berliners. In the West, the *Geschichtswerkstätten* had sought to destabilize ossified academic infrastructures, not reinforce them. From the eastern perspective, too, there was good reason for caution in building alliances with western organizations. Easterners brought their own ambitions, rather than simply copying the West German *Geschichtswerkstatt*'s values.[76] Students and young scholars shared the push to democratize historical research in the East. But they also treated the *Geschichtswerkstatt* framework as springboard from which to critique orthodox Marxist theory openly. They put it to work evening out caricatures of the East that often featured in western research. They used it to respond to western scholars who dominated research on the DDR by claiming expertise—many easterners thought unfairly. And they employed it to gauge the public reception of their research directly. The two groups had differing opinions on terminology: the definitions of Stalinism or dictatorship, for example. And they found themselves polarized over major historiographical debates like the totalitarianism thesis—that is, the question of whether and how to compare totalitarian regimes. These tensions drove a wedge between the eastern and western grassroots historical organizations, and the BGW's hopes for collaborations with the former East quickly deflated.[77]

We might return, here, to Michel de Certeau, who provided theoretical guidance about the promise of historical practice to *Geschichtswerkstatt* participants. If the narration of history is indeed performative, as Certeau argued, designed not only to produce believers of its narrative but also to prompt those believers to act on their ideas, one could argue that the BGW, in the early and mid-1980s, had engaged in a believable performance of history.[78] It participated in a broad critique of official historical research on National Socialism that challenged its failure to analyze Nazism's impact on everyday life. And it sought to correct for this failure by providing opportunities for both amateur and professional historians to explore the rise of Nazism in their own neighborhoods. That this intellectual moment culminated in the lively *Historikerstreit* of the late 1980s underscores that the BGW hit a nerve.

But the BGW proved surprisingly inflexible in its historical interests. When confronted with a wide array of new intellectual opportunities, the BGW fell back on the same set of historical questions that first motivated it, namely life during National Socialism. One of its first contributions to newly reunified Germany, for example, was to initiate a major study of Jews in Berlin's neighborhood of Kreuzberg.[79] To carry the metaphor of theatrical performance further, one might suggest that when society swapped out the old playbill for a new one at the end of the decade, the BGW failed to take notice that the script had changed. Interest in the German-German question suddenly replaced the history of National Socialism. Unable to engage with the historical rupture unfolding before it, the BGW found itself—metaphorically—performing Brahms, while everyone else had moved on to Schönberg. While the group's convincing historical performance led to action in the 1980s, its myopic interests prevented it from doing the same in the 1990s and onward.

Ignoramuses, Blockheads, and Know-It-Alls

The BGW's rocky attempts to carve out an intellectual home in post-Wall Germany were complicated by an untenable social dynamic that developed among its membership and in its relationships to other alternative organizations. The group's success in the mid-1980s generated administrative problems that it was unprepared to handle. Irreconcilable opinions about funding, professionalization, and group leadership; intransigence toward peer grassroots organizations; and the decline of some of its stronger projects led to the deterioration of the sustainable utopia wrapped up in the BGW's historical enterprise.

The first crisis was financial. Certainly, the BGW had never enjoyed total financial stability. In its heyday, however, it provided for its researchers and participants admirably. After registering with the state as an official organization in 1981 and later having been designated a nonprofit, the BGW secured considerable financial support from both governmental and nongovernmental sources.[80] Grants as high as one million DM and funding for several paid researchers allowed the BGW to maintain its intellectual independence.[81] But this independence had limits. In the years leading up to reunification, the organization found itself increasingly unable to raise its paid workers' wages. At best, it could offer only compensatory time off. Money gathered via annual membership dues failed to cover more than the group's fixed operational costs. This gap required intensified fundraising efforts, which pulled members away from their research. And the group became increasingly bureaucratic when it came to another major revenue source, namely its publications. In the wake of the dispute with Götz Aly over authorship in the T-4 exhibit, the BGW took strides with all subsequent projects to identify clearly who could claim copyright over and thus profit from each of its published works.[82]

Though reunification had little impact on the content of the BGW's research, it had a tangible effect on the group's financial situation. Amid the tumult, the BGW botched its state funding application in late 1989 and delayed its subsequent application in 1990. By the time the group finally got around to submitting its 1991 application, the unreliability of its funding had already sent the group into a tailspin. The BGW's executive committee began to exercise increasingly strict control over the group's finances, and the group recalibrated its commitments. It redirected its limited funds away from long-term initiatives like the archive project toward those whose progress had been more dramatically curtailed by the BGW's staunched income flow. But these changes were not enough to forestall an acute financial crisis. Group members were notified of its onset in 1992.[83]

The BGW's financial problems came to a head in the late 1990s when Berlin's tax office (*Finanzamt*) reassessed the tax obligations of registered non-profit organizations. The BGW fell under the *Finanzamt*'s gaze in 1998. Two separate audits revealed that the BGW was in danger of losing its tax-exempt status. The group managed to pull itself back from the brink by updating the language of its constitution to clarify its purpose and how it served the common good. It highlighted, for example, that its boat tours were educational events delivered in a scholarly manner and that its research activities would result in publications. The BGW's executive committee tended to understate the threat this tussle with the *Finanzamt* posed to the group. But it was a close call that underscored that the group's existence was hardly guaranteed.[84]

This nagging sense of precariousness helped to nurture a related crisis of professionalization. The BGW had always positioned itself as a nexus between lay and professional historians. It sought to bridge the methods of academic research—oral history, visual history, and the history of mentalities, for example—and informal local historical "forensics."[85] As the BGW developed a more authoritative presence in Berlin's scholarly circles, however, it grew more receptive to those academic practices it had once resisted. The creation of a professional historical journal topped the list. Where *Geschichtswerkstatt* participants had once criticized the tenacious pursuit of peer-reviewed publications as an emblem of an "ossified academic life," they later fought to win greater scholarly esteem for their organizational publication. Out of the original journal, *Geschichtswerkstatt,* the more formal *WerkstattGeschichte* was born.[86] Some members criticized this push for professionalization. One member cited critical theorist Oskar Negt, who recognized "among critical intellectuals an 'erosion of their self-understanding.' From 'the reservoir of disappointed, leftist intellectuals, influenced by an employment crisis [*Berufsnot*],'" he highlighted, emerged a new collection of intellectuals who measured their success in terms of "ice-cold realism" and "ever intensifying expediency." The drive to publish in outlets with specialized readerships exemplified this instrumentalization. It subjected authors to a major initiation ritual of the ivory tower and threatened the alternative discursive environment that the *Geschichtswerkstätten* hoped to create. In the minds of many members, the *Geschichtswerkstatt*'s journal no longer served the movement's goal of "the self-liberation of humanity [*Selbstbefreiung des Menschens*]." Instead, it provided line-items on curricula vitae.[87]

Concerns about professionalization gradually eclipsed some of the group's more substantive interests. For some members, this tendency amounted to a great betrayal of the BGW's original ambitions and led to a series of often insuperable interpersonal crises. Disagreements among members ignited where commitment to the principles of grassroots democracy clashed with the exigencies of administering a complex organization. The BGW's leadership, the Monday Group, became a flashpoint for such conflict. It had been open to anyone who wished to participate and ended each meeting, its members liked to note, with a genial trip to the bar.[88] The payout from this openness, however, never arrived. Instead of buttressing a democratic communicative infrastructure, BGW member Thomas Lindenberger argued in 1987, the Monday Group created a climate and workload that drove participants away. Though Lindenberger called for "glasnost" within the organization, his calls were too little, too late. The Monday Group witnessed a 50 percent decline in participation over several years.[89] Despite the executive committee's efforts to the contrary, a sense of hierarchy and operational opacity began to take hold among the BGW's general membership, who felt they exercised insufficient agency over the initiation of new projects.[90]

The Monday Group was hardly an unmitigated failure. In fact, its handiwork initiating a 1987 study of the "mental mobilization" of ordinary Germans at the outbreak of the First World War won it some noteworthy accolades. Research for "The August Experience 1914" would conclude in time for the seventy-fifth anniversary of the start of World War I.[91] To support a three-month-long exhibit of its research findings at the Kreuzberg art center, the *Künstlerhaus Bethanien,* the BGW sought funding from the *Stiftung Deutsche Klassenlotterie.* It came as a shock when, in February 1988, the BGW received the full amount it had requested. At an impressive 1.05 million DM, the grant was the largest of any BGW effort and won the undertaking the nickname "the million Mark project."[92]

The project's promise soon fizzled, however, as entropy began to take hold. The BGW earmarked considerable funding for a bulky group of administrators: a general project director, an artistic director, a content coordinator, an accountant, and five assistants to oversee research on intellectual, art historical, religious, cinematic, and pedagogical themes. Assembled to ensure the project's organization, intellectual diversity, and quality of research, the leadership of the "August Experience" was largely left to its own devices by the Monday Group. This autonomy backfired after the BGW failed to establish a consensus regarding the project's conceptual framework or methodology. In the absence of a coherent mission, participants had, at best, a hazy idea about their responsibilities. And coordinators had few answers to their questions. The unwieldy network of administrators ended up offering little more than a tangle of often irreconcilable opinions.[93] Resignation, laziness, even fear "mixed with frightful arrogance and a tendency to scheme," one project assistant explained. "It would take a Balzac," he complained, "to represent the complicated braid of motives and actions" that had formed among the project's participants. This atmosphere "turned social relations into a kind of war" instead of fostering the radical democratization and decentralization of historical knowledge that lay at the heart of the BGW's historiographical utopia.[94]

Compounding its leadership problems were problems with the project's participants, most of whom were volunteers. When the BGW hired a sixth paid assistant midway through 1988, it offended its unpaid researchers. Feeling undervalued, many of those working without remuneration chose to leave the research group.[95] To mitigate frustrations, the BGW elected two members in May 1988 to mediate between the August Experience project and the rest of the BGW. Just a few weeks later, however, both declared themselves powerless against the disaster that the project had become and abdicated their positions. In their footsteps followed four other project contributors, two of whom were so disillusioned with the BGW's recent trajectory that they exited not only the project but also the *Geschichtswerkstatt* entirely.

Having already used some of the allotted *Klassenlotterie* money, the project's organizers could no longer just abandon it. In a last-ditch attempt to save the "August Experience," the BGW split the contributors into two groups, based on the most antagonistic factions. One focused on the publication of a book; the other, on the preparation of an exhibit. Some viewed this move as kowtowing to intransigence, however, and it became yet another occasion for disaffected members—including some of the organization's most longstanding—to jump ship.[96]

The hobbled "August Experience" somehow managed to crawl to the finish line, resulting in both an exhibit and a publication in 1989.[97] But the BGW continued to reel from the turmoil the project's crises helped to create. Three years later, in 1992, the BGW descended into yet another personnel crisis, catalyzed by the retirement of Ray Rosdale from the Archive Group. Though Rosdale had served as one of the two unsuccessful ombudsmen amid the "August Experience" chaos, that failure hardly marred his ten-year-long service record to the BGW. When the Archive Group chose to replace him with someone less experienced, the decision incensed some fellow members. A seasoned BGW participant, Jürgen Karwelat, spoke with authority when he chastised the BGW for hiring "disinterested and narrow-minded specialists [*Fachidioten*]." He demanded that the group return to employing people clearly invested in the BGW's mission.[98] Shortly thereafter, the organization's archivist, Sonja Miltenberger, reached out to BGW members to clarify that the Archive Group hardly arrived at its decision recklessly. Her explanation was sensible, but she tempered her diplomacy with a not-so-subtle ad hominem attack. To the charge of being a *Fachidiot,* she argued that those who undervalued painstaking archival work suffered from "a capricious hodgepodge of stagnant prejudices, misunderstanding, resentment, [or] impatience" and deserved to be called "ignoramuses, blockheads, or know-it-alls." And to those who viewed the Archive Group—whose membership was largely female—as a "haven for effusive broads . . . who lack an eye for bigger connections, who get hung up on details" and "create rules that they themselves do not follow," Miltenberger lobbed charges of misogyny.[99] The Karwelat-Miltenberger exchange consummated the BGW's steady downward spiral.

The "City Tours by Boat" group also deteriorated beginning in the late 1980s, though not as a result of internal squabbling. While the 1986 tour season had booked the BGW's boats completely, the 1987 season began with lackluster turnout for two new tours through the Neukölln and Teltow canals. It remained unclear whether weak advertisement or disinterest among local residents was to blame.[100] Attendance yo-yoed over the next few years, but in 1993 the group took another serious hit as bad summer weather decimated participation and amplified the impact of declining tourism in Berlin after the excitement over reunification subsided.[101] Only half of their tours were occupied, and one member described the "sad high point" of the season as a dry but very cold night when they hosted five guests. In an attempt to fill their coffers, the BGW began to offer bus tours, but those saw equally poor attendance. Compounding disappointing public interest was a 50 percent drop in volunteers, as they took up full-time employment elsewhere or enrolled in university.[102] Though "City Tours by Boat" would remain the most consistent of the BGW's working groups, its decline was telling.[103]

The BGW's convulsions were not always turned upon itself. A bee flew into the BGW's bonnet in 1989 when the national *Geschichtswerkstatt* executive committee invited members to a workshop to plan for the fiftieth anniversary of the outbreak of the Second World War. The BGW objected not to the workshop itself but to the fact that it had been planned as a collaboration with the German Historical Museum (DHM). Refusing to countenance the idea that the DHM might actually share similar investments, the Monday Group penned a statement of disapproval that it presented at the 1989 gathering of independent historians, HistoryFest (*Geschichtsfest*), organized in Bonn by the national *Geschichtswerkstatt*.[104] But its opposition proved a nonstarter. That it generated little debate further angered the BGW, whose members expected attendees to prioritize grassroots historical activism rather than bowing to an institutional behemoth like the DHM.[105]

The BGW grew increasingly willing to pick fights, even with those with analogous investments. Another sponsor of alternative historical tours around Germany, *StattReisen*, for example, found itself in the BGW's crosshairs.[106] Given their commitment to using German topography as a "site of learning [*Lernort*]," it made sense for the two groups to use the Bonn HistoryFest as an opportunity to exchange wisdom.[107] Perhaps sensitized by its own recent decline, however, the BGW interpreted the occasion not as an exchange but as an exaltation of *StattReisen*'s successes. In the meeting's wake, the disgruntled BGW criticized *StattReisen* for giving in to commercial pressures, abandoning creative research in favor of a relentless tour schedule that turned a good profit, and forgetting to engage with other alternative organizations. At the same time, in a letter to its membership, the BGW lamented enviously that its own tours could never keep up with those of what they assumed was a better-endowed *StattReisen.*[108] For seven years, the BGW and *StattReisen*'s Berlin branch had maintained a mutually beneficial relationship. Now, the BGW's antagonism threatened to marginalize its accomplishments by alienating an organization that had happily incorporated the BGW's research findings into its own work.[109]

As ambitious as the BGW may have been at its founding in 1981, a decade and a half had provided enough time for disillusionment, calculated realism, and myopia to replace ambition. The group waged something of an aggressive slash-and-burn campaign, directed both inward and toward its allies. Though diplomacy tended to win out in the end, and the BGW mended relationships with many of those it alienated, the group clearly no longer occupied the position it had in the early 1980s. It began to lose its grasp on its mission. The collapse of the socialist project in the East complicated this constellation. Spun out of both the leftist ambitions and leftist failures associated with 1968, the BGW had always been a project on the left of the political spectrum. Its members were no revolutionary socialists, and their connections to the realities on the other side of the Iron Curtain were rather thin. Still, the ongoing project of state socialism offered hope that real social change might be possible from below. But when the Left's most ambitious experiment in utopian social alternatives crumbled, the BGW lost a major source of momentum. One member of the national executive committee wrote in 1994 of a "loss of hope and the deterioration of the goal [*Zielverfall*]." The organization had slowly succumbed to cynicism and mistrust of political action, embarrassment at having been duped by the optimism of the 1980s, and the resignation that "enormous public poverty"—social, cultural, and material—would replace the hopes of grassroots democratic culture.[110] A sense of impotence had taken hold. And the changing intellectual investments of the post-Soviet world amplified these problems. "If in the minds of social democratic and alternative intellectuals, the concept of the nation state had given way to a vision of a 'Europe of regions,'" Michael Wildt wrote of the previous decades, "the events of October 3, 1990 put the idea of the nation state firmly back on the agenda."[111] The project of writing local histories from below could hardly compete with new desires to work through national history via the German-German question.

In 1994, one frustrated member insisted it was "high time to lift our tired bones and start up the debate" about the content and methods of innovative historical work once again.[112] But the BGW struggled to pursue path-breaking research. Flagging interest in new projects was partially responsible. Members often committed to participating in projects when planning was still underway but disappeared when it was time to launch them. Intellectual path dependency, however, was also to blame. In the early 1980s, the BGW's work responded to a historiographical gap. That work sought to correct for the limited knowledge about how Nazism operated on the ground. Though by no means the only one, the BGW became a vocal player in the push to rethink the historiography of National Socialism over the course of the decade. In the extended historiographical denouement that followed, scholars expanded their methodological approaches to the history of National Socialism, adopting many of those championed by the BGW. The history of everyday life, the idea that the politics of power unfold on the register of the ordinary, and the impulse to sift through the details of the quotidian were taken up in many social science disciplines in universities throughout Germany.[113]

From one perspective, the growth of an influential professional intellectual community around these themes stands as one of the greatest accomplishments of historians like those of the BGW. Indeed, some former members and *Geschichtswerkstatt* affiliates ascended to the top of the university hierarchy: Adelheid von Saldern at the Leibniz Universität Hannover; Michael Wildt at Humboldt Universität; Thomas Lindenberger at the Zentrum für Zeithistorische Forschung in Potsdam and then at the Technische Universität Dresden; Alf Lüdtke at the Leibniz Universität Hannover and then the Universität Erfurt; Lutz Niethammer at the Universität Jena; and Hans Medick at the Universität Erfurt and then the Universität Göttingen, for example. And their work not only elevated *Alltagsgeschichte*, local history, and public history; they also became topical and methodological trendsetters in the academy. Lutz Niethammer contributed greatly to the use of oral history.[114] Alf Lüdtke, via his work on factory workers at the height of industrialization, popularized the concept of *Eigen-Sinn*—an obstinate sense of one's self-will—and created a new framework to understand resistance toward authoritarian figures.[115] And Michael Wildt has sketched out the lives and afterlives of the notions of *Volk* and *Volksgemeinschaft,* setting the stage for, among other things, interpretations of Germany's twenty-first-century resurgence of far right politics.[116] In short, practitioners of history from below, many of whom cut their teeth in the *Geschichtswerkstätten,* would go on to make some of the most important contributions to German historical scholarship in the late twentieth century.

But this gradual institutionalization of the methods and topics of *Alltagsgeschichte* and history from below also chipped away at the BGW's uniqueness. Unable to think in sustained ways beyond National Socialism, even as historiography moved on, the BGW lost the interest of its audience, the primary motor for its utopian project of grassroots historical engagement.[117] In an article in the *Frankfurter Rundschau* just a year and a half after reunification, one journalist quipped that the national *Geschichtswerkstatt* had grown too weak even to dissolve itself. Doing so would require a two-thirds majority of its membership, and the journalist reckoned that the organization could never muster such a turnout.[118] Plagued by interpersonal drama, an inability to update its research agenda, and difficulty rendering itself relevant to reunified Germany, the BGW's future looked bleak. But the final nail in its coffin, much like the Greens, took the form, ironically, of its own success in spreading its values and methods for an alternative form of historical engagement from below.

6

A Sustainable Aesthetics

Although not always so consciously apocalyptic as the Greens, West Germany's artists, by the second half of the 1980s, also understood themselves to occupy a precarious position. Many belonged to those generations of Germans born too late to have participated actively in National Socialism's brutality. Though their late birth may have implied something of a benediction, their genealogy nevertheless yoked them to Nazi crimes. Wedged between innocence and an inescapable inheritance of guilt, they launched an "obsessive quest to assume the burden of memory." They plunged headfirst into the urgent project of "reconstructing and recovering memory" of Germany's genocidal past.[1]

Among their preoccupations was the recognition that any attempt at redress for Holocaust violence had to counter the tendencies to anonymize its victims or collapse them into neat categories. For many West Germans, the 1985 Bitburg controversy made the dangerous implications of anonymity quite clear. It was only a short leap between the act of abstracting victims from their individual identities, on one hand, and the elision of victims of National Socialism with all victims of war (including Nazis themselves), on the other.[2] This tendency had replicated itself elsewhere in the stunted memorial politics of the Kohl administration as well. Three years before Bitburg the chancellor had agreed to reenvision Germany's small national monument to "the victims of war and tyranny," the *Neue Wache*. Though it would acknowledge a wide range of victim groups, from "fallen soldiers" to "the victims of violence," absent was a clear distinction between Nazi killers and Nazi victims. Public protests indicated that this dedication rang hollow.[3]

This opposition opened a space for new dialogue about the nature of victimhood. Many found a catalyst in President Richard von Weizsäcker, who offered his own delineation as a counterpoint to Kohl's tendency to blur categories of victimhood. Under the rubric of "the dead of the war and of the rule of tyranny," Weizsäcker acknowledged Jewish victims first. Next were those who suffered the war's consequences in the bloodlands of the Soviet Union and Poland. Soldiers followed, after which came those who died on account of their ethnic background, sexual orientation, mental or physical capacity, or political or religious convictions. Resistance fighters, German and otherwise, rounded out his list.[4] Weizsäcker attempted to acknowledge the range of experiences vis-à-vis National Socialism while also reserving a special position for those the Nazis pursued most doggedly.

For some, however, Weizsäcker's efforts stopped short of taking real strides to overcome the oblivion to which National Socialism consigned its victims. Writing in the red-green German daily *Die Tageszeitung* in 1986, the scholar of education and Green Party cultural leader Micha Brumlik called on Germans to avoid what he termed the "fascism of memory." With this phrase he signaled the commemorative stance that did to the memory of Holocaust victims what National Socialism did to their person. "Annihilation," Brumlik wrote,

> becomes an end; the murdered Jews become the Jewry. The abstraction into tragedy . . . only has the function of letting the horror of the actual events disappear under the veil of words. . . . It was possible to let millions of people be murdered by redefining them as abstract numbers. Attempting to understand their horrible fate by means of equally abstract concepts represents something in the same vein: treating the memory of the victims just as the murdered ones themselves were treated.[5]

To instrumentalize language of scale to convey the gravity of Nazi moral failure—these, after all, were crimes against *humanity*. To consolidate victims' stories and make them representative. These practices stripped victims of their identity and uniqueness once again. Instead, Brumlik tasked Germans with undoing what Hannah Arendt called "organized oblivion."[6] The president of the German Federation of Historians, Christian Meier, echoed these concerns when he asked Germans to see history "with the eyes of identity." The failure to think with such nuance, he augured, risked allowing an analogous violence to "come back to haunt us in a worse way." It would also prevent Germans from responding more appropriately to similarly "exacting demands that may some day be placed upon us."[7] In short, the postwar moral-political mantra "*Nie wieder Auschwitz* [Never again Auschwitz]" stipulated a new mnemonic politics. No ethical commemoration could consign Nazi victims to oblivion a second time.

As Germans reassessed how they thought about and spoke of these victims, they also reassessed where commemorations of them should take place. This spatial attentiveness makes sense. For most Germans, beyond immediate familial or other personal connections, their strongest tangible link to their history was topographical. Though their late birth may have saved them from direct involvement in the regime, it could not disconnect them from formerly National Socialist spaces. They began to push back against a long-standing postwar memorial paradigm that located the Nazi *Tatort*—the crime scene or, more literally, "the place of the act"—at a remove from daily life in Germany.[8] The camps had long served as the clearest evidence of Nazi destruction. Photographs of them had played an essential role in shaping quotidian German perspectives on guilt and the consequences of National Socialism in the early postwar period.[9] Though recent research has highlighted the truly massive network of Nazi camps and their tight proximity to everyday life even in Germany, with few exceptions the household names among them were located in the East: Auschwitz, Majdanek, Treblinka, Sobibor, Belzec, Chełmno.[10] Their position beyond German borders permitted among West Germans a sense of physical distance from their violence. Gradually, however, new generations of Germans foreshortened their mnemonic gaze. Starting in the late 1970s, West Germans began to shift their efforts to locate the Nazi *Tatort* locally, rather than projecting the site of Nazi terror abroad. They increasingly acknowledged that Nazism took root in environments they continued to occupy: where they lived, worked, and relaxed. They never experienced Nazism firsthand, but they continued to hear its echoes in those spaces. And they made it their task not to let those echoes fade away.

Not only did this climate of spirited engagement with Holocaust memory tend to attract spatial interventionists. The need for fresh commemorative practices also encouraged them to jettison mnemonic conventions. Who or what their memorials should commemorate, where, when, and how all underwent reassessment. The typical boundedness of both the commemorative site and the commemorative act came under fire. So did their remove from the spaces and rhythms of daily life. Underscoring the banality and proximity of Nazi violence—that its targets were mostly ordinary citizens inhabiting ordinary spaces—became a high priority. These investments collided with earlier spatial interventionist agendas. Artists had already become adept at using their work to intervene in public space. By provoking viewers into new relationships with that space, it endowed them with new agency. Now, the question was simply how to put that agency to use.

Some aspects of their answer looked entirely familiar. They intended their monuments to honor the dead and atone for National Socialist violence, for example. But other elements were radical. They brought the imperative to remember into the spaces and timeframes of ordinary Germans' daily lives. And they refused give this intervention finite boundaries. Instead, their monuments asked Germans to engage and reengage regularly in a commemorative act. This inbuilt motor would prevent remembrance from going dormant. The spatial interventionists, in other words, had developed a new utopia. It was modest, focusing solely on the act of Holocaust commemoration. But it harbored the sweeping ambition to fundamentally and sustainably rework how Germans, both as individuals and as a collective communicative network, engaged with their past. This chapter details the trajectory that led from the new spatial investments of artists like Joseph Beuys and Gunter Demnig in the first half of the 1980s to the utopian mnemonic agenda in the latter half. As the dust from the fall of the Berlin Wall began to settle, the spatial interventionists pushed their commemorative aesthetics into the spotlight in reunified Germany. Among the sustainable utopian projects of the late twentieth century, theirs has proved the most enduring.

Memorial as Work in Progress

In response to West Germany's new commemorative investments, an impatience developed toward the powerful social expectations for the structure, function, and location of national monuments. Those norms had originated at a time when the project of imagining the political and cultural cohesion of the nation had become an imperative. Traditional nineteenth-century monuments took a fairly standardized form. They were large, conspicuous, centrally located, and expensive. They occupied sites with clear boundaries. They tended to be set off from the mundane occurrences of everyday life in locations often distinguished by their prestige and prominence. And they circumscribed the commemorative act itself. One's entrance into and necessary departure from the monument's site gives the mnemonic performance a clear beginning and end. One generally does not dwell there at any real length, making a visit to a national monument spatially and temporally finite. These characteristics allowed such monuments to represent visually the strength and stability of nations whose material and administrative infrastructures were often far more tenuous.[11]

Beginning in the 1980s, however, artists began to challenge both the formal and the functional qualities of more traditional monuments. Their discontent generated a flurry of unconventional memorials and commemorative practices. Instead of imposing, positive forms, they experimented with quiet, understated, negative forms. In 1986, for example, the Association for the Preservation of Historical Monuments in Kassel selected the artist Horst Hoheisel's proposal for a reconstruction of the city's historic Aschrott Fountain. Financed at the turn of the century by Sigmund Aschrott—a Jew—the twelve-meter-tall sandstone obelisk fountain stood in the courtyard of Kassel's city hall. It symbolized Jewish presence at the heart of German society. But that location also made the fountain threatening to the Nazis, who destroyed it in 1939. Just shy of fifty years later, Hoheisel designed its re-inauguration. He inverted the original fountain's form such that its waters poured into the ground, rather than shooting upward. "The destruction of the sandstone form," Hoheisel explained, "was followed by the destruction of the human form. The only way I know to make this loss visible is through a perceptibly empty space." By pointing to the city's depths, the monument represented both the deep transgression of the Nazi era against the fabric of German society and the embeddedness of the Nazi annihilation of the Jews in Kassel's history.[12]

Two years after Kassel approved Hoheisel's design, West Berlin's Senate jumped on the negative form bandwagon. In its competition to design the city's Jewish Museum, it selected a proposal by the world-renowned Jewish American architect Daniel Libeskind. Down to its floor plan, the museum made the absence of Berlin's Jews central to its concept. To create the building's lightning bolt–shaped footprint, Libeskind plotted on a map the addresses of six prominent Berlin Jews. He connected them with an uneven Star of David and then deconstructed the shape, using the star's sides to determine the length of each of the museum's zigzagging walls. The museum's blueprint also incorporated five architectural empty spaces. Out of the Holocaust's complex act of annihilation, the architect explained of these voids, "comes that which cannot really be given by architecture." Through his design, Libeskind aimed to "bring to consciousness" a double act of erasure: not only the annihilation of Jewish life but also the ways that annihilation was subsequently rendered invisible.[13]

This same tension between presence and absence lay at the heart of a memorial installed by the German artist Jochen Gerz in the courtyard of Saarbrücken's old town hall in 1993. Gerz wanted to document all Jewish cemeteries in existence prior to the beginning of the Third Reich, many of which were destroyed by the Nazis. In total, he counted 2,146. To Gerz, cemeteries signaled that their inhabitants had once called that place home. To document the cemeteries was to acknowledge simultaneously the physical absence and the resilient cultural presence of Jews in Germany. Over several weeks (and under the cover of night because he lacked official permission to execute his project), Gerz removed 2,146 cobblestones from the town hall square. He engraved them with the location of an individual Jewish cemetery and replaced the stone engraved side down such that the completed installation would appear no different than the courtyard prior to his installation. What kind of monument was it, though, if no one could see it? This ambiguity fueled a dialogue that Gerz considered integral to contemporary Holocaust memorialization. The monument mattered because people talked about it. "It exists because we are here," Gerz argued. "Memory and remembrance can have no other place outside of us."[14]

Horst Hoheisel captured this same concern for localized discussions in his *Denk-Stein Sammlung* (*Thought Stones Collection*). Armed with a book featuring the names and fates of Kassel's Jews, Hoheisel visited local schools to discuss with students how members of Kassel's thriving Jewish community once populated the spaces the students now occupied. Since most students knew no Jews, Hoheisel invited each of them to select a name from the book, to research that person's life, and to write a short biography of their subject. Hoheisel then wrapped these handwritten life stories around cobblestones from the city. The collection found its home in Kassel's main train station, a hub of Jewish deportations and the beginning of the end of these life narratives.[15]

The critical, self-conscious, even transgressive elements that the designs from Hoheisel, Libeskind, and Gerz all shared won the attention of the literary scholar and specialist in Holocaust memory James Young. In a 1992 article, Young gave this phenomenon a name. Self-reflective, self-abnegating, even playful, what he called the "counter-monument" was "a monument against itself." It positioned itself "against the traditionally didactic function of monuments, against their tendency to displace the past they would have us contemplate—and finally, against the authoritarian propensity in all art that reduces viewers to passive spectators."[16] The counter-monument faced off, in other words, against the most conspicuous norms of national commemoration. As West Germans reevaluated what it meant to engage critically with the history of the Holocaust, the counter-monument movement argued for the impossibility of a true *Vergangenheitsbewältigung.* No monument could ever occasion the mastery of Germany's difficult past.

Young's term spawned a small cottage industry of scholarship. Researchers delighted at having a language with which to describe these practices.[17] The appeal of the counter-monument, as a conceptual framework, seems to have derived in part from its capaciousness. As scholars attempted to make sense of a transition period in monument making, this new category allowed them to underscore that centuries-old norms of commemoration had grown brittle. But the notion of the counter-monument proved emptier than the scholarly excitement around it might suggest. The contours of these unorthodox monuments varied widely. Some disappeared over time. Some did violence to the landscape they inhabited. Some invited their own defacement. Some created controversy over whether they even existed. In the end, the term indicated little more than a negation. The most one could say definitively was that a counter-monument was *not* a traditional monument.

Still, the desire to develop a theory that made sense of these negative mnemonic forms remained enticing. In 1997, Andreas Huyssen introduced the term "voids" to chronicle changes to Germany's urban landscape in the last decades of the twentieth century. The city had begun to reckon in very public ways with its essential absences. The absence of Jews from postwar Germany appeared as conspicuously empty spaces, such as in Libeskind's design for

Berlin's Jewish Museum. The vacancy of the threshold between former East and West Berlin, where the Berlin Wall's no-man's-land once stood, emphasized the ever-present but now "invisible history" of Germany's division. And the great holes in Berlin's former economic center, Potsdamer Platz—blocked from view by construction walls and teeming with cranes—marked reunified Germany's rapid efforts to correct for the absence of Western capitalist enterprises in the former East.[18] Whether they remained or were filled in, Huyssen claimed, voids highlighted the gaping wounds Germany had inflicted on itself over the previous century. They harbored resilient memories of their origins that would make simply forgetting those narratives quite difficult.

In a move that turned Young's and Huyssen's concepts on their heads, the historian Rudy Koshar used the term "traces" to illustrate the same phenomena but in positive terms. He wanted to highlight the ephemera of the past that linger just below the surface of the present. Beginning in the 1980s, memory work in Germany took the form of literal and metaphorical digging for those traces. The effort to fill the voids left by the past by uncovering the remnants it had deposited transformed the German landscape, Koshar argued. Traces gave this landscape a more diverse scale and range of historical meanings.[19] Ultimately, however, Koshar's analysis of traces as an alternative commemorative form returned to the same ideas that Young had popularized nearly a decade earlier. Koshar used the words of the French historian and pioneer in modern memory studies Pierre Nora to underscore that the hunt for traces marked a particular kind of historical investment, one "less interested in causes than in effects; less interested in actions remembered or even commemorated than in the traces left by those actions and in the interaction of those commemorations; less interested in events themselves than in the construction of events over time, in the disappearance and reemergence of their significations; less interested in 'what actually happened' than in its perpetual reuse and misuse, its influence on successive presents; less interested in traditions than in the way in which traditions are constituted and passed on."[20]

Concepts like traces, voids, and counter-monuments played a leading role in redirecting scholarly attention toward the range of innovative commemorative forms that emerged in the late twentieth century.[21] At the same time, however, these concepts shared three inadequacies. First, their great strength—their capacity—is also their weakness. Nearly anything, it seems, could be made to fit beneath their umbrella. Second, they prioritize form often at the expense of content. This tendency obscures the ways new commemorative methods, scales, temporalities, and agents could apply to contexts beyond the Holocaust. Finally, these concepts hide the geographical reach of the novel commemorative phenomena to which these terms first applied. In short, they have struggled to remain analytically forceful.

Just as the academic community began to shake up the discourse of memory, so too did the function and strictures of memory, commemorative practices, and monuments—including counter-monuments—come under increasing scrutiny in the artistic community. In West Germany, spatial interventionist artists began to push back against the practice of critique-via-negation. They increasingly refused to position themselves simply "against" the nineteenth-century nationalist monument-making tradition. This resistance led them to reevaluate the primarily spatial nature of their work. Not only did they prioritize creating art that would invite many people to participate in it, often by entering into conversation with one another; they also sought to create art with endurance, art that promised to shape society in the present and in the future. What began as art that encouraged its beholders to occupy public spaces in active ways became art that sought to extend that behavior in time. Their art could only effect radical social change if its mnemonic irritation was capable of reaching beyond its specific site, lingering beyond the visitor's initial encounter, and functioning even in the absence the artist's active influence. Ambitious memorials, in other words, started to become utopian ones.

In the early 1990s, artists began to win traction in their attempts to extend spatial interventionist practices across time. Among the pace-setters were the Berlin-based artist pair Renata Stih and Frieder Schnock. Their victory in a memorial design competition sponsored by the Berlin neighborhood of Schöneberg gave them an opportunity to create a monument that they hoped would permanently alter the ways residents talked and thought about the Holocaust. The opportunity emerged out of a Berlin *Geschichtswerkstatt* project. In the early 1980s, BGW members stumbled upon the rich history of the Jewish community that once flourished in Berlin's Bavarian Quarter but was later destroyed by the Nazis. After initiating a research project on the neighborhood, the group discovered that the extensive archival materials available exceeded its means to work through them.[22] Schöneberg's cultural affairs office (*Kunstamt*) stepped in and assumed responsibility for the project. The *Kunstamt*'s work resulted in a history of the persecution, exclusion, and elimination of Schöneberg's Jews told via local biographies.[23]

When the 1983 exhibit on the project's findings ended, its conclusion unleashed a debate about how to ensure locals would continue to think about this history. Consensus developed around the creation of a permanent monument in the neighborhood.[24] These conversations resulted in a four-year initiative to collect the names of six thousand Jews deported from the Bavarian Quarter. A temporary installation displayed the names on cardboard signs in front of seventy-six houses in the district. Motivated by the strong local response to this work, the Schöneberg district council voted in 1988 to erect a permanent version of the memorial on the plaza at the heart of the Bavarian Quarter and issued a call for design proposals. "The objective of the design competition," one journalist later explained, "was not to create a monument in the usual sense." Instead, the call for proposals appealed to a not-uncomplicated biblical metaphor. It demanded "stumbling stones [*Stolpersteine*] that would galvanize people as well as provoke conversations" about the legacy of the Nazi era among residents and visitors of Schöneberg.[25]

The Schöneberg city council awarded first prize to Stih and Schnock's *Places of Remembrance* (*Orte des Erinnerns*) (1993). The artists had drawn their inspiration from a 1981 publication, *Das Sonderrecht für die Juden im NS-Staat* (The Rights of Jews in the Nazi State), by the director of Jerusalem's Leo Baeck Institute, Joseph Walk.[26] Stih and Schnock proposed installing eighty small signs, roughly twenty by thirty inches, on lampposts throughout the neighborhood that depicted the gradual implementation of anti-Jewish legislation.[27] "At Bayerischer Platz, Jews may sit only on yellow marked park benches," reads one sign, with a pictogram of a red bench on the reverse side. Another displays a white letter "U" against a blue background, the symbol of Berlin's subway system. "Jews are permitted to use public transportation only to go to work. September 13, 1941," reads the opposite side. "Jews are expelled from all choral groups. August 16, 1933," reads another, with an image of a musical staff.[28]

The signs draw anti-Jewish policy out of the distant realm of legal history and into the daily lives of Berlin's residents. They might prompt one to think about the historical prohibition of riding the subway, for example, alongside

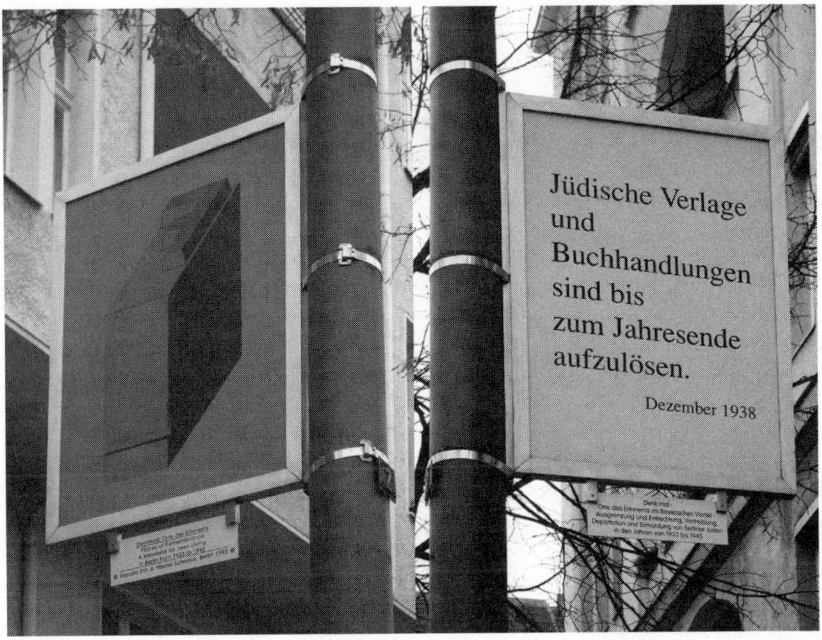

6.1 *Places of Remembrance* placard reads, "Jewish presses and bookstores must close by the end of the year. December 1938." © Renata Stih and Frieder Schnock, Berlin / VG Bild-Kunst Bonn-Berlin / ARS NYC.

one's own contemporary freedom to use public transportation. Stih and Schnock have likened their installation to a "*Kreuzweg*," or stations of the cross. One walks the stations. One reads the signs together with other passersby. One thinks through their meaning in a ritualized way. These acts, together, permit a form of meditative reparation performed collectively. "That's why we call it a social sculpture," Stih has explained, consciously mobilizing Joseph Beuys's concept, which became a conceptual launching pad for spatial interventionists looking to extend their projects' temporal reach. The artists aimed to provoke Berliners to reflect on the everyday social and spatial implications of National Socialism within their own communities. "We wanted . . . people [to] have it in their face every day," Stih explained of the horror of the Nazis' exclusionary policies toward Jews. Stih and Schnock intended their installation to become an "unavoidable

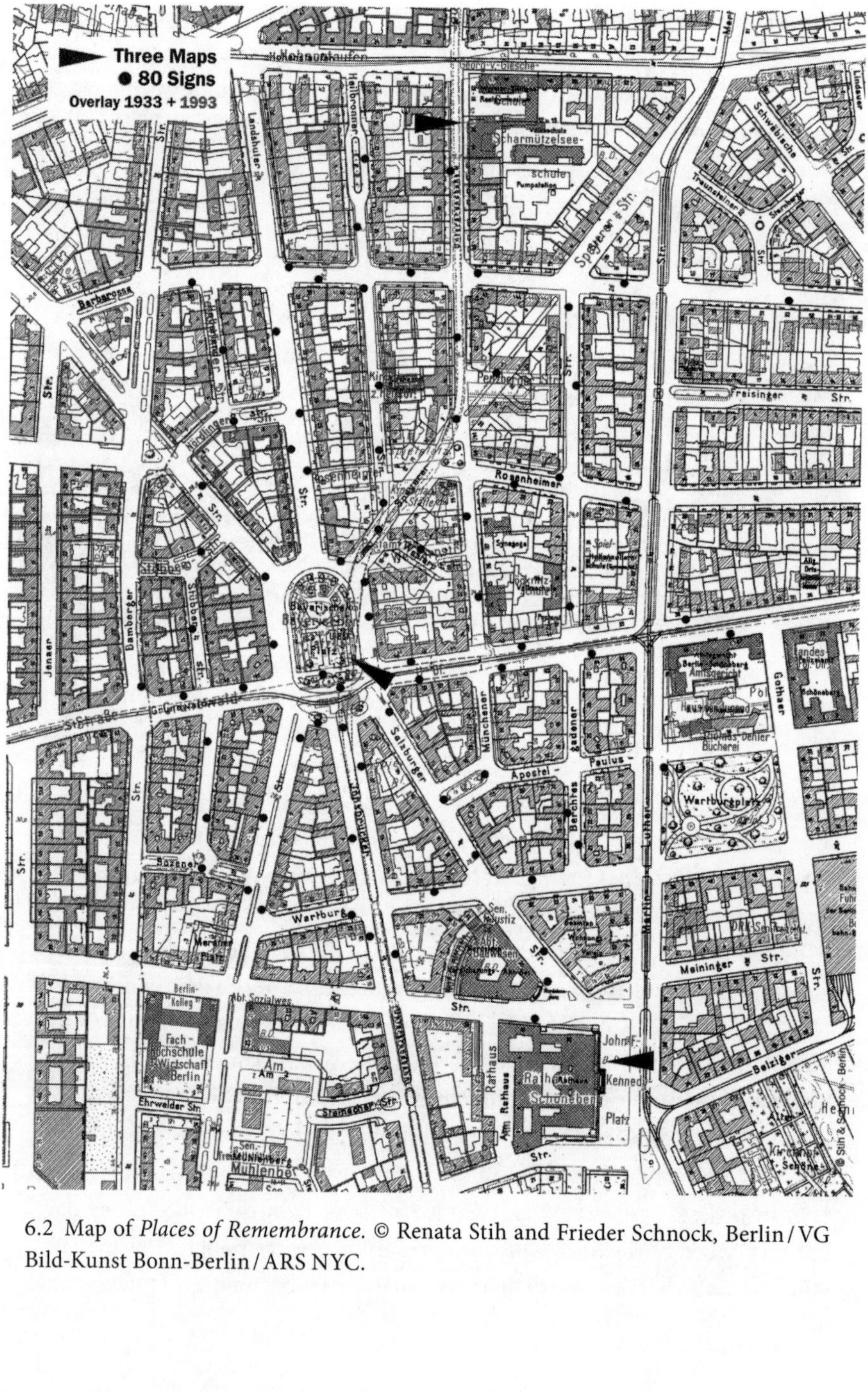

6.2 Map of *Places of Remembrance.* © Renata Stih and Frieder Schnock, Berlin / VG Bild-Kunst Bonn-Berlin / ARS NYC.

memorial" that forces passersby to consider the way spaces can facilitate oppression (or freedom). Unavoidability relied on the monument's decentralization. And decentralization, combined with irritation, would render the monument meaningful. The artists wanted to interrupt passersby, to administer their message "intravenously." The power of the project, Stih clarified, was that it "[gets] under your skin."[29] A snafu in the memorial's installation proved her right.

The artists began to install the first few signs a week before the piece's official inauguration in June 1993. Their work provoked several phone calls to the police reporting antisemitic activity in Schöneberg. The police responded swiftly. On June 6, the *Berliner Zeitung* reported that "signs reading 'Jews need a certificate of discharge in order to leave the neighborhood' have been removed from several streets in the Bavarian Quarter." The paper clarified that the installation "is part of an art campaign in the neighborhood, one of which local authorities were aware." Nevertheless, district administrators chose to remove the signs "on the grounds that they had overstepped the boundaries of tastefulness."[30] Even the head of Schöneberg's Jewish community failed to come to the memorial's aid, despite having sat on the jury that selected it. He had forgotten he voted for Stih and Schnock's proposal. Art can work in dangerous ways, and it was clear the city understood this power when its officials opted to store the signs with their other dangerous confiscated items, like drugs and weapons. The incident launched a battle over how to redeem the disgraced monument. It ended only when the artists agreed to append to each sign a smaller plaque that identified the memorial and explained its purpose—that is, only when they tempered its ability to provoke.[31]

Nearly three decades after its botched unveiling, the monument has seen better days. "Images are faded. Some placards have fallen victim to wind." And for years, the associated guidebook was out of print. Berlin's *Tageszeitung* suggested that the memorial owed its deterioration not to lack of funding but lack of interest.[32] Stih explains things differently. The monument's maintenance has flagged, she believes, because the city has yet to master the management of decentralized monuments. Oversight, care, and ongoing funding for the piece are nearly as decentralized as the monument itself. Officially, the city of Berlin owns it and has designated it a public state memorial (*Landesdenkmal*). But Schöneberg's *Kunstamt* manages it, while Stih and Schnock possess the copyright. Confusion reigns over who is obligated to mend broken signs, for example, and to whose standard.[33] Nevertheless, the memorial has continued to engage passersby and local residents alike. A new print run of the guidebook and an interactive smartphone app have fueled this interest. But, in some ways, the simple imperative of upkeep is what prevents locals from forgetting about the monument entirely. As much of a challenge as its form may create for its maintenance, in other words, the decentralized nature of the monument is what allows it to keep the abomination of racist legislation present in the minds of Schöneberg residents and visitors.

Stih and Schnock continued to test the ability of monuments to sustain conversations across time. Shortly after the unveiling of *Places of Remembrance,* they developed a memorial proposal called *Bus Stop. Bus Stop* (1995) generated equal controversy but no such administrative confusion, in part because it was never realized. Despite *Bus Stop*'s purely conceptual existence, it lives on—quite actively—in public consciousness.

Stih and Schnock submitted *Bus Stop* in 1994 as their entry in the competition to design Germany's national Holocaust monument, the *Memorial to the Murdered Jews of Europe.*[34] Though the initial impulse to create such a monument originated among a collection of citizens' initiatives in 1988, Kohl threw his endorsement behind the project in 1993. The proposed memorial offered a boon to his efforts to manage the Federal Republic's image abroad, which left his administration with few compunctions about effectively coopting this grassroots enterprise.[35] The monument's evolution was replete with controversy, and the final form it would take remained unclear for over a decade. But as it began to take shape, it became clear that it would possess the features of other top-down national memorial projects. The monument would occupy prime real estate, for example—the size of four football fields only meters from the Reichstag, the Brandenburg Gate, and Berlin's main public park, the Tiergarten. In other words, it would lie at the heart of both contemporary and historic Berlin.

This enticing blank canvas invited over five hundred suggestions for its final form.[36] Many of the 528 design proposals translated the plot's prestige into structural grandiosity.[37] They subscribed to the notion that only a truly monumental memorial befitted such a monumental site. "We know well the depth of Germany's guilt," Stih and Schnock wrote in a short piece for *Der Tagesspiegel* the year of the competition. It called for "great international art," they argued, and at a price.[38] The monument's estimated 16 million Mark (roughly $11 million) price tag backed up this assessment.[39] "One can't avoid the impression," Stih and Schnock elaborated,

> that a certain type of memorial was envisioned, one that reconciles the vast sorrow for the past with the size of the nation. . . . The only possible form for a memorial is "It must be big." Perhaps the historically significant area between the Brandenburg Gate, the new American embassy building, the Academy of Art, and Goethe's cool gaze down from his memorial all suggest the belief that physical size equals impact.[40]

The final monument, designed by American architect Peter Eisenman, certainly fits this bill. It features 2,711 large concrete blocks, some nearly sixteen feet tall, on an undulating terrain that occupies the entire plot of land.

Stih and Schnock's proposal, by contrast, adopted different priorities. Theirs aligned with those expressed by jury member (and scholar of countermonuments) James Young. "The ideal situation," Young explained, "would be the memorial as 'work in process,' in which every succeeding generation took part."[41] Stih and Schnock took this call to heart. They described their proposal, which made minimal use of the expansive empty plot, as a "non-monument" and "ephemeral memorial." Its transitory nature derived from the single bus terminal they placed at the center of the giant lot. Visitors would board buses departing regularly for former concentration camps and other existing memorials to Nazi brutality both within Germany and abroad. As a "reminder of the decades of urban destruction created by National Socialist rule," Stih and Schnock otherwise planned to leave the site's "desolate landscape" unaltered.[42] Echoing contemporary calls by *Geschichtswerkstatt* members, Active Museum supporters, and the Greens to treat the German landscape as a "history workshop" already filled with primary sources for historical learning, Stih and Schnock called on Germans to make use of existing commemorative possibilities rather than to create new ones. "One wishes," the artists wrote in 1995, "that instead of monumental stars of David, polished marble and deep trenches, there could be a discussion which excludes gigantomania. This is important for citizens' consciousness, so that they can and will confront the past in many places."[43] This wish clearly resonated with both a German public and an international one. At an exhibit in

April and May 1995, visitors to the state council building could view renderings for all 528 designs. The visitors' book at the exhibit documented the surprisingly enthusiastic public response to Stih and Schnock's entry:

> The only decent one is the Bus Stop! The rest are trite symbolism.
>
> Why no Bus Stop? All the others are the same and toot their own horns with flowery, pompous, holier-than-thou language.
>
> Against gigantomania and notions of redemption—so, THE BUS STOP!
>
> If you need a monument for the Holocaust as an indication (above all with a view to the future) that we want to remember, then, in my opinion, the Bus Stop is the only plausible one. Brisk business at a station like this would be, for me, a reassuring indication that noteworthy engagement with this history was taking place. And what if the busses were empty? A fascinating question! A decision in favor of realizing this proposal would be a courageous choice. But who is that brave?
>
> Hollywood designers on coke!!! Only the Bus Stop is legit.
>
> The banality and normality of the bus stop as an active memorial would best motivate a remembering that could engage present and future generations!
>
> I vote for the Bus Stop as a daily, perpetual reminder.
>
> I'm for the Bus Stop and for an active commemoration [*lebendiges Erinnern*].
>
> The Bus Stop is the only proposal that actually engaged meaningfully with the concept of a monument.[44]

Some visitors voiced their design preferences in terms of cost, arguing that the funds allotted for the monument would be better spent on the upkeep of existing historical sites. One pointed to the absurdity of the whole competition. "We should collect money for an even bigger plot of land. Then we could solicit even more megalomaniacal proposals. Then we would finally be sure that we have the biggest Holocaust monument in the universe. And what then? Delusions of grandeur [*Größenwahn*]."[45]

Stih and Schnock acknowledged these criticisms. They noted that "the idea of erecting a central monument for the millions of Jews murdered in Europe is not lacking in absurdity." Europe already had an abundance of what the artists described as "authentic sites for remembrance." They proposed *Bus*

Stop as a way to bridge the desire for a national memorial and the desire to learn, mourn, and commemorate at places where Nazi violence occurred:

> Bus Stop is a reaction to this inherent conflict in forms of remembrance. Bus Stop is a transitory monument. Its primary function is based on the dissolution of the conventional concept of a memorial. No site for ritualized remembrance is created. Instead, the idea is that one can go to the actual places of remembrance. In this manner, the otherwise passive visitor is forced to play an active role: In place of consumption, the acquisition of knowledge and the coming to terms with historical facts.[46]

Bus Stop presented itself as a monument for a new Germany with new commemorative needs.

Upon the creation of the national Holocaust memorial, scholar of memory Aleida Assmann argued that monuments enable a "trans-generational preservation of memory." They rescue historical moments from the oblivion of time and allow society to claim those moments as part of its collective past. Monuments thus bear upon national identity. Germany stood at a transitional moment in its national identity, Assmann noted, and monuments must help point that transition in the right direction, toward an identity "that is no longer ideologically but rather communicatively grounded."[47] Stih and Schnock touted *Bus Stop*'s ability to bring together strangers on long bus rides to sites within Europe's existing memory landscape. Guests' proximity to one another would provoke dialogue and facilitate a communal act of confronting the past.[48] Drawing consciously on Beuys's idea of a social sculpture, the artists' proposal rejected passive ritualized consumption of the past. Instead, they wanted visitors themselves to turn commemoration into a willful act of extended social transformation.[49] By asking ordinary Germans to confront the topographies of terror in their own proverbial backyards, Stih and Schnock intended *Bus Stop* to play a role in teaching Germans to recognize and, ideally, combat such violence in the future. The project was to become an ongoing actualization of the popular injunction "Never again [*Nie wieder*]."

A Utopia of Stumbling

As Stih and Schnock experimented with mnemonic irritants in Berlin, Gunter Demnig began to do the same in Cologne. Over the course of the 1990s, he initiated several memorial projects. Each rested on communicatively grounded confrontations with the past. Each took an increasingly prominent stance against the banal ritualization of commemoration and the kinds of passive interactions memorials often encourage among their visitors. And each made increasingly more central the task of ensuring that active commemorative behaviors would continue indefinitely. Demnig, in short, increasingly prioritized commemorative sustainability.

Like many of his contemporaries, Demnig found himself drawn to Holocaust commemoration. His work grew more and more attentive to the new mnemonic investments that were shaping West Germany's relationship to the Holocaust. The imperative to combat the fascism of memory in Holocaust commemoration generated a powerful and challenging question: How could West Germany possibly restore individuality to the Nazis' millions of victims? In an effort to answer this question, Demnig embarked on the utopian project of commemorating every individual victim of Nazi violence. His memorial initiative, which he called *Stolpersteine* (*Stumbling Stones*), would become his magnum opus.

Today, the *Stolpersteine* consist not of a single large commemorative site, but rather of tens of thousands of micro-sites scattered throughout Europe. Each monument consists of a brass-covered cobblestone roughly three inches cubed, engraved with the name, date of birth, date of death, and place of death of a single victim of Nazi persecution. The text on each stone begins the same: "Here lived . . ." Demnig places the stones flush with the sidewalk in front of the victim's last freely chosen residence. He called them *Stumbling Stones* not because one actually stumbles over them but because one stumbles over a memory whose unanticipated discovery invites a moment of reflection and participation.[50] Identifying victims by name, the stones cement the occurrence of each individual existence into the topography of everyday life. Remarkably, since the project's initiation in 1994, more than eighty thousand of these mini-monuments have been installed in twenty-six European countries.[51]

The number of stones has continued to climb rapidly because Demnig does not work alone.[52] Perhaps the most significant feature of the *Stolpersteine* is the massive transnational network of participants the memorial initiative has created. Each stone requires a sponsor; a financier; someone to research the victim's life; someone to make the stone, to advertise its installation, and to

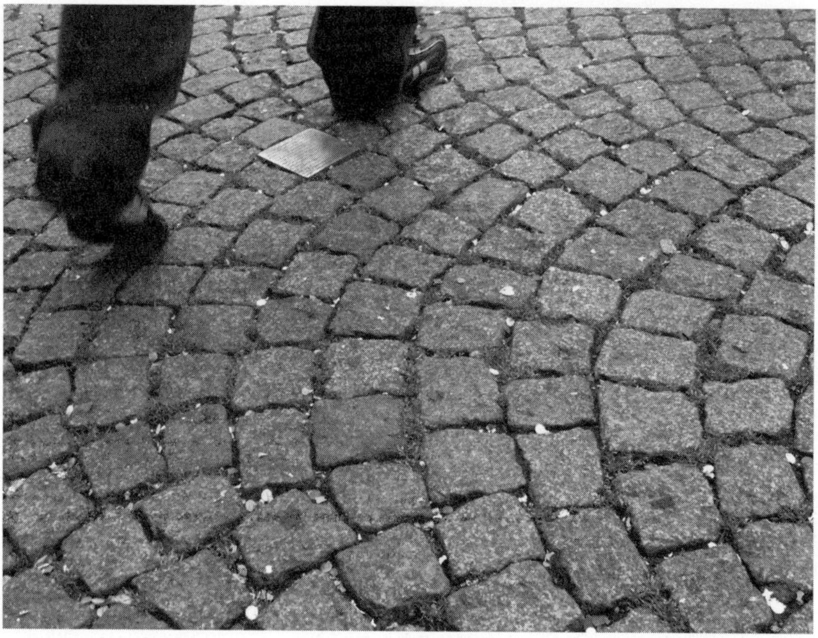

6.3 A pedestrian walks by a *Stolpersteine* prototype in front of Cologne's City Hall. © Jennifer L. Allen.

lay it; guests to attend the installation ceremony; and often individuals committed to the stone's upkeep after it is laid. The number of individuals behind those eighty thousand *Stumbling Stones* is, thus, far more numerous, making the *Stolpersteine* the largest grassroots memorial in the world.

The first steps toward what would become the *Stolpersteine* appeared in a temporary installation Demnig undertook in 1990. It had materialized out of Demnig's work with Kölner Rom, a Cologne-based association to promote understanding between Roma and Sinti people and non-Romani. For the installation, which would subsequently ignite Demnig's commitment to using his art to work through the traumas of National Socialism, he created a temporary monument marking the fiftieth anniversary of the experimental deportation of thousands of Cologne's Sinti and Roma.[53] (The Nazis would later use this technique to deport not only Sinti and Roma, but also millions of antifascist resisters, members of the queer community, people with disabilities, Jehovah's Witnesses, alternative thinkers and, of course, Jews from the heart of European cities to the camps.)[54] Using the same ink wheel from his

1980 *Duftmarken* installation between Kassel and Paris, Demnig inked the text "May 1940—1,000 Roma and Sinti" onto Cologne's streets. The words followed the path that more than 1,500 Roma and Sinti walked on 6 May 1940 as the Nazis herded them to the central deportation site at the Cologne exhibition grounds.[55] Demnig intended the minimalist printed trace to fight the ease with which Cologne's citizens could forget how the Nazis put the city's ordinary spaces to violent ends. It would operate as a provocation. Its purpose was to incite viewers to ask questions and, by seeking answers, to generate dialogue about the history the memorial commemorated.

With a permit to use chalk as his medium, Demnig had originally planned that his installation would foreground the transitory nature of memory. In an expression of the rebellious side for which Demnig had a reputation, however, he chose to replace the chalk with a more durable dispersion paint. Though the police detained Demnig as he laid his text trail—not an uncommon occurrence for the artist—their fortuitous decision not to search the trunk of his car meant that they discovered neither his clearly labeled medium nor his act of transgression.[56] Understandably, the temporary monument lasted longer than municipal authorities had anticipated. "The dry weather had done its part; everything stuck around a while, preserved," explained Rolf Sachsse, a photographer and writer with an interest in Demnig's work. "Then came the people and the dogs and the weather and only that remained which nothing else could wash away. And then came the authorities." But they responded in a way no one expected. In a reversal of their previous permit decision, which allowed the use of a temporary medium, they decided to award the trace the privileged status of a protected monument (*Denkmalschutz*). Then, in March 1993, Demnig received permission to install a permanent version of *1000 Roma and Sinti.* At twenty-three sites throughout the city, Demnig laid concrete plaques in which he embedded the same text in brass lettering.[57] Many informally called it the *Leidensweg*, or Way of Sorrows, a solemn nod to the Via Dolorosa in Jerusalem, the path Jesus allegedly walked both toward his crucifixion and after his resurrection.[58] Demnig, however, referred to the installation, which he laid in 1994, as "stumbling stones [*Stolpersteine*]."[59]

Demnig often recounts an exchange he had with an elderly woman while installing the *Leidensweg* as a defining moment in the development of his subsequent work. She described his project as "very nice" but claimed that no

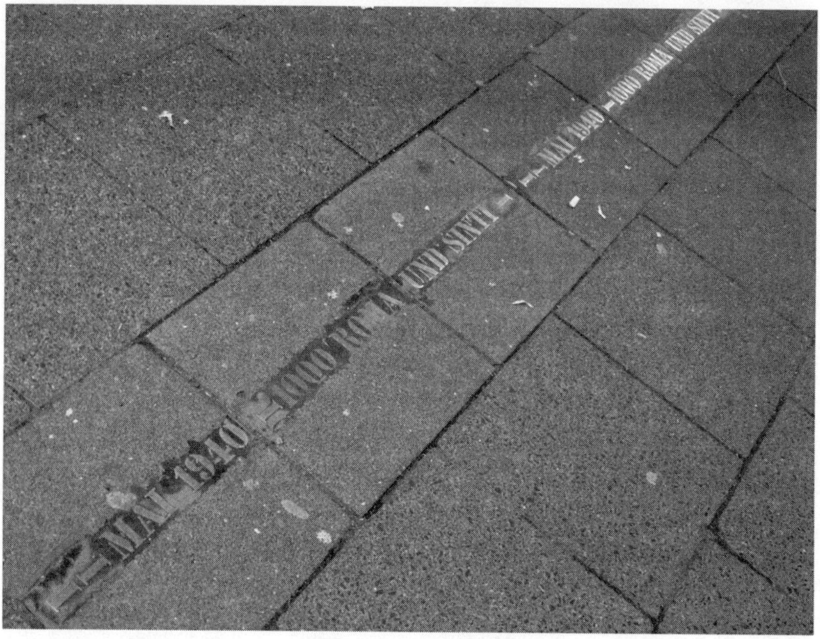

6.4 *1000 Roma and Sinti* memorial. © Jennifer L. Allen.

Sinti or Roma had lived in the area. Here, however, she was mistaken.[60] Her comment suggested to Demnig that engagement with the more mundane aspects of the Holocaust's history—despite prominent treatment in German media, politics, and schools—had not penetrated everyday life in Germany.[61] Germany's commemorative politics and landscape had abstracted and depersonalized the history of Nazi violence. They permitted Germans to forget the basic human arithmetic of genocide: that the targets of brutality were individuals with unique lives and that they lived in the same neighborhoods, streets, and homes that people continue to occupy today.[62] "Auschwitz was the destination, the end point," Demnig notes. "But the horror, the inconceivable began in apartments and houses."[63]

Shortly before this encounter, Demnig had been invited to contribute an entry to an edited volume of conceptual art titled *Delusions of Grandeur: Art Projects for Europe* (*Größenwahn: Kunstprojekte für Europa*). Soliciting contributions from two hundred artists in a score of different countries, the editors of the 1993 publication wanted art projects that could guide post–Cold War Europe through "an era of political reconfiguration." They described the initiative as an attempt to bridge politics and art through dialogue about their shared investment in realizing a united Europe. Contributors were invited to dream big dreams—even utopian ones. Many contributors even freely admitted that their proposals would never be realized. The collection's editors nevertheless intended the volume as "a treasure chest of inspiration" for those "active in the construction of Europe" and were careful not to preclude the success of any proposal. Over the next millennium, they suggested hopefully, perhaps some would come to fruition when intra-European conflict would no longer play such a constitutive role in the continent's political, social, and cultural life. At that moment, they predicted, "the concrete European utopia will finally have enabled new structures of social reality. In the meantime," however, they preferred to concentrate on a "politics of small steps and great visions."[64] Motivated by his *Leidensweg* encounter, Demnig oriented his submission toward commemorating the Holocaust's millions of victims not as an anonymous mass but as discrete individuals, torn one by one from the fabric of European society.

Demnig's contribution to the book drew from a monument prototype he had recently developed. During the three-year-long wait for municipal approval to lay the permanent version of the *Leidensweg,* Demnig illegally installed another memorial in the cobblestone plaza in front of Cologne's City Hall. On December 16, 1992, Demnig marked the fiftieth anniversary of Heinrich Himmler's order that all "gypsies" be deported from the Reich to Auschwitz-Birkenau. The tiny memorial consisted of a small brass-capped cobblestone. It bore on its face the text of Himmler's order and included a paper copy of the text in a hollowed-out cavity carved inside the stone. The shiny metal stone stood out among the plaza's uniform grayness. This anomaly served as a provocation to look. And those who looked could hardly avoid considering the responsibilities of political power amid their comings and goings from Cologne's seat of political authority.[65] Using this tiny memorial as a model, Demnig's entry in *Delusions of Grandeur* proposed to create a massive network of similar mini-monuments. But instead of Nazi orders, the text on each would list the identifying information of an individual Holocaust victim. As its title, Demnig recycled one he had used several times already: *Stolpersteine.*

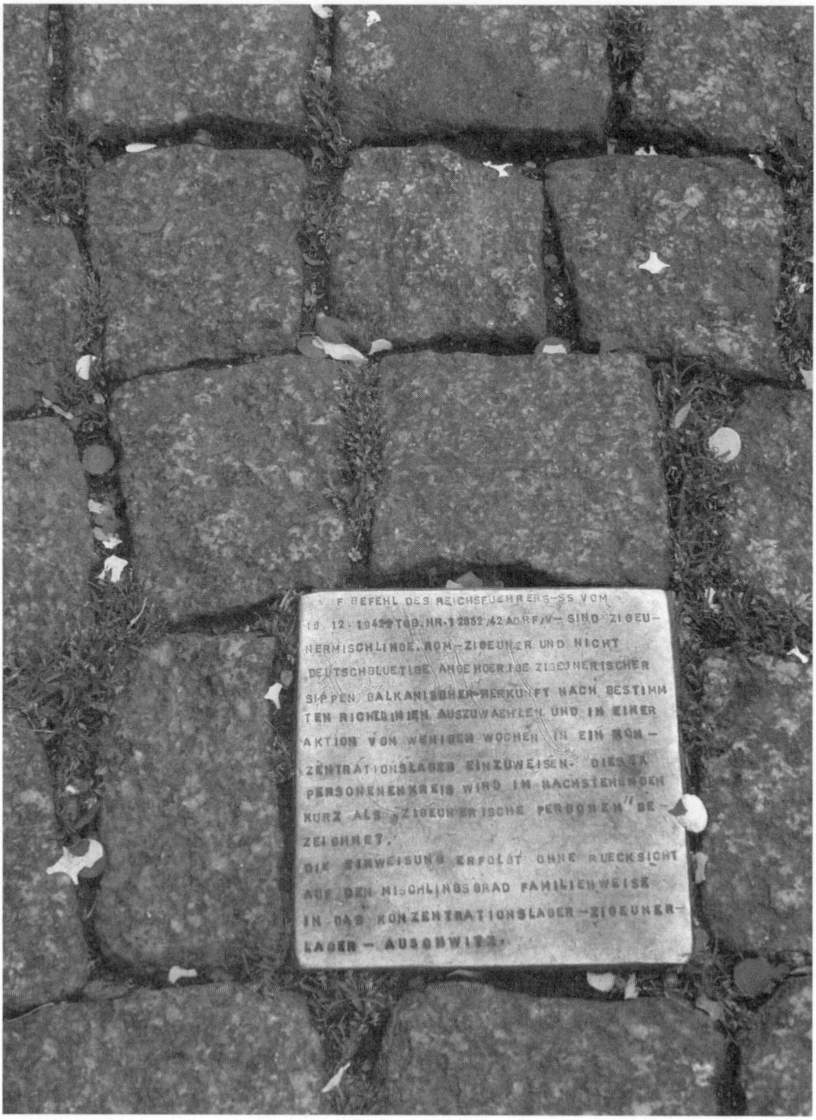

6.5 Memorial to the 1942 deportation order in Cologne. © Jennifer L. Allen.

With the publication of *Delusions of Grandeur,* the *Stolpersteine* remained "a purely conceptual work." The proposal to commemorate every single Holocaust victim, Demnig later quipped, was "surely delusional enough."[66] But the project's actual contours managed to cut through this delusional quality. It refused to underscore the Holocaust's gravity in terms of anonymous masses and instead worked to restore individual names to its victims. And it revealed the proximity of these victims by combating the tendency of larger, more centralized Holocaust memorials to permit their visitors "to forget that these horrors played out in neighborhoods, in streets, in apartments in which we live today." These features began to attract attention, starting with a small evangelical church community. While researching for *1000 Sinti and Roma,* Demnig made contact with Cologne's Antoniter Church. Antoniter had recently offered religious asylum to two Roma families threatened with deportation. In the wake of that decision, the church community initiated a longer conversation about the precarious living situation of Cologne's Romani population.[67] Noting that the Nazis killed far more than one thousand Sinti and Roma, Antoniter's head pastor, Kurt Pick, invited Demnig to begin to commemorate more of them by using the form of the *Stolpersteine.* Demnig balked, deterred precisely by the absurdity of trying to commemorate such an impossibly large number of individuals *as individuals.* He could never make millions of stones. But Pick reminded him that this limitation did not render him powerless. "Of course you can't make six million stones," the pastor advised the artist, "but if you want to set an example, you can still begin small."[68] This line of wisdom has since become something of a mantra for the project's supporters, and the encouragement sufficed to set Demnig's gears in motion. Using archival materials available through his connections with Kölner Rom, the artist created for the church 250 stones, each bearing the personal details of one Holocaust victim. From September to November 1994, Demnig displayed the stones in the Antoniter Church.[69]

Reflecting on the submissions to *Delusions of Grandeur,* art historian Manfred Schneckenburger asked whether Europeans have "not all been waiting for a long time for a new paradigm."[70] As Demnig's delusional monument began to jump off the pages of the edited volume and into the lived spaces of Cologne, it began to seem that his project might fill this need. Art in public space, Schneckenburger wrote, "possesses the capacity to tackle themes pointedly, both at their site and in their contemporary moment." Such interventions in public space, he argued,

> seize at once upon structure, topography, sociology, public attitudes, memories as concrete spaces, as concrete pasts. . . . Public art directs itself not at the psychology of the masses, but rather at the individual and his individual sensibility. . . . Art forms that seemed to have been discredited or abandoned entirely—monuments, memorials—have suddenly regained a form and a meaning. The old task of art in public space as the "Mnemonic of the Polity," per Gerhard Schröder, has generated a new paradigm.[71]

Schneckenburger suggested that Demnig possessed a gift in this regard, arguing that he had "mastered the greatest expanse of space, more than any other artist I know." One finds in Demnig's art, he elaborated, "an (ironic?) aesthetic dialectic between word and act." Demnig's work "does not dispense with the past through a kind of memorial pathos but instead brings it into everyday life in the present."[72] And so it would seem that Demnig, with the earliest iterations of the *Stolpersteine,* had pioneered a new kind of monument: a mini-memorial that could provoke commemoration spontaneously in the spaces and rhythms of everyday life.

In 1995, Demnig brought his decentralized memorial beyond Cologne for the first time. A young employee at Berlin's New Society for the Visual Arts (*Neue Gesellschaft für bildende Kunst,* NGBK), Matthias Reichelt invited Demnig to participate in an exhibition organized with the Schöneberg community arts gallery, the Haus am Kleistpark. The exhibit explored the theme of the Holocaust in art. Other participants included the American cartoonist Art Spiegelman, famous for his graphic novel *Maus,* which depicts interviews with the author's Polish-Jewish father about his experience in the concentration camps; the German photographer Reinhard Matz, who at the time was focused on representing monuments; German installation artist Beate Passow; and British artist Pam Skelton, whose work emphasized the problems of postwar geographies and temporalities. The exhibit's title, a play on words, revealed its dual ambitions. "*Künstler forschen nach Auschwitz*" suggested both artists working in the wake of Auschwitz as well as artists searching for the meaning of Auschwitz. The head of Schöneberg's *Kunstamt,*

Katharina Kaiser, explained that the galleries wanted to play a role in the process of reckoning with Nazi violence.[73] Reichelt elaborated that, "for us, it was not about finding artists interested in engaging the subject in monumental ways (as is the case, for example, with the Monument for the Murdered Jews of Europe). Rather, we sought artists who attempt, processually, to bring these difficult themes into closer proximity."[74] In this regard, they proved far more successful than they could have anticipated.

Demnig contributed to the exhibit a more conventional artwork that featured a scale electric model of a German Reichsbahn BR 53 train. A reproduction of an older project, *Lemniskate BR 53* showcased the kind of train that had transported deportees to the camps. The installation invited viewers to press a button that would set the model in motion. As the train began to chug along its track, an announcement over a loudspeaker detailed the gruesome history of the BR 53.[75] The point was to confront visitors unexpectedly with Holocaust history, to unsettle them, and to prompt them to react. (Demnig created the original *Lemniskate BR 53* in 1994, amid the excitement surrounding the *1000 Roma and Sinti* project and the Antoniter Church initiative. Becoming a bit predictable, he also called it a "*Stolperstein.*")[76]

Alongside *Lemniskate BR 53,* Reichelt encouraged Demnig to "give some thought to some kind of 'action'" that would complement his gallery piece.[77] Although Demnig worried that too little time remained to pull something together, they settled upon laying a small collection of *Stolpersteine* in Berlin's Kreuzberg neighborhood, on Oranienstraße near the NGBK itself.[78] Reichelt undertook the archival research to identify Jewish families that had lived on Oranienstraße. According to the deportation records he pulled from the finance ministry, fifteen apartments on the street had housed fifty-one Jewish residents. These numbers posed a problem for the NGBK, whose modest budget prohibited laying stones for all of them. But what initially appeared a modest fiscal dilemma catapulted them into a grievous moral dilemma. Reichelt drew an analogy between the task of selecting which victims to commemorate and the Final Solution's original selection of victims. For Reichelt, the correspondence was unacceptable, and he proposed they seek financial support from the Berlin Greens to complete the project in full.[79] While they did receive sufficient funding to create all fifty-one stones, they did not receive additional time. Only three months remained before the exhibit would open. "To get a permit approved" for a project of this sort, Demnig later explained, "one needs at least three years."[80] But, socialized in the protest generation of 1968, he possessed more than a mild irreverence toward authority and had become adept at dismissing bureaucratic hurdles.[81] In the end, he simply opted to forge ahead and laid the stones illegally.[82]

Demnig's decision to move forward without the appropriate permits inadvertently paved the way for a smoother approval process. For three months, the Oranienstraße stones escaped the notice of Berlin authorities. A summer construction project, however, generated unexpected attention for the memorial when city engineers made plans to remove that stretch of sidewalk. Confronted with fifty-one shiny stones bearing the names of concentration camp victims, the confused construction workers tasked with removing them refused on the premise that "these stones might be monuments." This civil engineering hiccup brought the stones to the attention of the Kreuzberg district council. With the support of a relatively progressive Green administration, all the stones were retroactively legalized and recognized as an official commemorative site (*Denkort*).[83]

Networking Memory

A curious kind of internationalism came to play a central role in the project's development. It grew only because people—first Germans, then increasingly individuals from around the world—committed themselves to ensuring it did.[84] The creation of a stone relies on a community first to articulate its desire for one. Community members, Demnig explained, must declare, "Yes, we want to realize this project."[85] Each stone then requires an individual or group to finance the cost of labor and supplies, currently 120€.[86] An extensive grassroots gift economy has thus become integral to the memorial's ability to expand. This patronage system first emerged out of a chance encounter by a South African anthropologist named Steven Robins. Robins's Jewish father had fled Nazi Germany in 1936 and later raised his family in South Africa under apartheid. White but also Jewish, Robins experienced apartheid with a strange version of what W. E. B. Du Bois, a century prior, called double consciousness. What South Africans saw as "white," and thus awarded the privileges of whiteness, would have been recognized as racially inferior and slated for extermination in Germany just a generation earlier. This tension left Robins with a "precarious sense of belonging and national identity." Listening to the testimonies of family members of apartheid victims prompted Robins to consider what he knew of his own family's tragic history and how he could commemorate it. While working as a guest faculty member at Berlin's Humboldt University in the late 1990s, he stumbled upon a set of Demnig's stones. They moved him. In the late 1990s, South Africa was only beginning to wrestle with the legacies of apartheid. This mode of commemorating millions of people excluded and then eliminated from the European civic body spoke to commemorative challenges similar to those facing the South African Truth and Reconciliation Commission, tasked with representing memories fragmented and lives shattered. Robins lobbied to place two stones in Berlin's Kreuzberg neighborhood to honor relatives who did not survive the camps.[87] The bureaucratic work required to install Robins's requested monuments legally raised the project's profile. That the stones could generate interest from a place as distant as South Africa inspired the Kreuzberg city council. The district of Kreuzberg decided to offer its full financial and administrative support to facilitate the installation of as many stones as possible. Neighboring Friedrichshain soon joined Kreuzberg, initiating a chain reaction of endorsement among Berlin's districts.[88] Robins's request and the press attention it generated, in other words, helped to formalize the project's patronage system, which has gradually gone global.[89]

The project's rapid growth prompted a critical reevaluation of its administrative framework. As Kurt Pick reminded Demnig in 1994, he could not fashion millions of stones himself. But he could certainly outsource the labor. So he did, to a growing network of international participants. In addition to funding the stone, someone needs to research the individual it commemorates. This process requires tracing the fate not only of the individual named on the stone but also of immediate family members so that the installation can, as far as possible, proceed with the blessing of the victim's relatives.[90] Research of this sort can prove quite laborious and often demands more than one researcher as well as a network of archivists who facilitate the historical investigation. In addition to financiers and researchers, the project requires someone to process its paperwork, since installations require permission in advance. Once the community receives a permit, someone must make the stone. Initially, Demnig did this work. Gradually, however, he began to divide the labor. In 2005, he invited a longtime colleague in Berlin, Michael Friedrichs-Friedländer, to craft stones as well.[91] Finally, the project requires someone to lay the stone. Though Demnig completes many installations himself in a grueling schedule that lands him in a different city often several times each week, the considerable interest has necessitated the involvement of others. The initiative operates entirely at the grassroots level. It runs on the fuel of popular contributions of both time and money. Municipal interventions are, in most instances, *pro forma.*

Some elements of the project's initial fantastic vision remain. "In Cologne," Demnig has mused, "one would have to pave whole streets with *Stolpersteine.* The project can at best set an example [*Zeichen setzen*]." But its massive network of participants tempers the absurdity of its objective. Youth in particular have demonstrated their willingness to shoulder the burden of memory. Demnig has often stressed the importance of school groups to the project's success. The Werner-Heisenberg-Schule in Leverkusen, for example, took over the project from the city, conducting archival research and coordinating municipal permit applications. And in Cologne, the Humboldt-Gymnasium organized sponsorship for thirty-three stones. Demnig has highlighted that young people often take a great interest in the biographies of those they commemorate. And they are also more likely, he argues, to draw lessons from the project, especially in the context of "the ever-increasing tendencies in all of Europe once again toward nationalism and intolerance toward foreigners."[92] Youth activists have also taken a lead on the monuments' upkeep. Throughout the year, but with special emphasis on International Holocaust Remembrance Day, they lead frequent initiatives to clean existing stones. Often, these efforts combine Holocaust remembrance with intercultural integration by involving multiethnic youth, including refugees.[93]

The project's remarkable growth belies its uneven popularity. As the mini-monuments have proliferated, so has opposition to them. German historian Harald Schmid has criticized the project on two counts. First, it fixates on commemorating victims to the exclusion of other memories. And, second, the memorial offers a one-dimensional engagement with Nazi atrocity. It teaches next to nothing about how the National Socialist power apparatus functioned in practice. The project would resonate quite differently—more meaningfully, even, he argues—were it to lay stones naming Nazi perpetrators instead of victims. Schmid has suggested that Germany can only hold to its imperative of "Never again!" if its citizens understand both how the Nazis slaughtered millions of individuals and who participated in this genocide.[94]

Others have charged the project with commemorative bullying. "The question," one historian has written, "is whether most communities permit the installation of *Stolpersteine* in their cities less out of enthusiasm than out of fear of negative effects" should they elect otherwise; indeed, public image may be at stake for many cities.[95] Still others have pointed to the problem of creating an aesthetics of superficiality, a commemorative cult akin to the gilt stars along Hollywood's Walk of Fame.[96]

Outside the ivory tower, opposition has proven less measured. In a suburb of Hamburg, the Christian Democratic Union together with the short-lived, right-wing populist Schill-Partei used their majority in the city council to reject a *Stolperstein* proposal on the (inaccurate) grounds that Demnig would turn a profit from the memorial. Only after public protests did they concede.[97] Some have balked at the placement of stones outside their homes for fear they might attract attention from the wrong sort of passersby.[98] One Berliner with political ties to the far right, for example, has made himself infamous by gouging deep gashes in stones near his home in Schöneberg.[99] A Cologne resident caused a commotion over the installation of a stone at the entrance to his property because he claimed it would distract from his garden.[100] Another person argued a stone would dramatically lower his property value because it would implicate his home in Nazi crimes.[101]

Many of these expressions of disapproval highlight the way the *Stumbling Stones* decouple commemoration from sites in which jurisdiction is clear and management fairly uncomplicated. Demnig had wanted to make the stones unavoidable, so he chose to install them directly before the front door of the apartment building or house. One could step over them or to one side, but they remained impossible to ignore. (Demnig also acknowledged the likelihood that passersby might simply step on the stones. Frequent foot traffic carried the advantage, however, that it would keep the stones polished, legible, and conspicuous.) The stones transport the mnemonic act into local landscapes governed, in practice, by more nebulous (though no less stringent) social expectations. They also differ from traditional local monuments in that they are designed to serve as commemorative disruptions amid everyday life. Although the stones occupy sidewalk space that, at least nominally, belongs to the city, both Demnig and residents themselves understand it as a liminal space. Here, the stones initiate an individualized, personal act of commemoration. However private the act itself, it remains publicly observable. And it takes place in a space neither fully public nor private, a threshold where the practical border between "mine" and "ours" often remains unclear. Demnig occasionally recalls a pivotal moment in Cologne in which one house owner took him to court on the grounds that the two *Stolpersteine* in front of his home lowered his property value by 100,000 Marks. The judge, however, ruled in Demnig's favor, arguing that "the sidewalk belongs to the city, and as such *Stolpersteine* are a gift of the building's residents to the city." The decision set a precedent for managing future conflicts.[102]

Just as this inconvenient topography has generated resistance, so has its unusual temporality of ongoing, spontaneous encounters with Holocaust history. Some *Stolpersteine* opponents have objected to the way the monuments bring the commemorative act not only into the space but also into the timeframe of daily life. One person refused to support the installation of stones for her parents because passersby would be forced to reckon with her parents' murder any time they saw the stones. She opposed the idea that their legacy would take the form of a permanent mnemonic raincloud over their neighborhood.[103] The *Stolpersteine* refuse to bracket commemoration from everydayness as an exceptional moment. They refuse to make willful visitation or willful evasion so simple. Instead, *Stolpersteine* render the commemorative act mundane, spontaneous, and often unavoidable.

The staunchest opposition to the stones, however, has come from Germany's Jewish communities, with the city of Munich leading the charge.[104] Much Jewish dissent has focused on the placement of the stones underfoot. Many regard the stones as ersatz gravestones (despite Demnig having discouraged this equivalency). To walk on a stone seen as such could be construed as an act of violence against the memory of the individual it commemorates.[105] Indeed, an offensive Nazi-era Austrian folk saying, for example, attributed the act of stumbling to having inadvertently encountered a Jewish burial site: "When one trips on a stone," read one 1930 encyclopedia of folk culture in the Sudetenland, "one exclaims, 'A Jew must be buried there.'"[106] Demnig consulted with Yad Vashem and others before initiating the project to ensure he would not violate Jewish law by placing names in the ground. He was given the green light. But that sanction remained unsatisfactory to many. In 2004, Munich's City Council—in consultation with the central organ of Jewish life in Munich, the Israelitische Kultusgemeinde—prohibited the installation of stones in the city. The decision stemmed, at least ostensibly, from the stones' embeddedness in everyday life. Their diffusion made it difficult to regulate those who interacted with them. The stones remained vulnerable to vandalism. Charlotte Knobloch, the leader of Munich's Jewish community and an aging survivor of the Nazi era, has served as a moral beacon for many of the city's leaders in their discussions. Rather than honoring the victims, she argues, the stones effectively permit their mnemonic desecration. A new stone remains a novelty for a brief period, during which it exists as an object of deliberate reverence. Those who do not stop when they pass may nevertheless step around a shiny cobblestone. But time assimilates it into the landscape. Dulled by the elements, even forgotten, the stone is eventually stepped on rather than around or over. And for Knobloch, to step on a *Stolperstein,* smearing it with filth, however inadvertently, is to debase the victim's memory in the same manner that the Nazis debased the victims themselves. Knobloch has even branded *Stolpersteine* advocates "*Gedenktäter,*" which translates loosely to "defilers of memory" or, more crudely, "memory Nazis."[107] Munich's former mayor, the Social Democrat Christian Ude, reinforced Knobloch's criticism, asserting that Munich, as the "Capital of the National Socialist Movement," bears a special responsibility to communicate atonement visibly and convincingly. To commemorate the Holocaust by laying a few small, mundane stones would downplay the gravity of National Socialism's impact.[108] In the intervening years since the city first issued its ban, it has sustained its opposition, though not without polarizing residents and officials. For this committed resistance, Munich has won for itself the unofficial title of "Capital of *Stumbling Stones* Opposition."[109]

Nevertheless, the city's long battle has revealed its limited ability to control the project. Supporters have found ways of working around the ban. In September 2007, Stolpersteine Initiative München, the main local group lobbying for the mini-monuments, began installing them on private property. Many of the stones remain visible from the street. And optimism that the city will eventually lift the ban has prompted supporters to fund the creation of more than three hundred additional *Stumbling Stones.* Until they too can find their final resting places, whether on private ground or public, they have been stored in a private cellar belonging to one of the initiative's members. Munich's vocal opposition has also ensured that conversations about the *Stolpersteine* remain present in the media. The inadvertent effect of this obstinacy has been to prevent the project's normalization. Demnig himself has acknowledged that only with confrontation "will the subject stay lively."[110] Its unresolved status remains an irritant to both supporters and detractors, which just fuels the project's longevity in public discourse and public consciousness.

Other cities with reservations about the project have used Munich as a reference point. The small town of Bad Tölz just outside of Munich, for example, has rejected the installation of *Stumbling Stones* on the premise that the town had very few Jewish residents, so their memorials would have been too dispersed to have an impact on the community. The absence of cobblestone-paved sidewalks in some areas of the town reinforced this decision. The alternative memorial the city adopted in June 2012, however, bore a striking resemblance to Demnig's project: ersatz cobblestones made of metal bear the names of victims, the dates of their birth and death, and their place of death. They are larger than Demnig's stones. They offer only the victim's first name and last initial instead of the full name, a compromise with data protection laws that permitted fuller research into the victim's life. They lie at the entrance to the Bad Tölz City Museum instead of before the victim's last freely chosen residence. And the installation has been dubbed a *Ge(h)denkstein*. The wordplay embedded in this neologistic compound noun underscores the stones' conventional memorial function. In German, both *Gedenkstein* and *Denkstein* indicate a small memorial plaque. But the monument's wordsmithing also promotes a now-familiar value. *Geh* is an imperative meaning "go" or "move." Together, the pun suggests something like a "go-and-think-about-it stone." It demands a dynamic, decentralized commemorative process.

Many highlight the *Stolpersteine*'s ability to provoke passersby not only into thought but also into dialogue about the history the stones record. In a book published by the small town of Elmshorn to document its efforts to install its own *Stolpersteine,* a leader of the initiative lauded the project for having enabled a kind of mutual understanding or rapprochement (*Verständigung*). "If one here follows the philosopher Jürgen Habermas," he noted, one interprets the Elmshorn monument-series as promoting "understanding-oriented communicative action." It "builds connections. Connections to those who wish to take in the perspective of the victims." Action-based art (*Aktionskunst*) "provokes . . . dialogue, encourages the public to participate, sets a chain of conversations in action, in which the process of critical reason is given voice [*kritische Vernunft zu Wort kommt*]."[111] The *Stolpersteine* project, Harald Schmid has argued, operates as a *perpetuum mobile.* It propels and sustains itself, growing ever larger through the organizational and communicative networks whose evolution it facilitates. International civic participations stand both as a condition and a consequence of the laying of *Stolpersteine.* The memorial enables an "activation of civic engagement 'at the site'" of historical meaning (*vor Ort*). Its massive human resources—a participatory network that reaches far beyond Demnig's personal orbit—render this mobilization normative, historically-politically charged (*geschichtspolitisch*), and radically democratic.[112] Others have also made note of the possibilities the project opens for grassroots civic engagement. The *Stolpersteine* "open up a sphere of action" toward the past. "No longer must one stand on the sidelines of time and bear the weight of the past; one can actually do something."[113]

Demnig emphasizes the importance of decentralization and democratization, but on different grounds. "This project . . . has become a social sculpture," he argues, using the language of Beuys. "It has fashioned a communicative network that exists by and large independently of me."[114] As a result, the project stands a good chance of sustaining itself even after Demnig and his current collaborators no longer drive it. In a sense, then, the *Stolpersteine* are not the product of a single creative genius. Demnig provided the idea and the initial infrastructure, essential elements without which the project may never have materialized. But the real creators of the massive grassroots memorial that the *Stolpersteine* have become are those ordinary participants who removed the proposal from the shelf of absurdity and remade it as a sustainable utopia. The project has thrived only by exploding beyond the orbit of the artist's control. That is, after all, the point of a successful social sculpture.

Stefanie Endlich, a scholar of art in public space, has placed special weight on this feature of the *Stolpersteine.* She argues that it sets decentralized grassroots projects like Demnig's apart from prior attempts to remake Germany's commemorative paradigm. The project occupies a liminal space between isolation and collaboration, between self-interest and beneficence, between the invisible and the visible, between repression and perception, and above all between reality and utopia.[115] The utopia is one that not only envisions but also attempts to enact a future in which German citizens engage actively with

Germany's difficult past both as individuals and as a collective communicative network.[116]

Demnig has lamented this utopian nature of his project in light of the continued aggression of extremist groups in Germany: "I wish my project were a little less contemporarily germane. But we should be laying many more *Stolpersteine* precisely because of this relevance."[117] Perhaps, Demnig suggested hopefully, "many individual memorials will have a greater effect than monuments largely kept at a distance. When set before your house door, repression [*Verdrängung*] becomes more challenging."[118] What, precisely, Demnig meant remains somewhat unclear. Repression of what sort? Challenging in what way and to whom? But others have since elaborated for him. One commentator highlighted that the liminal space the stones occupy "[challenges] our thoughts about the boundaries of private space, the threshold between house and street, . . . protection and exposure, individuality and anonymity, . . . privacy and . . . neighborliness."[119] The stones made Nazi violence harder to ignore, harder to forget, and harder to avoid taking a stand against.

The immediate power of the project rests in its ability to fragment mass atrocity, rendering it immediately tangible. "You can open a book and read six million murdered Jews," Demnig suggested after one stone-laying ceremony, "but to me, that's so abstract a number . . . it's beyond conception." The *Stolpersteine* project aims to overcome this conceptual defeatism.[120] "Abstraction," journalist Judith Miller has explained, "is memory's most ardent enemy." It "kills because it encourages distance, and often indifference. We must remind ourselves that the Holocaust was not six million." Rather, she argued, genocide takes place "one, plus one, plus one. . . . Only in understanding that civilized people must defend the one, by one, by one . . . can the Holocaust, the incomprehensible, be given meaning."[121] The *Stolpersteine* attempt to tackle in a sustainable way the utopian objective of honoring all of these "ones."

Conclusion

The Fate of Sustainable Utopia

One version of the history of utopia in the twentieth century leads straight to a dead end. It defines utopia based on the sweeping social engineering projects whose conceptual possibility Enlightenment attitudes toward future betterment first enabled. As a result, it struggles to escape the grave that the twentieth century's extreme violence dug for such programs. This narrative recasts radical dreams for a superlative future as either delusional musings or dangerous fallacies and consigns utopia to irrelevance. Reform remains possible, but the status quo holds immense power. In one form or another, liberal democracy and advanced capitalism seem here to stay, whether we like them or not. From a political perspective that lionizes this present, this reading permits triumphalism. Should one wish for any kind of radical alternative, however, this reading stokes a melancholy that sees only the choice between resignation and apathy. Disaffection can lead nowhere. Political disenfranchisement, social alienation, and cultural impotence take hold. Such a myth of endings found a home in considerable postwar scholarship of the Left.

Another version of this history becomes possible, though, with the concession that the concept of utopia itself has a history. When the concept of utopia is allowed to change, it reveals that, tempting though it may have been in the late twentieth century to throw out the baby with the utopian bathwater, ordinary Germans never seemed to countenance that possibility in earnest. From the century's violence, they had inherited an abiding cynicism toward totalizing utopias. But their suspicion toward the kinds of ends-oriented utopian programs that resulted in global bloodshed did not prompt them to give up entirely on dreaming dreams of a superlative future. Instead, they began to assign a new set of parameters to the radical alternatives they imagined. They began, in other words, to imagine new kinds of utopias.

Groups of artists, historians, and politicians each contributed to this process in their own way. They began by suiting up for battle against German hierarchies and fought using the weapons of localized, decentralized, democratic spaces of cultural engagement. The artists took on art in public space. Using their art to facilitate participatory, discursive, emancipatory experiences of public spaces, they aimed to fuel democratic agency in and over those spaces. The historians took on the narration of the past. By inviting local citizens to tell local histories "from below," they put theories about the production of authority to work developing historical scholarship with a grassroots democratic face. The politicians took on environmental politics through cultural initiatives. Creating a society that embraced the values of sustainability and grassroots democracy, they argued, required paying attention to art, aesthetics, and cultural institutions. The value of local experiences of culture lay in their ability to offer citizens opportunities to imagine and debate visions for a better world.

As these activists struggled against West Germany's aesthetic, intellectual, and political status quo, their objectives for their contributions to society began to shift. They adopted more radical aims. Making short-term changes no longer sufficed, and they refused to advocate merely for reform in the present. The goal became to make their respective corners of society fully democratic, socially integrated, just, and peaceful, both in the present and in the future. The West German Greens conceptualized "Green" cultural practices as serving as a long-term catechism for a thoroughgoing grassroots democratic political system in the Federal Republic. The Berlin History Workshop aimed to give local residents the tools to link their pasts with their present and in doing so to connect the ideals of their present to the realities of their future. The spatial interventionists reimagined the forms and practices of Holocaust commemorations in order to build a more socially conscious, ethical society for generations to come.

All three groups tried to implement programs and infrastructures that would make these new conditions durable but also adaptable. That is, they aimed for small-scale sustainable utopias. Their utopias assumed a new topography by engaging only finite aspects of society. They decentralized that engagement, replicating it at many analogous local sites that, together, constitute a large geography. This strong localization made it nearly impossible to administer these utopias from the top down. The spatial orientation of this new utopianism required, as a result, a new demographic orientation. It demanded the democratization of utopian practices via the contributions of many, mostly ordinary individuals who engaged in micro-actions repeated many times. The effect of these topographical and demographic shifts was that they endowed utopia with a new temporality as well. New utopians prioritized the means with which they pursued their projects as an expression of their ends. In a manner akin to the twentieth-century notion of environmental sustainability, they recognized their work as projects not only for the future but also for the present. By replicating extensively these small local behaviors, utopian undertakings attempted to approximate this future in the present. At the same time, this new utopianism insisted on the malleability of its objects. Utopias needed to be able to adapt to changing circumstances in order to achieve any kind of longevity.

The renewed ability to think in utopian terms or the hopes invested in sustainable utopian programs, however, should not be confused with the promise of their success. Modest though these utopias may have been, the irony of sustainable utopias is that their modesty often did not spare them from the possibility of failing to reach the benchmark of sustainability that their creators set for them. The trajectories of the Berlin *Geschichtswerkstatt*, the Greens, and the spatial interventionists each underscore this limitation.

How Sustainable a Sustainable Alternative?

One longtime member of the BGW argued that "the history of the Berlin *Geschichtswerkstatt* is a history of success."[1] By the 1990s, established academic institutions around Germany had taken up the *Geschichtswerkstatt*'s topical investments with the mainstreaming of confrontations with Germany's Nazi past. And they took up its methods as the history of everyday life won a place in universities and research centers alongside methods like social history, political history, or conceptual history. In a sense, the *Geschichtswerkstatt* had ensured its immortality. But these national triumphs spelled the group's local collapse. As its mode of doing history gained traction, the BGW watched members take their skills to more permanent, more lucrative employment.

These departures created a vacuum where the group's "old West Berlin 68er alpha members," as one critic described the BGW's founders, had failed to groom their replacements.[2] This flimsy line of succession created a domino effect. With no one prepared to carry the organization and its mission into a changing political and cultural milieu, the BGW lost not only its momentum but also nearly 40 percent of its membership between its heyday and the first years of the new millennium.[3] As the group failed to adapt to shifting circumstances, its volunteer base disappeared as well. As one member suggested, "an association with an executive committee and weekly meetings is just not hip any more."[4]

The BGW's printed and archival materials served as a modest buoy for the struggling organization. Open to the public a few hours each weekday, the Goltzstraße archive and informational center provided just enough of a repository of unique documents to prevent the group's descent into irrelevance within newly reunified Germany. The BGW has also added more than twenty publications since the fall of the Berlin Wall. It never fully managed to escape its obsession with the history of National Socialism, though, and nearly half of those publications take up the same themes it has wrestled with since its creation: the everyday life of Jewish residents in Berlin, forced labor and labor camps, or Polish women prisoners, for example.

The group has periodically ventured into newer territory and addressed issues of greater contemporary urgency in Germany. It published on the significance of the fall of the Berlin Wall, for example, and on freedom of travel in post–Cold War Europe after the 1995 establishment of the passport-free intra-European travel zone, the Schengen Area. It has also begun to experiment with mediating its work via digital technologies. Its website hosts a rudimentary online exhibit featuring interviews with Albanian women living in Berlin. The women discuss whether they have felt welcome in Berlin and the nature of their experiences. The BGW has also developed two smartphone apps that offer Berlin tours focusing on the history of forced labor. The apps give users access to witness testimonies, photographs, and primary source documents relevant to each historical site.

Perhaps the late BGW's most promising project, however, was a study of immigrants in Berlin that ran through 1994. Members had been deeply unsettled by the xenophobic riots in September 1991 in the Saxon town of Hoyerswerda just a few hours southeast of Berlin. The Hoyerswerda riots and the wave of racist nationalist expressions of solidarity that followed recalled National Socialism much too closely for comfort.[5] Fearing a resurgence of nationalism and racism, a handful of members joined forces to study immigration and foreign worker communities in Berlin from the construction of the Berlin Wall in 1961 through the years after its fall. The "Immi-Group," as its members called themselves, researched themes of housing, familial dynamics, work opportunities, and encounters with racism. Though somewhat limited by language barriers, they nevertheless conducted intergenerational family interviews with non-ethnic Germans who were longtime residents of Berlin. They intended these interviews as fodder for a traveling exhibit and a book. Both the exhibit and the book would demonstrate the conflicting manner in which Berlin had served, on one hand, as a meaningful hometown (*Heimatstadt*) to these workers while failing, on the other, to provide them with legal and social equality. In contrast to much of the BGW's previous work, the project oriented the organization's attentions solidly toward the present. Immi-Group members understood their work as a mouthpiece for immigrants in the city and as part of the BGW's continuing effort to fight racism in Germany from below. For these ambitions, the BGW received solid support both from the new Berlin administration and from the community. The *Stiftung Deutsche Klassenlotterie* awarded it nearly half a million Marks. A number of the city's districts expressed interest in hosting the final exhibit. And the Turkish Community of Berlin (*Türkische Gemeinde Berlin*) promised its cooperation.[6] Though the Immi-Group generated considerable interest among BGW members, interest did not translate to commitment. The exhibits ran, and the project generated a small set of publications, but with uninspiring book sales and flagging participation, the Immi-Group slowly dissolved after it concluded its scheduled exhibition cycle.[7] BGW members tried to revive the group on several occasions but could never get it off the ground again.[8]

The BGW continues to operate but only flaccidly. Of the nearly thirty books the organization has published since reunification, half were self-published. As funding has dried up, the group has increasingly run in an ad hoc way. Beyond the diligently maintained Goltzstraße information center, the BGW never devised a permanent arrangement that would ensure its existence after the project's original members moved on. Even more tellingly, it has thus far failed to respond in any significant way to the historical changes happening before its members' eyes. Both the backlash to the refugee crisis that gained momentum in Europe starting in 2015 and the resurgence of the far right have invited comparisons to subjects of more immediate interest to the BGW. Neither topic, however, has generated projects of a scale and seriousness analogous to those the BGW once undertook. These missed opportunities suggest that the organization has lost sight of its original alternative oppositional *raison d'être.*

The reason the BGW's sustainable utopian program proved not terribly sustainable likely stemmed from the group's failure to understand the true novelty of its work. The originality of a group that comprised community members as amateur historians doing "history from below" was lost on no one. But "it did not occur to us," one lifelong member explained in 2001, that Germany suffered from "a lack of social utopias."[9] BGW members never actually recognized their sustainable utopia for what it was. And this failure to understand the gap their work actually filled meant that they would also fail to realize when it no longer served this purpose.

The Greens have enjoyed greater longevity than the BGW, though not without hiccups and qualifications after they, too, found themselves hamstrung by their own successes. The party had fueled its rise with the fear of an imminent "crisis of humanity" that combined Europe's impending self-destruction at the hands of environmental degradation with the threat of nuclear energy and shortsighted oligarchical politics. Its members refused to insist on humanity's path dependency. Their optimism stemmed from their belief in the transformational power of culture. They understood it to possess the ability to facilitate new ways of thinking, feeling, and behaving. Art and culture could thus teach people to inhabit the world differently. By attempting to fashion Germany's "living conditions according to the inner principles and rules of art," the party believed it could foster a "Green" way of life, in which people would come to recognize that "ecology is more than environment."[10]

But as one artist and Green parliamentary representative remarked in 1995, quoting Weimar-era cabaret artist Karl Valentin, "art is nice, but it is a lot of work."[11] The Green's cultural program proved, in fact, too much work. The party attempted to obscure some of its failures. A 2005 document on the status of the party's cultural program suggested its task was "not about presenting a track record but rather about understanding a method."[12] Still, it was no secret that the Greens struggled to sustain the most radical aspects of the party's program under the pressure of both its mounting prominence and Germany's rapidly changing political and cultural climate.

The party's original aversion to Germany's parliamentary apparatus did not quite keep pace with the Greens' growing comfort as an increasingly conventional political party. In exchange for success, the Greens proved willing to trade fiery but inexperienced political hopefuls working on an unstable rotation cycle for a permanent salaried leadership with technical expertise, management skills, and a track record for turning aspirations into hard policy. Through it all, the party retained its rhetoric about fighting for a modern democratic state governed from the grassroots and continued to criticize the SPD and CDU as "over-adapted, over-generalized, over-institutionalized, and overloaded."[13] But members became more and more accepting of the technocracy growing within their own party. Though the Greens began as a "system of solidarity" led by amateur activists united by a shared set of environmental values and grassroots political methods, by the mid-1990s they had transformed into a "system of interests" oriented toward achieving parliamentary success.[14]

The party also shifted its relationship to its constituents. By bringing political practices into the everyday spaces of ordinary people's lives, the early Greens had intended to place practical political power permanently into the hands of Germans themselves. The party gradually tempered this emphasis on democracy from the grassroots. While the party's 1993 basic program (*Grundsatzprogramm*) still used the adjective "grassroots democratic [*basisdemokratisch*]," its next *Grundsatzprogramm* in 2002 omitted the language of grassroots democracy, preferring instead the more moderate language simply of *Demokratie*. Its 2020 *Grundsatzprogramm* revived the language of grassroots democracy, but only tepidly with one mention. "Our grassroots democratic party opens doors [*öffnet Zugänge*]," they argued. Just as quickly as it reappeared, however, it disappeared. The Greens' 2021 election program used "*Demokratie*" thirty-seven times and "*demokratisch*" thirty-one; neither "*Basisdemokratie*" nor "*basisdemokratisch*" appeared once.[15] Radical grassroots democratic practices began to fall by the wayside as the party recognized time as a precious political resource. Decision by social consensus came to seem profligate. And where the Greens had originally claimed that every person is an artist, they increasingly stressed the need for aesthetic education if social and cultural discourse were actually to become more open and more sophisticated. The party lobbied to provide such educational opportunities to its constituents, but it no longer emphasized allowing those constituents themselves to serve as the motor in creating them.[16]

Many of these same party members who tasked themselves with the administration of culture from below soon discovered that the demands of sustained parliamentary power proved boring and difficult in comparison to political activism. The early Greens were quick to insist, for example, that the public infrastructure of culture—library, music schools, or theaters, for example—should not be left to the free market.[17] Yet, when it came time to implement their program, they found themselves confronted with "a complex, overwhelmingly dry, increasingly juridified [*verrechtlichten*] subject matter." Somewhere along the path "from the Utopia of 'social sculpture' to the creation of a capital tax on art and cultural goods," party members had wandered off.[18] Despite all their pleas, by the middle of the 1990s the party had failed to establish a cultural bureau with any kind of staying power.[19]

The party was also waylaid by the political circumstances of 1989–1990. Its misreading of its constituency on the question of unification led to dismal results in the first federal elections for reunified Germany in December 1990. The West German Greens lost all their parliamentary seats, and Alliance 90, which became the Greens' sister party in the east, held on only by a thread. The sharp downsizing of its constituency plagued the party over the next decade as it attempted to regain its footing in the Bundestag. After the public rejected the Greens' opposition to German unification, the party tried to backtrack, toeing a more palatable line. Its members celebrated the public rallies held in the DDR in the days before the fall of the Wall as models of grassroots political decentralization. They compared the "politics of liberation" that featured in their updated party program to Alexanderplatz on 4 November 1989, when efforts to resist a "dead political system" grew out of "all the small and concrete life circumstances that accumulated" in the experiences of an entire population.[20] They tried to anchor the pursuit of a shared German culture at the heart of the new German constitution.[21] And they offered their support to grassroots efforts attempting to make sense of this shared culture. They stepped up in the debate about preserving East German monuments, for example, arguing that failing to allow the German people to decide which symbols of their complicated shared heritage to retain would lead to further repression, even barbarity.[22]

Though the Greens saw their attempts to foster cultural unity between East and West as a way to forge political unity, their 1990 election debacle left the party with only one real life vest: political coalitioning. The SPD, the Greens' longtime cautious ally, was the party's natural choice for a political partnership. But a red-green coalition meant that the Greens would be carried on the shoulders of giants.[23] This move required a great deal of compromise for the already hobbled party. Still, it opted for realism over dogmatism and for continued parliamentary power over allegiance to the idealistic principles of the Greens-as-protest-movement.[24] Coalitioning also buried Green radicalism a little deeper. The party rested in the hands of the SPD, after all, which had abandoned its own last vestiges of utopian thinking forty years earlier.

The Greens did not consign their sustainable utopian cultural program completely to oblivion. The party supported a project uncannily similar to the BGW's Mobile Museum called the Omnibus for Direct Democracy, for example. It drew inspiration from Joseph Beuys's 1972 documenta installation, *100 Days,* in which the artist sat for one hundred days in an office to talk with his visitors about direct democracy. More than a decade and a half later, one of Beuys's students, Johannes Stüttgen, sought to fuel his mentor's legacy by carrying the lessons of *7000 Oaks* and *100 Days* beyond Kassel. Stüttgen converted a bus in order to create what he described as a mobile social sculpture for the discussion of democratic practices. Intended to bring these conversations to all corners of Germany, the bus logged nearly 1,500 stops around the country in its first three years. It continues to pursue this mission today. Although *Omnibus* eventually gave up its political affiliations in favor of buttressing any initiatives that advanced the project of direct democracy, it was set into motion with support from the Greens.[25]

Still, the Greens found themselves on the defensive after their abysmal election results. The party's continued existence rested on a tenuous set of political alliances. From this position, its members got caught in a cycle of thinking and rethinking without any real forward motion. It took the confluence of impending global climate catastrophe, the global resurgence of the far right, and a global pandemic to reenergize not only German investment in the Greens but also the Greens' investment in their own historically radical political agenda: their 2021 election program declared that an "active cultural life is the basis of democratic society. This is where debates about how we want to live take place."[26] Only the threat of a multifaceted global dystopia, in other words, could save a Green sustainable utopia.

While the Berlin *Geschichtswerkstatt* and the German Greens floundered in reunified Germany, the spatial interventionists enjoyed more promising circumstances as the project of bringing commemoration of an unbelievable magnitude into the topographies and temporalities of everyday life won favor first in central Europe, then increasingly globally. The *Stolpersteine* have formed the vanguard of this international mnemonic movement, but the project has not grown without encountering obstacles. As of August 2021, the city of Munich remained opposed to the installation of stones. The fear of the "fascism of memory" has proven incredibly durable in the Bavarian capital, despite considerable popular protest to the contrary.[27] Demnig has also encountered backlash from other artists. Aschrott Fountain designer and fellow spatial interventionist Horst Hoheisel complained, for example, that Demnig's *Stolpersteine* plagiarized a design Hoheisel had submitted to the Bavarian Quarter monument competition.[28]

Copycat tendencies, however, cut both ways. Demnig lashed out against one imitation project in Vienna, the *Stones of Remembrance* (*Steine der Erinnerung*), founded in 2005. In an effort to rein in its coordinators, Demnig accused them of plagiarism, forbade them to lay stones anywhere but directly before house entryways, and threatened legal action should they fail to comply. Recognizing that he would likely lose the battle, he eventually backed away from this complicated attempt to reconcile an artist's intellectual property rights and the democratic nature of mourning mass trauma.[29] Together, the project's popularity and size shattered any real proprietary hopes Demnig might have had. Still, a fair degree of protectiveness has developed around the mini-monuments. One representative in Wuppertal, for example, received swift correction when he referred to a ground plaque for nineteenth-century working-class barricade fighters as a "*Stolperstein*."[30]

Though the popularity of the *Stolpersteine* within Europe stands out, Demnig's real impact lies in the uptake of his commemorative form globally. Seven thousand miles from Demnig's first stones, the city of Buenos Aires offered its own version of Demnig's decentralized, democratized commemorative practice. In 2005, a group of citizens in Argentina began to prepare for the thirtieth anniversary of the 1976 coup, which initiated a period of state terrorism during which left-wing activists, trade unionists, students, journalists, and others were "disappeared." Under the military junta of Jorge Raphael Videla, Roberto Viola, and Leopoldo Galtieri that ruled from 1976 to 1983, between thirteen thousand and thirty thousand alleged dissidents were kidnapped and killed, often tossed alive from airplanes over the Atlantic to drown, without leaving a trace of their fate.[31] To commemorate the thousands who lost their lives during this period, an informal association of mothers, young human rights workers, and some who refer to themselves simply as *vecinos,* or neighbors, began to weave the lives of these "disappeared" back into the social and cultural fabric of Buenos Aires. They embedded local walkways with tiles whose superficial appearance differs from the *Stolpersteine:* each is painted with a durable ferrous ceramic compound that gives it a green tint and then decorated with colorful glass. But the tiles follow the same basic form as Demnig's memorial. They feature the names of those killed and the dates of their disappearance. Many read "Here lived . . . ," though some stones are placed at sites of former employment, education, or political opposition, and the text is altered accordingly: "Here worked . . . ," "Here studied . . . ," or "Here resisted . . ." Their creators called them *Baldosas por la memoria,* or *Tiles of Remembrance.* Like the *Stolpersteine* and the other decentralized monuments that predate them, the *Tiles of Remembrance* originate out of grassroots community organization, intervene in quotidian spaces, and invite passersby to reckon with the history of mass death. Their numbers have continued to grow.[32]

The momentum of Demnig's enterprise continues to carry it further afield. In 2014, its influence appeared in Moscow in a project led by the international human rights organization Memorial. On December 10—International Human Rights Day—Memorial installed the first mini-monument of its project *Last Address* (Последний адрес), which commemorates victims murdered by the Stalin regime during the Great Terror in the late 1930s. Following Stalin's death, the state rehabilitated many of those murdered by the NKVD—a mass of victims numbering somewhere between 680,000 and 1.2 million. Although Russia holds an annual day of remembrance for victims of political repression (October 30) and has honored them with a general monument—the Solovetsky Stone in Moscow—to date, no national memorial exists for Stalin's purge victims. And if Memorial itself is any indication, opportunities for grassroots dialogue about government repression do not exactly receive a warm welcome in Russia. In recent years, the Putin administration has turned to intimidation tactics to muzzle Memorial.[33] This climate makes it all the more surprising, then, that the initiative has already received over 1,500 applications requesting that plaques naming a single victim of Soviet repression be installed on the façade of the building where the victim once lived. The plaques mobilize the same language as the *Stolpersteine,* beginning "Here lived . . ." and listing the life data of each victim. Their popularity is also surprising given that interested citizens must fund the plaque's creation themselves, the equivalent of roughly $80, and first obtain approval from the building's residents, a process that initiates a dialogue within the community about the history of government repression. The project's organizer, Sergey Parkhomenko, has spoken openly about the influence of the *Stolpersteine* on his own decentralized mini-monument effort. After an encounter with a collection of stones in Frankfurt in 2013, Parkhomenko decided that Russians should engage their history in the same way. Rather than despairing of the past, "the most important thing," he claimed, was for Russians "to act."[34]

The German *Stumbling Stones,* the Viennese *Stones of Remembrance,* the Argentine *Tiles of Remembrance,* and the Russian *Last Address* projects all rely on a modest use of text to bracket a life's absence from society and to invite passersby to participate in mnemonic work. In all but the Russian project, the involvement of the spectator begins with a short bow downward in order to read that text, an inadvertent act of reverence, but one certainly not lost on their creators.[35] Although their textual similarities clearly place these projects under the same umbrella, their textuality is not their pioneering feature. Similar individualized plaques have been a staple of memory landscapes for centuries. More important is their agenda of transgressive, grassroots, networked decentralization. These projects have given average citizens—sometimes even nonnationals—principal agency in the memorial process.

Spatial interventionism also readied fertile ground for a range of sustainable utopian art projects less explicitly reminiscent of the *Stolpersteine.* One Holocaust monument has quite literal roots that date to January 1943 on the Jewish holiday of Tu Bishvat, the New Year of the Trees. Irma Lauscher, a prisoner of the Theresienstadt concentration camp in what is today the Czech

Republic, persuaded a guard to smuggle a tiny sapling into the camp. The camp's Jewish children celebrated the holiday by planting the little red maple and kept it alive by sharing their meager water rations. Unlike the tree, most of these children did not live to see the war's end. Among the camp's survivors, however, was Lauscher herself, who informed Czech authorities about the tree after liberation. By then five feet tall, the tree was uprooted and replanted near the camp's former crematorium as a memorial to those who perished there.[36] Before her death in 1985, Lauscher requested of her friend Mark Talisman—then vice chair of the US Holocaust Memorial Council—that seeds from the tree be planted in memory of the children lost to Nazi inhumanity. Talisman agreed and annually sends seeds to people around the world to plant in their communities. As the story of the tree spread, far-flung communities took an interest in planting their own Tree of Life, as it was called. They began, often without sanction, to collect seeds and take cuttings from the original tree and to transplant them globally. Today, estimates put the progeny of the Theresienstadt tree at around six hundred, with roots in Jerusalem, central and southern England, Washington, DC, Philadelphia, San Francisco, northern Illinois, and Cincinnati, to name just a few.[37] Catastrophic flooding in 2002 unfortunately damaged the original tree's root system, and it died not long afterward.[38] The fate of the original Tree of Life, however, vitalized the larger memorial effort, a metaphor for the way the work of commemorating genocide passes from one generation to the next. The tree's work is connective and dialogic, a transgenerational, transnational, living monument.

The global affinity for this kind of grassroots, networked commemorative work was displayed prominently in 2013 in a brief but massive installation in Washington, DC. For three days, 1,018,260 bone-shaped sculptures covered the National Mall. Appropriately titled *One Million Bones,* the installation commemorated the lives lost in mass atrocities in places like Sudan, South Sudan, Democratic Republic of the Congo, Burma, Syria, and Somalia. Though temporary, the monument involved an extensive international collaborative effort. Each of the bones had been handmade by more than 150,000 participants from all fifty US states and thirty-one countries. Moreover, each bone was installed individually by thousands of volunteers from around the United States. The Art of Revolution, the artist group behind *One Million Bones,* described the installation as a collaborative site honoring both victims and survivors. Its organizers sought to offer a visual representation of the extensive global network invested in fighting genocide. Their claim to "[use] art to transform public opinion" and to "[inspire] creative action towards social change" clearly echoed the imperatives to which Joseph Beuys first gave voice half a century prior.[39]

Few other examples better demonstrate the magnetism of this form of commemoration, however, than the recent emergence of spatial interventionist monuments on the model of the *Stolpersteine* in the United States, which has long displayed an allergy to commemorating the injustice of slavery. In the wake of a series of highly publicized incidents of police violence against Black Americans and the election of Donald Trump to the presidency, several groups of American activists independently initiated their own decentralized grassroots monuments to slavery. The Vermont-based activist and philanthropist Paul Growald—a member by marriage of the Rockefeller family—launched the *Stopping Stones.* With explicit reference to Demnig's work, Growald has insisted on the urgent need for Americans to confront the history of dehumanization not as a distant phenomenon but as present in their local communities. And Growald has no interest in this project remaining provincial. His organization is currently developing an interactive online database for the mini-monuments that, if other projects are any indication, may help fuel international interest.[40] Lest one be inclined to dismiss such an effort as a burden for the American South, it is worth highlighting that Growald's project focuses on the history of slavery largely in northern states. The *Witness Stones,* which emerged concurrently with Growald's effort and also point to the *Stumbling Stones* as inspiration, commemorate the history of slavery in Connecticut.[41] An article in the *Washington Post* suggested that such projects may unlock the door to a new, productive confrontation with prejudice and bigotry in the United States.[42]

If American civil rights lawyer and MacArthur "Genius Grant" winner Bryan Stevenson gets his way, Americans throughout the United States will increasingly encounter such monuments to racial injustice more often and closer to home. On 26 April 2018, after years of planning, his nonprofit organization Equal Justice Initiative (EJI) inaugurated a national monument to commemorate lynching and, more generally, the violence committed against Black people in the United States. With a large forum, it honors the Black victims of the more than 4,400 lynchings that took place between 1877 and

1950. That square structure, located on a hill overlooking Montgomery, Alabama, houses eight hundred suspended columns, one for each of the counties in which EJI has documented lynchings. The columns bear the names of those 4,400 victims. At first glance, EJI's *Monument to Peace and Justice* resembles a more conventional national memorial. Two features, however, give the project both a broader reach and a more critical function. Surrounding the monument is a field of eight hundred duplicate columns. EJI has invited the respective counties to claim their twin monument and erect it at home. "Over time," EJI notes, "the national memorial will serve as a report on which parts of the country have confronted the truth of this terror and which have not."[43] A companion website, "Lynching in America," makes use of virtual space to share interactive maps, testimonies, and opportunities for further political engagement with the issue of racial injustice in the United States.[44] In a nation struggling awkwardly to find an effective way to address ongoing problems of racial injustice and inequality with deep historical roots, such grassroots commemorative forms with broad national and even international participation could show a way forward.

Perhaps the greatest indicator of the success of this transnational restive mnemonics lies in its uptake by governments and nongovernmental organizations. Between 2002 and 2006, for example, the city of Berlin immortalized the footprint of the Berlin Wall in the *Berlin Wall Trail* (*Mauerweg*). This monument to the division of Germany runs the entire ninety-six miles along which the Wall once stood. Where the city has slowly begun to recolonize the border's no-man's-land, the *Berlin Wall Trail* ensures that the city's inhabitants and visitors will continue to encounter traces of this Cold War history in their daily lives.[45] Similarly, a massive undertaking called the European Green Belt has brought together 150 governmental and nongovernmental organizations representing twenty-two countries to commemorate the Iron Curtain. The intra-European border created a long environmental scar where natural landscapes were eliminated to make way for artificial ones, with death strips, guard towers, and checkpoints.[46] In the same year that work began on the *Berlin Wall Trail,* these groups started to turn the more than 7,750-mile-long threshold between East and West into a nature preserve that runs from the Russian-Norwegian border in the Arctic Circle to the Turkish-Bulgarian border at the Black Sea. It operates as a "living memorial landscape" that marks the ecological impact of the Cold War.[47]

States and NGOs, in other words, have co-opted decentralized grassroots commemorative forms for use from above. Many have remained mum on the inspiration for this stylistic shift. Whether or not they consciously imitated alternative memorials, however, seems immaterial. More important is their apparent willingness to amend their respective memory landscapes in ways that imitate designs and agendas produced from below, rather than the other way around. The kind of commemorative act that spatial interventionist art demands does not take place as an exceptional, state-sponsored production. It operates as a popular act that we might understand, somewhat in the manner of Ernest Renan, as a post-nationalist "daily plebiscite"—a plebiscite that constitutes not a nation but a virtual, democratic, commemorative network. What was once a utopian commemorative project of a small set of artists has become a global initiative beyond their control.

Utopian Heists by the Right

Utopian revisionism has not been solely the purview of a left-liberal milieu, however. In the late twentieth century, the political Right also found itself afflicted with a powerful sense of disillusionment, disempowerment, and resignation. And it has responded in ways that should, by now, look familiar.

The milieu that had supported the early postwar New Right, including the rise of the postwar neo-Nazi party, the National Democratic Party of Germany (NPD), largely disintegrated in the 1970s and early 1980s. It bled constituents to the New Social Movements and left behind only a fragmented subculture with a kaleidoscope of ideological commitments. Growing increasingly fearful of a decline of German culture, those who remained sought to vitalize a new right-wing political-cultural current.[48] It expressed an affinity for nationalism, national homogeneity directed against immigrants and ethnic minorities, and antisemitism. It opposed sexual liberation and equality for queer citizens and espoused a commitment to the structures of a traditional family. It rejected the broad social project of the welfare state and European integration. On account of liberalism's ostensible tendency to render modernity individual and subjective and to destroy a sense of community (*Gemeinschaft[sgefühl]*), this new New Right rejected the politics of liberalism.[49] The content of its program, in other words, stands worlds away from the sustainable utopias on the Left.

But I want us to tread carefully in the conclusions we draw from this distance. While the late twentieth-century far right has regurgitated the values of its early twentieth-century predecessors, its proponents have simultaneously called for a recalibration of their program, methods, and public face to suit a more modern, digitally oriented society.[50] The results bear a striking—arguably frightening—resemblance to the impulses we have observed among activists of the Left. I join those scholars who have heard the echoes between these figures and those of the Right in the late twentieth century.[51] But this is not a book about the Right; tracing the sustainable utopias that have developed on the political Right is a project for another scholar. This is, however, a book whose inquiry into the resilience of hope also demands that we not take that resilience for granted. That work would be incomplete without acknowledging that, much like the activists of the late twentieth-century left-liberal milieu, the far right in the same moment found a similar solution to its stagnation by directing its activism against the trappings of representative democracy. It identified a way to empower forceful masses of ordinary people via the practices of radical democratization and decentralization, and it considered its activism increasingly longitudinally via the logic of sustainability.

Direct democracy appeared on the lips of the New Right as early as the 1970s. One of its intellectual guiding lights, Henning Eichberg, described the rejuvenation of the politics of the Right as hinging on efforts "to re-politicize the grassroots [*Basis*]" via a kind of "revolutionary democracy from below."[52] The New Right's commitment to the German *Volk* created a space in which it could prioritize the *Volk*'s right of self-determination (*Selbstbestimmungsrecht*) as a weapon against an "unduly powerful, centralized EU-bureaucracy."[53] In the 1980s, this affinity for the practices of direct democracy fueled efforts like the Citizens' Initiative for a Moratorium on Foreigners (*Bürgerinitiative Ausländerstopp*), which took aim at immigration and asylum policies using popular referenda.[54] And in 1992, one branch of the right-wing party the Republicans (*Republikaner*) argued that "plebiscite, referendum, and popular legislation [*Volksbegehren, Volksentscheid und Volksgesetzgebung*] at all levels" offered a path out of an oppressive oligarchical state toward one governed truly by the people.[55] A decade later, the NPD argued that plebiscitary democracy would "free German politics from the stranglehold of bloc parties and self-concerned interest groups."[56]

The breakout of the young far right political party Alternative for Germany (AfD) has elevated this rhetoric. The AfD has famously repurposed the slogan from the East German protests against the Berlin Wall and German division in 1989, "We are the people [*Wir sind das Volk*]," to campaign on the promise of restoring popular sovereignty.[57] Its 2016 party program emphasized that the strengthening of the European Union had rendered "a foundation of our state, an inviolable popular sovereignty, a mere fiction." Only when the *Volk* is enabled to make decisions about its state via direct democracy will the party find itself in a position to reintegrate into Germany's democratic system.[58] This *Volk*, however, hardly stands for a universalist, pluralist claim for equality. Instead, political theorist Jan-Werner Müller has argued, AfD actually means "We—and only we—represent the true people [*das wahre Volk*]."[59] Radical direct democracy with an exclusionary twist has found other disciples as well. A leader of the political-cultural youth opposition movement, the Identitarians—named for its focus on safeguarding its members' identity as Europeans—has argued that the group "adamantly [believes] that the *Volk* has the right not to co-determination but rather to full and complete self-determination. Direct democracy and popular referendums [*Volksabstimmungen*] are our ideals." Pointing an accusatory finger at representative democracy, the Identitarians argue that "the *Volk* can decide things a thousand times better than your ivory tower [*weltfremden*] parliamentarians."[60]

As with the sustainable utopians of the left, the far right has also sought to bolster the practices of direct democracy by expanding the range of spaces in which those practices are carried out. In 1988, one pivotal New Right intellectual, Karlheinz Weißmann, demanded that the Right get with the times by finding ways to dominate extra-political space. It lacked "street theater [*Straßentheater*]," he chided, "conservative songwriters, national bookstores, and the forest of brochures and leaflets used by the Left and alternative scene." These were tools that would offer access to a wider base and as such, Weißmann thought, could unleash "a cultural 'grassroots revolution [*Graswurzelrevolution*]' that would buttress a 'conservative movement from below.'"[61] In the years since Weißmann's assessment, the digital revolution dramatically expanded potential sites of political intervention. Newer venues like YouTube, Facebook, Instagram, and TikTok have allowed the far right to engage massive audiences via "pre-political or unpolitical spaces."[62] These new digital tools not only allow them to tailor their work to local communities.[63] They also offer an avenue by which activists can skirt the control exercised over more conventional outlets for public discourse.[64]

One lingering question is, of course, how long the new New Right's momentum will last. Its proponents have weighed this question via an abstract (admittedly stunted) interest in developing a more sustainable politics. Drawing on the theoretical scholarship of the early twentieth century's Conservative Revolution, the New Right has argued that to be conservative is "to create things that are worth preserving."[65] Weißmann, though, might have formulated this statement differently, replacing "things" (or ideas) with behaviors. "Metapolitical strategies," he argued, "only make sense as part of a larger political strategy," namely one that addresses "questions of practicality [*Machbarkeitsfragen*]." Metapolitics, he suggested, are urgently tied to "political praxis and its bearers."[66] The Identitarians have largely agreed. They chastise older activists and politicians on the right for always "waiting . . . for Day X, which will offer the sole opportunity for altering political power structures."[67] In contrast, they argue that their movement is one "of doing [*Tat*], not of waiting. One of action, not of reaction."[68] But both a successful metapolitics and a successful political praxis require patience to ensure their durability over time. "Metapolitics is a laborious thing," Weißmann warned. "It requires prolonged timelines [*gedehnte Fristen*] and . . . patience. Whoever thinks it can be forced, . . . whoever believes that everything depends on our words and not on preparation and deep breaths should stay far away."[69]

The far right activist Götz Kubitschek helped connect the dots between action in the present and the durability of its message. Cribbing from the small far left movement of the 1960s, Subversive Aktion, Kubitschek argued that only provocations could effect meaningful change in an ossified society.[70] He advocated what historian Volker Weiß has called "microrevolts," a series of small-scale actions designed to irritate those who witness them and to make it difficult not to react.[71] Echoing an investment of the spatial interventionists, Kubitschek celebrated the ability of such actions "to leave behind a trace [*Spur*]." Their value, he argued, lies in their ability to creep into the minds of their opponents. Not only do they irritate; they also leave no indication when the irritation will strike again. Such microrevolts "unsettle their targets sustainably [*nachhaltig*]" by creating a durable intervention in public consciousness.[72] This durability becomes a boon to the work of the far right, insofar as its proponents have committed themselves not to "short-term activism" but rather to "the long-term pursuit of their goal" and, in turn, "long-term success."[73] As the young leader of the Austrian Identitarians Markus Willinger has argued, their politics are "not for weeks or months, but for years and decades."[74] The logic of sustainability, in other words, has proved infectious across the political spectrum.

The Right's affinities for sustainable utopianism demonstrate the flexibility of this concept. Though its *content* differs greatly from the subjects of this book, activists on the Right have underscored that its *methods* can be easily exported to the other side of the political spectrum. Programs on the Right generally appear more capacious and more diffuse than those on the Left. Through their use of the practices of radical democratization and decentralization and the application of the logic of sustainability in pursuit of a superlative future, however, the New Right has made clear that these practices cannot be claimed solely as the purview of the Left.

Experimentation on the Right with this new kind of radical optimism demands far more than I can offer here, namely its own genealogy, one that can take into account more fully both the conceptual and practical burdens National Socialism left in its wake for those on the far right intent on realizing a vision for an ideal Germany. Still, no study of late twentieth-century utopian revisionism can ignore that left-wing activists share some essential elements of their ideological toolbox with activists of the Right.

The blossoming of the twenty-first-century far right notwithstanding, many of the sustainable utopias put forth in the late twentieth and early twenty-first century have, in the end, proven not so sustainable. The reasons for these failures, however, have tended not to lay in the ambitions of the programs themselves. They have faltered on account of thorny interpersonal politics. They have faltered after misjudging popular interest. They have faltered because the administration of utopias, even modest ones, carries immense challenges. Why, then, have the spatial interventionists flourished where the Berlin *Geschichtswerkstatt* and the Greens tended to struggle? One answer lies in the function of art. In a 1989 interview, Frankfurt School member Leo Löwenthal reflected on the manner in which art serves optimism. Art, he argued, "often has utopian elements in the sense that it depicts a semblance of a world . . . cured of its ailments." Of course, Löwenthal continued, art "knows fully that it is only a semblance." But this realization need not throw the beholder into despair. It "does not mean that the semblance will not be realized someday, somewhere; such is utopian hope."[75] Looking in the same direction as Löwenthal, one might understand the aesthetic medium of the spatial interventionists simply to have been more functionally aligned with the sustainable utopian project than the media of historical or political practice. Perhaps, however, one might still hold out hope for hope. Perhaps the strewn bits that remain of the sustainable utopian projects of the other grassroots democratic organizations might not spell their demise entirely. Writing of the melodramatic posthistorians in 1989, Lutz Niethammer asked how one battles despair. Perhaps, he wrote, "all he or she can do is try to gather together some little stones, without knowing whether they form part of a mosaic, or whether they will eventually appear as a mere scree devoid of form and plan."[76] Perhaps in his desire to admonish his hasty colleagues, however, Niethammer missed a key point, namely that the leaving behind of what he describes as a "strewn legacy" has a beneficial side. This legacy does not eliminate hope but rather disperses it to be picked up and carried by ordinary people who possess both the freedom and the responsibility to put it to use.

The ongoing appeal of the practices of sustainable utopianism, despite their failures, underscores the significance of this paradigm shift in the history of utopian thought. It emphasizes the relatively widespread commitment activists have continued to demonstrate toward dreaming big dreams, even when scholars and political figures have tried mightily to cut those dreams down to size. Its service to the ideals of peace, equity, and human rights, on one hand, and ethnic nationalism and other politics of exclusion, on the other, suggests that one should be neither too pessimistic nor too sanguine about the modern fate of utopian thought and practice.

Notes

Introduction

1. The 1983 coalition agreement between the Christian Democratic Union and the Free Democrats declared that Germany "is not a land of immigration. Thus, it must seize all measures acceptable on humanitarian grounds to prevent the influx of foreigners." See "Ergebnis der Koalitionsgespräche," *CDU-Extra*, October 1, 1982, 7. See also Andrea Dernbach, "'Wir sind kein Einwanderungsland,'" *Der Tagesspiegel*, December 7, 2006.

2. AfD Baden-Württemberg, "AfD Prof. Dr. Jörg Meuthen Videobotschaft 1 / 2016," YouTube video, January 20, 2016, www.youtube.com/watch?v=foBYtG3_roo.

3. Emily Schultheis, "Germany Is Testing the Limits of Democracy," *Atlantic*, February 25, 2019.

4. Jon Henley, "Merkel's Long Goodbye Will Be Severe Test for Troubled Continent," *Guardian*, October 29, 2018.

5. Michael Wildt, "Droht Deutschland ein neues 1933?" *Die Zeit*, September 8, 2018.

6. Loveday Morris, "Germany's Greens Look to Be Kingmakers in a Post-Merkel Era," *Washington Post*, March 15, 2021; Michael Birnbaum, Griff Witte, and James McAuley, "European Greens Surge as Voters Abandon Old Parties over Climate," *Washington Post*, May 27, 2019.

7. See, for example, "Alle reden vom Klimaschutz," *tagesschau.de*, May 27, 2019, www.tagesschau.de/inland/eu-wahl-reaktionen-101.html; Jon Henley, "European Elections: Triumphant Greens Demand More Radical Climate Action," *Guardian*, May 27, 2019; "Grüne: Europawahl Signal für mehr Klimaschutz," *Süddeutsche Zeitung*, May 26, 2019.

8. Ann-Katrin Müller, "AfD setzt auf Zweifel am Klimawandel," *Spiegel Online*, April 27, 2019, www.spiegel.de/politik/deutschland/afd-setzt-auf-zweifel-am-klimawandel-im-wahlkampf-a-1264532.html.

9. Susan Buck-Morss, *Dreamworld and Catastrophe: The Passing of Mass Utopia in East and West* (Cambridge, MA: MIT Press, 2000), ix.

10. Buck-Morss, *Dreamworld*, ix–xi.

11. Eric J. Hobsbawm, *The Age of Extremes: A History of the World, 1914–1991* (New York: Pantheon Books, 1994); Mary Nolan, "Gender and Utopian Visions in a Post-Utopian Era: Americanism, Human Rights, Market Fundamentalism," *Central European History* 44, no. 1 (2011): 13–36; Joachim C. Fest, *Der zerstörte Traum: Vom Ende des utopischen Zeitalters* (Berlin: Siedler, 1991); Russell Jacoby, *The End of Utopia: Politics and Culture in an Age of Apathy* (New York: Basic Books, 1999); Russell Jacoby, "Karl Popper, Isaiah Berlin, and the Anti-Utopian Refugees," in *The Temptation of Hope: Utopian Thinking and Imagination from Thomas More to Ernst Bloch—and Beyond*, ed. Jost Hermand and Klaus L. Berghahn, 49–64 (Bielefeld: Aisthesis, 2011); William W. Hagen, "Master Narratives beyond Postmodernity: Germany's 'Separate Path' in Historiographical-Philosophical Light," *German Studies Review* 30, no. 1 (2007): 1–32; C. M. Hann, *Postsocialism: Ideals, Ideologies, and Practices in Eurasia* (New York: Routledge, 2002); Valerie Bunce, "The Political Economy of Postsocialism," *Slavic Review* 58, no. 4 (1999): 756–793; Michael Burawoy and Katherine Verdery, eds., *Uncertain Transition: Ethnographies of Change in the Postsocialist World* (Lanham: Rowman and Littlefield, 1999); Manduhai Buyandelgeriyn, "Post-Post Transition Theories: Walking on Multiple Paths," *Annual Review of Anthropology* 37 (October 2008): 235–250; Daniel Bell, *The End of Ideology: On the Exhaustion of Political Ideas in the Fifties* (Glencoe: Free Press, 1960); Lutz Niethammer and Dirk van Laak, *Posthistoire: Has History Come to an End?* (London: Verso, 1992); Lutz Niethammer and Bill Templer, "Afterthoughts on Posthistoire," *History and Memory* 1, no. 1 (April 1989): 27–53; Francis Fukuyama, *The End of History and the Last Man* (New York: Free Press, 1992).

12. Judith Shklar, *After Utopia: The Decline of Political Faith* (Princeton, NJ: Princeton University Press, 1957), 271.

13. H. Stuart Hughes, "The End of Political Ideology," *Measure* 2 (Spring 1951): 146–158. See also Seymour Martin Lipset, *Political Man: The Social Bases of Politics* (Garden City, NY: Doubleday, 1960); Raymond Aron, *The Opium of the Intellectuals* (Garden City: Doubleday, 1957).

14. Bell, *End of Ideology*, 393.

15. Samuel Moyn, *The Last Utopia: Human Rights in History* (Cambridge, MA: Belknap Press of Harvard University Press, 2010), 8.

16. Jacoby, *End of Utopia*, 7.

17. Fest, *Der zerstörte Traum*.

18. Fukuyama, *End of History*. See also Francis Fukuyama, "The End of History?" *National Interest* 16 (Summer 1989): 3–18; Francis Fukuyama, "Reply to My Critics," *National Interest* 18 (Winter 1989–90): 21–28.

19. Buck-Morss, *Dreamworld*, ix–x.

20. Moyn, *Last Utopia*, 9, 213–214.

21. György Lukács, *The Theory of the Novel: A Historico-Philosophical Essay on the Forms of Great Epic Literature* (Cambridge, MA: MIT Press, 1971), 112ff.

22. Jacoby, *End of Utopia*, xi–xii.

23. Niethammer and van Laak, *Posthistoire*, 149–151.

24. Lutz Niethammer, Veronika Settele, and Paul Nolte, "Oral History in der deutschen Zeitgeschichte," *Geschichte und Gesellschaft* 43, no. 1 (2017): 110–145, 114.

25. See C. Wright Mills, "Letter to the New Left," *New Left Review* 1, no. 5 (October 1960): 18–23; Donald Clark Hodges, "The End of 'The End of Ideology,'" *American Journal of Economics and Sociology* 26, no. 2 (1967): 135–146.

26. Norbert Frei, *1968: Jugendrevolte und globaler Protest* (Munich: Deutscher Taschenbuch, 2008), 31. Ernst Bloch differentiated between the abstract utopias of idealistic reformers and what he understood as the concrete utopias of Marxism. See Klaus L. Berghahn, "'Concrete Utopia' and 'Exact Fantasy': Utopian Thinking and Imagination in Ernst Bloch's *The Principle of Hope*," in *The Temptation of Hope: Utopian Thinking and Imagination from Thomas More to Ernst Bloch—and Beyond*, ed. Jost Hermand and Klaus L. Berghahn, 67–76 (Bielefeld: Aisthesis, 2011). See also Ernst Bloch, *The Principle of Hope* (Cambridge, MA: MIT Press, 1986), 1–20.

27. Gerd-Rainer Horn, *The Spirit of '68: Rebellion in Western Europe and North America, 1956–1976* (Oxford: Oxford University Press, 2007), 154–155.

28. Sabine Von Dirke, *All Power to the Imagination! The West German Counterculture from the Student Movement to the Greens* (Lincoln: University of Nebraska Press, 1997), 33. On subjectivity and the 1960s, see Richard W. McCormick, *Politics of the Self: Feminism and the Postmodern in West German Literature and Film* (Princeton, NJ: Princeton University Press, 1991).

29. Tony Judt, *Postwar: A History of Europe since 1945* (New York: Penguin Press, 2005), 397.

30. Frei, *1968*, 195.

31. Wini Breines, *Community and Organization in the New Left, 1962–1968: The Great Refusal* (New York: Praeger, 1982), 6.

32. On the work of 1960s activists in West Germany, see Nick Thomas, *Protest Movements in 1960s West Germany: A Social History of Dissent and Democracy* (Oxford: Berg, 2003); Martin Klimke, *The Other Alliance: Student Protest in West Germany and the United States in the Global Sixties* (Princeton, NJ: Princeton University Press, 2010); Quinn Slobodian, *Foreign Front: Third World Politics in Sixties West Germany* (Durham, NC: Duke University Press, 2012).

33. Horn, *Spirit of '68*, 206. On the Generation of 1968's tendency to think in Manichaean terms, with utopia as one of its poles, see Hans Kundnani, *Utopia or Auschwitz: Germany's 1968 Generation and the Holocaust* (London: Hurst, 2009).

34. Herbert Marcuse, "The End of Utopia," in *Marxism, Revolution and Utopia: Collected Papers of Herbert Marcuse,* vol. 6, ed. Douglas Kellner and Clayton Pierce, 249–263 (Hoboken, NJ: Taylor and Francis, 2014).

35. Wolfgang Kraushaar, *Achtundsechzig: Eine Bilanz* (Berlin: Propyläen, 2008), 264–265.

36. Marcuse, "End of Utopia," 249.

37. Karl Mannheim, *Ideology and Utopia: An Introduction to the Sociology of Knowledge,* trans. Edward Shils (New York: Harcourt, Brace, 1952), 173, 176–177. Emphasis in original.

38. Marcuse, "End of Utopia," 251.

39. Marcuse, "End of Utopia," 254.

40. Breines, *Community and Organization in the New Left,* xi.

41. "Anmerkung der Redaktion," *Kursbuch* 11 (1968): 170–171.

42. Kraushaar, *Achtundsechzig,* 122.

43. Kraushaar, *Achtundsechzig,* 122, 258. See Marion Gräfin Dönhoff, "Die Rebellion der Romantiker," *Die Zeit,* January 5, 1968, www.zeit.de/1968/01/die-rebellion-der-romantiker.

44. Martin Klimke and Joachim Scharloth, "Utopia in Practise: The Discovery of Performativity in Sixties' Protest, Arts and Sciences," *Historein* 9 (2009): 46–56, 53.

45. Timothy Scott Brown, *Sixties Europe* (Cambridge: Cambridge University Press, 2020), 4.

46. See, for example, J. M. Winter, *Dreams of Peace and Freedom: Utopian Moments in the Twentieth Century* (New Haven: Yale University Press, 2006); Frank Biess, *German Angst: Fear and Democracy in the Federal Republic of Germany* (Oxford: Oxford University Press, 2020); Mia Lee, *Utopia and Dissent in West Germany: The Resurgence of the Politics of Everyday Life in the Long 1960s* (London: Routledge, 2019); Vladimir Tismaneanu, "Introduction," in *Promises of 1968: Crisis, Illusion, and Utopia,* ed. Vladimir Tismaneanu (Budapest: Central European University Press, 2011); Paul Berman, *A Tale of Two Utopias: The Political Journey of the Generation of 1968* (New York: W. W. Norton, 1996).

47. On postwar economic growth, see Hobsbawm, *Age of Extremes.* On the significance of 1979, see Frank Bösch, *Zeitenwende 1979: Als die Welt von heute begann* (Munich: C. H. Beck, 2019). Sven Reichardt, *Authentizität und Gemeinschaft: Linksalternatives Leben in den siebziger und frühen achtziger Jahren* (Berlin: Suhrkamp, 2014). On 1960s activism, see Horn, *Spirit of '68;* Arthur Marwick, *The Sixties: Cultural Revolution in Britain, France, Italy, and the United States, c. 1958–c. 1974* (Oxford: Oxford University Press, 1998); Martin Klimke and Joachim Scharloth, eds., *1968 in Europe: A History of Protest and Activism, 1956–1977* (New York: Palgrave Macmillan, 2008). On terrorism, see Karrin Hanshew, *Terror and Democracy in West Germany* (Cambridge: Cambridge University Press, 2012). On consumption patterns, see Alexander Sedlmaier, *Consumption and Violence: Radical Protest in*

Cold-War West Germany (Ann Arbor: University of Michigan Press, 2014); Axel Schildt and Detlef Siegfried, *Between Marx and Coca-Cola: Youth Cultures in Changing European Societies, 1960–1980* (New York: Berghahn Books, 2006).

48. Brown, *Sixties Europe,* 12–14. See also Timothy Scott Brown, *West Germany and the Global Sixties: The Anti-Authoritarian Revolt, 1962–1978* (Cambridge: Cambridge University Press, 2013).

49. Karl R. Popper, *The Open Society and Its Enemies* (Princeton, NJ: Princeton University Press, 1966).

50. Pierre Bourdieu, *Acts of Resistance: Against the New Myths of Our Time* (Cambridge: Polity Press, 1998), 12.

51. Geoff Eley, *Forging Democracy: The History of the Left in Europe, 1850–2000* (Oxford: Oxford University Press, 2002), 420–421.

52. Sven Reichardt and Detlef Siegfried, "Das Alternative Milieu: Konturen einer Lebensform," in *Das Alternative Milieu: Antibürgerlicher Lebensstil und linke Politik in der Bundesrepublik Deutschland und Europa 1968–1983,* ed. Sven Reichardt and Detlef Siegfried (Göttingen: Wallstein, 2010), 16–18. See also Reichardt, *Authentizität und Gemeinschaft.*

53. Berman, *Tale of Two Utopias,* 18–20.

54. The German historian Lucian Hölscher has called these "utopias of space [*Raumutopien*]" and "utopias of time [*Zeitutopien*]." Lucian Hölscher, "Utopie," *Utopian Studies* 7, no. 2 (1996): 1–65.

55. Winter, *Dreams of Peace,* 205–209.

56. Erik Olin Wright, *Envisioning Real Utopias* (London: Verso, 2010), 5–6, 373. On the origins of the term "real utopia," see Wolfgang Abendroth, "Aufgaben einer deutschen Linken," *Gesammelte Schriften,* 3:580, originally published in Horst Krüger, ed., *Was ist heute links? Thesen und Theorien zu einer politischen Position* (Munich: P. List, 1963), 130–157. See also Ernst Bloch, *Tübinger Einleitung in die Philosophie I* (Frankfurt am Main: Suhrkamp, 1963), 80.

57. Dennis Soron, "Back to the Future: The Contemporary Left and the Politics of Utopia," *Labour / Le Travail* 47 (2001): 203–216, 212. See Daniel Singer, *Whose Millennium? Theirs or Ours?* (New York: Monthly Review Press, 1999), 236.

58. Soron, "Back to the Future," 215; Singer, *Whose Millennium?* 252. Singer may have drawn inspiration from John Rawls, who used the same language of "realistic utopia" in his *Law of Peoples.* See John Rawls, *The Law of Peoples, with "The Idea of Public Reason Revisited"* (Cambridge, MA: Harvard University Press, 1999), especially 7, 11–12.

59. Singer, *Whose Millennium?* 260–263.

60. Ashlie Lancaster, "Instantiating Critical Utopia," *Utopian Studies* 11, no. 1 (2000): 109–119.

61. Charles Price, Donald Nonini, and Erich Fox Tree, "Grounded Utopian Movements: Subjects of Neglect," *Anthropological Quarterly* 81, no. 1 (December 2008): 127–159, 128.

62. Geoff Eley, "Leaving the Borderlands . . . but for Where? 1968 and the New Registers of Political Feeling," keynote address, Social Movements after '68: Germany, Europe, and Beyond Conference, Center for European Studies, Rutgers University, New Brunswick, NJ, November 7, 2018, 8.

63. Quoted in David Pinder, "In Defence of Utopian Urbanism: Imagining Cities after the 'End of Utopia,'" *Geografiska Annaler. Series B, Human Geography* 84, no. 3 / 4 (January 2002): 229–241, 238. See Leonie Sandercock, *Towards Cosmopolis: Planning for Multicultural Cities* (Chichester: J. Wiley, 1998), 8. See also David Pinder, *Visions of the City: Utopianism, Power and Politics in Twentieth-Century Urbanism* (Edinburgh: Edinburgh University Press, 2005).

64. See Paul Warde, "The Invention of Sustainability," *Modern Intellectual History* 8, no. 1 (April 2011): 153–170; Joachim Radkau, *Nature and Power: A Global History of the Environment,* trans. Thomas Dunlap (New York and Washington, DC: Cambridge University Press and German Historical Institute, 2008), 86–152, 195–249; S. Ravi Rajan, *Modernizing Nature Forestry and Imperial Eco-Development 1800–1950* (Oxford: Oxford University Press, 2006), 21–54. On the twentieth-century concept of sustainability, see World Commission on Environment and Development, *Our Common Future* (Oxford: Oxford University Press, 1987).

65. World Commission on Environment and Development, *Report of the World Commission on Environment and Development: Our Common Future* (1987), http://www.un-documents.net/wced-ocf.htm, 17.

66. Andreas Wirsching, *Abschied vom Provisorium: Geschichte der Bundesrepublik Deutschland 1982–1990,* vol. 6 (Stuttgart: Deutsche Verlags-Anstalt, 2006), 393.

67. Jenny Wüstenberg, *Civil Society and Memory in Postwar Germany* (Cambridge: Cambridge University Press, 2017), 62.

68. See, for example, Matthias Zimmer, *Nationales Interesse und Staatsräson: Zur Deutschlandpolitik der Regierung Kohl, 1982–1989* (Paderborn: F. Schöningh, 1992); Hans-Peter Schwarz, *Helmut Kohl: Eine politische Biographie* (Munich: Deutsche Verlags-Anstalt, 2012); Reimut Zohlnhöfer, *Die Wirtschaftspolitik der Ära Kohl: Eine Analyse der Schlüsselentscheidungen in den Politikfeldern Finanzen, Arbeit und Entstaatlichung, 1982–1998* (Leverkusen: Leske und Budrich, 2001); Göttrik Wewer, ed., *Bilanz der Ära Kohl. Christlich-liberale Politik in Deutschland 1982–1998: Ein Sonderband der Zeitschrift Gegenwartskunde* (Opladen: Leske und Budrich, 1998); Rupert Seuthe, *Geistig-moralische Wende? Der politische Umgang mit der NS-Vergangenheit in der Ära Kohl am Beispiel von Gedenktagen, Museums- und Denkmalprojekten* (Frankfurt am Main: P. Lang, 2001); Sabine Moller, *Die Entkonkretisierung der NS-Herrschaft in der Ära Kohl: Die Neue Wache. Das Denkmal für die ermordeten Juden Europas. Das Haus der Geschichte der Bundesrepublik Deutschland* (Hannover: Offizin, 1998); Karl-Rudolf Korte, *Deutschlandpolitik in Helmut Kohls Kanzlerschaft: Regierungsstil und Entscheid-*

ungen 1982–1989 (Stuttgart: Deutsche Verlags-Anstalt, 1988); Klaus Dreher, *Helmut Kohl: Leben mit Macht* (Stuttgart: Deutsche Verlags-Anstalt, 1998); Reinhard Appel, ed., *Helmut Kohl im Spiegel seiner Macht* (Bonn: Bouvier, 1990); Werner Süss, ed., *Die Bundesrepublik in den achtziger Jahren: Innenpolitik, politische Kultur, Aussenpolitik* (Opladen: Leske und Budrich, 1991).

69. Deutscher Bundestag, Plenarprotokoll 9 / 121, Stenographischer Bericht, 121. Sitzung, October 13, 1982, 7218.

70. Jeffrey K. Olick, *The Sins of the Fathers: Germany, Memory, Method* (Chicago: University of Chicago Press, 2016), 335. See also Wüstenberg, *Civil Society and Memory;* Edgar Wolfrum, *Geschichtspolitik in der Bundesrepublik Deutschland. Der Weg zur bundesrepublikanischen Erinnerung 1948–1990* (Darmstadt: Wissenschaftliche Buchgesellschaft, 1999), 316–345; Jan-Holger Kirsch, "'Hier geht es um den Kern unseres Selbstverständnisses als Nation.' Helmut Kohl und die Genese des Holocaust-Gedenkens als bundesdeutscher Staatsräson," *Potsdamer Bulletin für zeithistorische Studien* 43 / 44 (2008): 40–48; Moller, *Die Entkonkretisierung der NS-Herrschaft in der Ära Kohl.*

71. Andreas Wirsching refers to the years 1982–1990 as the "departure from the provisional." See Wirsching, *Abschied vom Provisorium.* For other periodizations, see Jennifer L. Allen, "Against the 1989–1990 Ending Myth," *Central European History* 52, no. 1 (March 2019): 131.

72. Jacob S. Eder, *Holocaust Angst: The Federal Republic of Germany and American Holocaust Memory since the 1970s* (New York: Oxford University Press, 2016), 84, 117–118.

73. Deutscher Bundestag, Plenarprotokoll 9 / 121, Stenographischer Bericht, 121. Sitzung, October 13, 1982, 7218, 7227.

74. Wolfrum, *Geschichtspolitik in der Bundesrepublik Deutschland,* 338.

75. Jan-Werner Müller, *Another Country: German Intellectuals, Unification and National Identity* (New Haven: Yale University Press, 2000), 8.

76. Helmut Schelsky, *Die skeptische Generation. Eine Soziologie der deutsche Jugend* (Düsseldorf: Eugen Diedrichs, 1957).

77. A. Dirk Moses, *German Intellectuals and the Nazi Past* (Cambridge: Cambridge University Press, 2007), esp. 55–73.

78. On the origins of this expression, see Christian Wicke, *Helmut Kohl's Quest for Normality: His Representation of the German Nation and Himself* (New York: Berghahn Books, 2015), 203n135.

79. Müller, *Another Country,* 16, 54–55.

80. Wirsching, *Abschied vom Provisorium,* 475. See also Olick, *Sins of the Fathers,* 328–329.

81. Deutscher Bundestag, Plenarprotokoll 9 / 121, Stenographischer Bericht, 121. Sitzung, October 13, 1982, 7227.

82. On the creation of and controversies surrounding the German Historical Museum in Berlin, see Christoph Stölzl and Rosmarie Beier-de-Haan, *Deutsches*

Historisches Museum: Ideen, Kontroversen, Perspektiven (Berlin: Propyläen, 1988).

83. BArch (Koblenz) N 1569/740, pag. 178–183, Bundesministerium für Raumordnung, Bauwesen und Städtebau, Pressemitteilung 54/88, June 10, 1988.

84. Eder, *Holocaust Angst,* 84, 117–118, 137–159. See also Katrin Pieper, *Die Musealisierung des Holocaust. Das Jüdische Museum Berlin und das U.S. Holocaust Memorial Museum in Washington D.C.: Ein Vergleich* (Cologne: Böhlau, 2006).

85. Charles S. Maier, *The Unmasterable Past: History, Holocaust, and German National Identity* (Cambridge, MA: Harvard University Press, 1988), 9–16. See also Geoffrey H. Hartman, ed., *Bitburg in Moral and Political Perspective* (Bloomington: Indiana University Press, 1986); Wolfrum, *Geschichtspolitik in der Bundesrepublik Deutschland,* 338–340.

86. Müller, *Another Country,* 59–63. Emphasis in original.

87. Maier, *Unmasterable Past.* See also Gerrit Dworok et al., "Holocaust Scholarship and Politics in the Public Sphere: Reexamining the Causes, Consequences, and Controversy of the *Historikerstreit* and the Goldhagen Debate," *Central European History* 50, no. 3 (2017): 375–403; James Knowlton and Truett Cates, trans., *Forever in the Shadow of Hitler?: Original Documents of the Historikerstreit, the Controversy Concerning the Singularity of the Holocaust* (Atlantic Highlands, NJ: Humanities Press, 1993).

88. Müller, *Another Country,* 60.

89. Christina Morina, *Legacies of Stalingrad: Remembering the Eastern Front in Germany since 1945* (Cambridge: Cambridge University Press, 2011), 232, 248n69. See also Hannes Heer and Klaus Naumann, eds., *Vernichtungskrieg: Verbrechen der Wehrmacht 1941–1944* (Hamburg: Hamburger Edition, 1995); Heribert Prantl, ed., *Wehrmachtsverbrechen: Eine deutsche Kontroverse* (Hamburg: Hoffmann und Campe, 1997); Hamburger Institut für Sozialforschung, ed., *Eine Ausstellung und ihre Folgen: Zur Rezeption der Ausstellung "Vernichtungskrieg: Verbrechen der Wehrmacht 1941 bis 1944"* (Hamburg: Hamburger Edition, 1999).

90. Daniel Jonah Goldhagen, *Hitler's Willing Executioners: Ordinary Germans and the Holocaust* (New York: Knopf, 1996).

91. Christopher R. Browning, *Ordinary Men: Reserve Police Battalion 101 and the Final Solution in Poland* (New York: HarperCollins, 1992).

92. Goldhagen, *Hitler's Willing Executioners,* 14.

93. See Julius H. Schoeps, ed., *Ein Volk von Mördern? Die Dokumentation zur Goldhagen-Kontroverse um die Rolle der Deutschen im Holocaust* (Hamburg: Hoffmann und Campe, 1996); Geoff Eley, ed., *The "Goldhagen Effect": History, Memory, Nazism—Facing the German Past* (Ann Arbor: University of Michigan Press, 2000); Norbert Frei, "Goldhagen, die Deutschen und die Historiker. Über die Repräsentation des Holocaust im Zeitalter der Visualisierung," in *Zeitgeschichte als Streitgeschichte: Grosse Kontroversen seit 1945,* ed. Martin Sabrow, Ralph Jessen, and Klaus Große Kracht, 138–151 (Munich: Beck, 2003); A. D. Moses,

"Structure and Agency in the Holocaust: Daniel J. Goldhagen and His Critics," *History and Theory* 37, no. 2 (1998): 194–219; Volker Ullrich, "Eine produktive Provokation. Die Rolle der Medien in der Goldhagen-Kontroverse," in *Zeitgeschichte als Streitgeschichte: Grosse Kontroversen seit 1945,* ed. Martin Sabrow, Ralph Jessen, and Klaus Große Kracht, 152–170 (Munich: Beck, 2003).

94. Frei, "Goldhagen, die Deutschen und die Historiker," 147.

95. Wolfrum, *Geschichtspolitik in der Bundesrepublik Deutschland,* 317.

96. Biess, *German Angst,* 292.

97. Reichardt, *Authentizität und Gemeinschaft,* 164–165.

98. Jürgen Habermas, "Die neue Unübersichtlichkeit. Die Krise des Wohlfahrtsstaates und die Erschöpfung utopischer Energien," *Merkur* 29 (1985): 1–14.

99. Wüstenberg, *Civil Society and Memory,* 62.

100. Uta G. Poiger, "Das Schöne und das Hässliche. Kosmetik, Feminismus und Punk in den siebziger und achtziger Jahren," in *Das Alternative Milieu: Antibürgerlicher Lebensstil und linke Politik in der Bundesrepublik Deutschland und Europa 1968–1983,* ed. Sven Reichardt and Detlef Siegfried (Göttingen: Wallstein, 2010), 231.

101. See Roger Fletcher, "Recent Developments in West German Historiography: The Bielefeld School and Its Critics," *German Studies Review* 7, no. 3 (October 1984): 451–480; Hans Medick, "'Missionaries in the Rowboat?' Ethnological Ways of Knowing as a Challenge to Social History," in *The History of Everyday Life: Reconstructing Historical Experiences and Ways of Life,* ed. Alf Lüdtke, 41–71 (Princeton, NJ: Princeton University Press, 1995).

102. E. Gene Frankland, Paul Lucardie, and Benoît Rihoux, eds., *Green Parties in Transition: The End of Grass-Roots Democracy?* (Burlington, VT: Ashgate, 2008); Margit Mayer and John Ely, *The German Greens: Paradox between Movement and Party* (Philadelphia: Temple University Press, 1998); E. Gene Frankland and Donald Schoonmaker, *Between Protest and Power: The Green Party in Germany* (Boulder, CO: Westview Press, 1992). On the iron law of oligarchy, see Robert Michels, *Political Parties: A Sociological Study of the Oligarchical Tendencies of Modern Democracy* (New York: Dover, 1959).

103. See, for example, Andrei S. Markovits and Philip S. Gorski, *The German Left: Red, Green and Beyond* (New York: Oxford University Press, 1993); E. Gene Frankland, "The Greening of the German Left," *Review of Politics* 56, no. 4 (October 1994): 813–815; John Ely, "Green Politics and the Transformation of the Left in Germany," *New German Critique* 72 (October 1997): 177–192.

104. Von Dirke, *All Power to the Imagination!*

105. On museum access see Petra Hornig, *Kunst im Museum und Kunst im öffentlichen Raum* (Wiesbaden: Springer Fachmedien, 2011); Florian Matzner, ed., *Public Art: Kunst im öffentlichen Raum* (Ostfildern-Ruit: Hatje Cantz, 2001); Volker Plagemann and Babette Peters, eds., *Kunst im öffentlichen Raum: Anstösse der 80er Jahre* (Cologne: DuMont, 1989); Henriette Steube, *Kunst in der Stadt*

1945 bis 1995: Eine Dokumentation zur Kunst im öffentlichen Raum in Hildesheim (Hildesheim: Gerstenberg, 1996); Walter Grasskamp, *Unerwünschte Monumente: Moderne Kunst im Stadtraum* (Munich: Schreiber, 1989); Walter Grasskamp, *Die unbewältigte Moderne: Kunst und Öffentlichkeit* (Munich: C. H. Beck, 1989). On memory debates, see Corinna Tomberger, *Das Gegendenkmal: Avantgardekunst, Geschichtspolitik und Geschlecht in der bundesdeutschen Erinnerungskultur* (Bielefeld: Transcript, 2007); Christoph Heinrich, *Strategien des Erinnerns: Der veränderte Denkmalbegriff in der Kunst der achtziger Jahre* (Munich: S. Schreiber, 1993); Detlef Hoffmann, "Erinnerungsarbeit der '*zweiten und dritten*' Generation und 'Spurensuche' in der zeitgenössischen Kunst," *Kritische Berichte* 2 (1988): 31–46.

1. The Rise of the Spatial Interventionists

1. See Hal Foster et al., *Art since 1900: Modernism, Antimodernism, Postmodernism* (New York: Thames and Hudson, 2004); Götz Adriani et al., *Joseph Beuys: Life and Works,* trans. Patricia Lech (Woodbury, NY: Barron's Educational Series, 1979).

2. As a darling of the avant-garde art world and committed proponent of democracy after the war, Beuys's early National Socialist inclinations tend to fade into the background of both scholarly and popular representations of his life. One controversial biography, however, has attempted to reassess these representations by foregrounding Beuys's continued flirtations with less progressive agendas after the war. See Hans Peter Riegel, *Beuys: Die Biographie* (Berlin: Aufbau, 2013).

3. See, for example, Omnibus für direkte Demokratie in Deutschland, *Projekte Erweiterte Kunst: Von Beuys aus* (Wangen: FIU, 1993).

4. Joseph Beuys and Harald Kimpel, eds., *1982–2002: 20 Jahre Joseph Beuys: "7000 Eichen—Stadtverwaldung statt Stadtverwaltung"* (Kassel: Kulturamt, 2003), 16.

5. Martin Warnke, "Kunst unter Verweigerungspflicht," in *Skupturenboulevard Kurfürstendamm Tauentzien, Kunst im öffentlichen Raum,* ed. Barbara Straka (Berlin: Neuer Berliner Kunstverein, 1987), 25. See also Beate Mielsch, "Die historischen Hintergründe der 'Kunst-am-Bau'-Regelungen," in *Kunst im öffentlichen Raum: Anstösse der 80er Jahre,* ed. Volker Plagemann et al. (Cologne: DuMont, 1989), 39–43; Claudia Büttner et al., eds., *Geschichte der Kunst am Bau in Deutschland* (Berlin: Bundesministerium für Verkehr, Bau und Stadtentwicklung, 2011); Sunke Herlyn et al., eds., *Kunst im Stadtbild: Von Kunst am Bau zu Kunst im öffentlichen Raum* (Bremen: Hauschild, 1976); Elisabeth Dühr, *Kunst am Bau/Kunst im öffentlichen Raum: Geschichte und Entwicklung öffentlicher Kunst im Spannungsfeld von Architektur, Städtebau und Kulturpolitik in der Bundesrepublik Deutschland* (Frankfurt am Main: Lang, 1991); Klaus Honnef, "Kunstwerke

im öffentlichen Raum repräsentativer Demokratien: 'Umwelt-Akzente' in Monschau, 1970," in *Kunst im öffentlichen Raum: Anstösse der 80er Jahre*, ed. Volker Plagemann and Babette Peters (Cologne: DuMont, 1989).

6. See Gerd Schwerhoff, "Spaces, Places, and the Historians: A Comment from a German Perspective," *History and Theory* 52, no. 3 (2013): 420–432; Doris Bachmann-Medick, "Der Spatial Turn als Cultural Turn," in *"Cultural Turns": Neuorientierungen in den Kulturwissenschaften* (Reinbek bei Hamburg: Rowohlt, 2011), 284–328; Karl Schlögel, *Im Raume lesen wir die Zeit: Über Zivilisationsgeschichte und Geopolitik* (Munich: Hanser, 2003), 19–24. On the problematic of territoriality, see Charles S. Maier, *Once within Borders: Territories of Power, Wealth, and Belonging since 1500* (Cambridge, MA: Belknap Press of Harvard University Press, 2016). On the popularity of *Kulturraumforschung*, see Stephan Güntzel, ed., *Topologie: Zur Raumbeschreibung in den Kultur- und Medienwissenschaften* (Bielefeld: Transcript, 2007).

7. Novalis wrote that "each person should be an artist. Everything can become beautiful art." Quoted in Herbert Uerlings, ed., *Novalis: Poesie und Poetik* (Tübingen: Niemeyer, 2004), 35.

8. BArch (Koblenz) N 1569/773-2, pag. 263–265, Die Grünen im Bundestag, Claudia Siede and Karlheinz Koinegg, "Jeder Mensch ein Künstler," July 1990.

9. Martin Jay, "'The Aesthetic Ideology' as Ideology; Or, What Does It Mean to Aestheticize Politics?," *Cultural Critique* 21 (April 1992): 41–61.

10. Tautologically, however, Beuys also claimed that the process of developing social consciousness was "in fact already a sculptural [*plastischer*] event." BArch (Koblenz) N 1569/773-2, pag. 263–265, Siede and Koinegg, "Jeder Mensch ein Künstler."

11. On West Germany's encounters with terrorism, see Karin Hanshew, *Terror and Democracy in West Germany* (Cambridge: Cambridge University Press, 2012).

12. Joseph Beuys and Clara Bodenmann-Ritter, *Jeder Mensch ein Künstler: Gespräche auf der Documenta 5/1972* (Frankfurt am Main: Ullstein, 1975).

13. Petra Hornig, *Kunst im Museum und Kunst im öffentlichen Raum* (Wiesbaden: Springer Fachmedien, 2011). See also Albrecht Göschel, "Identitäts- und Imagepolitik: Revision kulturpolitischer Reformen," *Jahrbuch für Kulturpolitik* 6 (2006): 235–243; Dieter Sauberzweig, *Urbanität und Kultur: Erfahrungen beim Deutschen Städtetag und in Berlin* (Essen: Klartext, 2005), 20ff.; Hilmar Hoffmann, "Kultur für alle. Als Prognose," *Kultur Politik Diskurs* 3 (2000): 15–22.

14. Hornig, *Kunst im Museum*, 16–18. On a pivotal moment in the effort to use *Kultur* to make the German city more humane, see Deutscher Städtetag, *Wege zur menschlichen Stadt* (Stuttgart: W. Kohlhammer, 1973).

15. On the development of public art, see Claudia Büttner, *Art Goes Public: Von der Gruppenausstellung im Freien zum Projekt im nicht-institutionellen Raum* (Munich: S. Schreiber, 1997); W. J. T. Mitchell, *Art and the Public Sphere*

(Chicago: University of Chicago Press, 1992); Grant Kester, "Aesthetic Evangelists: Conversion and Empowerment in Contemporary Community Art," *Afterimage* 22, no. 6 (January 1995): 5–11; Rosalyn Deutsche, *Evictions: Art and Spatial Politics* (Cambridge, MA: MIT Press, 1996); Stephan Schmidt-Wulffen, "On the 'Publicness' of Public Art and the Limits of the Possible," in *Public Art: Kunst im öffentlichen Raum,* ed. Florian Matzner (Ostfildern-Ruit: Hatje Cantz, 2001), 649.

16. Miwon Kwon, "One Place after Another: Notes on Site Specificity," *October* 80 (April 1997): 85. See also Douglas Crimp, *On the Museum's Ruins* (Cambridge, MA: MIT Press, 1993), 17; Rosalind Krauss, "Sculpture in the Expanded Field," in *The Anti-Aesthetic: Essays on Postmodern Culture,* ed. Hal Foster, 31–42 (Port Townsend: Bay Press, 1983); Mary Miss, "From Autocracy to Integration: Redefining the Objectives of Public Art," in *Insights/On Sites: Perspectives on Art in Public Places,* ed. Stacy Paleologos Harris (Washington, DC: Partners for Livable Places, 1984).

17. A new group of artists working under the broad rubric of "minimalism" took aim at the site of art in the postwar period. See Kwon, "One Place after Another," 85–110; Miwon Kwon, *One Place after Another: Site-Specific Art and Locational Identity* (Cambridge, MA: MIT Press, 2002); Erika Suderburg, ed., *Space, Site, Intervention: Situating Installation Art* (Minneapolis: University of Minnesota Press, 2000); Martin Hogue, "The Site as Project: Lessons from Land Art and Conceptual Art," *Journal of Architectural Education* 57, no. 3 (February 2004): 54–61; Jane McFadden, "Toward Site," *Grey Room* 27 (April 2007): 36–57.

18. Kwon, "One Place after Another," 85–86.

19. Brian O'Doherty, *Inside the White Cube: The Ideology of the Gallery Space* (San Francisco: The Lapis Press, 1976), 15.

20. O'Doherty, *Inside the White Cube,* 15, 34.

21. Kwon, "One Place after Another," 86.

22. "Administering" here connotes not only governance but control and a correlate lack of freedom, whereas the neologism *Verwaldung*—roughly, "enforesting" or "sylvanizing"—suggests something wild, free, earthy, and uninhibited. Beuys tapped into a long German tradition of escaping the confines of urban administration. See Walter Laqueur, *Young Germany: A History of the German Youth Movement* (New York: Basic Books, 1962); Simon Schama, *Landscape and Memory* (New York: A. A. Knopf, 1995); John A. Williams, *Turning to Nature in Germany: Hiking, Nudism, and Conservation, 1900–1940* (Stanford: Stanford University Press, 2007).

23. Quoted in Heiner Bastian, ed., *7000 Eichen* (Bern: Benteli, 1985), preface.

24. Wolfgang Schmidt, "Das Baumkataster '7000 Eichen' der Stadt Kassel," in *1982–2002: 20 Jahre Joseph Beuys: "7000 Eichen—Stadtverwaldung statt Stadtverwaltung,"* eds. Joseph Beuys and Harald Kimpel (Kassel: Kulturamt, 2003), 33.

25. Valentin Rothmaler et al., *Kunst wächst manchen über den Kopf: Zwei Spaziergänge zu 7000 Eichen von Joseph Beuys* (Kassel: Kassel Arbeitsgemeinschaft Freiraum und Vegetation, 1997), 6–7; Kai Uwe Schierz, "Von Bonifatius bis Beuys, oder: Vom Umgang mit heiligen Eichen," in *Bonifatius: Heidenopfer, Christuskreuz, Eichenkult,* ed. Hardy Eidam et al. (Erfurt: Stadtverwaltung Erfurt, 2004), 139–145.

26. "Mit grünen Augen betrachtet. Eine Diskussion über Kunst und ihre Verantwortung in der Gesellschaft anlässlich der Documenta 8 in Kassel," in *Öko-Kunst?: Zur Ästhetik der Grünen,* ed. Jost Hermand and Hubert Müller (Hamburg: Argument-Verlag, 1989), 89.

27. BArch (Koblenz) N 1569/771, pag. 30–34, Arbeitsgemeinschaft Kunst und Kultur, "Vom 'Öko-Kult' zur Öko-Kultur," May 19, 1988.

28. Wolfgang Hahn, "Gunter Demnig, Tausendsassa," in *Vor meiner Haustür—"Stolpersteine" von Gunter Demnig: Ein Begleitbuch,* ed. Joachim Rönneper (Gelsenkirchen: Arachne-Verlag, 2010), 114.

29. Brinda Sommer, "Stolpersteine wider das Vergessen. Gesellschaftliches Erinnern an den Nationalsozialismus im lokalen Kontext" (Magisterarbeit, Freie Universität Berlin, Fachbereich Politik- und Sozialwissenschaften, 2006), 127.

30. Florian Matzner, ed., *Public Art: Kunst im öffentlichen Raum* (Ostfildern-Ruit: Hatje Cantz, 2001), 17; Uta Franke and Gunter Demnig, "Am treffendsten läßt sich meine Berufsbezeichnung mit Bildhauer umschreiben, Uta Franke im Interview mit Gunter Demnig," in *Stolpersteine für die von den Nazis ermordeten ehemaligen Nachbarn aus Friedrichshain und Kreuzberg: Dokumentation, Texte, Materialien,* ed. Bettina Eisbrenner (Berlin: Neue Gesellschaft für bildende Kunst, 2002), 9.

31. See McFadden, "Toward Site," 37; Craig Owens, "Earthwords," *October* 18 (Fall 1979): 120–130; Crimp, *Museum's Ruins;* James Meyer, "The Functional Site; or, The Transformation of Site-Specificity," in *Space, Site, Intervention: Situating Installation Art,* ed. Erika Suderburg, 23–37 (Minneapolis: University of Minnesota Press, 2000).

32. Friedrich Wilhelm Martin Schnock, "Richard Long und der veränderte Skulpturbegriff" (Dissertation, Hochschule für bildende Künste, 1999).

33. Marie-Louise Geiseler, "Zeit/Raum/Natur-Erfahrung im Werk von Richard Long" (Dr. Phil. Dissertation, Humboldt-Universität zu Berlin, 2003), 17, 164–168.

34. Kwon, "One Place after Another," 100.

35. On Germany's "conquest of nature," see David Blackbourn, *The Conquest of Nature: Water, Landscape, and the Making of Modern Germany* (New York: W. W. Norton, 2006); Norbert Elias, *The Civilizing Process* (Oxford: Blackwell, 1994).

36. Gunter Demnig and Jürgen Rapp, "Gunter Demnig: Dezentrales Mahnmal. Ein Gespräch mit Jürgen Rapp," *Kunstforum International* 170 (2004): 229–231.

37. Hahn, "Gunter Demnig," 114.

38. Karlheinz Schmid, "Kunst-Tip des Monats: Gunter Demnig," *Pan* 10 (1988): 9.

39. NGBK, KfnA, pag. 137–138, Neuer Berliner Kunstverein, Spuren, Demnig 88, August 13, 1988, Rolf Sachsse, "Spur und Monument. Zwei plastische Grundbegriffe in Gunter Demnigs Arbeit."

40. Demnig participated in a growing national interest in traces in West Germany in the late twentieth century. See Rudy Koshar, *From Monuments to Traces: Artifacts of German Memory, 1870–1990* (Berkeley: University of California Press, 2000), 226–285.

41. NGBK, KfnA, pag. 137–138, Sachsse, "Spur und Monument."

42. Brinda Sommer, "Stolpersteine wider das Vergessen," 127.

43. Demnig and Rapp, "Gunter Demnig," 232.

44. Hahn, "Gunter Demnig," 114.

45. NGBK, KfnA, pag. 137–138, Sachsse, "Spur und Monument."

46. Brinda Sommer, "Stolpersteine wider das Vergessen," 127.

47. Sommer, "Stolpersteine wider das Vergessen," 127.

48. NGBK, KfnA, pag. 137–138, Sachsse, "Spur und Monument."

49. Hahn, "Gunter Demnig," 114.

50. Hahn, "Gunter Demnig," 114.

51. Demnig and Rapp, "Gunter Demnig," 235.

52. NGBK, KfnA, pag. 137–138, Sachsse, "Spur und Monument."

53. Rothmaler, *Kunst wächst*, 9.

54. BArch (Koblenz) N 1569 / 773-2, pag. 263–265, Siede and Koinegg, "Jeder Mensch ein Künstler." Siede and Koinegg distinguished these remarks from Hilmar Hoffmann's phrase "Culture for Everyone" (*Kultur für alle*), which they interpreted as stripping culture of its power by dissolving its boundaries completely.

55. See Martin Heidegger, "Building Dwelling Thinking," in *Poetry, Language, Thought*, trans. Albert Hofstadter (New York: Harper and Row, 1971), 155, 158. See also Jeff Malpas, *Heidegger's Topology: Being, Place, World* (Cambridge, MA: MIT Press, 2006); Jeff Malpas, *Heidegger and the Thinking of Place: Explorations in the Topology of Being* (Cambridge, MA: MIT Press, 2012); Theodore Schatzki, *Martin Heidegger: Theorist of Space* (Stuttgart: Steiner, 2007); Yoko Arisaka, "On Heidegger's Theory of Space: A Critique of Dreyfus," *Inquiry* 38, no. 4 (December 1995): 455–467; Edward Casey, "Heidegger in and out of Place," in *Heidegger: A Centenary Appraisal* (Pittsburgh: Simon Silverman Phenomenology Center, 1990).

56. This reasoning echoes Kant's understanding of absolute vs. relative or empirical space. See Michael Friedman, "Kant on Space, the Understanding, and the Law of Gravitation: 'Prolegomena' §38," *The Monist* 72, no. 2 (April 1989): 236–284; Edward S. Casey, "How to Get from Space to Place in a Fairly Short Stretch of

Time: Phenomenological Prolegomena," in *Senses of Place*, ed. Steven Feld and Keith H. Basso, 13–52 (Santa Fe: School of American Research Press, 1996).

57. The spatial interventionists might have agreed with Edmund Husserl that things are never simply given; they appear, rather, as the possibility of the experience of space. See, for example, Edmund Husserl, *Thing and Space: Lectures of 1907*, trans. Richard Rojcewicz (Dordrecht: Kluwer, 1997).

58. Natilee Harren, *Fluxus Forms: Scores, Multiples, and the Eternal Network* (Chicago: University of Chicago Press, 2020), 14.

59. Hal Foster, "What's Neo about the Neo-Avant-Garde?," *October* 70 (1994): 15. Among the most prominent critics was Peter Bürger. See Peter Bürger, "Avant-Garde and Neo-Avant-Garde: An Attempt to Answer Certain Critics of 'Theory of the Avant-Garde,'" trans. Bettina Brandt and Daniel Purdy, *New Literary History* 41, no. 4 (2010): 695–715.

60. Frances Stracey, *Constructed Situations: A New History of the Situationist International* (London: Pluto Press, 2014), 1–4, here 4.

61. Stracey, *Constructed Situations*, 7, 9. See also Nina Zimmer, *SPUR und andere Künstlergruppen: Gemeinschaftsarbeit in der Kunst um 1960 zwischen Moskau und New York* (Berlin: Reimer, 2002).

62. Stracey, *Constructed Situations*, 10–14, here 10.

63. Harren, *Fluxus Forms*, 34. On Happenings, see Catherine Spencer, *Beyond the Happening: Performance Art and the Politics of Communication* (Manchester: Manchester University Press, 2020); Robert E. Haywood, *Allan Kaprow and Claes Oldenburg: Art, Happenings, and Cultural Politics* (New Haven: Yale University Press, 2017).

64. Mia Lee, *Utopia and Dissent in West Germany: The Resurgence of the Politics of Everyday Life in the Long 1960s* (London: Routledge, 2019), 117–137.

65. Kristine Stiles, "Survival Ethos and Destruction Art," *Discourse* 14, no. 2 (1992): 74–102; Wolfgang Kraushaar, "Guitar Smashing: Gustav Metzger, the Idea of Auto-Destructive Works of Art, and Its Influence on Rock Music," in *The Global Sixties in Sound and Vision: Media, Counterculture, Revolt*, ed. Timothy Scott Brown and Andrew Lison, 119–134 (New York: Palgrave Macmillan US, 2014).

66. Harren, *Fluxus Forms*, 12, 18–19, 25, 159.

67. Kwon, "One Place after Another," 85–86; Michael Fried, *Absorption and Theatricality: Painting and Beholder in the Age of Diderot* (Berkeley: University of California Press, 1980).

68. O'Doherty, *Inside the White Cube*, 14.

69. Kwon, "One Place after Another," 87–88. Emphasis in the original.

70. Kwon, "One Place after Another," 89, 91.

71. Matzner, ed., *Public Art*, 17.

72. Daniel Buren, "Art–Architecture–City–Politics. An Interview with Jerôme Sans," in *Public Art: Kunst im öffentlichen Raum*, ed. Florian Matzner (Ostfildern-Ruit: Hatje Cantz, 2001), 162.

73. Michel de Certeau, *The Practice of Everyday Life* (Berkeley: University of California Press, 1984), 117.

74. Hannah Arendt, *The Origins of Totalitarianism* (New York: Harcourt Brace, 1968), 466.

75. Hannah Arendt, *The Human Condition* (Chicago: University of Chicago Press, 1958), 184.

76. Arendt, *The Origins of Totalitarianism,* 296–297.

77. Arendt, *The Origins of Totalitarianism,* 466.

78. Vito Acconci, "Leaving Home—Notes on Insertions into the Public," in *Public Art: Kunst im öffentlichen Raum,* ed. Florian Matzner (Ostfildern-Ruit: Hatje Cantz, 2001), 45.

79. O'Doherty, *Inside the White Cube,* 38–39.

80. Acconci, "Leaving Home," 45.

81. Kwon, "One Place after Another," 88. See Daniel Buren, "Function of the Museum," *Artforum* 12, no. 1 (September 1973): 68.

82. Kwon, "One Place after Another," 91. Emphasis in the original.

83. Franke and Demnig, "Am treffendsten," 9.

84. He was never prosecuted. Sommer, "Stolpersteine wider das Vergessen," 127.

85. Franke and Demnig, "Am treffendsten," 9.

86. Demnig and Rapp, "Gunter Demnig," 235.

87. Kwon, "One Place after Another," 95.

88. Jürgen Habermas, *The Structural Transformation of the Public Sphere: An Inquiry into a Category of Bourgeois Society,* trans. Thomas Burger (Cambridge, MA: MIT Press, 1989).

89. See Seyla Benhabib, *The Reluctant Modernism of Hannah Arendt* (Thousand Oaks, CA: Sage Publications, 1996), 199–200. On the rise of an auditory public, see also James H. Johnson, *Listening in Paris: A Cultural History* (Berkeley: University of California Press, 1996).

90. Benedict Anderson, *Imagined Communities: Reflections on the Origin and Spread of Nationalism* (London: Verso, 1991).

91. Kwon, "One Place after Another," 92–93.

92. Kwon, "One Place after Another," 92–93. Emphasis in the original.

93. Meyer, "Functional Site," 24.

94. Meyer, "Functional Site," 25. Emphasis in the original.

95. Kwon, "One Place after Another," 95–96.

96. Bettina Eisbrenner and Neue Gesellschaft für bildende Kunst, eds., *Stolpersteine für die von den Nazis ermordeten ehemaligen Nachbarn aus Friedrichshain und Kreuzberg: Dokumentation, Texte, Materialien* (Berlin: NGBK, 2002), 10. See also NGBK, KfnA, pag. 137–138, Sachsse, "Spur und Monument."

97. Johannes Stüttgen, "Das soll ein Zeichen sein für die Notwendigkeit eines gewaltigen Tuns. Vortrag zum Festakt in der Neuen Galerie der Staatlichen Mu-

seen Kassel am 28 September 2002," in *1982–2002: 20 Jahre Joseph Beuys: "7000 Eichen—Stadtverwaldung statt Stadtverwaltung,"* eds. Joseph Beuys and Harald Kimpel (Kassel: Kulturamt, 2003), 16, 20.

2. A Workshop of "History from Below"

1. Peter Schöttler, "Häretiker, Pfadfinder und Ideenbankier. Zum Tod von Raphael Samuel," *WerkstattGeschichte* 16 (1997): 66.

2. *WerkstattGeschichte,* issued by the *Verein für kritische Geschichtsschreibung,* first appeared in 1992 as the successor to *Geschichtswerkstatt,* published by Germany's national History Workshop between 1983 and 1992.

3. Schöttler, "Häretiker, Pfadfinder und Ideenbankier," 67–68. See Raphael Samuel, *Theatres of Memory* (London: Verso, 1994), particularly Samuel's introduction.

4. "'Ein kräftiger Schub für die Vergangenheit.' Spiegel-Report über die neue Geschichtsbewegung in der Bundesrepublik," *Spiegel,* June 6, 1983, 36.

5. "'Ein kräftiger Schub,'" 37.

6. On responses from professional historians to the History Movement, see Heinz Dieter Kittsteiner, "Die Krisis der Historiker-Zunft," in *Auf der Suche nach der verlorenen Wahrheit: Zum Grundlagenstreit in der Geschichtswissenschaft,* ed. Rainer Maria Kiesow and Dieter Simon, 71–86 (Frankfurt am Main: Campus, 2000); Hannes Heer and Volker Ullrich, "Die 'neue Geschichtsbewegung' in der Bundesrepublik. Antriebeskräfte, Selbstverständnis, Perspektiven," in *Geschichte entdecken: Erfahrungen und Projekte der neuen Geschichtsbewegung,* ed. Hannes Heer and Volker Ullrich (Reinbek bei Hamburg: Rowohlt, 1985), 20; Lutz Niethammer, "Anmerkungen zur Alltagsgeschichte," *Geschichtsdidaktik* 5, no. 3 (1980): 231–242; Detlev Peukert, "Arbeiteralltag—Mode oder Methode?," in *Arbeiteralltag in Stadt und Land. Neue Wege der Geschichtsschreibung,* ed. Heiko Haumann and Stefan Bajohr, 8–39 (Berlin: Argument-Verlag, 1982).

7. "'Ein kräftiger Schub,'" 36.

8. Peter Schöttler, "Die Geschichtswerkstatt e. V. zu einem Versuch, basisdemokratische Geschichtsinitiativen und -forschungen zu 'Vernetzen,'" *Geschichte und Gesellschaft* 10, no. 3 (January 1984): 422.

9. On the early network of *Geschichtswerkstätten* around the Federal Republic, see Adelheid von Saldern, "Stadtgedächtnis und Geschichtswerkstätten," *WerkstattGeschichte* 50 (2008): 54–68.

10. Alfred Georg Frei, "Geschichtswerkstätten als Zukunftswerkstätten. Ein Plädoyer für aufklärerische Geschichtsarbeit," in *Die andere Geschichte: Geschichte von unten, Spurensicherung, ökologische Geschichte, Geschichtswerkstätten,* ed. Gerhard Paul and Bernhard Schossig (Cologne: Bund-Verlag, 1986), 269. See also Geschichtswerkstatt e. V., "Selbstverständnispapier der Geschichtswerkstatt e. V.," *Geschichtsdidaktik* 9, no. 2 (1984): 193f.

11. For the history of *Geschichtswerkstätten* in other cities, see Jenny Wüstenberg, *Civil Society and Memory in Postwar Germany* (Cambridge: Cambridge University Press, 2017), 127–177.

12. Wüstenberg, *Civil Society and Memory.*

13. Ian Gwinn, "'A Different Kind of History Is Possible': The History Workshop Movement and the Politics of British and West German Historical Practice" (Ph.D. Dissertation, University of Liverpool, 2015).

14. Ursula Schröter, "Gründungsphase der Berliner Geschichtswerkstatt," in *Immer noch Lust auf Geschichte. 20 Jahre Berliner Geschichtswerkstatt e. V.* (Berlin: Berliner Geschichtswerkstatt e. V., 2001), 9.

15. Schröter, "Gründungsphase," 10–11.

16. On *Geschichtswerkstatt* participants throughout the Federal Republic, see Wüstenberg, *Civil Society and Memory,* 41–45.

17. Martin Düspohl, "20 Jahre Berliner Geschichtswerkstatt: Ein persönlicher Rückblick," in *Immer noch Lust auf Geschichte. 20 Jahre Berliner Geschichtswerkstatt e. V.* (Berlin: Berliner Geschichtswerkstatt e. V., 2001), 46–47.

18. Schröter, "Gründungsphase," 9–11.

19. BGWA, Gisela Wenzel, "'Grabe, wo du stehst.' Zwei Jahrzehnte Berliner Geschichtswerkstatt," Tagung der Geschichtswerkstätten, October 2003.

20. BGWA, Programm, September–December 1983.

21. "'Ein kräftiger Schub,'" 40. On the history of the History Movement, see Wüstenberg, *Civil Society and Memory,* 127–177; Eva Sperner, *Die neue Geschichtsbewegung. Geschichtswerkstätten und Geschichtsprojekte in der Bundesrepublik* (Bielefeld: Bundesarbeitskreis Arbeit und Leben, 1985).

22. See Adelheid von Saldern, "'Schwere Geburten.' Neue Forschungsrichtungen in der bundesrepublikanischen Geschichtswissenschaft (1960–2000)," *WerkstattGeschichte* 40 (2005): 12; Alfred Georg Frei, "Die Geschichtswerkstätten in der Krise," in *Alltagskultur, Subjektivität und Geschichte: Zur Theorie und Praxis von Alltagsgeschichte,* ed. Berliner Geschichtswerkstatt (Münster: Westfälisches Dampfboot, 1994), 318; Ralf Vandamme, *Basisdemokratie als zivile Intervention: Der Partizipationsanspruch der Neuen Sozialen Bewegungen* (Opladen: Leske und Budrich, 2000); Gerhard Schneider, "Schülerwettbewerb Deutsche Geschichte," *Geschichte entdecken: Erfahrungen und Projekte der neuen Geschichtsbewegung,* ed. Hannes Heer and Volker Ullrich (Reinbek bei Hamburg: Rowohlt, 1985). On the New Social Movements, see Sabine Von Dirke, *All Power to the Imagination! The West German Counterculture from the Student Movement to the Greens* (Lincoln: University of Nebraska Press, 1997); Peter H. Merkl, "How New the Brave New World? New Social Movements in West Germany," *German Studies Review* 10, no. 1 (1987): 127–147; Roland Roth, Dieter Rucht, and Sabine Berthold, eds., *Neue soziale Bewegungen in der Bundesrepublik Deutschland* (Frankfurt am Main: Campus, 1987); Karl-Werner Brand, *Neue soziale Bewegungen: Entstehung,*

Funktion und Perspektive neuer Protestpotentiale: Eine Zwischenbilanz (Opladen: Westdeutscher, 1982).

23. Roger Fletcher, "History from Below Comes to Germany: The New History Movement in the Federal Republic of Germany," *The Journal of Modern History* 60, no. 3 (September 1988): 562. See also Alf Lüdtke, ed., *The History of Everyday Life: Reconstructing Historical Experiences and Ways of Life* (Princeton, NJ: Princeton University Press, 1995); Peter Borscheid, "Alltagsgeschichte—Modetorheit oder neues Tor zur Vergangenheit?," in *Sozialgeschichte in Deutschland. Entwicklungen und Perspektiven im internationalen Zusammenhang, vol. 3,* ed. Wolfgang Schieder and Volker Sellin, 87–100 (Göttingen: Vandenhoeck und Ruprecht, 1987). On Broszat's support, see, for example, Martin Broszat, *Nach Hitler: Der schwierige Umgang mit unserer Geschichte* (Munich: Oldenbourg, 1987).

24. Wüstenberg, *Civil Society and Memory,* 128. See also von Saldern, "'Schwere Geburten,'" 13–15.

25. On the cultural significance of the eyewitness at the end of the twentieth century, see Carolyn J. Dean, *The Moral Witness: Trials and Testimony after Genocide* (Ithaca, NY: Cornell University Press, 2019), esp. 132–170.

26. Frei, "Geschichtswerkstätten in der Krise," 317–318.

27. Thomas Lindenberger and Michael Wildt, "Radical Plurality: History Workshops as a Practical Critique of Knowledge," *History Workshop Journal* 33, no. 1 (March 1992): 73, quoting Gustav Seibt, "Grabe wo du stehst. Die Kontroverse um die Alltagsgeschichte," *Frankfurter Allgemeine Zeitung,* September 22, 1987, 36.

28. Wüstenberg, *Civil Society and Memory,* 131–133.

29. Michael Wildt, "History Workshops in Germany: A Survey at the End of the German Post-War Era," in *History Workshop: A Collectanea, 1967–1991: Documents, Memoirs, Critique and Cumulative Index to History Workshop Journal,* ed. Raphael Samuel and History Workshop Centre for Social History, trans. Lyndal Roper (Oxford: History Workshop, 1991), 56.

30. On the agendas of politicians of the Left, see Frei, "Geschichtswerkstätten in der Krise," 318; Frei, "Geschichtswerkstätten als Zukunftswerkstätten," 258; Manfred Scharrer, *Macht Geschichte von unten. Handbuch für gewerkschaftliche Geschichte vor Ort* (Cologne: Bund-Verlag, 1988).

31. Fletcher, "History from Below," 560.

32. Frei, "Geschichtswerkstätten in der Krise," 318. See also Alfred G. Frei, "Geschichte aus den 'Graswurzeln'? Geschichtswerkstätten in der historischen Kulturarbeit," *Aus Politik und Zeitgeschichte* B 2 (1988): 35–46, here 40f.

33. Wildt, "History Workshops," 56.

34. See *Geschichtswerkstatt* 24, "Rifts: History from below in the West and the East" (1991).

35. Alf Lüdtke, "Introduction: What Is the History of Everyday Life and Who Are Its Practitioners," in *The History of Everyday Life: Reconstructing Historical*

Experiences and Ways of Life, ed. Alf Lüdtke (Princeton, NJ: Princeton University Press, 1995), 13. See also Gert Zang, *Die unaufhaltsame Annäherung an das Einzelne: Reflexionen über den theoretischen und praktischen Nutzen der Regional- und Alltagsgeschichte* (Konstanz: Eigenverlag Arbeitskreis für Regionalgeschichte, 1985).

36. See Dennis L. Dworkin, *Cultural Marxism in Postwar Britain: History, the New Left, and the Origins of Cultural Studies* (Durham, NC: Duke University Press, 1997), 44–45, 77–78. See also Lawrence Grossberg and Cary Nelson, "The Territory of Marxism," in *Marxism and the Interpretation of Culture*, ed. Lawrence Grossberg and Cary Nelson (Urbana: University of Illinois Press, 1988); Martin Jay, *Marxism and Totality: The Adventures of a Concept from Lukács to Habermas* (Berkeley: University of California Press, 1984); Michael Kenny, *The First New Left: British Intellectuals after Stalin* (London: Lawrence and Wishart, 1995).

37. They drew inspiration from the socialist humanist historiography in E. P. Thompson, *The Making of the English Working Class* (1963). Though Thompson lit the fire beneath the History Workshop, the affinity was not entirely reciprocal. Dworkin, *Cultural Marxism*, 189. See also E. P. Thompson, "E. P. Thompson: Recovering the Libertarian Tradition," *Leveller* 22 (1978): 20–22.

38. E. P. Thompson, *The Making of the English Working Class* (New York: Pantheon Books, 1964), 12–13.

39. They were influenced by Raymond Williams's understanding of culture as an entire way of life. See Raymond Williams, *Culture and Society, 1780–1950* (New York: Columbia University Press, 1958).

40. "'Ein kräftiger Schub,'" 40.

41. Richard J. Evans, "Die 'History Workshop'-Bewegung in England," in *Geschichte entdecken: Erfahrungen und Projekte der neuen Geschichtsbewegung*, ed. Hannes Heer and Volker Ullrich, 37–45 (Reinbek bei Hamburg: Rowohlt, 1985).

42. Ralphael Samuel, "Das britische Modell. Die englische History-Workshop-Bewegung und ihre Ziele," *Moderne Zeiten—Extra. Geschichtswerkstatt. Sondernummer* 4 (April 1984): 7–9.

43. Alfred Georg Frei, "Die Zukunft liegt in der Vergangenheit. Geschichtswerkstätten, Tendenzwende und demokratische Alternativen," *Moderne Zeiten—Extra. Geschichtswerkstatt. Sondernummer* 4 (April 1984): 5. Frei devoted more attention to the *Geschichtswerkstatt*'s international influences in a 1988 article. See Alfred G. Frei, "Alltag—Region—Politik. Anmerkungen zur 'neuen Geschichtsbewegung,'" *Geschichtsdidaktik* 2 (1984): 107–120.

44. The author of the chapter in which these references appeared was neither a member of the Berlin *Geschichtswerkstatt* nor a German. Anna Davin was an English historian active in the British History Workshop Movement. Perhaps to distinguish the two groups, Davin translated the British movement as *Geschichtsseminare* or "history seminars" rather than as *Geschichtswerkstätten*. See Anna Davin, "Frauen und Alltagsgeschichte," *Alltagskultur, Subjektivität und Geschichte:*

Zur Theorie und Praxis von Alltagsgeschichte, ed. Berliner Geschichtswerkstatt (Münster: Westfälisches Dampfboot, 1994), 41–43, 57n10–13.

45. Frei, "Geschichtswerkstätten in der Krise," 318. Frei highlights *The Making of the English Working Class,* which was translated to German in 1987 (*Die Entstehung der englischen Arbeiterklasse* [Frankfurt am Main: Suhrkamp, 1987]) as well as Thompson's *The Poverty of Theory* (1978), translated to German in 1980 (*Das Elend der Theorie. Zur Produktion geschichtlicher Erfahrung* [Frankfurt am Main: Campus, 1980]).

46. See BGWA, Rundbrief March 7, 1983; BGWA, Programm, September–December 1983; *Immer noch Lust auf Geschichte. 20 Jahre Berliner Geschichtswerkstatt e. V.* (Berlin: Berliner Geschichtswerkstatt e. V., 2001).

47. Wildt, "History Workshops," 56.

48. Raphael Samuel, "Oral History in Großbritannien," in *Lebenserfahrung und kollektives Gedächtnis: Die Praxis der "Oral History,"* ed. Lutz Niethammer and Werner Trapp (Frankfurt am Main: Syndikat, 1980); Raphael Samuel, "Die englische History-Workshop-Bewegung und ihre Ziele," *Journal für Geschichte* 1 (1981), reproduced in *Moderne Zeiten—Extra. Geschichtswerkstatt. Sondernummer* 4 (April 1984): 7–9.

49. See Evans, "'History Workshop'-Bewegung," 45.

50. On filmic confrontations with Nazi history, see Anton Kaes, *From Hitler to Heimat: The Return of History as Film* (Cambridge, MA: Harvard University Press, 1992).

51. In West Berlin alone there were more than fifty scheduled events on the subject of Hitler's ascension to power. "'Ein kräftiger Schub,'" 37.

52. Klaus Tenfelde, "Schwierigkeiten mit dem Alltag," *Geschichte und Gesellschaft* 10, no. 3 (January 1984): 381.

53. Gerhard Paul and Bernhard Schossig, "Geschichte und Heimat," in *Die andere Geschichte: Geschichte von unten, Spurensicherung, ökologische Geschichte, Geschichtswerkstätten,* ed. Gerhard Paul and Bernhard Schossig (Cologne: Bund-Verlag, 1986), 18.

54. Horst Waffenschmidt, "'Schaufenster des Staates.' Aus der Ansprache zur Eröffnung der Ausstellung 'Der Bundespräsident,'" *Das Parlament* 44 (November 1984): 10.

55. Dieter Emig and Alfred G. Frei, "'. . . die Fremdheit der Dinge und Personen aufheben.' Über Versuche, Heimat neu zu entdecken," in *Heimat: Analysen, Themen, Perspektiven,* ed. Bundeszentrale für politische Bildung, 307–328 (Bonn: Bundeszentrale für politische Bildung, 1990).

56. Frei, "Geschichtswerkstätten als Zukunftswerkstätten," 266. See Ernst Bloch, *Das Prinzip Hoffnung* (Frankfurt am Main: Suhrkamp, 1968), 1628. On the idea of *Heimat,* see Celia Applegate, *A Nation of Provincials: The German Idea of Heimat* (Berkeley: University of California Press, 1990). These groups rejected a notion of *Heimat* associated with Nazi blood and soil ideology. They interpreted

Heimat not as proof of heritage (*Herkunftsnachweis*) or as a means of exclusion (*Eingrenzung*), but as that place which made life possible (*Heimat als Lebensmöglichkeit*). Paul and Schossig, "Geschichte und Heimat," 23.

57. BGWA, Programm, September–December 1983. They joined more prominent historians like Reinhart Koselleck in calling for plural histories. See Reinhart Koselleck, *Sediments of Time: On Possible Histories,* ed. and trans. Sean Franzel and Stefan-Ludwig Hoffmann (Stanford, CA: Stanford University Press, 2018).

58. Sven Lindqvist, "Dig Where You Stand," *Oral History* 7, no. 2 (October 1979): 24. Lindqvist, a cultural attaché at the Swedish embassy in China from 1960 to 1961, also drew inspiration from the cultural campaign *yiku sitian,* which translates as "recalling past bitterness in order to savor the sweetness of the present." See Wing-chung Ho, "The (Un-)Making of the Shanghai Socialist 'Model Community': From the Monolithic to Heterogeneous Appropriation(s) of the Past," *Journal of Asian and African Studies* 39, no. 5 (October 2004): 380; Wing-chung Ho, "From Resistance to Collective Action in a Shanghai Socialist 'Model Community': From the Late 1940s to Early 1970s," *Journal of Social History* 40, no. 1 (October 2006): 86. See also Sven Lindqvist, "Grabe, wo du stehst. Das schwedische Beispiel," in *Geschichte entdecken: Erfahrungen und Projekte der neuen Geschichtsbewegung,* ed. Hannes Heer and Volker Ullrich (Reinbek bei Hamburg: Rowohlt, 1985).

59. He compared this project favorably with that of Maxim Gorky, whose campaign in the early years of the Russian Revolution encouraged research on the history of factories. Lindqvist, "Grabe, wo du stehst," 72–73. See Maxim Gorky, "The People Must Know Their History!," in *Culture and the People* (New York: International, 1939), 94–100.

60. Sven Lindqvist, *Gräv där du står: Hur man utforskar ett jobb* (Stockholm: Bonnier, 1978).

61. Lindqvist, "Grabe, wo du stehst," 74.

62. "'Ein kräftiger Schub,'" 40. See also Sven Lindqvist, "Grabe, wo du stehst," in *Geschichte von unten: Fragestellungen, Methoden und Projekte einer Geschichte des Alltags,* ed. Hubert Ch. Ehalt, 295–304 (Vienna: H. Böhlau, 1984). The complete handbook was published as Sven Lindqvist, *Grabe, wo du stehst: Handbuch zur Erforschung der eigenen Geschichte,* trans. Manfred Dammeyer (Bonn: Dietz, 1989).

63. Lüdtke, ed., *History of Everyday Life,* 16. Lüdtke's text was originally published in German as *Alltagsgeschichte: Zur Rekonstruktion historischer Erfahrungen und Lebensweisen* (Frankfurt am Main: Campus, 1989).

64. Schröter, "Gründungsphase," 11. See also "Salecina-Seminar. 10.-16. Juni 1984. Geschichte von unten. Faschismus und Widerstand," *Moderne Zeiten—Extra. Geschichtswerkstatt. Sondernummer* 4 (April 1984): 59.

65. See Jürgen Habermas, *Theory and Practice* (Boston: Beacon Press, 1973); Nicholas Lobkowicz, *Theory and Practice* (Notre Dame, IN: University of Notre Dame Press, 1968).

66. C. Wright Mills, "Letter to the New Left," *New Left Review* 1, no. 5 (October 1960): 21.

67. Belinda Davis, "What's Left? Popular Political Participation in Postwar Europe," *American Historical Review* 113, no. 2 (April 2008): 369.

68. Horst Mewes, "The German New Left," *New German Critique* 1 (December 1973): 36–37. See also Johano Strasser, "Weiterentwicklung der Doppelstrategie," *Juso, Zeitschrift der Jungsozialisten in der SPD* 3 / 4 (1973): 9; Norbert Gansel, "Die Strategie in der Diskussion der Jungsozialisten," in *Überwindet den Kapitalismus, oder Was wollen die Jungsozialisten?* (Reinbek bei Hamburg: Rowohlt Taschenbuch Verlag, 1971), 55.

69. Hanno Hochmuth, *Kiezgeschichte: Friedrichshain und Kreuzberg im geteilten Berlin* (Göttingen: Wallstein, 2017), 146–168.

70. Davis, "What's Left?," 370.

71. Wolfgang Kraushaar, "Denkmodelle der 68er-Bewegung," *Aus Politik und Zeitgeschichte* B 22–23 (2001): 26.

72. Davis, "What's Left?," 369–370. On alternative public spheres, see also Belinda Davis, "The City as Theater of Protest: West Berlin and West Germany, 1962–1983," in *The Spaces of the Modern City: Imaginaries, Politics, and Everyday Life*, ed. Gyan Prakash and Kevin M. Kruse, 247–274 (Princeton, NJ: Princeton University Press, 2008); Timothy Scott Brown, *West Germany and the Global Sixties: The Anti-Authoritarian Revolt, 1962–1978* (Cambridge: Cambridge University Press, 2013), 121–123; Sven Reichardt, "'Wärme' als Modus sozialen Verhaltens—Vorüberlegungen zu einer Kulturgeschichte des linksalternativen Milieus vom Ende der sechziger bis Anfang der achtziger Jahre," *vorgänge* 44, no. 171 / 172 (2005): 175–187.

73. Düspohl, "20 Jahre," 46.

74. See Helmut Dahmer, "Die Sinngebung des Sinnlosen," *Die Zeit*, October 26, 1984, 57f.; Axel Schildt, "Zur Einleitung," in *Geschichtswerkstätten gestern, heute, morgen: Bewegung, Stillstand, Aufbruch*, ed. Forschungsstelle für Zeitgeschichte in Hamburg (Munich: Dölling und Galitz, 2004), 18.

75. Frei, "Geschichtswerkstätten als Zukunftswerkstätten," 260–262. See Jörn Rüsen, "Geschichte als Aufklärung? Oder: Das Dilemma des historischen Denkens zwischen Herrschaft und Emanzipation," *Geschichte und Gesellschaft* 7, no. 2 (January 1981): 189–218. See also Immanuel Kant, "An Answer to the Question: What Is Enlightenment?," in *What Is Enlightenment? Eighteenth-Century Answers and Twentieth-Century Questions*, ed. and trans. James Schmidt (Berkeley: University of California Press, 1996), 58.

76. Lindenberger and Wildt, "Radical Plurality," 74.

77. Lüdtke, "Introduction," 25–27.

78. Geoff Eley, "Labor History, Social History, 'Alltagsgeschichte': Experience, Culture, and the Politics of the Everyday—a New Direction for German Social History?," *Journal of Modern History* 61, no. 2 (June 1989): 297–298. On the East

German approach to *Alltagsgeschichte,* see Gunther Heydemann, "Geschichtswissenschaft und Geschichtsverstandnis in der DDR seit 1945," *Aus Politik und Zeitgeschichte* B 13 (March 1987): 15–26.

79. Geoff Eley, "Foreword," in *The History of Everyday Life: Reconstructing Historical Experiences and Ways of Life,* ed. Alf Lüdtke (Princeton, NJ: Princeton University Press, 1995), vii.

80. Tenfelde, "Schwierigkeiten," 379; Eley, "Labor History, Social History, 'Alltagsgeschichte,'" 298.

81. BGWA, Gisela Wenzel, "'Grabe, wo du stehst.'"

82. Lüdtke, "Introduction," 15–16.

83. Lindenberger and Wildt, "Radical Plurality," 83.

84. Frei, "Geschichtswerkstätten in der Krise," 323; Alf Lüdtke, "Einleitung: Was ist und wer treibt Alltagsgeschichte," in *Alltagsgeschichte: Zur Rekonstruktion historischer Erfahrungen und Lebensweisen,* ed. Alf Lüdtke (Frankfurt am Main: Campus, 1989), 12. See also Carola Lipp, "Alltagskulturforschung im Grenzbereich von Volkskunde, Soziologie, und Geschichte. Aufstieg und Niedergang eines interdiziplinären Forschungskonzepts," *Zeitschrift für Volkskunde* 1 (1993): 24f.

85. Geoff Eley, "Wie denken wir über Politik? Alltagsgeschichte und die Kategorie des Politischen," in *Alltagskultur, Subjektivität und Geschichte: Zur Theorie und Praxis von Alltagsgeschichte,* ed. Berliner Geschichtswerkstatt (Münster: Westfälisches Dampfboot, 1994), 27–29. See also Alf Lüdtke, "Zur Einleitung," *Sozialwissenschaftliche Informationen für Unterricht und Studium* 6 (1997): 147.

86. Lüdtke, "Introduction," 6. See Friedrich Engels to Joseph Bloch, September 21–22, 1890, in Institut für Marxismus-Leninismus, ed., *Marx-Engels-Werke, vol. 37* (Berlin: Dietz, 1978), 463

87. Lipp, "Alltagskulturforschung," 78.

88. Schöttler, "Geschichtswerkstatt e. V.," 421.

89. Lipp, "Alltagskulturforschung," 79. See Henri Lefebvre, *Critique of Everyday Life* (London: Verso, 1991). The Frankfurt School's arguments bore on these conversations as well. See, for example, Theodor Adorno, "Résumé über die Kulturindustrie," in *Ohne Leitbild: Parva Aesthetica* (Frankfurt am Main: Suhrkamp, 1967), 60–70.

90. Lüdtke, "Introduction," 11. See also Rudolf Bahro, "Socialism, Ecology and Utopia," *History Workshop Journal* 16, no. 1 (September 1983): 94–95.

91. Lüdtke, "Introduction," 9–10. See Jürgen Kocka, "Geschichte als Aufklärung?," *Frankfurter Rundschau,* January 4, 1988; Hans-Ulrich Wehler, "Königsweg zu neuen Ufern oder Irrgarten der Illusionen? Die westdeutsche Alltagsgeschichte: Geschichte 'von innen' und 'von unten,'" in *Geschichte von unten—Geschichte von innen: Kontroversen um die Alltagsgeschichte,* ed. Franz-Josef Brüggemeier and Jürgen Kocka (Hagen: Fernuniversität-Gesamthochschule Hagen, 1985), 47

92. "'Ein kräftiger Schub,'" 41.

93. Hans-Ulrich Wehler, "Geschichte—von unten gesehen," *Die Zeit,* May 3, 1985.

94. "'Ein kräftiger Schub,'" 38.

95. Lüdtke, "Introduction," 12. Lüdtke drew, in particular, from Wehler, "Königsweg zu neuen Ufern." Peter Borscheid criticized Wehler in "Alltagsgeschichte—Modetorheit oder neues Tor zur Vergangenheit?," 85. Jürgen Kocka and Klaus Tenfelde have tried to clarify the position of the historical social sciences. See Jürgen Kocka, *Sozialgeschichte: Begriff, Entwicklung, Probleme* (Göttingen: Vandenhoeck und Ruprecht, 1986), esp. 152–160, 162–174; Tenfelde, "Schwierigkeiten," 376–394.

96. Wildt, "History Workshops," 59.

97. Lindenberger and Wildt, "Radical Plurality," 89.

98. Alfred Georg Frei, "Geschichtswerkstätten," in *Geschichte entdecken: Erfahrungen und Projekte der neuen Geschichtsbewegung,* ed. Hannes Heer and Volker Ullrich (Reinbek bei Hamburg: Rowohlt, 1985), 402–403.

99. Lindenberger and Wildt, "Radical Plurality," 90; Lüdtke, "Introduction," 30–32.

100. Lipp, "Alltagskulturforschung," 79. On West Germany's postwar intellectual movements, see Agnes Heller, "Existentialismus, Entfremdung, Postmodernismus, kulturelle Bewegungen als Ausdrucksmittel des Wandels der Verhaltensmuster im alltäglichen Leben," *Der Alltag* 4 (1987): 16–27.

101. Fletcher, "History from Below," 560.

102. Düspohl, "20 Jahre," 49. After receiving his degree, Düspohl, for example, took work in the cultural affairs office of Berlin's Kreuzberg neighborhood (*Kunstamt Kreuzberg*) and later became the leader of the Kreuzberg Museum, now the Friedrichshain-Kreuzberg Museum.

103. Lüdtke, "Introduction," 28.

104. Lindenberger and Wildt, "Radical Plurality," 87; Frei, "Geschichtswerkstätten in der Krise," 320. Practitioners of *Alltagsgeschichte* were reading Michel de Certeau, "Die Geschichte: Wissen und Fiktion," in *Die Zeichen der Historie: Beiträge zu einer semiologischen Geschichtswissenschaft,* ed. Georg Schmid, 29–50 (Vienna: H. Böhlau, 1986).

105. The majority of Berlin *Geschichtswerkstatt* members undertook their research for the group without pay. The exception were the few individuals who received compensation as part of the West German government's job creation efforts (*ABM-Stellen*). BGWA, Programm, September–December 1983.

106. Schöttler, "Geschichtswerkstatt e. V.," 421–424.

107. Schröter, "Gründungsphase," 12.

108. Frei, "Geschichtswerkstätten als Zukunftswerkstätten," 268–269. On Gramsci's idea of the organic intellectual, see Antonio Gramsci, "The Modern Prince," in *Selections from the Prison Notebooks of Antonio Gramsci,* ed. and

trans. Quintin Hoare and Geoffrey Nowell-Smith (New York: International, 1971).

109. "'Ein kräftiger Schub,'" 41.

110. Some took a phenomenological approach to everyday life. Husserl proved particularly appealing, with practitioners of *Alltagsgeschichte* drawing on pieces like "Die Krisis der europäischen Wissenschaften und die transzendentale Philosophie. Eine Einleitung in die phänomenologische Philosophie" in *Husserliana, vol. 6,* ed. Walter Biemel (The Hague: M. Nijhoff, 1976), 125f. Alfred Schütz's *Strukturen der Lebenswelt* and Peter Berger and Thomas Luckmann's 1969 volume *Die gesellschaftliche Konstruktion der Wirklichkeit. Eine Theorie der Wissenssoziologie* also played an important role. See Lipp, "Alltagskulturforschung," 80.

111. Eley, "Wie denken wir," 20. See Michel Foucault, "Body/Power," in *Power/Knowledge: Selected Interviews and Other Writings 1972–1977,* ed. Colin Gordon (New York: Pantheon, 1980), 60.

112. Attention to gender in history became an important component of the *Geschichtswerkstätten*'s rejection of the notion of a single dominant masculine reality. Ute Frevert, "German Women Historians' Meeting, 26–27 March 1977," *History Workshop Journal* 4, no. 1 (September 1977): 235–236; Dorothee Wierling, "The History of Everyday Life and Gender Relations: On Historical and Historiographical Relationships," in *The History of Everyday Life: Reconstructing Historical Experiences and Ways of Life,* ed. Alf Lüdtke (Princeton, NJ: Princeton University Press, 1995).

113. Eley, "Wie denken wir," 22. See also Geoff Eley, "Reading Gramsci in English: Observations on the Reception of Antonio Gramsci in the English-Speaking World, 1957–1982," *European History Quarterly* 14 (1984): 441–477.

114. Wildt, "History Workshops," 57.

115. Frei, "Geschichtswerkstätten in der Krise," 318. See also Alfred Georg Frei, *Antonio Gramsci, Theoretiker des demokratischen Übergangs zum Sozialismus* (Berlin [West]: DVK-Verlag, 1978).

116. See Antonio Gramsci, "State and Civil Society," in *Selections from the Prison Notebooks of Antonio Gramsci,* ed. and trans. Quintin Hoare and Geoffrey Nowell-Smith (New York: International, 1971), esp. 234–243. See also James Martin, *Antonio Gramsci: Intellectuals, Culture and the Party* (London: Routledge, 2002), 525–526.

117. Quoted in Lindenberger and Wildt, "Radical Plurality," 82–83. See Michel de Certeau, "Die Geschichte," 32, 35f.

118. Lindenberger and Wildt, "Radical Plurality," 84–86. See Wolfgang Welsch, *Unsere postmoderne Moderne* (Weinheim: VCH, 1987). On socialization from above, see Zang, *Die unaufhaltsame Annäherung,* 41–51.

119. Certeau, "Die Geschichte," 77–78.

120. Lindenberger and Wildt, "Radical Plurality," 85–86. They pointed to Lyotard's work on the delegitimization of the Western discourse of emancipa-

tion. See Jean-Francois Lyotard, *The Postmodern Condition: A Report on Knowledge,* trans. Geoff Bennington and Brian Massumi (Manchester: Manchester University Press, 1986).

121. Lindenberger and Wildt, "Radical Plurality," 74.

122. Lindenberger and Wildt, "Radical Plurality," 84–85. See also Thomas Lindenberger, "Werkstattgeflüster. Überlegungen zu Selbstverständnis und Praxis radikaldemokratischer Geschichtsforschung aus der Berliner Geschichtswerkstatt," in *Demokratie- und Arbeitergeschichte. Jahrbuch 3,* ed. Franz Mehring Gesellschaft, Stuttgart, 23–27 (Weingarten: Drumlin-Verlag, 1983).

123. Eley, "Wie denken wir," 27.

124. Lindenberger and Wildt, "Radical Plurality," 75. Karl Marx, "Theses on Feuerbach," in *The Marx-Engels Reader,* ed. Robert C. Tucker (New York: W. W. Norton, 1978), 144.

125. Frei, "Geschichtswerkstätten als Zukunftswerkstätten," 274.

126. Andreas Ludwig, "Historische Neugier und Projektpraxis," in *Projekt: Spurensicherung. Alltag und Widerstand im Berlin der 30er Jahre,* ed. Berliner Geschichtswerkstatt, 5–8 (Berlin: Elefanten Press, 1983).

127. Eley, "Wie denken wir," 18–19, 33. See also Geoff Eley, "Is All the World a Text? From Social History to the History of Society Two Decades Later," in *The Historic Turn in the Human Sciences,* ed. Terrence McDonald (Ann Arbor: University of Michigan Press, 1996); Hans Medick, "'Missionaries in the Rowboat?' Ethnological Ways of Knowing as a Challenge to Social History," in *The History of Everyday Life: Reconstructing Historical Experiences and Ways of Life,* ed. Alf Lüdtke, 41–71 (Princeton, NJ: Princeton University Press, 1995); Lynn Hunt, ed., *The New Cultural History* (Berkeley: University of California Press, 1989).

128. Udo Gößwald, "Historische Ausstellungen—Orte rekonstruierte Sinnlichkeit," in *Geschichte entdecken: Erfahrungen und Projekte der neuen Geschichtsbewegung,* ed. Hannes Heer and Volker Ullrich (Reinbek bei Hamburg: Rowohlt, 1985), 305–306. Gößwald drew from Georg Simmel. See Georg Simmel, "Der Fremde," *Philosophische Kultur* (Leipzig: Klinkhardt, 1911), 63.

129. Gößwald, "Historische Ausstellungen," 304. See Ernst Bloch, *Karl Marx und die Menschlichkeit* (Reinbeck bei Hamburg: Rowohlt, 1972), 83.

130. Gößwald, "Historische Ausstellungen," 309. Gößwald repurposed a line from Walter Benjamin's "Eine Todesnachricht," in *Berliner Kindheit um neunzehnhundert* (Frankfurt am Main: Suhrkamp, 2017).

131. Detlef Stender, "Vom Leben der toten Dinge: Schränke zum Kühlen als historische Quelle," in *Alltagskultur, Subjektivität und Geschichte: Zur Theorie und Praxis von Alltagsgeschichte,* ed. Berliner Geschichtswerkstatt (Münster: Westfälisches Dampfboot, 1994), 157. See also Gert Selle and Jutta Boehe, *Leben mit schönen Dingen—Anpassung und Eigensinn im Alltag des Wohnens* (Reinbek bei Hamburg: Rowohlt, 1986).

132. Lindenberger and Wildt, "Radical Plurality," 79.

133. Gerhard Paul and Bernhard Schossig, "Vorwort," in *Die andere Geschichte: Geschichte von unten, Spurensicherung, ökologische Geschichte, Geschichtswerkstätten,* ed. Gerhard Paul and Bernhard Schossig (Cologne: Bund-Verlag, 1986), 12.

134. BGWA, Gisela Wenzel, "'Grabe, wo du stehst.'"

135. Schröter, "Gründungsphase," 9.

136. Frei, "Geschichtswerkstätten," 401.

137. Schröter, "Gründungsphase," 11–12.

138. BGWA, Programm, September–December 1983.

139. BGWA, Informationen, 1984; Schröter, "Gründungsphase," 11–12.

140. Jürgen Karwelat, "Mittlerweile bin ich mein eigener Zeitzeuge," in *Immer noch Lust auf Geschichte. 20 Jahre Berliner Geschichtswerkstatt e. V.* (Berlin: Berliner Geschichtswerkstatt e. V., 2001), 58. See Thomas Nipperdey, *Deutsche Geschichte 1800–1866: Bürgerwelt und starker Staat* (Munich: C. H. Beck, 1983); Thomas Nipperdey, *Deutsche Geschichte, 1866–1918* (Munich: C. H. Beck, 1990).

141. BGWA, Gisela Wenzel, "'Grabe, wo du stehst.'"

142. BGWA, Gisela Wenzel, "'Grabe, wo du stehst.'" On witnessing, see Dean, *The Moral Witness;* Robin Wagner-Pacifici, "Witness to Surrender," in *Visual Worlds,* ed. John R. Hall, Blake Stimson, and Lisa Tamiris Becker (New York: Routledge, 2005).

143. Ludwig, "Historische Neugier," 5–8.

144. BGWA, Rundbrief, June 6, 1983, Joachim Stein, "Leserbrief." Some criticized the BGW's interest in the witness, highlighting problems associated with oral history. See BGWA, Rundbrief, April 18, 1983, Siegfried Heimann, "Leserbrief."

145. Ludwig, "Historische Neugier," 5–8.

146. BGWA, Programm, September–December 1983.

147. Schröter, "Gründungsphase," 12.

148. Andreas Ludwig, "Das '33-Projekt,'" in *Immer noch Lust auf Geschichte. 20 Jahre Berliner Geschichtswerkstatt e. V.* (Berlin: Berliner Geschichtswerkstatt e. V., 2001), 21–22.

149. BGWA, Rundbrief, June 6, 1983.

150. BGWA, Rundbrief, March 7, 1983.

151. Frauke Bollow and Elke Mocker, "Archivierung biographischer Quellen im Dokumentationszentrum für Alltags- und Regionalgeschichte der Berliner Geschichtswerkstatt," in *Alltagskultur, Subjektivität und Geschichte: Zur Theorie und Praxis von Alltagsgeschichte,* ed. Berliner Geschichtswerkstatt (Münster: Westfälisches Dampfboot, 1994), 224. See also Rudolf Lüscher, Werner Schweizer, Amalie Pinkus-De Sassi, and Theo Pinkus-De Sassi, *Leben im Widerspruch* (Zürich: Limmat-Verlag, 1987).

152. BGWA, Rundbrief, March 7, 1983.

153. Wüstenberg, *Civil Society and Memory*, 139–140. See also Bernd Hüttner, *Archive von unten: Bibliotheken und Archive der neuen sozialen Bewegungen und ihre Bestände* (Neu-Ulm: AG SPAK Bücher, 2003); Cornelia Wenzel and Jürgen Bacia, *Bewegung bewahren: Freie Archive und die Geschichte von unten* (Berlin: Archiv der Jugendkulturen, 2013); Axel Diederich, Waldemar Schindowski, and Rudolf de Jong, *Reader der "anderen" Archive* (Amsterdam: ID-Archiv im Internationalen Institut für Sozialgeschichte, 1990).

154. Aleida Assmann, *Cultural Memory and Western Civilization: Functions, Media, Archives* (New York: Cambridge University Press, 2011), 128, 331; Michel Foucault, *The Archaeology of Knowledge* (New York: Pantheon, 1972), 129.

155. BGWA, Programm, September–December 1983; BGWA, Informationen, 1984.

156. BGWA, Rundbrief, June 6, 1983.

157. Eva Brücker and the Arbeitsgruppe Lindenhof, "Gemeinnützige 'Siedlung Lindenhof' E.G.m.b.H. Berlin-Schöneberg," in *Projekt: Spurensicherung. Alltag und Widerstand im Berlin der 30er Jahre*, ed. Berliner Geschichtswerkstatt (Berlin [West]: Elefanten Press, 1983), 9–10.

158. Brücker, "Gemeinnützige," 10; Eva Brücker, "Das Lindenhof-Projekt: Alltagsgeschichte ist machbar," in *Immer noch Lust auf Geschichte. 20 Jahre Berliner Geschichtswerkstatt e. V.* (Berlin: Berliner Geschichtswerkstatt e. V., 2001), 28.

159. Brücker, "Lindenhof-Projekt," 28–29.

160. BGWA, Informationen, 1984.

161. Brücker, "Lindenhof-Projekt," 29–30.

162. Michael Meyer and Berliner Geschichtswerkstatt, *"Das war 'ne ganz geschlossene Gesellschaft hier": Der Lindenhof, eine Genossenschafts-Siedlung in der Großstadt* (Berlin: Nishen, 1987).

163. Berliner Geschichtswerkstatt, ed., *Spurensicherung in Schöneberg 1933: "Rote Insel," Lindenhof, "Jüdische Schweiz"* (Berlin: Berliner Geschichtswerkstatt, 1983). See also Herbert Böpple and Berliner Geschichtswerkstatt, *Die Rote Insel. Berlin-Schöneberg: Bruchstücke zu einer Stadtgeschichte* (Berlin: Nishen, 1987).

164. BGWA, Gisela Wenzel, "'Grabe, wo du stehst.'"

165. Andreas Sander, "Die 'Rote Insel,'" in *Immer noch Lust auf Geschichte. 20 Jahre Berliner Geschichtswerkstatt e. V.* (Berlin: Berliner Geschichtswerkstatt e. V., 2001), 26–27; BGWA, Informationen, 1984.

166. Sander, "Die 'Rote Insel,'" 26–27; BGWA, Informationen, 1984.

167. Schröter, "Gründungsphase," 12.

168. Karwelat, "Mittlerweile," 56.

169. BGWA, Informationen, 1984. A representative from the evening news broadcast by Radio Free Berlin attended the first tour. Karwelat, "Mittlerweile," 56.

170. BGWA, "Warum historische Stadtrundfahrten mit dem Schiff?," 1984; BGWA, Berliner Geschichtswerkstatt e. V. und Wasserstraßenhauptamt, Ministerium für Verkehr in Berlin (Ost), December 13, 1985, and April 25, 1986.

171. Düspohl, "20 Jahre," 47.

172. "'Ein kräftiger Schub,'" 36.

173. LArch Berlin, B Rep. 232–233, 1, Andreas Ludwig, Vorüberlegungen zu einer Konzeption für das "Aktive Museum—Faschismus und Widerstand in Berlin," August / September 1983.

174. See, for example, LArch Berlin, B Rep. 232–233, 1, Konzeptionsgruppe Aktives Museum, undated; LArch Berlin, B Rep. 232–33, 1, Aktives Museum, Berliner Geschichtswerkstatt, Rundbrief 3 / 1984, Andreas Ludwig, "Wie sollte ein Aktives Museum einmal werden?"; LArch Berlin, B Rep. 232–233, 1, Attendance List, Aktives Museum, May 25, 1984; LArch Berlin, B Rep. 232–233, 1, Heinz-Dieter Schilling, Einladung zur Vorstandssitzung, March 29, 1984.

175. LArch Berlin, B Rep. 232–233, 1, Udo Gößwald, September 29, 1983.

176. LArch Berlin, B Rep. 232–233, 1, Udo Gößwald, Protokoll der Mitgleiderversammlung, August 5, 1983; BGWA, Informationen, 1984; LArch Berlin, B Rep. 232–233, 1, Schoenberner und Schilling, November 10, 1983.

177. LArch Berlin, B Rep. 232–233, 2, Andreas Ludwig, Bernhard Müller, February 14, 1987.

178. LArch, B Rep. 232–33, 1, Aktives Museum, Berliner Geschichtswerkstatt, Rundbrief 3 / 1984, Andreas Ludwig, "Wie sollte ein Aktives Museum einmal werden?"

179. LArch Berlin, B Rep. 232–233, 1, Udo Gößwald, undated.

180. LArch, B Rep. 232–33, 1, Aktives Museum, Berliner Geschichtswerkstatt, Rundbrief 3 / 1984, Andreas Ludwig, "Wie sollte ein Aktives Museum einmal werden?"

181. LArch Berlin, B Rep. 232–233, 3, "Stellungnahme der AL Kreuzberg zum Ergebnis des Wettbewerbs Prinz-Albrecht-Gelände," June 7, 1984.

182. Susanne Führer, "Wie eine Bürgerinitiative buchstäblich Geschichte ausgrub. Christine Fischer-Defoy zu 25 Jahren 'Topographie des Terrors,'" *deutschlandfunkkultur.de*, July 4, 2012, www.deutschlandfunkkultur.de/wie-eine-buergerinitiative-buchstaeblich-geschichte-ausgrub.954.de.html?dram:article_id=211331. See also Karwelat, "Mittlerweile," 58.

183. On the Topography of Terror, see Wüstenberg, *Civil Society and Memory*, 102–121; Reinhard Rürup, *Topographie des Terrors. Gestapo, SS und Reichssicherheitshauptamt auf dem "Prinz-Albrecht-Gelände": Eine Dokumentation* (Berlin: Verlag Willmuth Arenhövel, 1987); Akademie der Künste Berlin, ed., *Zum Umgang mit dem Gestapo-Gelände: Gutachten im Auftrag der Akademie der Künste Berlin* (Berlin: Akademie der Künste, 1988).

184. BArch (Koblenz) N1569 / 740, pag. 51, "Zum geplanten 'Deutschen Historischen Museum,'" undated. Emphasis mine.

185. Schildt, "Zur Einleitung," 18.
186. BGWA, Programm, GeschichtsFest '84 in Berlin.
187. BGWA, Gisela Wenzel, "'Grabe, wo du stehst.'"

3. Green Culture

1. Andreas Wirsching et al., "The 1970s and 1980s as a Turning Point in European History?," *Journal of Modern European History* 9, no. 1 (April 2011): 9–10, 20. On the 1970s as a point of transformation in Europe, see Anselm Doering-Manteuffel and Lutz Raphael, *Nach dem Boom: Perspektiven auf die Zeitgeschichte seit 1970* (Göttingen: Vandenhoeck und Ruprecht, 2008); Philippe Chassaigne, *Les années 1970: Fin d'un monde et origine de notre modernité* (Paris: A. Colin, 2008); Konrad Hugo Jarausch, ed., *Das Ende der Zuversicht?: Die siebziger Jahre als Geschichte* (Göttingen: Vandenhoeck und Ruprecht, 2008); Thomas Raithel, Andreas Rödder, and Andreas Wirsching, eds., *Auf dem Weg in eine neue Moderne?: Die Bundesrepublik Deutschland in den siebziger und achtziger Jahren* (Munich: Oldenbourg, 2009); Frank Bösch, *Zeitenwende 1979: Als die Welt von heute begann* (Munich: C. H. Beck, 2019).

2. Der Bundeswahlleiter, *Ergebnisse früherer Bundestagswahlen* (Wiesbaden: Der Bundeswahlleiter, 2018). See also E. Gene Frankland and Donald Schoonmaker, *Between Protest and Power: The Green Party in Germany* (Boulder, CO: Westview Press, 1992), 25–30.

3. Andrei S. Markovits and Stephen J. Silvia, "The Identity Crisis of Alliance '90 / The Greens: The New Left at a Crossroad," *New German Critique* 72, no. 1 (October 1997): 127–128.

4. Arno Klönne, "Überlegungen zur sozialen Basis und politische Philosophie der grünen Partei," in *Von der Machbarkeit der Unmöglichen: Politische Gespräche über grüne Praxis und grüne Perspektiven,* ed. Sabine Stamer (Hamburg: Junius, 1985), 172.

5. Missing were Saarland, Nordrhein-Westfalen, and Schleswig-Holstein. See Bündnis 90 / Die Grünen, "Grüne Wahlergebnisse seit 1978—Bund und Länder (%)," December 8, 2017, cms.gruene.de/uploads/documents/Gruene-Wahlergebnisse.pdf.

6. Klönne, "Überlegungen," 172–173.

7. See Josef Chytry, *The Aesthetic State: A Quest in Modern German Thought* (Berkeley: University of California Press, 1989). On German philhellenism, see Suzanne L. Marchand, *Down from Olympus: Archaeology and Philhellenism in Germany, 1750–1970* (Princeton, NJ: Princeton University Press, 1996).

8. See Martin Jay, "'The Aesthetic Ideology' as Ideology; Or, What Does It Mean to Aestheticize Politics?," *Cultural Critique* 21 (April 1992): 41–61; Zygmunt Bauman, *Modernity and the Holocaust* (Ithaca, NY: Cornell University Press, 1989), 18.

9. These groups often chose to call themselves a "list" rather than a "party," in order to distance themselves from the political status quo. "*Bunt*" (multicolored) referred to the German practice of identifying political parties by colors. The *Bunte Liste* saw itself as open to members of any political coloration.

10. Frankland and Schoonmaker, *Between Protest and Power,* 126–130. See also Thomas Scharf, *The German Greens: Challenging the Consensus* (Oxford: Berg Publishers, 1994).

11. Die Grünen, *Das Bundesprogramm* (Bonn: Die Grünen, 1980). The Greens inherited the concept of grassroots democracy (*Basisdemokratie*) from the New Social Movements of the 1970s. See E. Gene Frankland, "The Evolution of the Greens in Germany: From Amateurism to Professionalism," in *Green Parties in Transition: The End of Grass-roots Democracy?,* ed. E. Gene Frankland, Paul Lucardie, and Benoît Rihoux (Surrey: Ashgate, 2008), 25–26.

12. Horst Bieber, "Sie eint nur der Protest. Aber die Parteigründung ist beschlossene Sache," *Die Zeit,* October 26, 1979.

13. See Frankland and Schoonmaker, *Between Protest and Power,* 16. See also Detlef Murphy and Roland Roth, "In viele Richtungen zugleich. Die Grünen—eine Artefakt der Fünf-Prozent-Klausel?" in *Neue soziale Bewegungen in der Bundesrepublik Deutschland,* ed. Roland Roth, Dieter Rucht, and Sabine Berthold, 303–324 (Frankfurt am Main: Campus, 1987).

14. Andrei S. Markovits, "Reflections and Observations on the 1983 Bundestag Elections and Their Consequences for West German Politics," *New German Critique* 28 (January 1983): 11–12. On the Greens' impact on the SPD, see Andrei S. Markovits, "The Vicissitudes of West German Social Democracy in the Crisis of the 1980s," *Studies in Political Economy* 19 (1986): 83–112, esp. 98–99. On the Greens' early opposition to NATO, see Hans-Georg Betz, "Strange Love? How the Greens Began to Love NATO," *German Studies Review* 12, no. 3 (October 1989): 487–505.

15. Frankland and Schoonmaker, *Between Protest and Power,* 79.

16. Frankland, "Evolution of the Greens," 26–35.

17. See Silke Mende, *Nicht rechts, nicht links, sondern vorn: Eine Geschichte der Gründungsgrünen* (Munich: Oldenbourg, 2011); Jürgen Hoffmann, *Die doppelte Vereinigung: Vorgeschichte, Verlauf und Auswirkungen des Zusammenschlusses von Grünen und Bündnis 90* (Opladen: Leske und Budrich, 1998), 76–94; Andrei S. Markovits and Philip S. Gorski, *Grün schlägt rot. Die deutsche Linke nach 1945* (Hamburg: Rotbuch, 1997), 181ff.; Dick Richardson, "The Green Challenge: Philosophical, Programmatic, and Electoral Considerations," in *The Green Challenge: The Development of Green Parties in Europe,* ed. Dick Richardson and Chris Rootes (London: Routledge, 1995), 4–22.

18. Robert Michels, *Political Parties: A Sociological Study of the Oligarchical Tendencies of Modern Democracy* (New York: Dover, 1959).

19. Markovits and Silvia, "Identity Crisis," 130. See also Joachim Raschke und Gudrun Heinrich, *Die Grünen. Wie sie wurden, was sie sind* (Cologne: Bund-Verlag, 1993).

20. Die Grünen, *Das Bundesprogramm,* 5, 42.

21. On the self's relationship to the world in the German intellectual tradition, see Jerrold E. Seigel, *The Idea of the Self: Thought and Experience in Western Europe since the Seventeenth Century* (New York: Cambridge University Press, 2005), 295–426, 537–602. See also Charles Taylor, *Sources of the Self: The Making of the Modern Identity* (Cambridge, MA: Harvard University Press, 1989).

22. Sabine Von Dirke, *All Power to the Imagination! The West German Counterculture from the Student Movement to the Greens* (Lincoln: University of Nebraska Press, 1997), 185. See Die Grünen, *Das Bundesprogramm,* 5; Thomas Poguntke, "The Organization of a Participatory Party: The German Greens," *European Journal of Political Research* 15, no. 6 (1987): 609–633.

23. On criticisms of the Green program, see, for example, "Grüne: Sehr interessante Kehrtwendung," *Spiegel,* June 27, 1982.

24. Manon Maren-Grisebach, *Philosophie der Grünen* (Munich: Olzog, 1982), 57.

25. Maren-Grisebach, *Philosophie,* 23. See also Siegfried Kracauer, *The Mass Ornament: Weimar Essays,* ed. and trans. Thomas Y. Levin (Cambridge, MA: Harvard University Press, 1995), 76, 83.

26. Ronald Inglehart, *Culture Shift in Advanced Industrial Society* (Princeton, NJ: Princeton University Press, 1990); Ronald Inglehart, *Modernization and Postmodernization: Cultural, Economic, and Political Change in 43 Societies* (Princeton, NJ: Princeton University Press, 1997), 131–159; Ronald Inglehart, *The Silent Revolution: Changing Values and Political Styles among Western Publics* (Princeton, NJ: Princeton University Press, 1977); Robyn Eckersley, *The Green State: Rethinking Democracy and Sovereignty* (Cambridge, MA: MIT Press, 2004).

27. On the rising expectations of the working class and the absence of a historically consistent understanding of "subsistence," see Eduard Bernstein, *Evolutionary Socialism: A Criticism and Affirmation* (New York: Schocken Books, 1961).

28. See Peter Flora and Jens Alber, "Modernization, Democratization and the Development of Welfare States in Western Europe," in *The Development of Welfare States in Europe and America,* ed. Peter Flora and Arnold J. Heidenheimer (New Brunswick: Transaction Books, 1981); Wilhelm P. Bürklin, "Governing Left Parties Frustrating the Radical Non-Established Left: The Rise and Inevitable Decline of the Greens," *European Sociological Review* 3, no. 2 (September 1987): 109–126; Hans-Joachim Veen, "The Greens as a Milieu Party," in *The Greens in West Germany: Organisation and Policy Making,* ed. and trans. Eva Kolinsky, trans. Lindsay Batson (Oxford: Berg, 1989).

29. Maren-Grisebach, *Philosophie,* 27.

30. Frankland and Schoonmaker, *Between Protest and Power,* 17.

31. Hans Jonas, *Das Prinzip Verantwortung: Versuch einer Ethik für die technologische Zivilisation* (Frankfurt am Main: Insel, 1979). On the Greens' affinity for Jonas, see Jost Hermand, *Im Wettlauf mit der Zeit: Anstösse zu einer ökologiebewussten*

Ästhetik (Berlin: Edition Sigma, 1991), 157; Norbert Walz, "Die Erlösung der Natur," *Widerspruch* 38 (2002): 53.

32. See Roland Schmidt, "Zur alternativen Kultur. Erscheinungsbild und Strukturen," *Aus Politik und Zeitgeschichte* B 11 (March 1983): 54. Schmidt cites Bloch from *Das Prinzip Hoffnung, 1. Band* (Frankfurt am Main: Suhrkamp, 1977), 163.

33. Tilman Spengler, "Der Bauch als Avantgarde—Über den aufrechten Niedergang der Theorie," *Kursbuch* 65 (1981): 183.

34. Schmidt, "Zur alternativen Kultur," 53. See also Jörg Bopp, "Trauer-Power. Zur Jugendrevolte 1981," *Kursbuch* 65 (1981): 151–168. On the concept of authenticity in the alternative culture of the 1970s and 1980s, see Sven Reichardt, *Authentizität und Gemeinschaft: Linksalternatives Leben in den siebziger und frühen achtziger Jahren* (Berlin: Surhkamp, 2014); Joachim C. Häberlen, Mark Keck-Szajbel, and Kate Mahoney, eds., *The Politics of Authenticity: Countercultures and Radical Movements across the Iron Curtain, 1968–1989* (New York: Berghahn, 2018).

35. See Schmidt, "Zur alternativen Kultur," 50–51; Bopp, "Trauer-Power," 155f. See also Benny Härlin, "Von Haus zu Haus. Berliner Bewegungsstudien," *Kursbuch* 65 (1981): 15; Adolf Muschg, "Die Macht der Phantasie. Über die Ästhetik des Jugendprotests—am Beispiel der Züricher 'Bewegung,'" in *Aussteigen oder rebellieren. Jugendliche gegen Staat und Gesellschaft,* ed. Michael Haller (Reinbek bei Hamburg: Rowohlt, 1981), 183f.

36. Norbert Kostede, "The Greens and Intellectuals," in *The Greens in West Germany: Organisation and Policy Making,* ed. and trans. Eva Kolinsky (Oxford: Berg, 1989), 127–128.

37. Kostede, "Greens," 123, 137–138. See also Niklas Luhmann, *Ökologische Kommunikation. Kann die moderne Gesellschaft sich auf ökologische Gefährdungen einstellen?* (Opladen: Westdeutscher, 1986).

38. Peter Altendorfer, "Die Kunstbanausen: Über das (Nicht)Verhältnis der Grünen zur Kunst und Kultur. Versuch einer Herausforderung," *Kunstforum International* 93 (1988): 123–125.

39. Von Dirke, *All Power to the Imagination!,* 186–188, 193. See also Jost Hermand and Hubert Müller, eds., *Öko-Kunst? Zur Ästhetik der Grünen* (Hamburg: Argument-Verlag, 1989).

40. BArch (Koblenz) N 1569/774, pag. 127–133, Hajo Cornel, "Zwei Jahre AL-Kulturpolitik: Eine Bilanz," July 1983.

41. The BAG-Kultur was founded in January 1984 at the Green Cultural Congress in Hamburg. See Josef Boyer, Helge Heidemeyer, and Tim B. Peters, *Die Grünen im Bundestag: Sitzungsprotokolle und Anlagen 1983–1987* (Düsseldorf: Droste, 2008), 620, 631; Kulturbereich der Alternativen Liste, "Der Kulturbereich der Alternativen Liste stellt vor," in *Zum Thema: Kulturpolitik,* ed. Hajo Cornel et al. (Berlin: Die Alternative Liste Berlin, 1985).

42. BArch (Koblenz) N 1569/774, pag. 192–193, Klaus W. Becker, BAG Kultur, "Antrag an die Fraktion: Ein Votum für die Kultur," September 28, 1985.

43. BArch (Koblenz) N 1569/771, pag. 333–338, Annemarie Borgmann, "Von Adorno bis Zadek: Keine Problem! Aber: Kultur fängt vorher an . . . Ein Stück Brachland grüner Politik," 1985.

44. On the trajectory of the concept of *Kultur* in Germany, see Wolf Lepenies, *The Seduction of Culture in German History* (Princeton, NJ: Princeton University Press, 2006).

45. Norbert Elias, *The Civilizing Process* (Oxford: Blackwell, 1994), 6, 23–24.

46. Peter Gay, *Weimar Culture: The Outsider as Insider* (New York: Harper and Row, 1968); Helmut Lethen, *Cool Conduct: The Culture of Distance in Weimar Germany* (Berkeley: University of California Press, 2002); Lepenies, *The Seduction of Culture;* Jonathan O. Wipplinger, *The Jazz Republic: Music, Race, and American Culture in Weimar Germany* (Ann Arbor: University of Michigan Press, 2017); Mark Christian Thompson, *Anti-Music: Jazz and Racial Blackness in German Thought between the Wars* (Albany: State University of New York Press, 2018).

47. Uta G. Poiger, *Jazz, Rock, and Rebels: Cold War Politics and American Culture in a Divided Germany* (Berkeley: University of California Press, 2000); David Robb, *Protest Song in East and West Germany since the 1960s* (Rochester, NY: Camden House, 2007). On the mobilization of humor in art to work through flagging faith in oppositional aesthetics, see Gregory H. Williams, *Permission to Laugh: Humor and Politics in Contemporary German Art* (Chicago: University of Chicago Press, 2012).

48. Poiger, *Jazz, Rock, and Rebels;* Victoria de Grazia, *Irresistible Empire: America's Advance through Twentieth-Century Europe* (Cambridge, MA: Belknap Press of Harvard University Press, 2005).

49. Eckard Holler, "Soziokultur als Gegenkonzept zur etablierten Elitekultur?," *Das Argument* 151 (May/June 1985): 399.

50. Sabine Weißler, "Grüne Selbstverständlichkeiten: Zum Problem grün-alternativer Kulturprogramme," *Alternative Kommunalpolitik* 3 (1984): 23–24.

51. Hilmar Hoffmann, *Kultur für alle. Perspetiven und Modelle* (Frankfurt am Main: S. Fischer Verlag, 1979); Hilmar Hoffmann, *Kultur für morgen* (Frankfurt am Main: Fischer Taschenbuch Verlag, 1985).

52. Hermann Glaser, *Kleine Kulturgeschichte der Bundesrepublik Deutschland 1945–1989* (Bonn: Bundeszentrale für politische Bildung, 1991), 366.

53. BArch (Koblenz) N 1569/770, pag. 173–175, Christoph Schröder, "Zu einem 'grünen' Kulturbegriff," September 16, 1985.

54. Hajo Cornel et al., eds., *Zum Thema: Kulturpolitik* (Berlin: Die Alternative Liste Berlin, 1985), 8–9.

55. BArch (Koblenz) N 1569/774, pag. 190, Annemarie Borgmann, Kulturpolitische Debatte der Fraktion, October 1, 1985.

56. BArch (Koblenz) N 1569/770, pag. 173–175, Christoph Schröder, "Zu einem 'grünen' Kulturbegriff," September 16, 1985.

57. BArch (Koblenz) N 1569/772, pag. 52–53, Heidemarie Dann, "Thesen zur Kulturpolitik," January 14, 1985.

58. In Hamburg in January 1984, in Frankfurt in June 1984, and in Marburg in October 1984.

59. BArch (Koblenz) N 1569/774, pag. 171, Fachgruppe Kultur der GAL Hamburg, Invitation to the first Green-Alternative Bundeskongress on Kulturpolitik, January 1984. See also AGG, Kul 105–12, Grüne und Alternative in den Räten Nordrhein-Westfalens, “Arbeitsmappe. Grün-alternativer Bundeskongreß zur Kulturpolitik, 27.-29.1.1984,” Hamburg, 1984.

60. “Alternativen in der Kulturpolitik. Bestandsaufnahme und Neuansätze eines unterbelichteten Politikfeldes,” *Alternative Kommunalpolitik* 3 (1984): 17.

61. Deutscher Bundestag, Plenarprotokoll 10/99, Stenographische Berichte, 99. Sitzung, November 9, 1984. See also Deutscher Bundestag, Drucksachen 10/382, 10/785, 10/2236, 10/2237, 10/2262, 10/2279, and 10/2280. Together, these inquiries and statements formed the impetus for the Bundestag debate.

62. Deutscher Bundestag, Plenarprotokoll 10/99, Stenographische Berichte, 99. Sitzung, November 9, 1984, 7186.

63. Schmidt, “Zur alternativen Kultur,” 51. For the arguments of Schmidt’s interlocutors, see Wolfgang Kraushaar, “Thesen zum Verhältnis von Alternativ- und Fluchtbewegung,” in *Autonomie oder Getto? Kontroversen über die Alternativbewegung,* ed. Wolfgang Kraushaar, 8–67 (Frankfurt am Main: Verlag Neue Kritik, 1978); Claus Offe, “Konkurrenzpartei und kollektive politische Identität,” in *Parlamentarisches Ritual und politische Alternativen,* ed. Roland Roth, 26–42 (Frankfurt am Main: Campus, 1980).

64. Schmidt, “Zur alternativen Kultur,” 41–42. Schmidt mobilizes Habermas’s understanding of protest as “resistance against the tendency to colonize the lifeworld.” See Jürgen Habermas, *Theory of Communicative Action, vol. 2* (Boston: Beacon, 1987).

65. Hajo Cornel, “‘Rahmenbedingungen für eine Kultur im Widerspruch.’ Finanzielle, bürokratische und ideologische Fesseln der kommunalen Kulturpolitik,” *Alternative Kommunalpolitik* 3 (1984): 21.

66. Weißler, “Grüne Selbstverständlichkeiten,” 23–24.

67. Maren-Grisebach, *Philosophie,* 126–131.

68. Weißler, “Grüne Selbstverständlichkeiten,” 23–24. On the concept of *Selbermachen,* see Reinhild Kreis, *Selbermachen: Eine andere Geschichte des Konsumzeitalters* (Frankfurt am Main: Campus, 2020); Reinhild Kreis, “Heimwerken als Protest. Instandbesetzer und Wohnungsbaupolitik in West-Berlin während der 1980er-Jahre,” *Zeithistorische Forschungen/Studies in Contemporary History* 14 (2017): 41–67.

69. Sigmund Freud, *Civilization and Its Discontents,* trans. James Strachey (New York: W. W. Norton, 1989), 69–70, 78, 81–82.

70. Carl Amery, “Die philosophischen Grundlagen und Konsequenzen der Alternativbewegung,” in *Die Grünen: Personen, Projekte, Programme,* ed. Hans-Werner Lüdke and Olaf Dinné (Stuttgart-Degerloch: Seewald, 1980). On the im-

portance of positive, life-affirming utopia over negative utopia, see Herbert Marcuse, *Eros and Civilization: A Philosophical Inquiry into Freud* (Boston: Beacon Press, 1966), 83–84.

71. Amery, "Philosophischen Grundlagen," 20–21. Amery published his lecture as *Das ökologische Problem als Kulturauftrag* (Oldenburg: Bibliotheks- und Informationssystem der Universität Oldenburg, 1988).

72. Wolf-Dieter Hasenclever, "Ökologischer Humanismus," in *Die Grünen: Personen, Projekte, Programme,* ed. Hans-Werner Lüdke and Olaf Dinné (Stuttgart-Degerloch: Seewald, 1980), 46. See Ernst Bloch, *Das Prinzip Hoffnung. Gesamtausgabe, vol. 5* (Frankfurt am Main: Suhrkamp, 1977), 816.

73. Hasenclever, "Ökologischer Humanismus," 42, 50–51. On Schweitzer's philosophy of "reverence for life," see Albert Schweitzer, "The Ethics of Reverence for Life," *The Philosophy of Civilization* (Buffalo: Prometheus, 1987), 307–329.

74. BArch (Koblenz) N 1569/771, pag. 333–338, Annemarie Borgmann, "Von Adorno bis Zadek."

75. Weißler, "Grüne Selbstverständlichkeiten," 23–24.

76. Maren-Grisebach, *Philosophie,* 76–77.

77. Schmidt, "Zur alternativen Kultur," 41. See Thomas Ziehe und Herbert Stubenrauch, *Plädoyer für ungewöhnliches Lernen. Ideen zur Jugendsituation* (Reinbek bei Hamburg: Rowohlt, 1982), 25ff.

78. Von Dirke, *All Power to the Imagination!,* 185.

79. Schmidt, "Zur alternativen Kultur," 52. Schmidt drew the braid metaphor from Peter Brückner, "Thesen zur Diskussion der 'Alternativen,'" in *Autonomie oder Getto? Kontroversen über die Alternativbewegung,* ed. Wolfgang Kraushaar (Frankfurt am Main: Verlag Neue Kritik, 1978), 68. On the common agenda of the Alternative Movement, see Bundesministerium für Jugend, Familie und Gesundheit, "Zur alternativen Kultur in der Bundesrepublik Deutschland." *Aus Politik und Zeitgeschichte* B 39 (1981): 3–15.

80. Schmidt drew on Urs Jaeggi, "Drinnen und draußen," in *Stichworte zur 'Geistigen Situation der Zeit,' vol. 2,* ed. Jürgen Habermas, 443–473 (Frankfurt am Main: Suhrkamp, 1979).

81. Christiane Zieseke, "Dezentrale Kultur—Stiefkind etablierter Kulturpolitik," in *Zum Thema: Kulturpolitik,* ed. Hajo Cornel et al. (Berlin: Die Alternative Liste Berlin, 1985), 18.

82. Sabine Weißler, "Vom Umgang mit Geschichte," in *Zum Thema: Kulturpolitik,* ed. Hajo Cornel et al. (Berlin: Die Alternative Liste Berlin, 1985), 15–16; Weißler, "Grüne Selbstverständlichkeiten," 23–24.

83. Uwe Fricke, "Kultur—Ästhetik—Kunst," in *Zum Thema: Kulturpolitik,* ed. Hajo Cornel et al. (Berlin: Die Alternative Liste Berlin, 1985), 32–33.

84. Abgeordnetenhaus Berlin, Drucksache 9/35, Große Anfrage im Abgeordnetenhaus zur Breker-Ausstellung. The parliamentary debate in response to this

inquiry was held on June 25, 1981. See also William Saroyan, "Zeitmosaik," *Die Zeit,* May 22, 1981.

85. The Greens' first few years in the Berlin Senate saw the party's involvement in debates about the film scene in Berlin (debated on October 8, 1981); the status of a fiftieth anniversary project with the Berliner *Kulturrat* (Abgeordnetenhaus Berlin, Drucksache 9 / 188, debated on November 12, 1981, and 9 / 330, debated on March 24, 1982); funding and support for independent theater groups (debated in the cultural subcommittee in May 1982); support for artists (debated on January 20, 1983); funding for the annual Independent Berlin Art Exhibit (debated February 10, 1983); reading culture (Abgeordnetenhaus Berlin, Drucksache 9 / 2231, debated on October 25, 1984); and literary production (Abgeordnetenhaus Berlin, Drucksache 9 / 1415).

86. The Greens initially held only nine seats, a small number compared to the SPD's fifty-one and the CDU's sixty-five.

87. BArch (Koblenz) N 1569 / 774, pag. 127–133, Hajo Cornel, "Zwei Jahre AL"; Kulturbereich der Alternativen Liste, "Der Kulturbereich der Alternativen Liste stellt vor."

88. Wirsching et al., "The 1970s and 1980s as a Turning Point," 13.

89. Hajo Cornel, "Kultur," in *Handbuch für alternative Kommunalpolitik,* ed. Wolfgang Pohl et al. (Bielefeld: AJZ, 1985), 292–299.

90. BArch (Koblenz) N 1569 / 774, pag. 153, Christiane Zieseke, Berliner Kulturrat, September 22, 1982.

91. BArch (Koblenz) N 1569 / 774, pag. 127–133, Hajo Cornel, "Zwei Jahre AL." See also Kulturbereich der Alternativen Liste, "Der Kulturbereich der Alternativen Liste stellt vor"; Abgeordnetenhaus Berlin, Drucksache 9 / 188, Antrag, "50 Jahre Machtergreifung durch die NSDAP" (debated on November 12, 1981); Abgeordnetenhaus Berlin, Drucksache 9 / 330 (debated on March 24, 1982).

92. See Abgeordnetenhaus Berlin, Drucksache 9 / 619 (debated on June 24, 1982).

93. BArch (Koblenz) N 1569 / 774, pag. 153, Christiane Zieseke, Berliner Kulturrat, September 22, 1982.

94. BArch (Koblenz) N 1569 / 774, pag. 127–133, Hajo Cornel, "Zwei Jahre AL."

95. LArch Berlin, B Rep. 232–233, 1 Actives Museum Faschismus und Widerstand e. V., Gründung des Vereins, May 25, 1984.

96. BArch (Koblenz) N 1569 / 774, pag. 143, Roland Stelter, January 19, 1983.

97. LArch Berlin, B Rep. 232–233, 1 Actives Museum Faschismus und Widerstand e. V., Gründung des Vereins, May 25, 1984.

98. Jost Hermand, *Orte, irgendwo: Formen utopischen Denkens* (Königstein im Taunus: Athenäum, 1981), 134–135. See also Jost Hermand, *Grüne Utopien in Deutschland: Zur Geschichte des ökologischen Bewußtseins* (Frankfurt am Main: Fischer Taschenbuch Verlag, 1991).

99. Maren-Grisebach, *Philosophie,* 132–134.

100. On the Alternative Movement's response to the creation of the German Historical Museum, see AGG, B.II.1-2744; LArch Berlin, B. Rep. 232–233, 1–3, and 6; BArch (Koblenz) N 1569 / 740–741.

101. See, for example, AGG B.II.1, Die Grünen im Bundestag 1983–1990, 5683, Gedenkstätte für die Opfer des Nationalsozialismus auf dem Synagogenplatz Bonn.

102. AGG A-Düllmann, Gina, 64, Gedenkstätte, Bd. II, Pressemitteilung Nr. 579 / 85, "Nationale Gedenkstätte ist überflüssig," November 2, 1984; Deutscher Bundestag, Plenarprotokoll 10 / 99, Stenographische Berichte, 99. Sitzung, November 9, 1984, 7195D.

103. Kulturbereich der Alternativen Liste, "Der Kulturbereich der Alternativen Liste stellt vor," 11.

104. AGG A-Düllmann, Gina, 64, Gedenkstätte, Bd. II, Deutscher Bundestag, Drucksache 10 / 4521, Antrag der Fraktion Die Grünen, Geplante zentrale Mahn- und Gedenkstätte im Regierungsviertel in Bonn, December 11, 1985.

105. Kulturbereich der Alternativen Liste, "Der Kulturbereich der Alternativen Liste stellt vor."

106. Weißler, "Vom Umgang mit Geschichte," 14–16. For federal parliamentary documents that present Green views on other old or traditional spaces, see Drucksachen 10 / 382, 10 / 785, 10 / 2236, 10 / 2237, 10 / 2262, 10 / 2279, and 10 / 2280; at the regional level in Berlin see 9 / 1674, and 9 / 1675.

107. On early postwar local politics in Berlin, see, for example, Timothy Moss, "Divided City, Divided Infrastructures: Securing Energy and Water Services in Postwar Berlin," *Journal of Urban History* 35, no. 7 (2009): 923–942.

108. Scharf, *German Greens,* 28–38. On local political apathy during the postwar years, see Jutta Beyer and Everhard Holtmann, "'Sachpolitik,' Partizipation und Apathie in der Nachkriegsgesellschaft," in *Politische Kultur in Deutschland: Bilanz und Perspektiven der Forschung,* ed. Dirk Berg-Schlosser and Jakob Schissler, 144–154 (Opladen: Westdeutscher, 1987).

109. Deutscher Bundestag, Plenarprotokoll 10 / 99, Stenographische Berichte, 99. Sitzung, November 9, 1984; BArch (Koblenz) N1569 / 770, pag. 241–278.

110. Volker Gransow, "A Greening of German-German Relations?," in *The Greens in West Germany: Organisation and Policy Making,* ed. Eva Kolinsky (Oxford: Berg, 1989), 149.

111. BArch (Koblenz) N 1569 / 774, pag. 161, 21. Sitzung, Haushaltsrede on Kulturpolitik, Peter Finger, March 26, 1982.

112. Weißler, "Grüne Selbstverständlichkeiten," 23–24.

113. See David Templin, *Freizeit ohne Kontrollen: Die Jugendzentrumsbewegung in der Bundesrepublik der 1970er Jahre* (Göttingen: Wallstein, 2015).

114. See, for example, the Greens' major interpellation (*große Anfrage*) in the Berlin Abgeordnetenhaus about cultural houses and sociocultural centers in Berlin: Abgeordnetenhaus Berlin, Drucksache 9 / 1343 (debated on October 20,

1983). On the Greens' unsuccessful attempt in 1983–1984 to save the Kunst- und Kulturzentrum in Kreuzberg, see Kulturbereich der Alternativen Liste, "Der Kulturbereich der Alternativen Liste stellt vor."

115. BArch (Koblenz) N 1569 / 774, pag. 134, Jürgen Kunze, AL für Demokratie und Umweltschutz Berlin, May 30, 1984.

116. BArch (Koblenz) N 1569 / 774, pag. 177–179, Axel Stozenwaldt, Protokoll der BAG-Kultur, September 8–9, 1985.

117. BArch (Koblenz) N 1569 / 772, pag. 52–53, Heidemarie Dann, "Thesen zur Kulturpolitik," January 14, 1985.

118. "Wahlprogramm—Kultur," in *Zum Thema: Kulturpolitik,* ed. Hajo Cornel et al. (Berlin: Die Alternative Liste Berlin, 1985), 38–39.

119. BArch (Koblenz) N 1569 / 774, pag. 177–179, Axel Stozenwaldt, Protokoll der BAG-Kultur, September 8–9, 1985.

120. Maren-Grisebach, *Philosophie,* 134.

121. BArch (Koblenz) N 1569 / 772, pag. 52–53, Heidemarie Dann, "Thesen zur Kulturpolitik," January 14, 1985.

122. See Stephen Milder, *Greening Democracy: The Anti-Nuclear Movement and Political Environmentalism in West Germany and Beyond, 1968–1983* (Cambridge: Cambridge University Press, 2017); Volker Hauff, *Global denken, lokal handeln: Ein politisches Fazit* (Cologne: Kiepenheuer und Witsch, 1992); Lutz Mez, "Von den Bürgerinitiativen zu den Grünen: Zur Entstehungsgeschichte der 'Wahlalternativen' in der Bundesrepublik Deutschland," in *Neue soziale Bewegungen in der Bundesrepublik Deutschland,* ed. Roland Roth, Dieter Rucht, and Sabine Berthold, 263–276 (Frankfurt am Main: Campus, 1987); Karl-Werner Brand, *Neue soziale Bewegungen: Entstehung, Funktion und Perspektive neuer Protestpotentiale: Eine Zwischenbilanz* (Opladen: Westdeutscher, 1982); Dieter Rucht, *Von Wyhl nach Gorleben: Bürger gegen Atomprogramm und nukleare Entsorgung* (Munich: Beck, 1980); Fritjof Capra and Charlene Spretnak, *Green Politics: The Global Promise* (New York: Dutton, 1984).

123. Scharf, *German Greens;* Hauff, *Global denken,* 108–113.

124. BArch (Koblenz) N 1569 / 774, pag. 127–133, Hajo Cornel, "Zwei Jahre AL."

125. See Veen, "Greens as a Milieu Party," 31. See also M. Rainer Lepsius, "Parteiensystem und Sozialstruktur. Zum Problem der Demokratisierung der deutschen Gesellschaft," in *Deutsche Parteien vor 1918,* ed. Gerhard A. Ritter (Cologne: Kiepenheuer und Witsch, 1973).

126. Veen, "Greens as a Milieu Party," 50–51, 53.

127. Frankland and Schoonmaker, *Between Protest and Power,* 126. See also Rudolf van Hüllen, *Ideologie und Machtkampf bei den Grünen. Untersuchung zur programmatischen und innerorganisatorischen Entwicklung einer deutschen "Bewegungspartei"* (Bonn: Bouvier, 1990).

128. On two major camps, see Hajo Cornel, "'Rahmenbedingungen für eine Kultur im Widerspruch,'" 18–22; C. J. Schröder, "Kunst als Klassenkampf oder

Kultur für alle? Der Richtungsstreit in der grün-alternativen Kulturpolitik," *grüner basisdienst* 3 (1985): 23–27; C. J. Schröder, "Drei Fallen einer grün-alternativen Kulturpolitik," *Kultur und Gesellschaft* 4 (1984).

129. BArch (Koblenz) N 1569 / 774, pag. 192–193, Klaus W. Becker, BAG Kultur, "Antrag an die Fraktion."

4. A Sustainable Cultural Politics

1. Berlin's Alternative List, for example, issued sixty-five minor interpellations on the theme of cultural politics between 1985 and 1989. BArch (Koblenz) N 1569 / 774, pag. 120–123, Alternative Liste, *Zum Thema: Kultur,* 1989.

2. Dennis Soron, "Back to the Future: The Contemporary Left and the Politics of Utopia," *Labour / Le Travail* 47 (2001): 216.

3. Joachim Raschke, "Jenseits der Volkspartei," *Das Argument* 25, no. 137 (1983): 54–64.

4. E. Gene Frankland and Donald Schoonmaker, *Between Protest and Power: The Green Party in Germany* (Boulder, CO: Westview Press, 1992), 2, 75–79. On the issue of gender parity, see Beate Hoecker and Bundeszentrale für politische Bildung, "Frauen in der Politik—Dossier Frauen," November 5, 2009, www.bpb.de/gesellschaft/gender/frauen-in-deutschland/49362/frauen-in-der-politik. On the Greens' sartorial presence in parliament, see "Ärger um die Kleiderordnung im Bundestag: Nur ohne meine Krawatte," *sueddeutsche.de,* February 16, 2011, www.sueddeutsche.de/politik/aerger-um-die-kleiderordnung-im-bundestag-nur-ohne-meine-krawatte-1.1061031.

5. Elim Papadakis, "Green Issues and Other Parties: Themenklau or New Flexibility?," in *The Greens in West Germany: Organisation and Policy Making,* ed. Eva Kolinsky (Oxford: Berg, 1989), 66.

6. Since the beginning of the 1980s, the SPD lost thirty-two seats in the Bundestag, which marked a total loss of forty-four seats since 1972, the height of their federal elections returns. They also lost their coalition partner, the Free Democrats.

7. Samuel Moyn, *The Last Utopia: Human Rights in History* (Cambridge, MA: Belknap Press of Harvard University Press, 2010), 9.

8. Moyn, *Last Utopia,* 225–227.

9. Yosef Jabareen, "A New Conceptual Framework for Sustainable Development," *Environment, Development and Sustainability* 10, no. 2 (April 2008): 179, 186.

10. World Commission on Environment and Development, *Report of the World Commission on Environment and Development: Our Common Future* (1987), www.un-documents.net/wced-ocf.htm, 13, 16–17.

11. World Commission on Environment and Development, *Report,* 6, 246.

12. As evidence, the commission pointed to heartening global developments: decreasing infant mortality alongside rising life expectancy, literacy, and global

food production. See World Commission on Environment and Development, *Report,* 11–12, 28.

13. World Commission on Environment and Development, *Report,* 29, 39.

14. Andrew Dobson, *Green Political Thought* (London: Routledge, 2000), 206–207.

15. Marius de Geus, *Ecological Utopias: Envisioning the Sustainable Society* (Utrecht: International, 1999), 260.

16. Jabareen, "A New Conceptual Framework for Sustainable Development," 189.

17. Marc Antrop, "Sustainable Landscapes: Contradiction, Fiction or Utopia?," *Landscape and Urban Planning* 75, no. 3–4 (March 2006): 187–197.

18. Patrik Baard and Karin Edvardsson Björnberg, "Cautious Utopias: Environmental Goal-Setting with Long Time Frames," *Ethics, Policy and Environment* 18, no. 2 (May 2015): 193.

19. Papadakis, "Green Issues," 72–77.

20. Matthias Kaelberer, "The Emergence of Green Parties in Western Europe," *Comparative Politics* 25, no. 2 (January 1993): 240.

21. Andrei S. Markovits and Philip S. Gorski, *The German Left: Red, Green and Beyond* (New York: Oxford University Press, 1993), 205–208; Papadakis, "Green Issues," 63. See also Sozialdemokratische Partei Deutschlands, *Frieden mit der Natur, für eine umweltverträgliche Industriegesellschaft, beschlossen auf dem Bundesparteitag, Essen* (Bonn: SPD, 1984), 2; Sozialdemokratische Partei Deutschlands, *Irsee Draft of New SPD Manifesto* (Bonn: SPD, 1986), 58.

22. Markovits and Gorski, *German Left,* 270, 272. On the broad political recognition of the urgency of environmental issues, see Volker Hauff, *Global denken, lokal handeln: Ein politisches Fazit* (Cologne: Kiepenheuer und Witsch, 1992), 139–162.

23. Papadakis, "Green Issues," 67–69. See also Thomas Poguntke, "New Politics and Party Systems: The Emergency of a New Type of Party?," *West European Politics* 10, no. 1 (1986), 82; Claus Offe, "New Social Movements: Changing the Boundaries of Institutional Politics," *Social Research* 52, no. 4 (1985): 860.

24. Kaelberer, "Emergence," 238. See also Papadakis, "Green Issues." On the Greens' descent into crisis, see Markovits and Gorski, *German Left,* 191–192.

25. Stephen Milder, *Greening Democracy: The Anti-Nuclear Movement and Political Environmentalism in West Germany and Beyond, 1968–1983* (Cambridge: Cambridge University Press, 2017).

26. On Hauff's environmental political agendas, see Volker Hauff and World Commission on Environment and Development, *Unsere gemeinsame Zukunft: Der Brundtland-Bericht der Weltkommission für Umwelt und Entwicklung* (Greven: Eggenkamp, 1987), xi–xvii.

27. On *Themenklau,* see Papadakis, "Green Issues," 61–85.

28. On the Greens' fears of becoming "*stinknormal,*" see Wolf-Dieter Hasenclever, "Die Grünen sind eine stinknormale Partei geworden," in *Die Grünen: 10 be-*

wegte Jahre, ed. Michael Schroeren (Vienna: Ueberreuter, 1990); Antje Vollmer, "Die Grünen brauchen eine Kulturrevolution. Die Grünen-Bundestagsabgeordnete Antje Vollmer über die Schwierigkeiten ihrer Partei," *Spiegel,* March 14, 1988. See also Frankland and Schoonmaker, *Between Protest and Power,* 108–110.

29. Susan Buck-Morss, *Dreamworld and Catastrophe: The Passing of Mass Utopia in East and West* (Cambridge, MA: MIT Press, 2000), 101.

30. BArch (Koblenz) N 1569 / 772, pag. 3–7, Claudia Siede, Redeentwurf zur kulturpolitischen Debatte im Deutschen Bundestag, October 31, 1990.

31. Martin Fischer, "'Schlechtgemachte Bilder, schlechtgemachtes Fernsehen, schlechtgeführte Ehen, . . .' Auf den Spuren grüner Kulturpolitik am Beispiel der Bundesrepublik Deutschland," in *Nur kein Rhabarber! Auseinandersetzungen mit grüner Politik in Österreich,* ed. Karl Lind (Vienna: Grün-Alternativ-Verlag, 1988), 127.

32. Matthias Greffrath, "Die missbrauchte Kraft des Schönen. Auf dem Weg in die 'Kulturgesellschaft,'" *Die Zeit,* November 25, 1988, 65.

33. Buck-Morss, *Dreamworld,* 12.

34. David Pinder, "In Defence of Utopian Urbanism: Imagining Cities after the 'End of Utopia,'" *Geografiska Annaler. Series B, Human Geography* 84, no. 3 / 4 (January 2002): 233.

35. BArch (Koblenz) N 1569 / 772, pag. 24–26, Kulturbüro / Claudia Siede on behalf of Antje Vollmer, Die Grünen im Bundestag, "Kultur und Ökologie. Plädoyer für eine Neubewertung," January 22, 1990.

36. BArch (Koblenz) N 1569 / 771, pag. 310–324, "Kommunale Kulturpolitik," September 15, 1987.

37. See Sven Reichardt, *Authentizität und Gemeinschaft: Linksalternatives Leben in den siebziger und frühen achtziger Jahren* (Berlin: Suhrkamp, 2014), 67.

38. BArch (Koblenz) N 1569 / 740, pag. 67–69, Udo Knapp, Sabine Weißler, Christiane Zieseke, "Warum wollen die Herren Kohl, Hassemer, Momper, Momsen, Fichter und Hoffmann-Axthelm Geschichte in ein Deutsches Historisches Museum einsperren?," September 1, 1985. See also BArch (Koblenz) N 1569 / 740, pag. 390–417.

39. LArch Berlin, B Rep. 232–233, 1, Protokoll, 1. Sitzung der Konzeptgruppe Verein Aktives Museums, October 27, 1983.

40. BArch (Koblenz) N 1569 / 772, pag. 55–62, Karlheinz Koinegg, Claudia Siede, Kulturbüro, Die Grünen im Bundestag, "Ein Leben für die Kartoffel. Grüne, Kunst, und Grünenkunst," August 1989.

41. BArch (Koblenz) N 1569 / 783, pag. 9–10, Uli Trostowitsch, Hubert Müller, Die Grünen in Kassel, Einladung zum Grünen Kunst- und Kultur-Gespräch, "Grünes Kunst- und Kulturgespräch zur documenta acht," July 3, 1987.

42. Lurton Blassingame, "Sustainable Cities: Oxymoron, Utopia, or Inevitability?," *Social Science Journal* 35, no. 1 (1998): 2.

43. Pinder, "In Defence of Utopian Urbanism," 238.

44. BArch (Koblenz) N 1569/771, pag. 49–64, Claudia Siede, "Plädoyer für eine grüne Chorprobe. Bausteine zu einer grünen Kultur," March 6, 1988.

45. Blassingame, "Sustainable Cities," 3.

46. Vollmer, "Die Grünen brauchen eine Kulturrevolution."

47. Micha Brumlik, "Kulturpolitik als Ermöglichung von Bildung," *Kommune* 7 (1989): 46. When this article was published, Brumlik was serving as the spokesperson for cultural matters for the Green Party in Frankfurt.

48. On Breton, imagination, and utopia, see Russell Jacoby, *The End of Utopia: Politics and Culture in an Age of Apathy* (New York: Basic Books, 1999), 180. See also André Breton, "Manifesto of Surrealism," in *Manifestos of Surrealism* (Ann Arbor: University of Michigan Press, 1972 [1924]), 4–5. For imagination's role in the Student Movement, see Ingrid Gilcher-Holtey, *Die Phantasie an die Macht: Mai 68 in Frankreich* (Frankfurt am Main: Suhrkamp, 1995); Karl Heinz Bohrer, "1968: Die Phantasie an die Macht? Studentenbewegung—Walter Benjamin—Surrealismus," *Geschichte und Gesellschaft. Sonderheft* 17 (January 1998): 288–300. See also Herbert Marcuse, *Eros and Civilization: A Philosophical Inquiry into Freud* (Boston: Beacon Press, 1966), esp. 172–185.

49. On the projects that interested the Greens in the middle of the decade, see Hajo Cornel et al., eds., *Zum Thema: Kulturpolitik* (Berlin: Die Alternative Liste Berlin, 1985).

50. BArch (Koblenz) N 1569/740, pag. 178–183, Bundesministerium für Raumordnung, Bauwesen und Städtebau, Pressemitteilung 54/88, June 10, 1988.

51. See LArch Berlin, B Rep. 232–233, 6, Mitgliederrundbrief Nr. 4, June 1988.

52. LArch Berlin, B Rep. 232–233, 1, May 25, 1984.

53. LArch Berlin, B Rep. 232–233, 1, Hajo Cornel, Alternative Liste, Fraktion des Abgeordnetenhauses von Berlin, to Gerhard Schoenberner, Heinz-Dieter Schilling, Aktives Museum, July 21, 1983; LArch Berlin, B Rep. 232–233, 2, Heinz-Dieter Schilling, November 13, 1985. On the Active Museum's willingness to work with leftist political parties, especially the Greens, see LArch Berlin, B Rep. 232–233, 2, Diskussionspapier: Ergebnisse der Arbeitsgruppe "Konzeption," April 28, 1988.

54. Frankland and Schoonmaker, *Between Protest and Power*, 74–75.

55. On the history of German efforts to conceive of nature as inclusive of human artifice, see Jens Lachmund, *Greening Berlin: The Co-Production of Science, Politics, and Urban Nature* (Cambridge, MA: MIT Press, 2013).

56. BArch (Koblenz) N 1569/730, pag. 26–34, Große Anfrage des Abgeordneten Sauermilch und der Fraktion Die Grünen, "Zivilisationsbedingte Schäden an Gebäuden, Kulturdenkmälern, und Ingenieurbauwerken," undated.

57. Michael Stürmer, "Geschichte in geschichtslosem Land," *Frankfurter Allgemeine Zeitung*, April 25, 1986. On the implications of this stance, see Geoff Eley, "Nazism, Politics and the Image of the Past: Thoughts on the West German

Historikerstreit 1986–1987," *Past and Present* 121 (1988): 171–208, esp. 194ff.; Aleida Assmann, *Geschichte im Gedächtnis: Von der individuellen Erfahrung zur öffentlichen Inszenierung* (Munich: C. H. Beck, 2007), 189; Charles S. Maier, *The Unmasterable Past: History, Holocaust, and German National Identity* (Cambridge, MA: Harvard University Press, 1988), 184n23. On the Greens' response to this idea, see BArch (Koblenz) N 1569/741, pag. 164–191, Die Grünen im Bundestag, ed., *Wider die Entsorgung der deutschen Geschichte. Streitschrift gegen die geplanten historischen Museen in Berlin (W) und Bonn* (Bonn: Die Grünen, 1986).

58. LArch Berlin, B Rep. 232–233, 2, Planungssitzung zum Gestapogelände, September 7, 1987.

59. BArch (Koblenz) N 1569/740, pag. 201–202, October 27, 1987. See also LArch Berlin, B Rep. 232–233, 3, Hilde Schramm, Annette Ahme, Entwurf des Aufrufs: Wir wollen mit Geschichte leben. Aber ohne Deutsches Historisches Museum, October 28, 1987.

60. See BArch (Koblenz) N 1569/740, pag. 51, undated.

61. BArch (Koblenz) N 1569/740, pag. 47, Der Sozialdemokratischer Bundestagsfraktion, January 15, 1986; BArch (Koblenz) N 1569/740, pag. 48–49, December 4, 1985. See also Drucksache 10/47 (May 24, 1985), Response to Kleine Anfrage Nr. 890 des Abgeordneten Dietrich Pawlowski (FDP), October 17, 1985.

62. BArch (Koblenz) N 1569/740, pag. 201–202, October 27, 1987. See also LArch Berlin, B Rep. 232–233, 3, Hilde Schramm, Annette Ahme, Entwurf des Aufrufs: Wir wollen mit Geschichte leben.

63. On engagement with the historical palimpsest in Germany's built landscape, see Daniela Sandler, *Counterpreservation: Architectural Decay in Berlin since 1989* (Ithaca, NY: Cornell University Press, 2016).

64. BArch (Koblenz) N 1569/741, pag. 164–191, Die Grünen im Bundestag, ed., *Wider die Entsorgung der deutschen Geschichte.*

65. BArch (Koblenz) N 1569/740, pag. 390–417, Die Grünen im Bundestag, Fraktion der Alternativen Liste Berlin, "Warum soll die deutsche Geschichte in ein Deutsches Historisches Museum eingesperrt werden? Einladung zum Weiterdenken," 1985.

66. BArch (Koblenz) N 1569/741, pag. 113–117, Lutz Niethammer, "Fünf Bemerkungen zur Gründung des DHM in Berlin," Kurzfassung zum Gespräch in Bonn am October 21, 1987.

67. BArch (Koblenz) N 1569/774, pag. 38–63, Die Grünen im Römer, November 17, 1986.

68. BArch (Koblenz) N 1569/740, pag. 51, undated.

69. BArch (Koblenz) N 1569/771, pag. 232–236, Han-Christian Ströbele to die Grünen im Landtag Stuttgart, May 14, 1986, a response to BArch (Koblenz) N 1569/771, pag. 229–231.

70. LArch Berlin, B Rep. 232–233, 1, Gerhard Schoenberner, March 21, 1984.

71. Inspiration for the museum's conceptual foundation came, in part, from a paper written by Thomas Vogel, titled "The Meaning of Site." LArch Berlin, B Rep. 232–233, 1, Thomas Vogel, Aktion Sühnezeichen, January 26, 1984.

72. LArch Berlin, B Rep. 232–233, 1, Gerhard Schoenberner, March 21, 1984.

73. BArch (Koblenz) N 1569/740, pag. 390–417, Die Grünen im Bundestag, Fraktion der Alternativen Liste Berlin, "Warum soll die deutsche Geschichte in ein Deutsches Historisches Museum eingesperrt werden?"

74. "Wie ein riesiges Gefängnis. Die Entwürfe zum Historischen Museum sind jetzt ausgestellt," *Tagesspiegel,* June 1988, 26.

75. BArch (Koblenz) N 1569/741, pag. 24–25, Thesenpapier, October 21, 1987.

76. "Gedenkstätten: Verfluchter Ort," *Spiegel,* May 28, 1984.

77. LArch Berlin, B Rep. 232–233, 3, Stellungnahme der AL Kreuzberg zum Ergebnis des Wettbewerbs Prinz-Albrecht-Gelände, June 7, 1984.

78. The designers included East German communists under this rubric of "terror." See Benedikt Erenz, "Der Ort, der stört," *Die Zeit,* September 2, 1988; "Gedenkstätten: Verfluchter Ort," *Spiegel,* May 28, 1984.

79. LArch Berlin, B Rep. 232–233, 3, Stellungnahme der AL Kreuzberg zum Ergebnis des Wettbewerbs Prinz-Albrecht-Gelände, June 7, 1984.

80. LArch Berlin, B Rep. 232–233, 3, Stellungnahme der AL Kreuzberg zum Ergebnis des Wettbewerbs Prinz-Albrecht-Gelände, June 7, 1984.

81. LArch Berlin, B Rep. 232–233, 1, Andreas Ludwig, "Vorüberlegungen zu einer Konzeption für das Aktive Museum Faschismus und Widerstand in Berlin," August/September 1983.

82. BArch (Koblenz) N 1569/740, pag. 390–417, Die Grünen im Bundestag, Fraktion der Alternativen Liste Berlin, "Warum soll die deutsche Geschichte in ein Deutsches Historisches Museum eingesperrt werden?"

83. BArch (Koblenz) N 1569/740, pag. 201–202, October 27, 1987. See also LArch Berlin, B Rep. 232–233, 3, October 3, 1987; BArch (Koblenz) N 1569/774, pag. 120–123, Alternative Liste, *Zum Thema: Kultur,* 1989.

84. LArch Berlin, B Rep. 232–233, 1, Andreas Ludwig, "Vorüberlegungen zu einer Konzeption für das Aktive Museum."

85. LArch Berlin, B Rep. 232–233, 1, Konzept für das Aktive Museum, Diskussionsstand, September 16, 1983.

86. BArch (Koblenz) N 1569/740, pag. 390–417, Die Grünen im Bundestag, Fraktion der Alternativen Liste Berlin, "Warum soll die deutsche Geschichte in ein Deutsches Historisches Museum eingesperrt werden?"; LArch Berlin, B Rep. 232–233, 1, Andreas Ludwig and Andreas Heinemann-Grudder, "'Aktives Museum': Ein Ort selbsttätiger Aneignung der Geschichte," undated.

87. LArch Berlin, B Rep. 232–233, 1, Berliner *Geschichtswerkstatt* Rundbrief March 1984, Andreas Ludwig, "Wie sollte ein Aktives Museum einmal werden?" Ludwig's article was circulated to the members of the Aktives Museum.

88. BArch (Koblenz) N 1569/740, pag. 390–417, Die Grünen im Bundestag, Fraktion der Alternativen Liste Berlin, "Warum soll die deutsche Geschichte in ein Deutsches Historisches Museum eingesperrt werden?"

89. LArch Berlin, B Rep. 232–233, 1, Andreas Ludwig, "Vorüberlegungen zu einer Konzeption für das Aktive Museum."

90. BArch (Koblenz) N 1569/741, pag. 44, Rede der Abg. Antje Vollmer zu DHM, October 27, 1989. See also Deutscher Bundestag, Drucksache 11/5487, Antrag der Fraktion die Grünen, Überarbeitung des Konzeptes zum "Europäischen Forum für Geschichte und Gegenwart," October 26, 1989; BArch (Koblenz) N 1569/741, pag. 48–51, Vorschlag der AL-Fraktion im Abgeordnetenhaus zum weiteren Umgang mit dem DHM, undated; BArch (Koblenz) N 1569/741, pag. 46, October 26, 1989.

91. BArch (Koblenz) N 1569/740, pag. 390–417, Die Grünen im Bundestag, Fraktion der Alternativen Liste Berlin, "Warum soll die deutsche Geschichte in ein Deutsches Historisches Museum eingesperrt werden?"

92. On the problems of cultural agency, see, for example, Eberhard Lämmert, "Wem gehört die Geschichte? Über den vernünftigen Umgang mit der Vergangenheit," *Die Zeit,* January 22, 1988.

93. Norbert Frei, *1968: Jugendrevolte und globaler Protest* (Munich: Deutscher Taschenbuch, 2008). The twentieth anniversary of the Student Movement in 1988 meant that its legacy was present in the minds of the Greens during this period. See BArch (Koblenz) N 1569/773-2, Veröffentlichungen und Dokumentationen zur Kulturpolitik, 1986–1990.

94. Karin Hanshew, *Terror and Democracy in West Germany* (Cambridge: Cambridge University Press, 2012).

95. Roland Roth, Dieter Rucht, and Sabine Berthold, eds., *Neue soziale Bewegungen in der Bundesrepublik Deutschland* (Frankfurt am Main: Campus, 1987); Ruud Koopmans, *Democracy from Below: New Social Movements and the Political System in West Germany* (Boulder, CO: Westview Press, 1995).

96. Frankland and Schoonmaker, *Between Protest and Power,* 117. Among their most enduring contributions beyond the realm of culture was their demand that women participate equally in politics. See BArch (Koblenz) N 1569/740, pag. 54, Kleine Anfrage Nr. 871, Abg. Christiane Zieseke, "Sachverständigenkommission für das DHM," October 14, 1985.

97. BArch (Koblenz) N 1569/774, pag. 38–63, Die Grünen im Römer, November 17, 1986.

98. BArch (Koblenz) N 1569/730, pag. 6, Resolution zum Erhalt der sozialistischen Denkmale in der DDR, Summer 1990. The federal Greens' cultural bureau under Antje Vollmer and Claudia Siede, for example, went to battle over the removal of monuments from the German Democratic Republic and advocated initiating open, public conversations about how to process the physical and conceptual remnants of East Germany. See BArch (Koblenz) N 1569/730, pag. 2–3,

September 3, 1990; BArch (Koblenz) N 1569/730, pag. 6, Resolution zum Erhalt der sozialistischen Denkmale in der DDR, Summer 1990. See also Matthias Flügge, "Bildersturm," *Kunst Intern* (1987).

99. BArch (Koblenz) N 1569/740, pag. 186, *Das Parlament* 46–47 (November 1987): 12.

100. BArch (Koblenz) N 1569/772, pag. 55–62, Karlheinz Koinegg, Claudia Siede, "Ein Leben für die Kartoffel."

101. BArch (Koblenz) N 1569/740, pag. 186, *Das Parlament* 46–47 (November 1987): 12. The Greens interrogated the majority leadership on these issues. They received only oblique, uncontroversial answers.

102. See BArch (Koblenz) N 1569/740, pag. 207–208, Abgeordnetenhaus von Berlin, Ausschuß für Bundesangelegenheiten und gesamtberliner Fragen, gemeinsame Sitzung mit dem Ausschuß für innerdeutsche Beziehungen des Deutschen Bundestages, October 14, 1987; BArch (Koblenz) N 1569/740, pag. 73–75, Hans-Christian Ströbele, Errichtung eines "Historischen Museums" in Berlin zur 750 Jahr Feier, July 26, 1985.

103. BArch (Koblenz) N 1569/740, pag. 390–417, Die Grünen im Bundestag, Fraktion der Alternativen Liste Berlin, "Warum soll die deutsche Geschichte in ein Deutsches Historisches Museum eingesperrt werden?"

104. BArch (Koblenz) N 1569/740, pag. 201–202, October 27, 1987. See also LArch Berlin, B Rep. 232–233, 3, October 3, 1987.

105. BArch (Koblenz) N 1569/741, pag. 32, Pressemitteilung, Arbeitsgruppe Alternative Deutschlandpolitik in der AL, Offene deutsche Frage läßt Bau des DHM nicht zu, October 21, 1989.

106. BArch (Koblenz) N 1569/741, pag. 164–191, Die Grünen im Bundestag, ed., *Wider die Entsorgung der deutschen Geschichte.*

107. See BArch (Koblenz) N 1569/740, pag. 32, Kleine Anfrage der Abgeordneten Christiane Zieseke, Einrichtung eines DHM in Berlin, October 6, 1986. For the response from Berlin's Senator for Cultural Affairs, Volker Hassemer, see BArch (Koblenz) N 1569/740, pag. 33–35, November 11, 1986.

108. BArch (Koblenz) N 1569/741, pag. 113–117, Lutz Niethammer, "Fünf Bemerkungen zur Gründung des DHM in Berlin."

109. BArch (Koblenz) N 1569/771, pag. 39–48, Rainer Zech, "Aus der Sackgasse der Selbstfesselung zu veränderten Politikformen. Beispiele aus der Basispolitik einer stadtteilbezogenen Friedensinitiative," June 16, 1988.

110. BArch (Koblenz) N 1569/741, pag. 44, Rede der Abg. Antje Vollmer zu DHM, October 27, 1989. See also Deutscher Bundestag, Drucksache 11/5487, Antrag der Fraktion die Grünen, Überarbeitung des Konzeptes zum "Europäischen Forum für Geschichte und Gegenwart," October 26, 1989; BArch (Koblenz) N 1569/741, pag. 48–51, Vorschlag der AL-Fraktion im Abgeordnetenhaus zum weiteren Umgang mit dem DHM; BArch (Koblenz) N 1569/741, pag. 46, October 26, 1989.

111. LArch Berlin, B Rep. 232–233, 1, response from Aktives Museum to inquiry from May 17, 1984, undated.

112. LArch Berlin, B Rep. 232–233, 3, Christiane Zieseke, "B 750, E 88 . . . Thesen zur Situation der Kulturpolitik und Chancen für Initativen (1989)," April 14, 1988.

113. LArch Berlin, B Rep. 232–233, 1, Berliner *Geschichtswerkstatt* Rundbrief March 1984, Andreas Ludwig, "Wie sollte ein Aktives Museum einmal werden?"; LArch Berlin, B Rep. 232–233, 1, Andreas Ludwig, "Vorüberlegungen zu einer Konzeption für das 'Aktive Museum.'" See also "Ehemaliges Konzentrationslager Neuengamme wird Mahnmal. Hamburger Senat will Teile unter Denkmalschutz stellen / Grün-Alternative Liste hält Pläne für nicht ausreichend," *Frankfurter Rundschau,* February 16, 1984. The Greens, as much as they disapproved of many of their political opponents, remained—at least in word—receptive to dialogue that included them. See BArch (Koblenz) N 1569 / 740, pag. 59, Heidi Bischoff-Pflanz, Alternative Liste für Demokratie und Umweltschutz, Fraktion des Abgeordnetenhauses, Berlin to Walter Momper, SPD-Fraktion, November 1985; BArch (Koblenz) N 1569 / 740, pag. 67–69; BArch (Koblenz) N 1569 / 740, pag. 390–417, September 1, 1985.

114. LArch Berlin, B Rep. 232–233, 3, Christiane Zieseke, "B 750, E 88."

115. On opposition to reunification from the Left, see A. Dirk Moses, *German Intellectuals and the Nazi Past* (Cambridge: Cambridge University Press, 2007), 229–245; Jan-Werner Müller, *Another Country: German Intellectuals, Unification and National Identity* (New Haven, CT: Yale University Press, 2000), 121–129.

116. The Greens' demise was not total. In the 1990 elections they still held seats in nine of the eleven original West German state parliaments, and the Eastern Greens held seats in four of the five newly assimilated state parliaments.

117. John Ely, "Green Politics and the Transformation of the Left in Germany," *New German Critique* 72 (October 1997): 180; Joachim Hirsch, *Der Sicherheitsstaat: Das "Modell Deutschland," seine Krise und die neuen sozialen Bewegungen* (Frankfurt am Main: Europäische Verlagsanstalt, 1980).

118. BArch (Koblenz) N 1569 / 771, pag. 30–34, AG Kunst und Kultur, Kassel, "Vom 'Öko-Kult' zur Öko-Kultur," May 19, 1988.

119. BArch (Koblenz) N 1569 / 740, pag. 137, Die Grünen im Bundestag. Pressemitteilung Nr. 283 / 86, Historiker erklären sich zu Kohls Staatsgeschichtsschreibern, April 28, 1986. See also Walter Benjamin, "Theses on the Philosophy of History," in *Illuminations,* ed. Hannah Arendt, trans. Harry Zohn (New York: Harcourt, Brace and World, 1968), 255.

120. Manfred Kunk, "Zwischen Kulturutopie und Kulturinstitution. Zum Stellenwert soziokultureller Zentren," *Alternative Kommunale Kulturpolitik* 1 (1988): 37–39. See also BArch (Koblenz) N 1569 / 771, pag. 35, "Entwurf für Perspektiven: Kultur: Die Grünen wollen künftig stärker mitmischen," *Hessische-Niedersächsische Allgemeine,* June 9, 1988.

5. A Sustainable Historical Practice

1. Thomas Lindenberger, “Wer hat Angst vor den Barfußhistorikern? Plaedoyer für einen rationalen Dialog,” *Geschichtsdidaktik. Probleme, Projekte, Perspektiven* 11, no. 1 (1986): 17–20.

2. BGWA, Rundbrief 1987 / 1, June 1987, 12.

3. Alfred G. Frei, “Geschichte aus den ‘Graswurzeln’? Geschichtswerkstätten in der historischen Kulturarbeit,” *Aus Politik und Zeitgeschichte* B 2 (1988): 39, 45–46. See also BArch (Koblenz), N1569 / 740, pag. 218–241, January 8, 1988. See also Ingrid Laurien, “Flucht aus der Geschichte in die Geschichte?,” *L'80. Zeitschrift für Literatur und Politik* 39 (1986): 75–84; Joachim Raschke, *Soziale Bewegungen. Ein historisch-systematischer Grundriß* (Frankfurt am Main: Campus, 1987), 446.

4. Hans-Ulrich Wehler, “Geschichte—von unten gesehen,” *Die Zeit,* May 3, 1985; Hans-Ulrich Wehler, “Im Gespräch. Geschichte ganz unten,” *Bayerische Rundfunk,* July 16, 1987.

5. Frei, “Geschichte aus den ‘Graswurzeln’?,” 43. See also BArch (Koblenz), N1569 / 740, pag. 218–241, January 8, 1988.

6. Jenny Wüstenberg, “Vom alternativen Laden zum Dienstleistungsbetrieb: The Berliner Geschichtswerkstatt. A Case Study in Activist Memory Politics,” *German Studies Review* 32, no. 3 (2009): 590–618.

7. Jürgen Karwelat, *Wahnsinn: Erinnerung an den Berliner Mauerfall vom 9. November 1989* (Berlin: Berliner Geschichtswerkstatt, 1999).

8. See Krijn Thijs, “Klopfzeichen und Feierkonkurrenz. Die 750-Jahr-Feier 1987 in Ost- und West-Berlin,” in *Deutschland Archiv 2017* (Bonn: Bundeszentrale für politische Bildung, 2018), 88–99; Krijn Thijs, *Drei Geschichten, eine Stadt: Die Berliner Stadtjubilaen von 1937 und 1987* (Cologne: Bohlau, 2008); Katie Trumpener, “Goethe in Chains. West Berlin ‘at 750’: The Politics of Commemoration,” *Telos* 74 (December 1987): 79–108; Peter Jelavich, “The Berlin Jubilee: Which History to Celebrate?,” *German Politics and Society* 12 (1987): 11–17.

9. LArch Berlin, B Rep. 232–233, 5, Bernhard Müller, “Neu in Berlin: Das Mobile Museum,” undated.

10. BGWA, Rundbrief 1987 / 1, June 1987, “Forum ’87,” 11.

11. Precedents existed for such an initiative. Among the most proximate was the phenomenon of the mobile library. See Johannes von Freymann and Detlef Schwarz, *Fahrbibliotheken in Deutschland: Struktur- und Betriebsdaten* (Berlin: Deutsches Bibliotheksinstitut, 1997); Miriam Hölscher and Corinna Sepke, *Moving Libraries: Mobile Bibliothekskonzepte als Antwort auf die Herausforderungen der modernen Informationsgesellschaft* (Wiesbaden: Dinges und Frick, 2010).

12. LArch Berlin, B Rep. 232–233, 5, Bernhard Müller, “Neu in Berlin: Das Mobile Museum,” undated.

13. LArch Berlin, B Rep. 232–233, 2, undated.

14. LArch Berlin, B Rep. 232–233, 5, Bernhard Müller, “Neu in Berlin: Das Mobile Museum,” undated.

15. Henry Friedlander, *The Origins of Nazi Genocide: From Euthanasia to the Final Solution* (Chapel Hill: University of North Carolina Press, 1995).

16. LArch Berlin, B Rep. 232–233, 5, Bernhard Müller, "Neu in Berlin: Das Mobile Museum," undated. See also LArch Berlin, B Rep. 232–233, 2, undated.

17. LArch Berlin, B Rep. 232–233, 2, undated.

18. LArch Berlin, B Rep. 232–233, 5, Terminkalendar, Vergessene Geschichte? Tiergartenstraße 4 Euthanasie-Aktionen 1939–1945, undated.

19. LArch Berlin, B Rep. 232–233, 2, Protokoll des Vorstandssitzung Aktives Museum, February 10, 1987.

20. LArch Berlin, B Rep. 232–233, 5, Presseerklärung, Das mobile Museum, Bernhard Müller, "Mord an 200.000 Kranken. Erinnerung und Mahnung," undated. See also LArch Berlin, B Rep. 232–233, 5, Christine Fischer-Defoy, August 31, 1988; LArch Berlin, B Rep. 232–233, 5, "Richard Serra entwirft Gedenktafel für Euthanasie-Opfer," *Tagesspiegel*, September 2, 1988, 14.

21. LArch Berlin, B Rep. 232–233, 5, Das mobile Museum, Text-Vorschlag, Gedenkstein, Tiergartenstrasse 4, undated. Some called for a stronger statement. In a draft of the text, one member had crossed out "Remember," arguing that "it should read PILLORY [*anprangern*]!"

22. LArch Berlin, B Rep. 232–233, 5, Bernhard Müller, September 1, 1988.

23. LArch Berlin, B Rep. 232–233, 5, Bernhard Müller, September 28, 1987.

24. LArch Berlin, B Rep. 232–233, 6, Aktives Museum Mitglieder Rundbrief Nr. 1, Anne von Törne, "'T-4'-Ausstellung," December 1987.

25. LArch Berlin, B Rep. 232–233, 5, Presseerklärung, Das mobile Museum, Bernhard Müller, "Mord an 200.000 Kranken. Erinnerung und Mahnung," undated.

26. Götz Aly, *Aktion T4, 1939–1945: Die "Euthanasie"-Zentrale in der Tiergartenstrasse 4* (Berlin: Hentrich, 1987). The book was available for purchase at the T-4 exhibit.

27. LArch Berlin, B Rep. 232–233, 5, Thomas Lutz, Aktion Sühnezeichen, zu Götz Aly, September 2, 1987.

28. LArch Berlin, B Rep. 232–233, 5, Götz Aly, September 4, 1987.

29. LArch Berlin, B Rep. 232–233, 5, Das mobile Museum to Götz Aly, Vertragsentwurf als Ergebnis des Gespräches am September 7, 1987.

30. BGWA, Rundbrief 1988 / 3, Bernhard Müller, "Sackgassen? Projektverlauf," 9–10.

31. Berliner Geschichtswerkstatt, ed., *Sackgassen: Keine Wendemöglichkeit für Berliner Strassennamen* (Berlin: Nishen, 1988).

32. BGWA, Rundbrief 1988 / 3, Bernhard Müller, "Sackgassen? Projektverlauf," 10.

33. Only in 2012, for example—twenty-five years after the BGW first directed its attention to the Lichtenstein Bridge—did the group finally succeed in convincing the city to rename it the Rosa Luxemburg Bridge. BGWA, Rundbrief 1987 / 1, June 1987, 12.

34. BGWA, Rundbrief 1988 / 3, Bernhard Müller, "Sackgassen? Projektverlauf," 12. See also LArch Berlin, B Rep. 232–233, 5, Ausstellung, Steglitz, Schloßstraße, September 6–16, 1988; Jürgen Karwelat, "Der Druck der öffentlichen Straße," *die tageszeitung,* March 18, 1994; BGWA, Rundbrief 1994 / 1.

35. LArch Berlin, B Rep. 232–233, 6, Aktives Museum Mitglieder Rundbrief Nr. 1, December 1987, Anne von Törne, "'T-4'-Ausstellung." For the BGW's ongoing engagement with Japan, see BGWA, Rundbrief 1988 / 3, 20–28.

36. LArch Berlin, B Rep. 232–233, 5, Das mobile Museum, Einladung zur Ausstellungseröffnung, November 3, 1988.

37. BGWA, Rundbrief 1988 / 3, 7–8.

38. Stephanie Endlich, "Ein "dezentrales Monument"? Anmerkungen zu einem ungewöhnlichen Denkmalskonzept," in *Stolpersteine für die von den Nazis ermordeten ehemaligen Nachbarn aus Friedrichshain und Kreuzberg: Dokumentation, Texte, Materialien,* ed. Bettina Eisbrenner and Neue Gesellschaft für bildende Kunst (Berlin: NGBK, 2002), 29–30.

39. BGWA, Rundbrief 1988 / 3, "Projektgruppe AIDS: Koch-Rezepte gegen Pimmelpanik," 16–19.

40. BGWA, Rundbrief 1991 / 3, May 18, 1991, 14.

41. LArch Berlin, B Rep. 232–233, 2, Aktives Museum, Protokoll der Mitgliederversammlung, May 19, 1988.

42. BGWA, Rundbrief 1991 / 3, May 18, 1991, 14–15. See also "Chronik der Projekte des Vereins," in *Immer noch Lust auf Geschichte. 20 Jahre Berliner Geschichtswerkstatt e. V.,* ed. Berliner Geschichtswerkstatt e. V. (Berlin: Berliner Geschichtswerkstatt e. V., 2001), 7.

43. BGWA, Rundbrief 1991 / 3, May 18, 1991, 15.

44. BGWA, 1985 / 86, Informationen und Programm, "Berliner Nachkriegsgeschichte am Beispiel Wedding."

45. BGWA, Rundbrief 1987 / 1, June 1987. See also Berliner Geschichtswerkstatt, ed., *Der Wedding—Hart an der Grenze: Weiterleben in Berlin nach dem Krieg* (Berlin: Nishen, 1987).

46. At a 1988 meeting, BGW members expressed eagerness to meet with a representative from the DDR's Contemporary Video Archive as the BGW systematized its multimedia holdings. BGWA, Rundbrief 1988 / 3.

47. BGWA, Rundbrief 1988 / 3, "Russen in Karlshorst!!!," 15.

48. BGWA, Rundbrief 1989 / 2, "Mitgliederversammlung der Geschichtswerkstatt. Das Protokoll." See also Berliner Geschichtswerkstatt, ed., *Russen-Bilder, Berlin 1945* (Berlin: Berliner Geschichtswerkstatt e. V., 1988).

49. Thomas Lindenberger and Michael Wildt, "Radical Plurality: History Workshops as a Practical Critique of Knowledge," *History Workshop Journal* 33, no. 1 (March 1992): 80.

50. This invitation came as the result of a conversation that began with the 1986 Cultural Convention between East and West Germany. BGWA, Rundbrief 1988 / 3, "Rote Insel in Prenzlauer Berg," 14–15.

51. BGWA, Rundbrief 1988 / 3, "Rote Insel in Prenzlauer Berg," 14; BGWA, Rundbrief 1989 / 3, Gisela Wenzel, "Rote Insel in Prenzlauer Berg," 13–14.

52. BGWA, Rundbrief 1989 / 3, Gisela Wenzel, "Rote Insel in Prenzlauer Berg," 13–14.

53. BGWA, Rundbrief 1989 / 3, Gisela Wenzel, "Rote Insel in Prenzlauer Berg," 14; BGWA, Rundbrief 1988 / 3, "Rote Insel in Prenzlauer Berg," 14; BGWA, Rundbrief 1987 / 1, June 1987, "Die Rote Insel. Berlin-Schöneberg. Bruchstücke zu einer Stadtgeschichte," 8–9. See also Herbert Böpple and Berliner Geschichtswerkstatt, *Die Rote Insel: Berlin-Schöneberg: Bruchstücke zu einer Stadtgeschichte* (Berlin: Nishen, 1987).

54. BGWA, Rundbrief 1989 / 3, Gisela Wenzel, "Rote Insel in Prenzlauer Berg," 14–15.

55. Wolfgang Kil, "Geschichte von unten," *Sonntag*, July 2, 1989.

56. BGWA, Rundbrief 1989 / 3, "Rote Insel in Prenzlauer Berg," 14–15.

57. BGWA, Berliner Geschichtswerkstatt e. V. und Wasserstraßenhauptamt, Ministerium für Verkehr in Berlin (Ost), December 13, 1985; April 25, 1986; and June 10, 1986.

58. BGWA, Rundbrief 1999 / 1, Karin Winklhöfer and Jürgen Karwelat, "15 Jahre Dampfergruppe. Seit 1984—und noch nicht untergegangen. 15 Jahre historische Stadtrundfahrten mit der Berliner Geschichtswerkstatt," 21.

59. BGWA, Historische Stadtrundfahrten mit dem Schiff, April–September 1992; BGWA, Rundbrief 1999 / 1, Karin Winklhöfer and Jürgen Karwelat, "15 Jahre Dampfergruppe," 21.

60. BGWA, Historische Stadtrundfahrten mit dem Schiff, April–September 1992.

61. BGWA, Rundbrief 1999 / 1, Karin Winklhöfer and Jürgen Karwelat, "15 Jahre Dampfergruppe," 21.

62. BGWA, Rundbrief 1988 / 3, Bernhard Müller, "Sackgassen? Projektverlauf," 12.

63. Jürgen Karwelat, "Schon wieder 'ne Luise? Berliner Straßenumbenennungen—Die Zwischenbilanz ergibt: Viele Chancen vertan," *die tageszeitung*, March 13, 1992.

64. BGWA, Rundbrief 1991 / 3, Cord Pagenstecher and Jürgen Karwelat, "Sommerspaß auf der Oberbaumbrücke: Open-Air-Ausstellung," May 18, 1991.

65. BGWA, Rundbrief 1998 / 2, Angela Martin, "Märzfeiern in Zeiten des Kalten Krieges. Der 100. Jahrestag der 1848er-Revolution in Ost- und West-Berlin," 35–36.

66. Martin Düspohl, "20 Jahre Berliner Geschichtswerkstatt: Ein persönlicher Rückblick," in *Immer noch Lust auf Geschichte. 20 Jahre Berliner Geschichtswerkstatt e. V.* (Berlin: Berliner Geschichtswerkstatt e. V., 2001), 50.

67. Jürgen Karwelat, "Mittlerweile bin ich mein eigener Zeitzeuge," in *Immer noch Lust auf Geschichte. 20 Jahre Berliner Geschichtswerkstatt e. V.* (Berlin: Berliner Geschichtswerkstatt e. V., 2001), 59–60.

68. Düspohl, "20 Jahre," 50.

69. Karwelat, "Mittlerweile," 59. See Konrad Hugo Jarausch, *The Rush to German Unity* (New York: Oxford University Press, 1994).

70. BGWA, Rundbrief 1999 / 1, Jürgen Karwelat and Marcel Munte, "Projekt 9 November 1989—Hoffentlich wird es ein Buch," 23–24.

71. BGWA, Rundbrief 1991 / 3, May 18, 1991, 17–19; Karwelat, "Mittlerweile," 59.

72. Axel Doßmann, "Geschichtswerkstatt-Initiativen im Osten—ein ernüchterndes Fazit," in *Alltagskultur, Subjektivität und Geschichte: Zur Theorie und Praxis von Alltagsgeschichte,* ed. Berliner Geschichtswerkstatt (Münster: Westfälisches Dampfboot, 1994), 333.

73. Michael Wildt, "History Workshops in Germany: A Survey at the End of the German Post-War Era," trans. Lyndal Roper, in *History Workshop: A Collectanea, 1967–1991: Documents, Memoirs, Critique and Cumulative Index to History Workshop Journal,* ed. Raphael Samuel and History Workshop Centre for Social History (Oxford: History Workshop, 1991), 61.

74. BGWA, Rundbrief 1993 / 3, October 1, 1993, Felix Mühlberg, "Ostberliner Geschichtswerkstatt e. V. Ein Beitrag zur Arbeit der OBGW," 14–15, 19. The OBGW registered as an official association in Charlottenburg. But, in a move Mühlberg claimed was not a typo, the organization was listed as the East Berlin Gerichts*werkstatt,* or court workshop, rather than Geschichts*werkstatt.*

75. BGWA, Rundbrief 1991 / 3, May 18, 1991, "Ost-West-Kontakte," 19.

76. Harald Dehne, "W(a)ende für / gegen eine Geschichtswerkstatt in der DDR?," *Geschichtswerkstatt* 20 (1990).

77. Doßmann, "Geschichtswerkstatt-Initiativen im Osten," 328–332. See also Alexander von Plato, "Notizen zu einer 'Geschichte von unten' in Ost und West," *Geschichtswerkstatt* 24, 1990.

78. Lindenberger and Wildt, "Radical Plurality," 82–83. See Michel de Certeau, "Die Geschichte: Wissen und Fiktion," in *Die Zeichen der Historie: Beiträge zu einer semiologischen Geschichtswissenschaft,* ed. Georg Schmid (Vienna: H. Böhlau, 1986), 32, 35f.

79. Düspohl, "20 Jahre," 50.

80. BGWA, Informationen und Programm, 1985 / 86.

81. After relative success securing paid positions in divided Germany, the BGW struggled after the fall of the Berlin Wall to obtain funding for a position to research East Berlin. See BGWA, Rundbrief 1993 / 3, October 1, 1993, Michael Pfleghar, "Arbeitsbericht zur ABM-Stelle in der BGW vom 1.3.1991 bis 28.2.1993," 8. See also BGWA, Rundbrief 1987 / 1, June 1987, Thomas Lindenberger, "Von der Sowjetunion lernen . . . Anmerkungen zur letzten MV der Berliner Geschichtswerkstatt," 24.

82. BGWA, Rundbrief 1989 / 2, "Mitgliederversammlung der Geschichtswerkstatt—das Protokoll."

83. BGWA, Rundbrief 1992 / 1, 3–4; BGWA, Rundbrief 1989 / 3, Andreas Ludwig, "Institutionalisierung," 3.

84. BGWA, Rundbrief 1998 / 2, "Das Finanzamt prüft und befindet: die Gemeinnützigkeit des Vereins ist in Gefahr," 2–4. Such existential uncertainty also developed at the national level.

85. BGWA, Gisela Wenzel, "'Grabe, wo du stehst.' Zwei Jahrzehnte Berliner Geschichtswerkstatt," Tagung der Geschichtswerkstätten, October 2003. See also Alfred Georg Frei, "Die Geschichtswerkstätten in der Krise," in *Alltagskultur, Subjektivität und Geschichte: Zur Theorie und Praxis von Alltagsgeschichte,* ed. Berliner Geschichtswerkstatt (Münster: Westfälisches Dampfboot, 1994), 317; Alf Lüdtke, "Rekonstruktion von Alltagswirklichkeit—Entpolitisierung der Sozialgeschichte?," in *Klassen und Kultur: Sozialanthropologische Perspektiven in der Geschichtsschreibung,* ed. Robert M. Berdahl et al. (Frankfurt am Main: Syndikat, 1982), 332.

86. Frei, "Geschichtswerkstätten in der Krise," 316–317, 320–321. See also Alfred Georg Frei and Michael Wildt, "Hirsebrei und Seifenblasen. Die Geschichtswerkstätten und ihre Kritiker," *L'80. Zeitschrift für Literatur und Politik* 39 (1986): 64–72, here 71.

87. Frei, "Geschichtswerkstätten in der Krise," 321.

88. BGWA, Informationen, 1984.

89. BGWA, Rundbrief 1987 / 1, June 1987, Thomas Lindenberger, "Von der Sowjetunion lernen," 20, 22; BGWA, Rundbrief, March 7, 1983.

90. BGWA, Rundbrief 1991 / 3, May 18, 1991, "Montagsgruppe / Vorstand," 13.

91. BGWA, Rundbrief 1988 / 3, "Projekt 1914. Lehrer und Krieg," 5.

92. BGWA, Rundbrief, Sonderausgabe 1988, Augusterlebnisse: 1914 und 1989: Das Projekt, die Krise, die Lösung, 2–3, 5.

93. BGWA, Rundbrief, Sonderausgabe 1988, Augusterlebnisse, 2–3, 5–6, 56, 58.

94. BGWA, Rundbrief, Sonderausgabe 1988, Augusterlebnisse, 8.

95. BGWA, Rundbrief, Sonderausgabe 1988, Augusterlebnisse, 3. See also BGWA, Rundbrief 1993 / 3, October 1, 1993, Michael Pfleghar, "Arbeitsbericht zur ABM-Stelle," 8–9.

96. BGWA, Rundbrief, Sonderausgabe 1988, Augusterlebnisse, 3, 5.

97. Berliner Geschichtswerkstatt, ed., *August 1914: Ein Volk zieht in den Krieg* (Berlin: Nishen, 1989).

98. BGWA, Rundbrief 1992 / 1, Jürgen Karwelat, "'Alarmglocken sollten klingeln.' Kritik an der Archivgruppe," 5.

99. BGWA, Rundbrief 1992 / 1, Sonja Miltenberger, "Frust der gemeinen Archivarin," 6.

100. BGWA, Rundbrief 1987 / 1, June 1987, "Saisonstart der Dampfergruppe," 3.

101. Claire Colomb, *Staging the New Berlin: Place Marketing and the Politics of Urban Reinvention Post-1989* (London: Routledge, 2012), 123.

102. BGWA, Rundbrief 1993 / 3, October 1, 1993, Manuela Dörnenburg, "Dampfergruppe, Saisonbericht und Buchprojekt," 12; BGWA, Rundbrief 1993 / 3, October 1, 1993, Sonja Miltenberger, "Protokoll der MVV vom 3.7.1993," 17.

103. BGWA, Rundbrief 1999 / 1, Karin Winklhöfer and Jürgen Karwelat, "15 Jahre Dampfergruppe," 22.

104. Düspohl, "20 Jahre," 49. See also BGWA, *Moderne Zeiten—Extra. Geschichtswerkstatt. Sondernummer* 4 (April 1984); BGWA, Geschichtswerkstatt Rundbrief 4, August 1984; Alfred Georg Frei, "Spannungsfelder. Geschichtsfest Berlin," *Journal für Geschichte* 4 (1984) 4–7; Anthony McElligott, "The German History Workshop Festival in Berlin May–June 1984," *German History* 2 (1985): 21–29.

105. BGWA, Rundbrief 1989 / 2, "Geschichtsfest Bonn 1989."

106. See Katja Schmid, "Das Gästeführungswesen im Wandel: Analyse von Angebotsformen und Organisationsstrukturen in deutschen Städten und Gemeinden" (Diplomarbeit, Universität Trier, 1998), 80f.

107. Düspohl, "20 Jahre," 47–48.

108. BGWA, Rundbrief 1989 / 2, Gisela Hahn, "Geschichtsfest Bonn: Alternative Stadtrundfahrten Bestätigungesfeld für Geschichtswerkstätten."

109. BGWA, Rundbrief 1989 / 3, Martin Düspohl, "StattReisen und Geschichtswerkstätten. Entgegnung zum Artikel von Gisela Hahn im GW-Rundbrief 2 / 89 über einen Workshop beim Geschichtsfest '89 in Bonn," 20–21.

110. Frei, "Geschichtswerkstätten in der Krise," 128.

111. Wildt, "History Workshops," 61.

112. BGWA, Rundbrief 1994 / 1, Bernhard Müller, "Einladung zu einem Werkstattgespräch zum Thema 50 Jahre Kriegsende 1995," 11.

113. See Frei, "Geschichtswerkstätten in der Krise," 319. See also Carola Lipp, "Alltagskulturforschung im Grenzbereich von Volkskunde, Soziologie, und Geschichte. Aufstieg und Niedergang eines interdiziplinären Forschungskonzepts," *Zeitschrift für Volkskunde* 1 (1993): 1–33; BGWA, Rundbrief 1987 / 1, June 1987; BGWA, Rundbrief 1994 / 1, "Mitteilung aus dem Vorstand—Laden in der Malplaquetstraße," 2.

114. See his extensive multivolume oral history project, "Lebensgeschichte und Sozialkultur im Ruhrgebiet 1930–1960." See also Lutz Niethammer, *Ego-Histoire? Und andere Erinnerungs-Versuche* (Vienna: Böhlau, 2002).

115. Alf Lüdtke, *Eigen-Sinn: Fabrikalltag, Arbeitererfahrungen und Politik vom Kaiserreich bis in den Faschismus* (Hamburg: Ergebnisse, 1993). See also Belinda J. Davis, Thomas Lindenberger, and Michael Wildt, eds., *Alltag, Erfahrung, Eigensinn: Historisch-anthropologische Erkundungen* (Frankfurt am Main: Campus, 2008).

116. Michael Wildt, *Volksgemeinschaft als Selbstermächtigung: Gewalt gegen Juden in der deutschen Provinz 1919 bis 1939* (Hamburg: Hamburger Edition, 2007). See also Frank Bajohr and Michael Wildt, eds., *Volksgemeinschaft: Neue Forschungen zur Gesellschaft des Nationalsozialismus* (Frankfurt am Main: Fischer Taschenbuch Verlag, 2012); Michael Wildt, *Volk, Volksgemeinschaft, AfD* (Hamburg: Hamburger Edition, 2017).

117. See, for example, Frei, "Geschichtswerkstätten in der Krise," 319.

118. Harald Gesterkamp, "'Barfußhistoriker' ohne Boden," *Frankfurter Rundschau*, April 23, 1992. See also BGWA, Rundbrief 1992/1, 13.

6. A Sustainable Aesthetics

1. Froma Zeitlin, "The Vicarious Witness: Belated Memory and Authorial Presence in Recent Holocaust Literature," *History and Memory* 10, no. 2 (1998): 6, 15.

2. Bill Niven, *Facing the Nazi Past: United Germany and the Legacy of the Third Reich* (London: Routledge, 2002), 105.

3. See, for example, *Süddeutsche Zeitung*, May 2, 1985, May 6, 1985, and May 8, 1985; *Frankfurter Allgemeine Zeitung*, May 9, 1985. On the controversies surrounding the Neue Wache, see Sabine Moller, *Die Entkonkretisierung der NS-Herrschaft in der Ära Kohl: Die Neue Wache. Das Denkmal für die ermordeten Juden Europas. Das Haus der Geschichte der Bundesrepublik Deutschland* (Hannover: Offizin, 1998); Jörg Fessmann, ed., *Streit um die Neue Wache: Zur Gestaltung einer zentralen Gedenkstätte* (Berlin: Akademie der Künste, 1993); Christoph Stölzl and Jürgen Tietz, *Die Neue Wache Unter den Linden: Ein deutsches Denkmal im Wandel der Geschichte* (Berlin: Koehler und Amelang, 1993).

4. Jeffrey K. Olick, *The Sins of the Fathers: Germany, Memory, Method* (Chicago: University of Chicago Press, 2016), 359–367; Jeffrey Herf, *Divided Memory: The Nazi Past in the Two Germanys* (Cambridge, MA: Harvard University Press, 1997), 355–359; Christina Morina, *Legacies of Stalingrad: Remembering the Eastern Front in Germany since 1945* (Cambridge: Cambridge University Press, 2011), 227; Jan-Holger Kirsch, *"Wir haben aus der Geschichte gelernt": Der 8. Mai als politischer Gedenktag in Deutschland* (Cologne: Böhlau, 1999). See also Richard von Weizsäcker, *A Voice from Germany: Speeches by Richard von Weizsäcker*, trans. Karin von Abrams (London: Weidenfeld and Nicholson, 1985), 45.

5. Micha Brumlik, "New Myth of State: The Eastern Front. The Most Recent Development in the Discipline of History in the Federal Republic of Germany," in *Forever in the Shadow of Hitler?: Original Documents of the Historikerstreit, the Controversy Concerning the Singularity of the Holocaust*, trans. James Knowlton and Truett Cates (Atlantic Highlands: Humanities Press, 1993), 48.

6. Hannah Arendt, *The Origins of Totalitarianism* (New York: Harcourt Brace, 1968), 452.

7. Christian Meier, "Condemning and Comprehending," *Forever in the Shadow of Hitler?: Original Documents of the Historikerstreit, the Controversy Concerning the Singularity of the Holocaust*, trans. James Knowlton and Truett Cates (Atlantic Highlands: Humanities Press, 1993), 33.

8. Rudy Koshar, *From Monuments to Traces: Artifacts of German Memory, 1870–1990* (Berkeley: University of California Press, 2000), 154. On wartime

destruction, see Steven Brakman, Harry Garretsen, and Marc Schramm, "The Strategic Bombing of German Cities during World War II and Its Impact on City Growth," *Journal of Economic Geography* 4 (2004): 205.

9. See Barbie Zelizer, *Remembering to Forget: Holocaust Memory through the Camera's Eye* (Chicago: University of Chicago Press, 1998), 92; Hannah Arendt, "The Aftermath of Nazi Rule: Report from Germany," *Commentary* 10, no. 4 (1950): 349.

10. Nikolaus Wachsmann, *KL: A History of the Nazi Concentration Camps* (New York: Farrar, Straus and Giroux, 2015).

11. Jennifer L. Allen, "National Commemoration in an Age of Transnationalism," *The Journal of Modern History* 91, no. 1 (2019): 109–148.

12. Horst Hoheisel, *Aschrottbrunnen* (Frankfurt am Main: Fritz Bauer Institut, 1998), 7, 31.

13. Daniel Libeskind, *Erweiterung des Berlin Museums mit Abteilung Jüdisches Museum,* ed. Kristin Feireiss (Berlin: Ernst und Sohn, 1992), 59–61.

14. Jochen Gerz, *2146 Steine: Mahnmal gegen Rassismus Saarbrücken* (Stuttgart: Gerd Hatje Verlag, 1993), 11–13.

15. James E. Young, *At Memory's Edge: After-Images of the Holocaust in Contemporary Art and Architecture* (New Haven, CT: Yale University Press, 2000), 102–103.

16. James E. Young, "The Counter-Monument: Memory against Itself in Germany Today," *Critical Inquiry* 18 (1992): 274.

17. See, for example, Anna Sheftel, "'Monument to the International Community, from the Grateful Citizens of Sarajevo': Dark Humour as Counter-Memory in Post-Conflict Bosnia-Herzegovina," *Memory Studies* 5 (2012): 145–164; Cecily Harris, "German Memory of the Holocaust: The Emergence of Counter-Memorials," *Penn History Review* 17 (2010): 212–227; Corinna Tomberger, "The Counter-Monument: Memory Shaped by Male Post-War Legacies," in *Memorialization in Germany since 1945,* ed. William John Niven and Chloe E. M. Paver (Basingstoke: Palgrave Macmillan, 2010), 224–232; Richard Crownshaw, "The German Countermonument: Conceptual Indeterminacies and the Retheorisation of the Arts of Vicarious Memory," *Forum for Modern Language Studies* 44 (2008): 212–227; Corinna Tomberger, *Das Gegendenkmal: Avantgardekunst, Geschichtspolitik und Geschlecht in der bundesdeutschen Erinnerungskultur* (Bielefeld: Transcript, 2007); Noam Lupu, "Memory Vanished, Absent, and Confined: The Countermemorial Project in 1980s and 1990s Germany," *History and Memory* 15 (2003): 130–164.

18. Andreas Huyssen, "The Voids of Berlin," *Critical Inquiry* 24 (1997): 57–81.

19. Koshar, *From Monuments to Traces,* 228.

20. Quoted in Koshar, *From Monuments to Traces,* 283–284. See also Pierre Nora, "From Lieux de mémoire to Realms of Memory," in *Realms of Memory:*

Rethinking the French Past, vol. 1 (New York: Columbia University Press 1996), xxiv.

21. This same period witnessed the rapid international expansion of the academic field of memory studies, or what the historian Jay Winter has called a "memory boom." Jay Winter, "The Memory Boom in Contemporary Historical Studies," *Raritan* 21, no. 1 (Summer 2001): 52–66. For an indictment of this scholarly fixation, see Kerwin Klein, "On the Emergence of Memory in Historical Discourse," *Representations* 69 (2000): 127–150. See also Pierre Nora, "Between Memory and History: Les Lieux de Mémoire," *Representations* 26 (1989): 7–24.

22. See Birgit Menzel and Werner Süß, "Das Bayrische Viertel—'Die Jüdische Schweiz.' Etappen eines Vernichtungsprozesses," in *Leben in Schöneberg/Friedenau 1933–45*, ed. Gisela Wenzel, 39–44 (Berlin: Kunstamt Schöneberg, 1983).

23. Kunstamt Schöneberg and Gedenkstätte Haus der Wannsee-Konferenz, *Orte des Erinnerns, vol 2. Jüdisches Alltagsleben im Bayerischen Viertel, eine Dokumentation* (Berlin: Edition Hentrich, 1995).

24. Kunstamt Schöneberg and Gedenkstätte Haus der Wannsee-Konferenz, *Orte des Erinnerns, vol. 1. Das Denkmal im Bayerischen Viertel, Beitrag zur Debatte um Denkmale und Erinnerung* (Berlin: Edition Hentrich, 1994).

25. "Stolpersteine im Bayerischen Viertel. Jüdische Geschichte in Berlin—ungewöhnlich dokumentiert," *Unabhängige Jüdische Stimme* 2, no. 3 (1993): 8–9. The metaphor of the stumbling stone has appeared in both Jewish and Christian thought to signify something that provokes a sin. For references in the Hebrew Bible, see Leviticus 19:14 and Isaiah 8:13–15; in the New Testament, Matthew 18:7 and Romans 9:30–33, among others.

26. Renate Stih and Frieder Schnock, interviewed by the author, May 8, 2013, Berlin. See Joseph Walk, *Das Sonderrecht für die Juden im NS-Staat: Eine Sammlung der gesetzlichen Maßnahmen und Richtlinien, Inhalt und Bedeutung* (Heidelberg and Karlsruhe: Müller Juristischer, 1981). Walk, whose approval they solicited prior to the project's installation, suggested he could not think of a better end for his research. Stih and Schnock personal archive, letter from Joseph Walk, undated.

27. "Stolpersteine im Bayerischen Viertel," 8–9. See also Senatsverwaltung für Bau- und Wohnungswesen Berlin, *Offener Kunstwettbewerb. "Kunst im Stadtraum." Mahnen und Gedenken im Bayerischen Viertel. Ausschreibung 1. Phase* (Berlin: Senatsverwaltung für Bau- und Wohnungswesen Berlin, 1991); Senatsverwaltung für Bau- und Wohnungswesen Berlin, *Offener Kunstwettbewerb. "Kunst im Stadtraum." Mahnen und Gedenken im Bayerischen Viertel. Protokoll der Preisgerichtssitzung und Bericht der Vorprüfung* (Berlin: Senatsverwaltung für Bau- und Wohnungswesen Berlin, 1991); Senatsverwaltung für Bau- und Wohnungswesen Berlin, *Offener Kunstwettbewerb. "Kunst im Stadtraum." Mahnen und Gedenken im Bayerischen Viertel. Protokoll der Preisgerichtssitzung und Bericht*

der Vorprüfung. 2. Phase (Berlin: Senatsverwaltung für Bau- und Wohnungswesen Berlin, 1992).

28. Renata Stih and Frieder Schnock, *Orte des Erinnerns: Places of Remembrance in Berlin* (Berlin: Stih und Schnock, 2009), 12–13.

29. Renate Stih and Frieder Schnock, interviewed by the author, May 8, 2013, Berlin.

30. "Kurz und knapp. Plakate abgenommen," *Berliner Zeitung,* June 5/6, 1993, 17. See also Ulrich Clewing, "Anwohner hielten das Mahnmal für antisemitische Propaganda. Berlin: Missverständnisse um Denkmal für Juden," *art. Das Kunstmagazin* 8 (1993): 193.

31. Renate Stih and Frieder Schnock, interviewed by the author, May 8, 2013, Berlin.

32. Brigitte Werneburg, "Armes Berlin," *taz,* June 9, 2008.

33. Renate Stih and Frieder Schnock, interviewed by the author, May 8, 2013, Berlin.

34. Senatsverwaltung für Bau- und Wohnungswesen Berlin, *Künstlerischer Wettbewerb. Denkmal für die ermordeten Juden Europas. Kurzdokumentation* (Berlin: Senatsverwaltung für Bau- und Wohnungswesen Berlin, 1995), 9.

35. Hans-Georg Stavginski, *Das Holocaust-Denkmal: Der Streit um das "Denkmal für die ermordeten Juden Europas" in Berlin (1988–1999)* (Paderborn: Schöningh, 2002); Bürgerinitiative Perspektive Berlin, *Ein Denkmal für die ermordeten Juden Europas. Dokumentation 1988–1995* (Berlin: Bürgerinitiative Perspektive Berlin e. V., 1995). See also Jacob S. Eder, *Holocaust Angst: The Federal Republic of Germany and American Holocaust Memory since the 1970s* (New York: Oxford University Press, 2016), 192–193; Jenny Wüstenberg, *Civil Society and Memory in Postwar Germany* (Cambridge: Cambridge University Press, 2017), 123.

36. Senatsverwaltung für Bau- und Wohnungswesen Berlin, *Künstlerischer Wettbewerb,* 15.

37. See Senatsverwaltung für Bau- und Wohnungswesen Berlin, *Künstlerischer Wettbewerb,* 54ff.

38. Stih and Schnock personal archive, Renata Stih and Frieder Schnock, "Under Goethe's Cool Gaze. Controversial Holocaust Memorial: Size at What Price?," *Tagesspiegel,* trans. Renata Stih and Frieder Schnock, January 19, 1995.

39. Marlies Emmerich, "Ausstellung zum Holocaust-Denkmal eröffnet. 200 000 Mark gespendet: Eine Pflicht zur Erinnerung," *Berliner Zeitung,* April 11, 1995.

40. Stih and Schnock personal archive, Stih and Schnock, "Under Goethe's Cool Gaze."

41. Stih and Schnock personal archive, Stih and Schnock, "Under Goethe's Cool Gaze."

42. Renata Stih and Frieder Schnock, *Bus Stop,* trans. Steve Sokol (Berlin: Neue Gesellschaft für bildende Kunst, 1995).

43. Stih and Schnock personal archive, Stih and Schnock, "Under Goethe's Cool Gaze."

44. Renata Stih and Frieder Schnock, *Bus Stop Fahrplan, 1. Auflage,* ed. Leonie Baumann (Berlin: NGBK, 1995), 106–110. See also Stih and Schnock personal archive, Visitors' Book.

45. Stih and Schnock, *Bus Stop Fahrplan,* 107–109. See also Stih and Schnock personal archive, Visitors' Book.

46. Stih and Schnock, *Bus Stop.*

47. Senatsverwaltung für Wissenschaft, Forschung und Kultur, *Colloquium. Denkmal für die ermordeten Juden Europas. Dokumentation* (Berlin: Senatsverwaltung für Wissenschaft, Forschung und Kultur, 1997), 8.

48. Stih and Schnock personal archive, Stih and Schnock, "Under Goethe's Cool Gaze."

49. Stih and Schnock, *Bus Stop.*

50. It remains unclear how consciously Demnig channeled the biblical metaphor.

51. Stolpersteine Initiative für München e. V., "Stolpersteine: The World's Largest Project of Commemoration," www.stolpersteine-muenchen.de/english. As a project with a massive, decentralized, largely ad hoc management system, the *Stolpersteine* have proven hard to keep track of. The Stolpersteine Twitter account (@_Stolpersteine_) generally offers up-to-date statistics.

52. On Demnig's decision to begin outsourcing the responsibility for crafting the stones, see Harald Schmid, "Stolpersteine und Erinnerungskultur—Eine Zwischenbilanz," Tagung: Stolpersteine. Irritationen der Erinnerung. Evangelische Akademie der Nordkirche, Hamburg, September, 9–10, 2011, www.akademie-nek.de/h/stolpersteine_96.php, 7.

53. NS-Dokumentationszentrum (Historisches Archiv der Stadt Köln) and Karola Fings, *Stolpersteine: Gunter Demnig und sein Projekt = Gunter Demnig and His Project* (Cologne: Emons, 2007), 14; Joachim Rönneper, *Vor meiner Haustür—"Stolpersteine" von Gunter Demnig: Ein Begleitbuch* (Gelsenkirchen: Arachne-Verlag, 2010), 116f.

54. That Demnig began with Romani victims should not escape notice. Although approximately 90 percent of Demnig's work commemorates Jewish victims, neither spotlighting particular groups nor their hierarchization have played a role in his projects. See Beate Meyer, "Stolpersteine in Hamburg. Individualisiertes Erinnern in alltäglichen Lebensräumen," in *"Mein Täubchen aus dem Felsenspalt, im Hohlhort des Berghanges, lass Dein Antlitz mich schauen, Deine Stimme mir ertönen . . ." (gemäß das Hohelied 2,14): Becoming Visible: Jüdisches Leben in Deutschland seit 1990,* ed. Miryam Gilis-Karlebakh and Barbara Vogel (Munich: Dölling und Galitz, 2011), 70; NGBK, KfnA, 78, Gunter Demnig, May 1994; NGBK, KfnA, 53, Gunter Demnig, undated.

55. NGBK, KfnA, 78, Gunter Demnig, May 1994; NGBK, KfnA, 53 Gunter Demnig, undated.

56. Kurt Holl and Corinna Kawaters, *Ein Strich durchs Vergessen: 1000 Roma und Sinti—Mai 1940* (Cologne: Rom e. V., 1997), 7, 23.

57. NGBK, KfnA, 66, Rolf Sachsse, 1991.

58. NGBK, KfnA, 67–70, Stadt Köln, Dauerhafte Sicherung des Weges durch den Künstler Herr Gunter Demnig, March 18, 1993.

59. Kurt-Werner Pick, "Stolpersteine. Spuren gegen das Vergessen. Ein Kunstprojekt an der Antoniterkirche," *Antoniter Nachrichten* (March 1994): 5. See also NGBK, KfnA, 78, Gunter Demnig, May 1994; NGBK, KfnA, 53, Gunter Demnig, undated.

60. Uta Franke, *Stolpersteine: Idee, Vorgeschichte und Entwicklung eines Projektes. Interviews von Uta Franke mit Gunter Demnig* (Cologne: self-pub., 2003), 4–5. See also Bettina Eisbrenner and Neue Gesellschaft für bildende Kunst, eds., *Stolpersteine für die von den Nazis ermordeten ehemaligen Nachbarn aus Friedrichshain und Kreuzberg: Dokumentation, Texte, Materialien* (Berlin: NGBK, 2002), 11–12.

61. German sociologist Harald Welzer describes this phenomenon as the "collateral damage" of successful education in Holocaust history. Harald Welzer, "Collateral Damage of History Education: National Socialism and the Holocaust in German Family Memory," *Social Research* 75 (2008): 287–314.

62. Gunter Demnig, "Projekt Stolpersteine," in *Größenwahn: Kunstprojekte für Europa*, ed. Gabriele Lindinger and Karlheinz Schmid (Regensburg: Lindinger und Schmid, 1993), 61. See also Pick, "Stolpersteine," 6. On the importance of naming and the dead, see Thomas Laqueur, *The Work of the Dead: A Cultural History of Mortal Remains* (Princeton, NJ: Princeton University Press, 2015), 363–488.

63. Franke, *Stolpersteine*, 4–5. See also Eisbrenner and Neue Gesellschaft für bildende Kunst, *Stolpersteine*, 11–12.

64. Gabriele Lindinger and Karlheinz Schmid, eds., *Größenwahn: Kunstprojekte für Europa* (Regensburg: Lindinger und Schmid, 1993), 11, 15.

65. Holl and Kawaters, *Ein Strich durchs Vergessen*, 8–9, 14.

66. Gunter Demnig and Jürgen Rapp, "Gunter Demnig: Dezentrales Mahnmal. Ein Gespräch mit Jürgen Rapp," *Kunstforum International* 170 (2004): 232.

67. Demnig, "Projekt Stolpersteine," 61. See also Pick, "Stolpersteine," 6–7.

68. Demnig and Rapp, "Gunter Demnig," 232; Franke, *Stolpersteine*, 7.

69. Uta Franke and Gunter Demnig, "Am treffendsten läßt sich meine Berufsbezeichnung mit Bildhauer umschreiben, Uta Franke im Interview mit Gunter Demnig," in *Stolpersteine für die von den Nazis ermordeten ehemaligen Nachbarn aus Friedrichshain und Kreuzberg: Dokumentation, Texte, Materialien*, ed. Bettina Eisbrenner and Neue Gesellschaft für bildende Kunst (Berlin: Neue Gesellschaft für bildende Kunst, 2002), 12.

70. Manfred Schneckenburger, "Delta im Einheitsstrom. Zur Kunst der neunziger Jahre," in *Größenwahn: Kunstprojekte für Europa*, ed. Gabriele Lindinger and Karlheinz Schmid (Regensburg: Lindinger und Schmid, 1993), 18–19.

71. Schneckenburger, "Delta im Einheitsstrom," 20–21.

72. Manfred Schneckenburger, "Gunter Demnig—Vergangenheit, trittfest gemacht," *Kölner Skizzen* 15, no. 4 (1993): 7.

73. NGBK, KfnA, 114, Katharina Kaiser, April 18, 1996.

74. NGBK, KfnA, 13, Matthias Reichelt to Heiner Hepper, April 29, 1996.

75. NGBK, KfnA, 56, Matthias Reichelt to Gunter Demnig, October 31, 1995. On the Lemniskate BR 53, see also NGBK, KfnA, 78, Gunter Demnig May 1994; NGBK, KfnA, 39–41, Gunter Demnig to Matthias Reichelt, February 27, 1996.

76. NGBK, KfnA, 39–41, Gunter Demnig to Matthias Reichelt, February 27, 1996.

77. NGBK, KfnA, 56, Matthias Reichelt to Gunter Demnig, October 31, 1995.

78. NGBK, KfnA, 46–49, Gunter Demnig to Matthias Reichelt, November 5, 1995.

79. NGBK, KfnA, 45, Matthias Reichelt to Gunter Demnig, December 5, 1995. On the dilemma of reproducing the act of selection by placing *Stolpersteine,* see Harald Stingele and Die AnStifter, *Stuttgarter Stolpersteine: Spuren vergessener Nachbarn. Ein Kunstprojekt füllt Gedächtnislücken* (Filderstadt: Markstein, 2007), 18; Eisbrenner and Neue Gesellschaft für bildende Kunst, *Stolpersteine,* 20.

80. Eisbrenner and Neue Gesellschaft für bildende Kunst, *Stolpersteine,* 14–15.

81. Brinda Sommer, *Gesellschaftliches Erinnern an den Nationalsozialismus: Stolpersteine wider das Vergessen* (Berlin: Institut für Museumsforschung, Staatliche Museen zu Berlin, Preußischer Kulturbesitz, 2007), 38; Kirsten Serup-Bilfeldt and Elke Heidenreich, *Stolpersteine: Vergessene Namen, verwehte Spuren. Wegweiser zu Kölner Schicksalen in der NS-Zeit* (Cologne: KIWI, 2003), 156.

82. Demnig was no stranger to crossing bureaucratic t's and dotting clerical i's. For the NGBK installation, Demnig would have had a good working knowledge of how to obtain permission to install the stones. See, for example, documentation of his *Einreise '88* (*Entry '88*) project in 1988. NGBK, KfnA: 1988, 131–138: Neuer Berliner Kunstverein, Spuren, Demnig 88, August 13, 1988, Barbara Straka, "Grenzüberschreitender Verkehr. Gunter Demnigs Projekt 'Einreise' und die Kunst des Spurenlesens."

83. Personal correspondence with Matthias Reichelt, March 26, 2013; NGBK, KfnA, 1–2, Finanzplan, "Künstler forschen nach Auschwitz," November 21, 1996. See also Eisbrenner and Neue Gesellschaft für bildende Kunst, *Stolpersteine,* 14–15. Reichelt has been careful to note that the workers' decision cannot necessarily be read as an expression of empathy or reverence. More likely, their refusal originated out of fear of inadvertently desecrating a Holocaust monument.

84. On Demnig's increasing reliance on a large network of institutions and individuals, see NS-Dokumentationszentrum and Fings, *Stolpersteine,* 15; Rönneper, *Vor meiner Haustür,* 117; Wolfgang Jorzig, "Stolpern heißt auch, darauf stoßen. Erinnerungsmale. Kunst im öffentlichen Raum," *Schriftenreihe des Vereins "Gegen Vergessen—Für Demokratie"* 36 (März 2003): 6–8.

85. Demnig and Rapp, "Gunter Demnig," 234.

86. "Technical Aspects," www.stolpersteine.eu/en/technical-aspects. These stones are affordable compared to other copycat projects, including one with a price tag of 670€ per stone. Steine der Erinnerung, "Mein Beitrag," www.steinedererinnerung.net/mein-beitrag.

87. Archiv FHXB, Steven Robins, "Silence in My Father's House: Holocaust Memory and Jewish Belonging after Apartheid. A Proposal for an Installation at the Holocaust Center," undated.

88. Franke and Demnig, "Am treffendsten," 20.

89. Demnig credits the 2002 publication of an article in the Deutsche Bahn magazine *Mobil* with generating a large wave of attention. See Sigrid Rahlfes, "Die Spur der Steine," *Mobil,* November 2002. See also Demnig and Rapp, "Gunter Demnig," 234.

90. Not every effort to reach living relatives is successful. In a number of cases, relatives have discovered stones have been laid for family members without their permission—and not always to their pleasure.

91. Schmid, "Stolpersteine und Erinnerungskultur," 7.

92. Franke, *Stolpersteine,* 7, 14–15.

93. See, for example, Civic Engagement: Ziviles Engagement und Studium verbinden, "#Mitmachaktion: Stolpersteine putzen," December 14, 2020, civic-engagement.blogs.uni-hamburg.de/mitmachaktion-4; BundJugend, "Aktionsidee: Stolpersteine putzen und gemeinsam Erinnerung wachhalten," January 27, 2020, blog.bundjugend.de/aktionsidee-stolpersteine-putzen-und-gemeinsam-erinnerung-wachhalten; Stolpersteine für München, September 23, 2020, www.facebook.com/photo?fbid=10157183587566682&set=g.57104271651.

94. Schmid, "Stolpersteine und Erinnerungskultur," 13–15. See also Harald Schmid, "Perpetuum mobile der Erinnerungskultur? Die Stolpersteine zwischen Innovation und Inflation," paper presented at the conference Steine des Anstoßes oder normiertes Ritual? Zur Rolle des Stolperstein-Projekts in den Erinnerungskonflikten der Gegenwart, Berlin, February 21, 2019.

95. Ulrike Schrader, "Die 'Stolpersteine' oder Von der Leichtigkeit des Gedenkens: Einige kritische Anmerkungen," *Geschichte im Westen: Zeitschrift für Landes- und Zeitgeschichte* 21 (2006): 175–176.

96. Franke and Demnig, "Am treffendsten," 20.

97. Schmid, "Stolpersteine und Erinnerungskultur," 8. See also "Nur in Bergedorf darf es keine Stolpersteine geben," *Die Welt,* January 30, 2003, 38; "Bergedorf: Streit um Stolpersteine," *Hamburger Abendblatt,* July 4, 2003, 15.

98. Franke and Demnig, "Am treffendsten," 20.

99. Matthias Reichelt, interviewed by the author, April 29, 2013, Berlin. See also Carsten Kloth, "Gleditschstraße: Stolpersteine in Schöneberg beschädigt," *Tagesspiegel,* October 31, 2010.

100. Schmid, "Stolpersteine und Erinnerungskultur," 8.

101. Sommer, *Gesellschaftliches Erinnern*, 90–91.

102. Sommer, *Gesellschaftliches Erinnern*, 90–91.

103. Schrader, "Die 'Stolpersteine,'" 176n8.

104. Göttingen and Kassel, for example, both delayed installations after Jewish groups voiced their disapproval. Schmid, "Stolpersteine und Erinnerungskultur," 8. See also Reimar Paul, "Kultusgemeinde kritisiert Stolpersteine," *Tageszeitung*, July 22, 2006; Christina Hein, "Stolperstein schlägt Wellen. Die Stadt Kassel unterstützt künftig die Gedenkstein-Aktion von Gunter Demnig," *Hessische-Niedersächsische Allgemeine*, May 27, 2011.

105. Franke, *Stolpersteine*, 8; Stingele and Die AnStifter, *Stuttgarter Stolpersteine*, 16.

106. G. Jungbauer, *Sudetendeutsche Zeitschrift für Volkskunde, vol. 3–4* (Prague: Dr. G. Jungbauer, 1930), 257. See also Verein für Volkskunde, *Österreichische Zeitschrift für Volkskunde, vol. 31–33* (Vienna: Verein für Volkskunde, 1926), 46; Christian Berger, *Zwölf Wiener Geschichten über bedeutende Tote und ihre Gräber* (Bielefeld: Neues Literaturkontor, 1997), 87; Ingke Brodersen, Klaus Humann, and Susanne von Paczensky, *1933, wie die Deutschen Hitler zur Macht verhalfen: Ein Lesebuch für Demokraten* (Reinbek bei Hamburg: Rowohlt, 1983), 300.

107. Jan Bielicki, "'Es ist Zeit, gegen Rechtsradikale aufzustehen.' Interview mit Charlotte Knobloch," *Süddeutsche Zeitung*, February 12, 2005, 45.

108. Schmid, "Stolpersteine und Erinnerungskultur," 9. Schmid highlights the minutes from the meeting of the Munich City Council on June 16, 2004. See also Igal Avidan, "In München stolpert man nicht gerne," *sueddeutsche.de*, May 17, 2010, www.sueddeutsche.de/kultur/im-kino-stolperstein-in-muenchen-stolpert-man-nicht-gerne-1.536809.

109. Schmid, "Stolpersteine und Erinnerungskultur," 9–10. In a similar vein, Joachim Rönneper refers to Munich as the *Stolpersteine Sonderweg*. Rönneper, *Vor meiner Haustür*.

110. "Stolpersteine eines Künstlers," *Kölner Stadt-Anzeiger*, January 5, 1995.

111. Rudi Arendt, "Aktionskunst schafft Verbindungen: 'Stolpersteine in Elmshorn—Gegen das Vergessen,'" in *Stolpersteine in Elmshorn—Gegen das Vergessen: Eine Kunstaktion*, ed. Gunter Demnig and Bert C. Biehl (Elmshorn: Kiel Landeszentrale für politische Bildung, 2008), 10ff.

112. Schmid, "Stolpersteine und Erinnerungskultur," 12.

113. Jürgen-Wolfgang Goette, *Stolpersteine Erich-Mühsam-Preis 2009 an Gunter Demnig* (Lübeck: EMG, 2009), 32.

114. Barbara Günther and Landeszentrale für politische Bildung, *Stolpersteine in Hamburg-Harburg und Hamburg-Wilhelmsburg biographische Spurensuche* (Hamburg: Landeszentrale für politische Bildung, 2012), 16.

115. Stephanie Endlich, "Ein 'dezentrales Monument'? Anmerkungen zu einem ungewöhnlichen Denkmalskonzept," in *Stolpersteine für die von den Nazis*

ermordeten ehemaligen Nachbarn aus Friedrichshain und Kreuzberg: Dokumentation, Texte, Materialien, ed. Bettina Eisbrenner and Neue Gesellschaft für bildende Kunst (Berlin: NGBK, 2002), 33.

116. Leonie Baumann, "Ein kleiner Stein zwischen Kunst, Geschichte und Zukunft," in *Stolpersteine für die von den Nazis ermordeten ehemaligen Nachbarn aus Friedrichshain und Kreuzberg: Dokumentation, Texte, Materialien*, ed. Bettina Eisbrenner and Neue Gesellschaft für bildende Kunst (Berlin: NGBK, 2002), 8.

117. Franke and Demnig, "Am treffendsten," 20.

118. Demnig, "Projekt Stolpersteine," 61. Elsewhere, Demnig notes the attentiveness in Jewish philosophy to the relationship between traversing (*Begehen*) and reading. He points to Derrida's essay on Edmund Jabès in *Writing and Difference* (London: Routledge and Kegan Paul, 1978), esp. 80, 87.

119. Endlich, "Ein 'dezentrales Monument'?," 31.

120. scrapheaper, "'Stolpersteine': Gedenken im Alltag," YouTube video, May 7, 2011, www.youtube.com/watch?v=hziXzDDGayY.

121. Judith Miller, *One, by One, by One: Facing the Holocaust* (New York: Simon and Schuster, 1990), 287.

Conclusion: The Fate of Sustainable Utopia

1. Jürgen Karwelat, "Mittlerweile bin ich mein eigener Zeitzeuge," in *Immer noch Lust auf Geschichte. 20 Jahre Berliner Geschichtswerkstatt e. V.* (Berlin: Berliner Geschichtswerkstatt e. V., 2001), 57.

2. Cord Pagenstecher, "'. . . da sind wir keine Ausländer mehr.' Eingewanderte ArbeiterInnen in Berlin 1961–1993," in *Immer noch Lust auf Geschichte. 20 Jahre Berliner Geschichtswerkstatt e. V.* (Berlin: Berliner Geschichtswerkstatt e. V., 2001), 44.

3. Karwelat, "Mittlerweile," 56. See also Jenny Wüstenberg, "Vom alternativen Laden zum Dienstleistungsbetrieb: The Berliner Geschichtswerkstatt. A Case Study in Activist Memory Politics," *German Studies Review* 32, no. 3 (2009): 608ff.

4. Pagenstecher, "'. . . da sind wir,'" 44.

5. BGWA, Rundbrief 1992 / 1, Michael Pfleghar, "Projektbericht: 'Alltagsgeschichte der Arbeitsimmigranten und Arbeitsimmigrantinnen und ihrer Familien in Berlin seit 1961,'" 9; BGWA, Rundbrief 1991 / 3, "Project report: 'Alltagsgeschichte,'" May 18, 1991. See also Elke Allinger and Berliner Geschichtswerkstatt, *. . . da sind wir keine Ausländer mehr: Eingewanderte ArbeiterInnen in Berlin 1961–1993* (Berlin: Berliner Geschichtswerkstatt, 1993).

6. BGWA, Rundbrief 1991 / 3, May 18, 1991, Projekt "Geschichte der ausländischen ArbeitsimmigrantInnen in West-Berlin seit 1961," 5; Pagenstecher, "'. . . da sind wir,'" 41–45; BGWA, Rundbrief 1993 / 3, October 1, 1993, Sonja Miltenberger, "Protokoll der MVV vom 3.7.1993," 17–18.

7. See, for example, Kathrin Roller, *Frauenmigration und Ausländerpolitik im Deutschen Kaiserreich. Polnische Arbeitsmigrantinnen in Preußen* (Berlin: D. Bertz, 1994); Cord Pagenstecher, "Die 'Illusion' der Rückkehr. Zur Mentalitätsgeschichte von 'Gastarbeit' und Einwanderung," *Soziale Welt* 47, no. 2 (1996): 149–179.

8. Pagenstecher, "'. . . da sind wir,'" 41–45; BGWA, Rundbrief 1994 / 1, Ursula Trüper, "Protokoll der MVV," 17; BGWA, Rundbrief 1994 / 1, K. Roller, "Eine Idee und ein Aufruf," 14.

9. Martin Düspohl, "20 Jahre Berliner Geschichtswerkstatt: Ein persönlicher Rückblick," in *Immer noch Lust auf Geschichte. 20 Jahre Berliner Geschichtswerkstatt e. V.* (Berlin: Berliner Geschichtswerkstatt e. V., 2001), 49.

10. BArch (Koblenz), N 1569 / 773-2, pag. 263–265, Claudia Siede and Karlheinz Koinegg, Die Grünen im Bundestag, "Jeder Mensch ein Künstler," July 1990.

11. Albert Schmidt, "Bündnisgrüne Kulturpolitik zwischen Skepsis und Erwartung," in *Zwischen Leuchtturmprogramm und Warnblinkanlage. Bündnisgrüne Kulturpolitik auf Bundesebene. Dokumentation des kulturpolitischen Ratschlags am 8. Juli 1995 in Bonn*, ed. Bündnis 90 / Die Grünen Bundestagsfraktion and Bernd Wagner (Bonn: Bündnis 90 / Die Grünen, 1995), 8.

12. Antje Vollmer, ed., *Politik mit Kultur* (Berlin: Bündnis 90 / Die Grünen—Bundestagsfraktion, 2005), 2.

13. Bündnis 90 / Die Grünen, *Die Zukunft ist grün. Grundsatzprogramm von Bündnis 90 / Die Grünen* (Berlin: Bündnis 90 / Die Grünen, 2002).

14. E. Gene Frankland, "The Evolution of the Greens in Germany: From Amateurism to Professionalism," in *Green Parties in Transition: The End of Grass-roots Democracy?*, ed. E. Gene Frankland, Paul Lucardie, and Benoît Rihoux (Surrey: Ashgate, 2008), 35. See also Angelo Panebianco, *Political Parties: Organization and Power* (Cambridge: Cambridge University Press, 1988), 17ff.

15. Bündnis 90 / Die Grünen, *Politische Grundsätze* (Berlin: Bündnis 90 / Die Grünen, 1993); Bündnis 90 / Die Grünen, *Die Zukunft ist grün;* Bündnis 90 / Die Grünen, *". . . zu achten und zu schützen." Veränderung schafft Halt. Grundsatzprogramm* (Berlin: Bündnis 90 / Die Grünen, 2020), 9; Bündnis 90 / Die Grünen, *Deutschland. Alles ist drin. Programmentwurf zur Bundestagswahl 2021* (Berlin: Bündnis 90 / Die Grünen, 2021).

16. Claudia Roth, "Kreativitätspolitik im Übergang zur Wissensgesellschaft. Verschiedene Politik- und Aufgabenfelder miteinander in Beziehung setzen," in *Kulturpolitik der Parteien: Visionen, Programmatic, Geschichte und Differenzen*, ed. Olaf Zimmermann and Theo Geißler (Berlin: Deutscher Kulturrat, 2008), 94. See also Helga Trüpel, "Plädoyer für eine 'kleine' Kulturpolitik," in *Zwischen Leuchtturmprogramm und Warnblinkanlage. Bündnisgrüne Kulturpolitik auf Bundesebene. Dokumentation des kulturpolitischen Ratschlags am 8. Juli 1995 in Bonn*, ed. Bündnis 90 / Die Grünen Bundestagsfraktion and Bernd Wagner (Bonn: Bündnis 90 / Die Grünen, 1995), 11.

17. Katrin Göring-Eckardt, "'Die K-Frage'—Kultur diesseits und jenseits der Ökonomie. Kulturpolitik als bevorzugter Bereich kreativen und politischen Denkens," in *Kulturpolitik der Parteien: Visionen, Programmatic, Geschichte und Differenzen,* ed. Olaf Zimmermann and Theo Geißler (Berlin: Deutscher Kulturrat, 2008), 98.

18. Eva Krings, "Politikfeld Kultur. Anforderungen an Bündnis 90 / Die Grünen," in *Zwischen Leuchtturmprogramm und Warnblinkanlage. Bündnisgrüne Kulturpolitik auf Bundesebene. Dokumentation des kulturpolitischen Ratschlags am 8. Juli 1995 in Bonn,* ed. Bündnis 90 / Die Grünen Bundestagsfraktion and Bernd Wagner (Bonn: Bündnis 90 / Die Grünen, 1995), 18.

19. Schmidt, "Bündnisgrüne Kulturpolitik zwischen Skepsis und Erwartung," 5.

20. BArch (Koblenz), N 1569 / 773-2, pag. 263–265, Claudia Siede and Karlheinz Koinegg, Die Grünen im Bundestag, "Jeder Mensch ein Künstler," July 1990.

21. BArch (Koblenz), N 1569 / 772, pag. 3–7, Claudia Siede, Redeentwurf zur kulturpolitischen Debatte im Deutschen Bundestag, October 31, 1990.

22. See, for example, BArch (Koblenz), N 1569 / 730, pag. 2–3, September 3, 1990, Kulturbüro / Claudia Siede, Antje Vollmer to Arbeitsgruppe "Sozialistische Denkmale in der DDR," Kunsthistorisches Institut Bonn; BArch (Koblenz), N 1569 / 730, pag. 6, Summer 1990, Arbeitsgruppe "Sozialistische Denkmale in der DDR," Kunsthistorisches Institut Bonn, Resolution zum Erhalt der sozialistischen Denkmale in der DDR; BArch (Koblenz), N 1569 / 730, pag. 7–9, August 7, 1990, Einladung, Diskussionsveranstaltung und Pressekonferenz, Ausstellung, "Erhalten, zerstören, verändern? Denkmäler der DDR in Ost-Berlin. Zum Beispiel Ernst Thälmann. Meinung vor Ort"; Göring-Eckardt, "'Die K-Frage.'"

23. Andrei S. Markovits and Stephen J. Silvia, "The Identity Crisis of Alliance '90 / The Greens: The New Left at a Crossroad," *New German Critique* 72, no. 1 (October 1997): 119–120.

24. On the Greens' difficulty swallowing this compromise, see, for example, Carl Amery, "Rat eines Ratlosen," in *Zwischen Leuchtturmprogramm und Warnblinkanlage. Bündnisgrüne Kulturpolitik auf Bundesebene. Dokumentation des kulturpolitischen Ratschlags am 8. Juli 1995 in Bonn,* ed. Bündnis 90 / Die Grünen Bundestagsfraktion and Bernd Wagner (Bonn: Bündnis 90 / Die Grünen, 1995), 13. Also Frankland, "Evolution of the Greens," 35.

25. BArch (Koblenz), N 1569 / 773-2, pag. 263–265, Claudia Siede and Karlheinz Koinegg, Die Grünen im Bundestag, "Jeder Mensch ein Künstler," July 1990. See also Omnibus für direkte Demokratie in Deutschland, *Projekte Erweiterte Kunst: Von Beuys aus* (Wangen: FIU, 1993).

26. Bündnis 90 / Die Grünen, *Deutschland. Alles ist drin. Programmentwurf zur Bundestagswahl 2021* (Berlin: Bündnis 90 / Die Grünen, 2021), 109.

27. Terry Swartzberg, "Aufhebung des Verbots von Stolpersteinen in München," www.change.org/p/aufhebung-des-verbots-von-stolpersteinen-in-m%C3%

BCnchen-stolpersteine-m%C3%BCnchen; Igal Avidan, "In München stolpert man nicht gerne," *sueddeutsche.de,* May 17, 2010, www.sueddeutsche.de/kultur/im-kino-stolperstein-in-muenchen-stolpert-man-nicht-gerne-1.536809.

28. NGBK, KfnA, 108, Horst Hoheisel to Katharina Kaiser, June 5, 1996. Hoheisel would later prove cagier about this connection. Personal correspondence with Horst Hoheisel, May 9, 2013.

29. Elisabeth Ben David-Hindler and Joachim Rönneper, "Verein 'Steine der Erinnerung.' Wien—Briefwechsel," in *Vor meiner Haustür—"Stolpersteine" von Gunter Demnig: Ein Begleitbuch,* ed. Joachim Rönneper (Gelsenkirchen: Arachne-Verlag, 2010). See also Jennifer L. Allen, "National Commemoration in an Age of Transnationalism," *Journal of Modern History* 91, no. 1 (2019): 138–139.

30. Ulrike Schrader, "Die 'Stolpersteine' oder Von der Leichtigkeit des Gedenkens: Einige kritische Anmerkungen," *Geschichte im Westen: Zeitschrift für Landes- und Zeitgeschichte* 21 (2006): 178.

31. See Alison Brysk, *The Politics of Human Rights in Argentina: Protest, Change, and Democratization* (Stanford, CA: Stanford University Press, 1994); Antonius C. G. M. Robben, *Political Violence and Trauma in Argentina* (Philadelphia: University of Pennsylvania Press, 2005).

32. See, for example, Estela Schindel, "Piedras, Plazas, y Performances: Modos Activos de la Memoria en Buenos Aires," in *Memorias Urbanas en Diálogo: Berlín y Buenos Aires,* ed. Peter Birle, Vera Carnovale, Elke Gryglewski, and Estela Schindel, 387–403 (Buenos Aires: Buenos Libros Santiago, Chile Fundación, Heinrich Böll, Cono Sur, 2010); Cristina Inés Bettanin and Laura Schenquer, "Baldosas por la Memoria: Marcas Territoriales en las Calles de Buenos Aires," *Conversaciones del Cono Sur* 1 (2015): 3–7; Cristina Inés Bettanin, "Iniciativas Comunitarias: Las Baldosas por la Memoria en la Ciudad de Buenos Aires," *Trabajo Social* 16 (2014): 65–78; Barrios X Memoria y Justicia and Instituto Espacio para la Memoria, *Baldosas X la memoria* (Buenos Aires: Instituto Espacio para la Memoria, 2008); Manuel Tufró and Luis Sanjurjo, "Descentralizar la memoria. Dos lógicas de intervención sobre el espacio urbano en la ciudad de Buenos Aires," *Universitas Humanística* 70 (2010): 119–132.

33. Editorial Board, "Russia Cracks Down on an Important Voice for Human Rights," *Washington Post,* November 11, 2015; Priyanka Boghani, "Putin's Legal Crackdown on Civil Society," *PBS: Frontline,* January 13, 2015, www.pbs.org/wgbh/frontline/article/putins-legal-crackdown-on-civil-society.

34. Masha Lipman, "Humble Memorials for Stalin's Victims in Moscow," *New Yorker,* December 13, 2014.

35. Schrader, "Die 'Stolpersteine,'" 173–181.

36. Much myth and disagreement surround the history of the tree. The best sources remain news articles in the local press in areas where descendants of the tree have been planted. See Marc Settle, "'Tree of Life' Planted for Peace." *BBC,* September 21, 2009, news.bbc.co.uk/2/hi/uk_news/8263288.stm; Debbie Cohen,

"Children's Tree from Theresienstadt May Sprout in S.F." *jweekly.com,* March 22, 1996. www.jweekly.com/includes/print/2794/article/children-s-tree-from-theresienstadt-may-sprout-in-s-f.

37. Settle, "'Tree of Life.'"

38. Památník Terezín, *Terezin Memorial: Annual Report for 2008* (Terezin: Památník Terezín, 2008), 6.

39. Kate Torgovnick May, "One Million Bones on the National Mall, All Countable in This Gigapixel Image," TED Blog, June 27, 2013, blog.ted.com/2013/06/27/one-million-bones-on-the-national-mall-all-countable-in-this-gigapixel-image; email correspondence with project coordinator, Susan McAllister, March 19, 2014. See also "The Art of Revolution," theartofrevolution.squarespace.com.

40. "Stopping Stones," stoppingstones.org.

41. Witness Stones Project, "What Is the Witness Stones Project?," witnessstonesproject.org/what-is-the-witness-stones-project.

42. Peter Cole, "How a Small Stone Could Help America Reckon with Its Worst History," *Washington Post,* February 6, 2018.

43. Equal Justice Initiative, "The National Memorial to Peace and Justice," museumandmemorial.eji.org/memorial. See also Campbell Robertson, "History of Lynchings in the South Documents Nearly 4,000 Names," *New York Times,* February 10, 2015.

44. Equal Justice Initiative, "Lynching in America: Confronting the Legacy of Racial Terror," lynchinginamerica.eji.org. See also Megan Rose Dickey, "Equal Justice Initiative, Backed by Google.org, Launches 'Lynching in America,'" *techcrunch.com,* June 13, 2017, techcrunch.com/2017/06/13/lynching-in-america-equal-justice-initiative.

45. On the multilayered symbolism of the Berlin Wall, see Brian Ladd, *The Ghosts of Berlin: Confronting German History in the Urban Landscape* (Chicago: University of Chicago Press, 1998), 7–39.

46. See Astrid M. Eckert, *West Germany and the Iron Curtain: Environment, Economy, and Culture in the Borderlands* (New York: Oxford University Press, 2019).

47. European Green Belt, "European Green Belt Initiative," www.europeangreenbelt.org.

48. Gideon Botsch, *Die extreme Rechte in der Bundesrepublik Deutschland 1949 bis heute* (Darmstadt: Wissenschaftliche Buchgesellschaft, 2013), 60–61, 65, 72; Cas Mudde, *The Ideology of the Extreme Right* (Manchester: Manchester University Press, 2000).

49. On the ideas the New Right has inherited from its forebears, see Klaus-Peter Hufer, *Neue Rechte, altes Denken: Ideologie, Kernbegriffe und Vordenker* (Weinheim: Beltz Juventa, 2018), 78–125, here 132.

50. Hufer, *Neue Rechte,* 130. On the rise of populism that drove these adjustments, see Helmut Dubiel, "Gespenst des Populismus," in *Populismus und Aufklärung,* ed. Helmut Dubiel, 33–50 (Frankfurt am Main: Suhrkamp, 1986).

51. See, for example, Edna Bonhomme, "The Disturbing Rise of 'Femonationalism,'" *The Nation*, May 7, 2019; Claus Leggewie, "Die anderen 68er. Die Neuen Rechten und ihre deutsch-französischen Väter," *Le Monde diplomatique*, August 10, 2017, monde-diplomatique.de/artikel/!5438005; Clemens Heni, *Salonfähigkeit der neuen Rechten: "Nationale Identität," Antisemitismus und Antiamerikanismus in der politischen Kultur der Bundesrepublik Deutschland 1970–2005: Henning Eichberg als Exempel* (Marburg: Tectum, 2007), 348. On the general transformation of postwar conservatism in Europe, see Anna von der Goltz and Britta Waldschmidt-Nelson, eds., *Inventing the Silent Majority in Western Europe and the United States: Conservatism in the 1960s and 1970s* (New York: Cambridge University Press, 2017).

52. Quoted in Thomas Wagner, *Die Angstmacher: 1968 und die Neuen Rechten* (Berlin: Aufbau, 2017), 47. See Eichberg's writing under the pseudonym Hartwig Singer, "Antwort an einen Konservativen," *Nationalismus heute. Junge Kritik, Beiheft des Studenten-Anzeigers* 1 (1970): 36.

53. Michael Wildt, *Volk, Volksgemeinschaft, AfD* (Hamburg: Hamburger Edition, 2017), 97.

54. Gunther Jürgens, *Direkte Demokratie in den Bundesländern: Gemeinsamkeiten—Unterschiede—Erfahrungen. Vorbildfunktion für den Bund?* (Stuttgart: Boorberg, 1993), 195–196, 213–214. On the far right's tendency to connect immigrants and asylum seekers, on one hand, and security, order, and the well-being of the German citizen, on the other, see Dirk Aschwanden, *Jugendlicher Rechtsextremismus als gesamtdeutsches Problem* (Baden-Baden: Nomos, 1995).

55. Klaus Kunze, "Plebiszite als Weg aus dem Parteienstaat," *Junge Freiheit* 10 (1992): 24.

56. Quoted in Wagner, *Angstmacher*, 175. See also NPD-Parteivorstand, *Argumente für Kandidaten und Funktionsträger. Handreichung für die öffentliche Auseinandersetzung* (Berlin: Nationaldemokratische Partei Deutschlands, 2006), 32.

57. See, for example, the chants at the far right rally in the town of Chemnitz in August 2018. Kate Connolly, "Fear in Chemnitz: 'I'm Used to Neo-Nazis, but Not My Neighbour Mixing with Them in Broad Daylight,'" *Guardian*, August 31, 2018.

58. Alternative für Deutschland, "Programm für Deutschland. Das Grundsatzprogramm der Alternative für Deutschland," April–May 2016, cdn.afd.tools/wp-content/uploads/sites/111/2018/01/Programm_AfD_Online-PDF_150616.pdf.

59. Jan-Werner Müller, *Was ist Populismus?: Ein Essay* (Berlin: Suhrkamp, 2016), 26. See also Wildt, *Volk, Volksgemeinschaft, AfD*, 97–98; Hufer, *Neue Rechte*, 15.

60. Markus Willinger, *Die identitäre Generation: Eine Kriegserklärung an die 68er* (London: Arktos Media, 2013), 36–37.

61. Quoted in Wagner, *Angstmacher*, 97. See Karlheinz Weißmann, "Die konservative Option. Vorschläge für eine andere Politik," *Criticón* 113 (1989): 129–133;

Helmut Kellershohn, ed., *Das Plagiat. Der völkische Nationalismus der Jungen Freiheit* (Duisburg: Duisburger Institut für Sprach- und Sozialforschung, 1994), 34f. On the New Right's attempts to communicate with a wider base, see Botsch, *Die extreme Rechte,* 117–118.

62. Aschwanden, *Jugendlicher Rechtsextremismus,* 131–143. See also Julian Bruns, Kathrin Glösel, and Natascha Strobl, *Die Identitären: Handbuch zur Jugendbewegung der Neuen Rechten in Europa* (Münster: UNRAST, 2017), 84.

63. Botsch, *Die extreme Rechte,* 4. See also Bruns, Glösel, and Strobl, *Die Identitären.*

64. Willinger, *Die identitäre Generation,* 101.

65. Volker Weiß, *Die autoritäre Revolte: Die Neue Rechte und der Untergang des Abendlandes* (Stuttgart: Klett-Cotta, 2017), 124. See Arthur Moeller van den Bruck, *Das Dritte Reich* (Hamburg: Hanseatische Verlagsanstalt, 1931), 202.

66. Karlheinz Weißmann, "Politik und Metapolitik," *Sezession* 57 (2013): 41.

67. Wagner, *Angstmacher,* 210. See Martin Sellner, "Gewaltlose Disziplin," *Sezession,* February 16, 2017, sezession.de/56991/gewaltlose-disziplin.

68. Willinger, *Die identitäre Generation,* 100.

69. Weißmann, "Politik und Metapolitik," 41. See also Weiß, *Die autoritäre Revolte,* 85.

70. See Götz Kubitschek, "Konservativ-Subversive Aktion," *Sezession* 25 (2008): 56.

71. Weiß, *Die autoritäre Revolte,* 119, 122; Bruns, Glösel, and Strobl, *Die Identitären,* 283.

72. See Kubitschek, "Konservativ-Subversive Aktion," 56.

73. Bruns, Glösel, and Strobl, *Die Identitären,* 245.

74. Willinger, *Die identitäre Generation,* 98.

75. Leo Löwenthal and Frithjof Hager, *Geschichte denken: Ein Notizbuch für Leo Löwenthal* (Leipzig: Reclam, 1992), 34. On the theme of despair, see Robyn Marasco, *The Highway of Despair: Critical Theory after Hegel* (New York: Columbia University Press, 2015).

76. Lutz Niethammer and Dirk van Laak, *Posthistoire: Has History Come to an End?* (London: Verso, 1992), 1.

Archives and Primary Sources

Archives

Abgeordnetenhaus Berlin, Drucksachen
Archiv des Friedrichshain-Kreuzberg Museums—Archiv FHXB
  Steven Robins
Archiv Grünes Gedächtnis—AGG
  A-Düllmann, Gina, 64: Gedenkstätte, Bd. II
  B.II.1—Die Grünen im Bundestag 1983–1990, 2744
  B.II.1—Die Grünen im Bundestag 1983–1990, 5683
Archiv der Neuen Gesellschaft für bildende Kunst—NGBK
  Künstler forschen nach Auschwitz
  Presse, Künstler forschen nach Auschwitz
Berliner Geschichtswerkstatt Archiv—BGWA
Bundesarchiv-Koblenz—BArch (Koblenz)
  N 1569, Nachlass Antje Vollmer
    730 Denkmalschutz, Mahnmal, 1984–1990
    740 Diskussion um die Planung eines Deutschen Historischen Museums in Berlin, 1985–1987
    741 Diskussionen um die Planung von Deutschen Historischen Museen—Geschichte und nationale Identität, 1987–1990
    770 Kulturpolitik der Grünen—Ostdeutsche Kulturarbeit, 1984–1988
    771 Grüne Kulturpolitik, 1985–1988
    772 Kuturbegriff und Kulturverständnis der Grünen, 1985–1990
    773-1 Veröffentlichungen und Dokumentationen zur Kulturpolitik, 1986–1990
    773-2 Veröffentlichungen und Dokumentationen zur Kulturpolitik, 1986–1990
    774 Kulturpolitik der Grünen auf Landes- und Bundesebene, 1983–1989
    783 Kunst- und Kulturverständnis / Kulturpolitik der Grünen, 1987–1988
Deutscher Bundestag, Drucksachen and Plenarprotokolle
Landesarchiv-Berlin—LArch Berlin

B. Rep. 232–233, Actives Museum Faschismus und Widerstand e. V.
1 Gründung des Vereins, 1983–1984
2 Protokolle der Mitgliederversammlungen und Vorstandssitzungen, 1984–1988
3 Korrespondenzen und Einladungen A–F, 1984–1989
5 Korrespondenzen und Einladungen M–Z, 1986–1989
6 Mitgliederrundbrief 1–13, 1987–1991
27 Korrespondenz zur Arbeit des Vereins Aktives Museum, 1990–1991
Personal Archive of Renata Stih and Frieder Schnock

Newspapers and Periodicals

Der Alltag
Alternative Kommunale Kulturpolitik
Alternative Kommunalpolitik
Antoniter Nachrichten
Das Argument
art. Das Kunstmagazin
The Atlantic
Aus Politik und Zeitgeschichte
Berliner Zeitung
CDU-Extra
Criticón
Frankfurter Allgemeine Zeitung
Frankfurter Rundschau
Geschichte und Gesellschaft
Geschichtsdidaktik
Geschichtswerkstatt
grüner basisdienst
The Guardian
Hamburger Abendblatt
Hessische-Niedersächsische Allgemeine
History Workshop Journal
Journal für Geschichte
Junge Freiheit
Juso, Zeitschrift der Jungsozialisten in der SPD
Kölner Skizzen
Kölner Stadt-Anzeiger
Kommune
Kultur Politik Diskurs
Kultur und Gesellschaft
Kunstforum International
Kunst Intern

Kursbuch
L'80. Zeitschrift für Literatur und Politik
Mobil
Moderne Zeiten
New Yorker
New York Times
Oral History
Pan
Das Parlament
Schriftenreihe des Vereins "Gegen Vergessen—Für Demokratie"
Sezession
Sonntag
Soziale Welt
Der Spiegel / Spiegel Online
Süddeutsche Zeitung/sueddeutsche.de
Der Tagesspiegel
Die Tageszeitung / taz
Unabhängige Jüdische Stimme
Washington Post
Die Welt
WerkstattGeschichte
Die Zeit

Published Primary Sources

AfD Baden-Württemberg. "AfD Prof. Dr. Jörg Meuthen Videobotschaft 1 / 2016." YouTube video, January 20, 2016. www.youtube.com/watch?v=foBYtG3_roo.

Akademie der Künste Berlin, ed. *Zum Umgang mit dem Gestapo-Gelände: Gutachten im Auftrag der Akademie der Künste Berlin.* Berlin: Akademie der Künste, 1988.

"Alle reden vom Klimaschutz." *tagesschau.de,* May 27, 2019. www.tagesschau.de/inland/eu-wahl-reaktionen-101.html.

Allinger, Elke and Berliner Geschichtswerkstatt. . . . *Da sind wir keine Ausländer mehr: Eingewanderte ArbeiterInnen in Berlin 1961–1993.* Berlin: Berliner Geschichtswerkstatt, 1993.

Altendorfer, Peter. "Die Kunstbanausen: Über das (Nicht)Verhältnis der Grünen zur Kunst und Kultur. Versuch einer Herausforderung." *Kunstforum International* 93 (1988): 123–125.

Alternative für Deutschland. "Programm für Deutschland. Das Grundsatzprogramm der Alternative für Deutschland." April–May 2016. cdn.afd.tools/wp-content/uploads/sites/111/2018/01/Programm_AfD_Online-PDF_150616.pdf.

"Alternativen in der Kulturpolitik. Bestandsaufnahme und Neuansätze eines unterbelichteten Politikfeldes." *Alternative Kommunalpolitik* 3 (1984).

Aly, Götz. *Aktion T4, 1939–1945: Die "Euthanasie"-Zentrale in der Tiergartenstrasse 4*. Berlin: Hentrich, 1987.

Amery, Carl. "Die philosophischen Grundlagen und Konsequenzen der Alternativbewegung." In *Die Grünen: Personen, Projekte, Programme*, edited by Hans-Werner Lüdke and Olaf Dinné, 9–21. Stuttgart-Degerloch: Seewald, 1980.

———. *Das ökologische Problem als Kulturauftrag*. Oldenburg: Bibliotheks- und Informationssystem der Universität Oldenburg, 1988.

———. "Rat eines Ratlosen." In *Zwischen Leuchtturmprogramm und Warnblinkanlage. Bündnisgrüne Kulturpolitik auf Bundesebene. Dokumentation des kulturpolitischen Ratschlags am 8. Juli 1995 in Bonn*, edited by Bündnis 90 / Die Grünen, Bundestagsfraktion and Bernd Wagner, 13–15. Bonn: Bündnis 90 / Die Grünen, 1995.

"Anmerkung der Redaktion." *Kursbuch* 11 (1968): 170–171.

Arendt, Rudi. "Aktionskunst schafft Verbindungen: 'Stolpersteine in Elmshorn—Gegen das Vergessen.'" In *Stolpersteine in Elmshorn—Gegen das Vergessen: Eine Kunstaktion*, edited by Gunter Demnig and Bert C. Biehl, 8. Elmshorn: Kiel Landeszentrale für politische Bildung, 2008.

"Ärger um die Kleiderordnung im Bundestag: Nur ohne meine Krawatte." *sueddeutsche.de*, February 16, 2011. www.sueddeutsche.de/politik/aerger-um-die-kleiderordnung-im-bundestag-nur-ohne-meine-krawatte-1.1061031.

"The Art of Revolution." Accessed April 10, 2021. theartofrevolution.squarespace.com.

Avidan, Igal. "In München stolpert man nicht gerne." *sueddeutsche.de*, May 17, 2010. www.sueddeutsche.de/kultur/im-kino-stolperstein-in-muenchen-stolpert-man-nicht-gerne-1.536809.

Bahro, Rudolf. "Socialism, Ecology and Utopia." *History Workshop Journal* 16, no. 1 (September 1983): 91–99.

Barrios X Memoria y Justicia and Instituto Espacio para la Memoria (Argentina). *Baldosas X la memoria*. Buenos Aires: Instituto Espacio para la Memoria, 2008.

Bastian, Heiner, ed. *7000 Eichen*. Bern: Benteli, 1985.

Baumann, Leonie. "Ein kleiner Stein zwischen Kunst, Geschichte und Zukunft." In *Stolpersteine für die von den Nazis ermordeten ehemaligen Nachbarn aus Friedrichshain und Kreuzberg: Dokumentation, Texte, Materialien*, edited by Bettina Eisbrenner and Neue Gesellschaft für bildende Kunst, 28–36. Berlin: NGBK, 2002.

Ben David-Hindler, Elisabeth, and Joachim Rönneper. "Verein 'Steine der Erinnerung.' Wien—Briefwechsel." In *Vor meiner Haustür—"Stolpersteine" von Gunter Demnig: Ein Begleitbuch*, edited by Joachim Rönneper, 18–20. Gelsenkirchen: Arachne-Verlag, 2010.

Berliner Geschichtswerkstatt, ed. *Spurensicherung in Schöneberg 1933: "Rote Insel," Lindenhof, "Jüdische Schweiz."* Berlin: Berliner Geschichtswerkstatt, 1983.

———. *Der Wedding—Hart an der Grenze: Weiterleben in Berlin nach dem Krieg.* Berlin: Nishen, 1987.

———. *Russen-Bilder, Berlin 1945.* Berlin: Berliner Geschichtswerkstatt e. V., 1988.

———. *Sackgassen: Keine Wendemöglichkeit für Berliner Strassennamen.* Berlin: Nishen, 1988.

———. *August 1914: Ein Volk zieht in den Krieg.* Berlin: Nishen, 1989.

———. *Alltagskultur, Subjektivität und Geschichte: Zur Theorie und Praxis von Alltagsgeschichte.* Münster: Westfälisches Dampfboot, 1994.

———. *Immer noch Lust auf Geschichte. 20 Jahre Berliner Geschichtswerkstatt e. V.* Berlin: Berliner Geschichtswerkstatt e. V., 2001.

Bettanin, Cristina Inés. "Iniciativas Comunitarias: Las Baldosas por la Memoria en la Ciudad de Buenos Aires." *Trabajo Social* 16 (2014): 65–78.

Bettanin, Cristina Inés, and Laura Schenquer. "Baldosas por la Memoria: Marcas Territoriales en las Calles de Buenos Aires." *Conversaciones del Cono Sur* 1 (2015): 3–7.

Beuys, Joseph, and Clara Bodenmann-Ritter. *Jeder Mensch ein Künstler: Gespräche auf der Documenta 5/1972.* Frankfurt am Main: Ullstein, 1975.

Bieber, Horst. "Sie eint nur der Protest. Aber die Parteigründung ist beschlossene Sache." *Die Zeit,* October 26, 1979.

Bielicki, Jan. "'Es ist Zeit, gegen Rechtsradikale aufzustehen' Interview mit Charlotte Knobloch." *Süddeutsche Zeitung,* February 12, 2005.

Birnbaum, Michael, Griff Witte, and James McAuley. "European Greens Surge as Voters Abandon Old Parties Over Climate." *Washington Post,* May 27, 2019. www.washingtonpost.com/world/europe/european-greens-surge-as-voters-abandon-old-parties-over-climate/2019/05/27/185be506-8085-11e9-b585-e36b16a531aa_story.html.

Boghani, Priyanka. "Putin's Legal Crackdown on Civil Society." *PBS: Frontline,* January 13, 2015, www.pbs.org/wgbh/frontline/article/putins-legal-crackdown-on-civil-society.

Bollow, Frauke, and Elke Mocker. "Archivierung biographischer Quellen im Dokumentationszentrum für Alltags- und Regionalgeschichte der Berliner Geschichtswerkstatt." In *Alltagskultur, Subjektivität und Geschichte: Zur Theorie und Praxis von Alltagsgeschichte,* edited by Berliner Geschichtswerkstatt, 223–232. Münster: Westfälisches Dampfboot, 1994.

Bopp, Jörg. "Trauer-Power. Zur Jugendrevolte 1981." *Kursbuch* 65 (1981): 151–168.

Böpple, Herbert, and Berliner Geschichtswerkstatt. *Die Rote Insel: Berlin-Schöneberg: Bruchstücke zu einer Stadtgeschichte.* Berlin: Nishen, 1987.

Borscheid, Peter. "Alltagsgeschichte—Modetorheit oder neues Tor zur Vergangenheit?" In *Sozialgeschichte in Deutschland. Entwicklungen und Perspektiven im internationalen Zusammenhang, Band III: Soziales Verhalten und soziale*

Aktionsformen in der Geschichte, edited by Wolfgang Schieder and Volker Sellin, 87–100. Göttingen: Vandenhoeck und Ruprecht, 1987.

Boyer, Josef, Helge Heidemeyer, and Tim B. Peters. *Die Grünen im Bundestag: Sitzungsprotokolle und Anlagen 1983–1987.* Düsseldorf: Droste, 2008.

Broszat, Martin. *Nach Hitler: Der schwierige Umgang mit unserer Geschichte.* Munich: Oldenbourg, 1987.

Brücker, Eva. "Das Lindenhof-Projekt: Alltagsgeschichte ist machbar." In *Immer noch Lust auf Geschichte. 20 Jahre Berliner Geschichtswerkstatt e. V.*, 28–30. Berlin: Berliner Geschichtswerkstatt e. V., 2001.

Brücker, Eva, and the Arbeitsgruppe Lindenhof. "Gemeinnützige 'Siedlung Lindehof' E.G.m.b.H. Berlin-Schöneberg." In *Projekt: Spurensicherung. Alltag und Widerstand im Berlin der 30er Jahre,* edited by Berliner Geschichtswerkstatt, 9–48. Berlin (West): Elefanten Press, 1983.

Brückner, Peter. "Thesen zur Diskussion der 'Alternativen.'" In *Autonomie oder Getto? Kontroversen über die Alternativbewegung,* edited by Wolfgang Kraushaar, 68–85. Frankfurt am Main: Verlag Neue Kritik, 1978.

Brüggemeier, Franz-Josef. *Leben vor Ort: Ruhrbergleute und Ruhrbergbau 1889–1919.* Munich: C. H. Beck, 1983.

Brumlik, Micha. "Kulturpolitik als Ermöglichung von Bildung." *Kommune* 7 (1989).

———. "New Myth of State: The Eastern Front. The Most Recent Development in the Discipline of History in the Federal Republic of Germany." In *Forever in the Shadow of Hitler?: Original Documents of the Historikerstreit, the Controversy Concerning the Singularity of the Holocaust,* translated by James Knowlton and Truett Cates, 45–49. Atlantic Highlands: Humanities Press, 1993.

Bundesministerium für Jugend, Familie und Gesundheit. "Zur alternativen Kultur in der Bundesrepublik Deutschland." *Aus Politik und Zeitgeschichte* B 39 (1981): 3–15.

BundJugend. "Aktionsidee: Stolpersteine putzen und gemeinsam Erinnerung wachhalten." January 27, 2020. blog.bundjugend.de/aktionsidee-stolpersteine-putzen-und-gemeinsam-erinnerung-wachhalten.

Bündnis 90 / Die Grünen. *Politische Grundsätze.* Berlin: Bündnis 90 / Die Grünen, 1993.

———. *Die Zukunft ist grün. Grundsatzprogramm von Bündnis 90 / Die Grünen.* Berlin: Bündnis 90 / Die Grünen, 2002.

———. "Grüne Wahlergebnisse seit 1978—Bund und Länder (%)." December 8, 2017. cms.gruene.de/uploads/documents/Gruene-Wahlergebnisse.pdf.

———. *". . . zu achten und zu schützen." Veränderung schafft Halt. Grundsatzprogramm.* Berlin: Bündnis 90 / Die Grünen, 2020.

———. *Deutschland. Alles ist drin. Programmentwurf zur Bundestagswahl 2021.* Berlin: Bündnis 90 / Die Grünen, 2021.

Bürgerinitiative Perspektive Berlin. *Ein Denkmal für die ermordeten Juden Europas. Dokumentation 1988–1995.* Berlin: Bürgerinitiative Perspektive Berlin e. V., 1995.

Certeau, Michel de. *The Practice of Everyday Life.* Berkeley: University of California Press, 1984.

———. "Die Geschichte, Wissen und Fiktion." In *Die Zeichen der Historie: Beiträge zu einer semiologischen Geschichtswissenschaft,* edited by Georg Schmid, 29–50. Vienna: H. Böhlau, 1986.

"Chronik der Projekte des Vereins." In *Immer noch Lust auf Geschichte. 20 Jahre Berliner Geschichtswerkstatt e. V.,* edited by Berliner Geschichtswerkstatt e. V., 5–8. Berlin: Berliner Geschichtswerkstatt e. V., 2001.

Civic Engagement: Ziviles Engagement und Studium verbinden. "#Mitmachaktion: Stolpersteine putzen." December 14, 2020. civic-engagement.blogs.uni-hamburg.de/mitmachaktion-4.

Clewing, Ulrich. "Anwohner hielten das Mahnmal für antisemitische Propaganda. Berlin: Missverständnisse um Denkmal für Juden." *art. Das Kunstmagazin* 8 (1993): 193.

Cohen, Debbie. "Children's Tree from Theresienstadt May Sprout in S.F." *jweekly.com,* March 22, 1996. www.jweekly.com/includes/print/2794/article/children-s-tree-from-theresienstadt-may-sprout-in-s-f.

Cole, Peter. "How a Small Stone Could Help America Reckon with Its Worst History." *Washington Post,* February 6, 2018. www.washingtonpost.com/news/made-by-history/wp/2018/02/06/how-a-small-stone-could-help-america-reckon-with-its-worst-history.

Connolly, Kate. "Fear in Chemnitz: 'I'm Used to Neo-Nazis, but Not My Neighbour Mixing with Them in Broad Daylight.'" *The Guardian,* August 31, 2018. www.theguardian.com/world/2018/aug/31/germany-chemnitz-far-right-neo-nazis-not-neighbour.

Cornel, Hajo. "'Rahmenbedingungen für eine Kultur im Widerspruch.' Finanzielle, bürokratische und ideologische Fesseln der kommunalen Kulturpolitik." *Alternative Kommunalpolitik* 3 (1984): 18–22.

———. "Kultur." In *Handbuch für alternative Kommunalpolitik,* edited by Wolfgang Pohl et al., 292–299. Bielefeld: AJZ, 1985.

Cornel, Hajo, et al., eds. *Zum Thema: Kulturpolitik.* Berlin: Die Alternative Liste Berlin, 1985.

Dahmer, Helmut. "Die Sinngebung des Sinnlosen." *Die Zeit,* October 26, 1984.

Davin, Anna. "Frauen und Alltagsgeschichte." In *Alltagskultur, Subjektivität und Geschichte: Zur Theorie und Praxis von Alltagsgeschichte,* edited by Berliner Geschichtswerkstatt, 37–58. Münster: Westfälisches Dampfboot, 1994.

Dehne, Harald. "W(a)ende für / gegen eine Geschichtswerkstatt in der DDR?" *Geschichtswerkstatt* 20 (1990): 80–82.

Demnig, Gunter. "Projekt Stolpersteine." In *Größenwahn: Kunstprojekte für Europa,* edited by Gabriele Lindinger and Karlheinz Schmid, 60–61. Regensburg: Lindinger und Schmid, 1993.

Demnig, Gunter, and Jürgen Rapp. "Gunter Demnig: Dezentrales Mahnmal. Ein Gespräch mit Jürgen Rapp." *Kunstforum International* 170 (2004): 228–235.

Der Bundeswahlleiter. *Ergebnisse früherer Bundestagswahlen.* Wiesbaden: Der Bundeswahlleiter, 2018.

Dernbach, Andrea. "'Wir sind kein Einwanderungsland.'" *Der Tagesspiegel,* December 7, 2006. www.tagesspiegel.de/politik/wir-sind-kein-einwanderungsland/783936.html.

Deutscher Städtetag. *Wege zur menschlichen Stadt. Vorträge, Aussprachen und Ergebnisse der 17. Hauptversammlung des Deutschen Städtetages vom 2. bis 4. Mai 1973 in Dortmund.* Stuttgart: W. Kohlhammer, 1973.

Dickey, Megan Rose. "Equal Justice Initiative, Backed by Google.org, Launches 'Lynching in America.'" *techcrunch.com,* June 13, 2017. techcrunch.com/2017/06/13/lynching-in-america-equal-justice-initiative.

Die Grünen. *Das Bundesprogramm.* Bonn: Die Grünen, 1980.

Die Grünen, Bundesarbeitsgemeinschaft Kultur. *Dem Struwwelpeter durch die Haare gefahren: Auf dem Weg zu einer grünen Kulturpolitik.* Bonn: Die Grünen, 1987.

Die Grünen im Bundestag, ed. *Wider die Entsorgung der deutschen Geschichte. Streitschrift gegen die geplanten historischen Museen in Berlin (W) und Bonn.* Bonn: Die Grünen, 1986.

Dönhoff, Marion Gräfin. "Die Rebellion der Romantiker." *Die Zeit,* January 5, 1968. www.zeit.de/1968/01/die-rebellion-der-romantiker.

Doßmann, Axel. "Geschichtswerkstatt-Initiativen im Osten—ein ernüchterndes Fazit." In *Alltagskultur, Subjektivität und Geschichte: Zur Theorie und Praxis von Alltagsgeschichte,* edited by Berliner Geschichtswerkstatt, 328–336. Münster: Westfälisches Dampfboot, 1994.

Dubiel, Helmut. "Gespenst des Populismus." In *Populismus und Aufklärung,* edited by Helmut Dubiel, 33–50. Frankfurt am Main: Suhrkamp, 1986.

Düspohl, Martin. "20 Jahre Berliner Geschichtswerkstatt: Ein persönlicher Rückblick." In *Immer noch Lust auf Geschichte. 20 Jahre Berliner Geschichtswerkstatt e. V.,* 46–51. Berlin: Berliner Geschichtswerkstatt e. V., 2001.

Editorial Board. "Russia Cracks Down on an Important Voice for Human Rights." *Washington Post,* November 11, 2015. www.washingtonpost.com/opinions/a-voice-that-must-not-be-stilled/2015/11/11/c1d4fb3c-87ea-11e5-9a07-453018f9a0ec_story.html.

Ehalt, Hubert Ch., ed. *Geschichte von unten: Fragestellungen, Methoden und Projekte einer Geschichte des Alltags.* Vienna: H. Böhlau, 1984.

"Ehemaliges Konzentrationslager Neuengamme wird Mahnmal. Hamburger Senat will Teile unter Denkmalschutz stellen / Grün-Alternative Liste hält Pläne für nicht ausreichend." *Frankfurter Rundschau,* February 16, 1984.

"'Ein kräftiger Schub für die Vergangenheit.' Spiegel-Report über die neue Geschichtsbewegung in der Bundesrepublik." *Der Spiegel,* June 6, 1983, 36–42.

Eisbrenner, Bettina, and Neue Gesellschaft für bildende Kunst, eds. *Stolpersteine für die von den Nazis ermordeten ehemaligen Nachbarn aus Friedrichshain und Kreuzberg: Dokumentation, Texte, Materialien.* Berlin: NGBK, 2002.

Eley, Geoff. "Wie denken wir über Politik? Alltagsgeschichte und die Kategorie des Politischen." In *Alltagskultur, Subjektivität und Geschichte: Zur Theorie und Praxis von Alltagsgeschichte,* edited by Berliner Geschichtswerkstatt, 17–36. Münster: Westfälisches Dampfboot, 1994.

Emig, Dieter, and Alfred G. Frei. "'. . . die Fremdheit der Dinge und Personen aufheben.' Über Versuche, Heimat neu zu entdecken." In *Heimat: Analysen, Themen, Perspektiven,* edited by Bundeszentrale für politische Bildung, 307–328. Bonn: Bundeszentrale für politische Bildung, 1990.

Emmerich, Marlies. "Ausstellung zum Holocaust-Denkmal eröffnet. 200 000 Mark gespendet: Eine Pflicht zur Erinnerung." *Berliner Zeitung,* April 11, 1995.

Endlich, Stephanie. "Ein 'dezentrales Monument'? Anmerkungen zu einem ungewöhnlichen Denkmalskonzept." In *Stolpersteine für die von den Nazis ermordeten ehemaligen Nachbarn aus Friedrichshain und Kreuzberg: Dokumentation, Texte, Materialien,* edited by Bettina Eisbrenner and Neue Gesellschaft für bildende Kunst. Berlin: NGBK, 2002.

"Entwurf für Perspektiven: Kultur: Die Grünen wollen künftig stärker mitmischen." *Hessische-Niedersächsische Allgemeine,* June 9, 1988.

Equal Justice Initiative. "Lynching in America: Confronting the Legacy of Racial Terror." Accessed April 10, 2021. lynchinginamerica.eji.org.

———. "The National Memorial to Peace and Justice." Accessed April 10, 2021. museumandmemorial.eji.org/memorial.

Erenz, Benedikt. "Der Ort, der stört." *Die Zeit,* September 2, 1988.

"Ergebnis der Koalitionsgespräche." *CDU-Extra,* October 1, 1982.

European Green Belt. "European Green Belt Initiative." Accessed April 10, 2021. www.europeangreenbelt.org.

Evans, Richard J. "Die 'History Workshop'-Bewegung in England." In *Geschichte entdecken: Erfahrungen und Projekte der neuen Geschichtsbewegung,* edited by Hannes Heer and Volker Ullrich, 37–45. Reinbek bei Hamburg: Rowohlt, 1985.

Fischer, Martin. "'Schlechtgemachte Bilder, schlechtgemachtes Fernsehen, schlechtgeführte Ehen . . .' Auf den Spuren grüner Kulturpolitik am Beispiel der Bundesrepublik Deutschland." In *Nur kein Rhabarber! Auseinandersetzungen mit grüner Politik in Österreich,* edited by Karl Lind, 123–139. Vienna: Grün-Alternativ-Verlag, 1988.

Fletcher, Roger. "Recent Developments in West German Historiography: The Bielefeld School and Its Critics." *German Studies Review* 7, no. 3 (October 1984): 451–480.

Flügge, Matthias. "Bildersturm." *Kunst Intern* (1987).

Franke, Uta. *Stolpersteine: Idee, Vorgeschichte und Entwicklung eines Projektes. Interviews von Uta Franke mit Gunter Demnig.* Cologne: self-pub., 2003.

Franke, Uta, and Gunter Demnig. "Am treffendsten läßt sich meine Berufsbezeichnung mit Bildhauer umschreiben, Uta Franke im Interview mit Gunter Demnig." In *Stolpersteine für die von den Nazis ermordeten ehemaligen Nachbarn aus Friedrichshain und Kreuzberg: Dokumentation, Texte, Materialien,* edited by Bettina Eisbrenner and Neue Gesellschaft für bildende Kunst, 9–22. Berlin: NGBK, 2002.

Frei, Alfred Georg. *Antonio Gramsci, Theoretiker des demokratischen Übergangs zum Sozialismus.* Berlin (West): DVK-Verlag, 1978.

———. "Alltag—Region—Politik. Anmerkungen zur 'neuen Geschichtsbewegung.'" *Geschichtsdidaktik* 2 (1984): 107–120.

———. "Spannungsfelder. Geschichtsfest Berlin." *Journal für Geschichte* 4 (1984): 4–7.

———. "Die Zukunft liegt in der Vergangenheit. Geschichtswerkstätten, Tendenzwende und demokratische Alternativen." *Moderne Zeiten—Extra. Geschichtswerkstatt. Sondernummer* 4 (April 1984): 3–6.

———. "Geschichtswerkstätten." In *Geschichte entdecken: Erfahrungen und Projekte der neuen Geschichtsbewegung,* edited by Hannes Heer and Volker Ullrich, 400–404. Reinbek bei Hamburg: Rowohlt, 1985.

———. "Geschichtswerkstätten als Zukunftswerkstätten. Ein Plädoyer für aufklärerische Geschichtsarbeit." In *Die andere Geschichte: Geschichte von unten, Spurensicherung, ökologische Geschichte, Geschichtswerkstätten,* edited by Gerhard Paul and Bernhard Schossig, 258–280. Cologne: Bund-Verlag, 1986.

———. "Geschichte aus den 'Graswurzeln'? Geschichtswerkstätten in der historischen Kulturarbeit." *Aus Politik und Zeitgeschichte* B 2 (1988): 35–46.

———. "Die Geschichtswerkstätten in der Krise." In *Alltagskultur, Subjektivität und Geschichte: Zur Theorie und Praxis von Alltagsgeschichte,* edited by Berliner Geschichtswerkstatt, 315–327. Münster: Westfälisches Dampfboot, 1994.

Frei, Alfred Georg, and Michael Wildt. "Hirsebrei und Seifenblasen. Die Geschichtswerkstätten und ihre Kritiker." *L'80. Zeitschrift für Literatur und Politik* 39 (1986): 64–72.

Frevert, Ute. "German Women Historians' Meeting, 26–27 March 1977." *History Workshop Journal* 4, no. 1 (September 1977): 235–236.

Fricke, Uwe. "Kultur—Ästhetik—Kunst." In *Zum Thema: Kulturpolitik,* edited by Hajo Cornel et al., 31–33. Berlin: Die Alternative Liste Berlin, 1985.

Gansel, Norbert. "Die Strategie in der Diskussion der Jungsozialisten." In *Überwindet den Kapitalismus, oder Was wollen die Jungsozialisten?* edited by Norbert Gansel, 79–100. Reinbek bei Hamburg: Rowohlt, 1971.

"Gedenkstätten: Verfluchter Ort." *Der Spiegel,* May 28, 1984.

Gerz, Jochen. *2146 Steine: Mahnmal gegen Rassismus Saarbrücken.* Stuttgart: Gerd Hatje Verlag, 1993.

Geschichtswerkstatt e. V. "Selbstverständnispapier der Geschichtswerkstatt e. V." *Geschichtsdidaktik* 9, no. 2 (1984): 193–194.

Gesterkamp, Harald. "'Barfußhistoriker' ohne Boden." *Frankfurter Rundschau,* April 23, 1992.

Goette, Jürgen-Wolfgang. *Stolpersteine Erich-Mühsam-Preis 2009 an Gunter Demnig.* Lübeck: EMG, 2009.

Göring-Eckardt, Katrin. "'Die K-Frage'—Kultur diesseits und jenseits der Ökonomie. Kulturpolitik als bevorzugter Bereich kreativen und politischen Denkens." In *Kulturpolitik der Parteien: Visionen, Programmatic, Geschichte und Differenzen,* edited by Olaf Zimmermann and Theo Geißler, 97–99. Berlin: Deutscher Kulturrat, 2008.

Gorky, Maxim. "The People Must Know Their History!" In *Culture and the People,* 94–100. New York: International Publishers, 1939.

Gößwald, Udo. "Historische Ausstellungen—Orte rekonstruierte Sinnlichkeit." In *Geschichte entdecken: Erfahrungen und Projekte der neuen Geschichtsbewegung,* edited by Hannes Heer and Volker Ullrich, 304–309. Reinbek bei Hamburg: Rowohlt, 1985.

Greffrath, Matthias. "Die missbrauchte Kraft des Schönen. Auf dem Weg in die 'Kulturgesellschaft.'" *Die Zeit,* November 25, 1988, Feuilleton, 65–66.

"Grüne: Europawahl Signal für mehr Klimaschutz." *Süddeutsche Zeitung,* May 26, 2019. www.sueddeutsche.de/politik/wahlen-gruene-europawahl-signal-fuer-mehr-klimaschutz-dpa.urn-newsml-dpa-com-20090101-190526-99-386734.

"Grüne: Sehr interessante Kehrtwendung." *Der Spiegel,* June 27, 1982. http://www.spiegel.de/spiegel/print/d-14345177.html

Günther, Barbara, and Landeszentrale für politische Bildung. *Stolpersteine in Hamburg-Harburg und Hamburg-Wilhelmsburg biographische Spurensuche.* Hamburg: Landeszentrale für politische Bildung, 2012.

Hahn, Wolfgang. "Gunter Demnig, Tausendsassa." In *Vor meiner Haustür—"Stolpersteine" von Gunter Demnig: Ein Begleitbuch,* edited by Joachim Rönneper, 114–115. Gelsenkirchen: Arachne-Verlag, 2010.

Hamburger Institut für Sozialforschung, ed. *Eine Ausstellung und ihre Folgen: Zur Rezeption der Ausstellung "Vernichtungskrieg. Verbrechen der Wehrmacht 1941 bis 1944."* Hamburg: Hamburger Edition, 1999.

Hasenclever, Wolf-Dieter. "Ökologischer Humanismus." In *Die Grünen: Personen, Projekte, Programme,* edited by Hans-Werner Lüdke and Olaf Dinné, 42–52. Stuttgart-Degerloch: Seewald, 1980.

———. "Die Grünen sind eine stinknormale Partei geworden." In *Die Grünen: 10 bewegte Jahre,* edited by Michael Schroeren, 135–145. Vienna: Ueberreuter, 1990.

Hauff, Volker. *Global denken, lokal handeln: Ein politisches Fazit.* Cologne: Kiepenheuer und Witsch, 1992.

Hauff, Volker, and World Commission on Environment and Development. *Unsere gemeinsame Zukunft: Der Brundtland-Bericht der Weltkommission für Umwelt und Entwicklung.* Greven: Eggenkamp, 1987.

Heer, Hannes, and Klaus Naumann, eds. *Vernichtungskrieg: Verbrechen der Wehrmacht 1941–1944.* Hamburg: Hamburger Edition, 1995.

Heer, Hannes, and Volker Ullrich. "Die 'neue Geschichtsbewegung' in der Bundesrepublik. Antriebeskräfte, Selbstverständnis, Perspektiven." In *Geschichte entdecken: Erfahrungen und Projekte der neuen Geschichtsbewegung,* edited by Hannes Heer and Volker Ullrich, 9–36. Reinbek bei Hamburg: Rowohlt, 1985.

Hein, Christina. "Stolperstein schlägt Wellen. Die Stadt Kassel unterstützt künftig die Gedenkstein-Aktion von Gunter Demnig." *Hessische-Niedersächsische Allgemeine,* May 27, 2011.

Heller, Agnes. "Existentialismus, Entfremdung, Postmodernismus, kulturelle Bewegungen als Ausdrucksmittel des Wandels der Verhaltensmuster im alltäglichen Leben." *Der Alltag* 4 (1987): 16–27.

Henley, Jon. "Merkel's Long Goodbye Will Be Severe Test for Troubled Continent." *The Guardian,* October 29, 2018. www.theguardian.com/world/2018/oct/29/angela-merkel-to-step-down-vacuum-eu-politics.

———. "European Elections: Triumphant Greens Demand More Radical Climate Action." *The Guardian,* May 27, 2019. www.theguardian.com/environment/2019/may/28/greens-eu-election-mandate-leverage-climate-policy.

Herlyn, Sunke, et al., eds. *Kunst im Stadtbild: Von Kunst am Bau zu Kunst im öffentlichen Raum: Katalog zur gleichnamigen Ausstellung in der Universität Bremen vom 8.–30. Juni 1976.* Bremen: Hauschild, 1976.

Hermand, Jost, and Hubert Müller, eds. *Öko-Kunst?: Zur Ästhetik der Grünen.* Hamburg: Argument-Verlag, 1989.

Heydemann, Gunther. "Geschichtswissenschaft und Geschichtsverstandnis in der DDR seit 1945." *Aus Politik und Zeitgeschichte* B 13 (March 1987): 15–26.

Hoffmann, Hilmar. *Kultur für alle. Perspetiven und Modelle.* Frankfurt am Main: S. Fischer Verlag, 1979.

———. *Kultur für morgen.* Frankfurt am Main: Fischer Taschenbuch Verlag, 1985.

———. "Kultur für alle. Als Prognose." *Kultur Politik Diskurs* 3 (2000): 15–22.

Hoheisel, Horst. *Aschrottbrunnen.* Frankfurt am Main: Fritz Bauer Institut, 1998.

Holl, Kurt, and Corinna Kawaters. *Ein Strich durchs Vergessen: 1000 Roma und Sinti—Mai 1940.* Cologne: Rom e. V., 1997.

Holler, Eckard. "Soziokultur als Gegenkonzept zur etablierten Elitekultur?" *Das Argument* 151 (May / June 1985): 398–404.

———. "Grüne Kulturpolitik und kulturelle Bewegung 'von unten.'" In *Öko-Kunst? Zur Ästhetik der Grünen,* edited by Jost Hermand and Hubert Müller, 55–70. Hamburg: Argument-Verlag, 1989.

Jaeggi, Urs. "Drinnen und draußen." In *Stichworte zur 'Geistigen Situation der Zeit,' vol. 2. Politik und Kultur,* edited by Jürgen Habermas, 443–473. Frankfurt am Main: Suhrkamp, 1979.

Jorzig, Wolfgang. "Stolpern heißt auch, darauf stoßen. Erinnerungsmale—Kunst im öffentlichen Raum." *Schriftenreihe des Vereins "Gegen Vergessen—Für Demokratie"* 36 (March 2003): 6–8.

Jungbauer, G. *Sudetendeutsche Zeitschrift für Volkskunde, vol. 3–4.* Prague: Dr. G. Jungbauer, 1930.

Karwelat, Jürgen. "Schon wieder 'ne Luise? Berliner Straßenumbenennungen—Die Zwischenbilanz ergibt: Viele Chancen vertan." *die tageszeitung,* March 13, 1992.

———. "Der Druck der öffentlichen Straße." *die tageszeitung,* March 18, 1994.

———. *Wahnsinn: Erinnerung an den Berliner Mauerfall vom 9. November 1989.* Berlin: Berliner Geschichtswerkstatt, 1999.

———. "Mittlerweile bin ich mein eigener Zeitzeuge." In *Immer noch Lust auf Geschichte. 20 Jahre Berliner Geschichtswerkstatt e. V.,* 56–61. Berlin: Berliner Geschichtswerkstatt e. V., 2001.

Kaschuba, Wolfgang. "Mythos oder Eigensinn, Volkskultur zwischen Volkskunde und Sozialgeschichte." In *Volkskultur in der Moderne. Probleme und Perspektiven empirischer Kulturforschung,* edited by Utz Jeggle and Hermann Bausinger, 469–507. Reinbek bei Hamburg: Rowohlt, 1986.

Kil, Wolfgang. "Geschichte von unten." *Sonntag,* July 2, 1989.

Klönne, Arno. "Überlegungen zur sozialen Basis und politische Philosophie der grünen Partei." In *Von der Machbarkeit der Unmöglichen: Politische Gespräche über grüne Praxis und grüne Perspektiven,* edited by Sabine Stamer, 171–179. Hamburg: Junius, 1985.

Kloth, Carsten. "Gleditschstraße: Stolpersteine in Schöneberg beschädigt." *Der Tagesspiegel,* October 31, 2010. www.tagesspiegel.de/berlin/polizei-justiz/gleditschstrasse-stolpersteine-in-schoeneberg-beschaedigt/1970952.html.

Knowlton, James, and Truett Cates, trans. *Forever in the Shadow of Hitler?: Original Documents of the Historikerstreit, the Controversy Concerning the Singularity of the Holocaust.* Atlantic Highlands: Humanities Press, 1993.

Kocka, Jürgen. "Geschichte als Aufklärung?" *Frankfurter Rundschau,* January 4, 1988.

Krings, Eva. "Politikfeld Kultur. Anforderungen an Bündnis 90 / Die Grünen." In *Zwischen Leuchtturmprogramm und Warnblinkanlage. Bündnisgrüne Kulturpolitik auf Bundesebene. Dokumentation des kulturpolitischen Ratschlags am 8. Juli 1995 in Bonn,* edited by Bündnis 90 / Die Grünen, Bundestagsfraktion and Bernd Wagner, 16–19. Bonn: Bündnis 90 / Die Grünen, 1995.

Kubitschek, Götz. "Konservativ-Subversive Aktion." *Sezession* 25 (2008): 56.

Kulturbereich der Alternativen Liste. "Der Kulturbereich der Alternativen Liste stellt vor." In *Zum Thema: Kulturpolitik,* edited by Hajo Cornel et al., 7–12. Berlin: Die Alternative Liste Berlin, 1985.

Kunk, Manfred. "Zwischen Kulturutopie und Kulturinstitution. Zum Stellenwert soziokultureller Zentren." *Alternative Kommunale Kulturpolitik* 1 (1988): 37–39.

Kunstamt Schöneberg and Gedenkstätte Haus der Wannsee-Konferenz. *Orte des Erinnerns, Band 1. Das Denkmal im Bayerischen Viertel, Beitrag zur Debatte um Denkmale und Erinnerung.* Berlin: Edition Hentrich, 1994.

———. *Orte des Erinnerns, Band 2. Jüdisches Alltagsleben im Bayerischen Viertel, eine Dokumentation.* Berlin: Edition Hentrich, 1995.

Kunze, Klaus. "Plebiszite als Weg aus dem Parteienstaat." *Junge Freiheit* 10 (1992): 23–24.

"Kurz und knapp. Plakate abgenommen." *Berliner Zeitung,* June 5 / 6, 1993.

Lämmert, Eberhard. "Wem gehört die Geschichte? Über den vernünftigen Umgang mit der Vergangenheit." *Die Zeit,* January 22, 1988, 36.

Laurien, Ingrid. "Flucht aus der Geschichte in die Geschichte?" *L'80. Zeitschrift für Literatur und Politik* 39 (1986): 75–84.

Libeskind, Daniel. *Erweiterung des Berlin Museums mit Abteilung Jüdisches Museum,* edited by Kristin Feireiss. Berlin: Ernst und Sohn, 1992.

Lindenberger, Thomas. "Werkstattgefluster. Überlegungen zu Selbstverständnis und Praxis radikaldemokratischer Geschichtsforschung aus der Berliner Geschichtswerkstatt." In *Demokratie- und Arbeitergeschichte. Jahrbuch 3,* edited by Franz Mehring Gesellschaft, Stuttgart, 23–27. Weingarten: Drumlin-Verlag, 1983.

———. "Wer hat Angst vor den Barfußhistorikern? Plaedoyer für einen rationalen Dialog." *Geschichtsdidaktik. Probleme, Projekte, Perspektiven* 11, no. 1 (1986): 17–20.

Lindenberger, Thomas, and Michael Wildt. "Radical Plurality: History Workshops as a Practical Critique of Knowledge." *History Workshop Journal* 33, no. 1 (March 1992): 73–99.

Lindinger, Gabriele, and Karlheinz Schmid, eds. *Größenwahn: Kunstprojekte für Europa.* Regensburg: Lindinger und Schmid, 1993.

Lindqvist, Sven. *Gräv där du står: Hur man utforskar ett jobb.* Stockholm: Bonnier, 1978.

———. "Dig Where You Stand." *Oral History* 7, no. 2 (October 1979): 24–30.

———. "Grabe, wo du stehst." In *Geschichte von unten: Fragestellungen, Methoden und Projekte einer Geschichte des Alltags,* edited by Hubert Ch. Ehalt, 295–304. Vienna: H. Böhlau, 1984.

———. "Grabe, wo du stehst. Das schwedische Beispiel." In *Geschichte entdecken: Erfahrungen und Projekte der neuen Geschichtsbewegung,* edited by Hannes Heer and Volker Ullrich, 72–74. Reinbek bei Hamburg: Rowohlt, 1985.

———. *Grabe, wo du stehst: Handbuch zur Erforschung der eigenen Geschichte,* translated by Manfred Dammeyer. Bonn: Dietz, 1989.

Lipman, Masha. "Humble Memorials for Stalin's Victims in Moscow." *New Yorker,* December 13, 2014. www.newyorker.com/news/news-desk/humble-memorials-stalins-victims-moscow.

Lüdtke, Alf. "Rekonstruktion von Alltagswirklichkeit—Entpolitisierung der Sozialgeschichte?" In *Klassen und Kultur: Sozialanthropologische Perspektiven in der Geschichtsschreibung,* edited by Robert M. Berdahl et al., 321–353. Frankfurt am Main: Syndikat, 1982.

Lüdtke, Alf, ed., *Alltagsgeschichte: Zur Rekonstruktion historischer Erfahrungen und Lebensweisen.* Frankfurt am Main: Campus, 1989.

———. *The History of Everyday Life: Reconstructing Historical Experiences and Ways of Life.* Princeton, NJ: Princeton University Press, 1995.

Ludwig, Andreas. "Historische Neugier and Projektpraxis." In *Projekt: Spurensicherung. Alltag und Widerstand im Berlin der 30er Jahre,* edited by Berliner Geschichtswerkstatt, 5–8. Berlin: Elefanten Press, 1983.

———. "Das '33-Projekt.'" In *Immer noch Lust auf Geschichte. 20 Jahre Berliner Geschichtswerkstatt e. V.,* 20–24. Berlin: Berliner Geschichtswerkstatt e. V., 2001.

Lüscher, Rudolf, Werner Schweizer, Amalie Pinkus-De Sassi, and Theo Pinkus-De Sassi. *Leben im Widerspruch.* Zürich: Limmat-Verlag, 1987.

Marcuse, Herbert. "The End of Utopia." In *Marxism, Revolution and Utopia: Collected Papers of Herbert Marcuse, vol. 6,* edited by Douglas Kellner and Clayton Pierce, 249–263. Hoboken: Taylor and Francis, 2014.

Maren-Grisebach, Manon. *Philosophie der Grünen.* Munich: Olzog, 1982.

Medick, Hans. "'Missionaries in the Rowboat?' Ethnological Ways of Knowing as a Challenge to Social History." In *The History of Everyday Life: Reconstructing Historical Experiences and Ways of Life,* edited by Alf Lüdtke, 41–71. Princeton, NJ: Princeton University Press, 1995.

Meier, Christian. "Condemning and Comprehending." In *Forever in the Shadow of Hitler?: Original Documents of the Historikerstreit, the Controversy Concerning the Singularity of the Holocaust,* translated by James Knowlton and Truett Cates, 24–33. Atlantic Highlands: Humanities Press, 1993.

Menzel, Birgit, and Werner Süß. "Das Bayrische Viertel—'Die Jüdische Schweiz.' Etappen eines Vernichtungsprozesses." In *Leben in Schöneberg/Friedenau 1933–45,* edited by Gisela Wenzel, 39–44. Berlin: Kunstamt Schöneberg, 1983.

Meyer, Michael, and Berliner Geschichtswerkstatt. *"Das war 'ne ganz geschlossene Gesellschaft hier": Der Lindenhof, eine Genossenschafts-Siedlung in der Großstadt.* Berlin: Nishen, 1987.

"Mit grünen Augen betrachtet. Eine Diskussion über Kunst und ihre Verantwortung in der Gesellschaft anlässlich der Documenta 8 in Kassel." In *Öko-Kunst?: Zur Ästhetik der Grünen,* edited by Jost Hermand and Hubert Müller, 71–94. Hamburg: Argument-Verlag, 1989.

Moeller van den Bruck, Arthur. *Das Dritte Reich.* Hamburg: Hanseatische Verlagsanstalt, 1931.

Morris, Loveday. "Germany's Greens Look to Be Kingmakers in a Post-Merkel Era." *Washington Post,* March 15, 2021. www.washingtonpost.com/world/germany-greens-merkel-elections/2021/03/15/c1073f16-835d-11eb-be22-32d331d87530_story.html.

Müller, Ann-Katrin. "AfD setzt auf Zweifel am Klimawandel." *Spiegel Online,* April 27, 2019. www.spiegel.de/politik/deutschland/afd-setzt-auf-zweifel-am-klimawandel-im-wahlkampf-a-1264532.html.

Müller, Friedrich-Thorsten. "Rechte der Kinder verteidigen." *Junge Freiheit* 14 (2013): 9.

Niethammer, Lutz. "Anmerkungen zur Alltagsgeschichte." *Geschichtsdidaktik* 5, no. 3 (1980): 231–242.

Niethammer, Lutz, ed. *"Die Jahre weiß man nicht, wo man die heute hinsetzen soll." Faschismuserfahrungen im Ruhrgebiet.* Berlin and Bonn: Dietz, 1983.

———. *"Hinterher merkt man, daß es richtig war, daß es schiefgegangen ist." Nachkriegserfahrungen im Ruhrgebiet.* Berlin and Bonn: Dietz, 1983.

Niethammer, Lutz, and Dirk van Laak. *Posthistoire: Has History Come to an End?* London: Verso, 1992.

Niethammer, Lutz, and Alexander von Plato, eds. *"Wir kriegen jetzt andere Zeiten." Auf der Suche nach der Erfahrung des Volkes in nachfaschistischen Ländern.* Berlin and Bonn: Dietz, 1985.

NPD-Parteivorstand. *Argumente für Kandidaten und Funktionsträger. Handreichung für die öffentliche Auseinandersetzung.* Berlin: Nationaldemokratische Partei Deutschlands, 2006.

NS-Dokumentationszentrum (Historisches Archiv der Stadt Köln) and Karola Fings. *Stolpersteine: Gunter Demnig und sein Projekt = Gunter Demnig and His Project.* Cologne: Emons, 2007.

"Nur in Bergedorf darf es keine Stolpersteine geben." *Die Welt,* January 30, 2003.

Offe, Claus. "Konkurrenzpartei und kollektive politische Identität." In *Parlamentarisches Ritual und politische Alternativen,* edited by Roland Roth, 26–42. Frankfurt am Main: Campus, 1980.

Omnibus für direkte Demokratie in Deutschland. *Projekte Erweiterte Kunst: Von Beuys aus.* Wangen: FIU, 1993.

Opresni, Miriam. "Bergedorf: Streit um Stolpersteine." *Hamburger Abendblatt,* July 4, 2003.

Pagenstecher, Cord. "Die 'Illusion' der Rückkehr. Zur Mentalitätsgeschichte von 'Gastarbeit' und Einwanderung." *Soziale Welt* 47, no. 2 (1996): 149–179.

———. "'. . . da sind wir keine Ausländer mehr.' Eingewanderte ArbeiterInnen in Berlin 1961–1993." In *Immer noch Lust auf Geschichte. 20 Jahre Berliner Geschichtswerkstatt e. V.,* 41–45. Berlin: Berliner Geschichtswerkstatt e. V., 2001.

Památník Terezín. *Terezin Memorial: Annual Report for 2008*. Terezin: Památník Terezín, 2008.

Paul, Reimar. "Kultusgemeinde kritisiert Stolpersteine." *Tageszeitung*, July 22, 2006.

Peukert, Detlev. "Arbeiteralltag—Mode oder Methode?" In *Arbeiteralltag in Stadt und Land. Neue Wege der Geschichtsschreibung, Argument Sonderband 94*, edited by Heiko Haumann and Stefan Bajohr, 8–39. Berlin: Argument-Verlag, 1982.

Pick, Kurt-Werner. "Stolpersteine. Spuren gegen das Vergessen. Ein Kunstprojekt an der Antoniterkirche." *Antoniter Nachrichten* (March 1994): 4–7.

Prantl, Heribert, ed. *Wehrmachtsverbrechen: Eine deutsche Kontroverse*. Hamburg: Hoffmann und Campe, 1997.

Rahlfes, Sigrid. "Die Spur der Steine." *Mobil* (November 2002): 13.

Raschke, Joachim. "Jenseits der Volkspartei." *Das Argument* 25, no. 137 (1983): 54–64.

"Richard Serra entwirft Gedenktafel für Euthanasie-Opfer." *Tagesspiegel*, September 2, 1988.

Robertson, Campbell. "History of Lynchings in the South Documents Nearly 4,000 Names." *New York Times*, February 10, 2015. www.nytimes.com/2015/02/10/us/history-of-lynchings-in-the-south-documents-nearly-4000-names.html.

Roller, Kathrin. *Frauenmigration und Ausländerpolitik im Deutschen Kaiserreich. Polnische Arbeitsmigrantinnen in Preußen*. Berlin: D. Bertz, 1994.

Rönneper, Joachim. *Vor meiner Haustür—"Stolpersteine" von Gunter Demnig: Ein Begleitbuch*. Gelsenkirchen: Arachne-Verlag, 2010.

Roth, Claudia. "Kreativitätspolitik im Übergang zur Wissensgesellschaft. Verschiedene Politik- und Aufgabenfelder miteinander in Beziehung setzen." In *Kulturpolitik der Parteien: Visionen, Programmatic, Geschichte und Differenzen*, edited by Olaf Zimmermann and Theo Geißler, 94–96. Berlin: Deutscher Kulturrat, 2008.

Rürup, Reinhard. *Topographie des Terrors. Gestapo, SS und Reichssicherheitshauptamt auf dem "Prinz-Albrecht-Gelände": Eine Dokumentation*. Berlin: Verlag Willmuth Arenhövel, 1987.

Rüsen, Jörn. "Geschichte als Aufklärung? Oder: Das Dilemma des historischen Denkens zwischen Herrschaft und Emanzipation." *Geschichte und Gesellschaft* 7, no. 2 (January 1981): 189–218.

"Salecina-Seminar. 10.-16. Juni 1984. Geschichte von unten. Faschismus und Widerstand." *Moderne Zeiten—Extra. Geschichtswerkstatt. Sondernummer* 4 (April 1984): 59.

Samuel, Raphael. "General Editor's Introduction: People's History." In *Village Life and Labour*, edited by Raphael Samuel, xx–xxi. London: Routledge and Kegan Paul, 1975.

———. "Oral History in Großbritannien." In *Lebenserfahrung und kollektives Gedächtnis: Die Praxis der "Oral History,"* edited by Lutz Niethammer and Werner Trapp, 55–73. Frankfurt am Main: Syndikat, 1980.

———. "History Workshop 1: Truth is Partisan." *New Statesman* (February 15, 1980): 247–249.

———. "Die englische History-Workshop-Bewegung und ihre Ziele." *Journal für Geschichte* 1 (1981): 7–9.

———. "Das britische Modell. Die englische History-Workshop-Bewegung und ihre Ziele." *Moderne Zeiten—Extra. Geschichtswerkstatt. Sondernummer* 4 (April 1984): 7–9.

Sander, Andreas. "Die 'Rote Insel.'" In *Immer noch Lust auf Geschichte. 20 Jahre Berliner Geschichtswerkstatt e. V.*, 25–27. Berlin: Berliner Geschichtswerkstatt e. V., 2001.

Saroyan, William. "Zeitmosaik." *Die Zeit*, May 22, 1981.

Scharrer, Manfred. *Macht Geschichte von unten. Handbuch für gewerkschaftliche Geschichte vor Ort.* Cologne: Bund-Verlag, 1988.

Schindel, Estela. "Piedras, Plazas, y Performances: Modos Activos de la Memoria en Buenos Aires." In *Memorias Urbanas en Diálogo: Berlín y Buenos Aires*, edited by Peter Birle, Vera Carnovale, Elke Gryglewski, and Estela Schindel, 387–403. Buenos Aires: Buenos Libros Santiago, Chile Fundación, Heinrich Böll, Cono Sur, 2010.

Schmid, Karlheinz. "Kunst-Tip des Monats: Gunter Demnig." *Pan* 10 (1988): 9.

Schmidt, Albert. "Bündnisgrüne Kulturpolitik zwischen Skepsis und Erwartung." In *Zwischen Leuchtturmprogramm und Warnblinkanlage. Bündnisgrüne Kulturpolitik auf Bundesebene. Dokumentation des kulturpolitischen Ratschlags am 8. Juli 1995 in Bonn*, edited by Bündnis 90 / Die Grünen, Bundestagsfraktion and Bernd Wagner, 5–8. Bonn: Bündnis 90 / Die Grünen, 1995.

Schmidt, Roland. "Zur alternativen Kultur. Erscheinungsbild und Strukturen." *Aus Politik und Zeitgeschichte* B 11 (March 1983): 41–54.

Schneckenburger, Manfred. "Delta im Einheitsstrom. Zur Kunst der neunziger Jahre." In *Größenwahn: Kunstprojekte für Europa*, edited by Gabriele Lindinger and Karlheinz Schmid, 18–23. Regensburg: Lindinger und Schmid, 1993.

———. "Gunter Demnig—Vergangenheit, trittfest gemacht." *Kölner Skizzen* 15, no. 4 (1993): 6–15.

Schneider, Gerhard. "Schülerwettbewerb Deutsche Geschichte." In *Geschichte entdecken: Erfahrungen und Projekte der neuen Geschichtsbewegung*, edited by Hannes Heer and Volker Ullrich, 391–395. Reinbek bei Hamburg: Rowohlt, 1985.

Schnock, Friedrich Wilhelm Martin. "Richard Long und der veränderte Skulpturbegriff." Dissertation. Hochschule für bildende Künste, 1999.

Schöttler, Peter. "Die Geschichtswerkstatt e. V. zu einem Versuch, basisdemokratische Geschichtsinitiativen und -forschungen zu 'Vernetzen.'" *Geschichte und Gesellschaft* 10, no. 3 (January 1984): 420–424.

———. "Häretiker, Pfadfinder und Ideenbankier. Zum Tod von Raphael Samuel." *WerkstattGeschichte* 16 (1997): 63–69.

Schrader, Ulrike. "Die 'Stolpersteine' oder Von der Leichtigkeit des Gedenkens: Einige kritische Anmerkungen." *Geschichte im Westen: Zeitschrift für Landes- und Zeitgeschichte* 21 (2006): 173–181.

Schröder, C. J. "Drei Fallen einer grün-alternativen Kulturpolitik." *Kultur und Gesellschaft* 4 (1984).

———. "Kunst als Klassenkampf oder Kultur für alle? Der Richtungsstreit in der grün-alternativen Kulturpolitik." *grüner basisdienst* 3 (1985): 23–27.

Schröter, Ursula. "Gründungsphase der Berliner Geschichtswerkstatt." In *Immer noch Lust auf Geschichte. 20 Jahre Berliner Geschichtswerkstatt e. V.*, 9–12. Berlin: Berliner Geschichtswerkstatt e. V., 2001.

Schultheis, Emily. "Germany Is Testing the Limits of Democracy." *The Atlantic*, February 25, 2019. www.theatlantic.com/international/archive/2019/02/german-intel-chief-plan-surveil-far-right-afd/583456.

Schweitzer, Albert. "The Ethics of Reverence for Life." In *The Philosophy of Civilization*, 307–329. Buffalo: Prometheus Books, 1987.

Scrapheaper. "'Stolpersteine': Gedenken im Alltag." YouTube video, May 7, 2011. www.youtube.com/watch?v=hziXzDDGayY.

Seibt, Gustav. "Grabe wo du stehst. Die Kontroverse um die Alltagsgeschichte." *Frankfurter Allgemeine Zeitung*, September 22, 1987.

Selle, Gert, and Jutta Boehe. *Leben mit schönen Dingen—Anpassung und Eigensinn im Alltag des Wohnens*. Reinbek bei Hamburg: Rowohlt, 1986.

Sellner, Martin. "Gewaltlose Disziplin." *Sezession*, February 16, 2017. sezession.de/56991/gewaltlose-disziplin.

Senatsverwaltung für Bau- und Wohnungswesen Berlin. *Offener Kunstwettbewerb. "Kunst im Stadtraum." Mahnen und Gedenken im Bayerischen Viertel. Ausschreibung 1. Phase*. Berlin: Senatsverwaltung für Bau- und Wohnungswesen Berlin, 1991.

———. *Offener Kunstwettbewerb. "Kunst im Stadtraum." Mahnen und Gedenken im Bayerischen Viertel. Protokoll der Preisgerichtssitzung und Bericht der Vorprüfung*. Berlin: Senatsverwaltung für Bau- und Wohnungswesen Berlin, 1991.

———. *Offener Kunstwettbewerb. "Kunst im Stadtraum." Mahnen und Gedenken im Bayerischen Viertel. Protokoll der Preisgerichtssitzung und Bericht der Vorprüfung. 2. Phase*. Berlin: Senatsverwaltung für Bau- und Wohnungswesen Berlin, 1992.

———. *Künstlerischer Wettbewerb. Denkmal für die ermordeten Juden Europas. Kurzdokumentation*. Berlin: Senatsverwaltung für Bau- und Wohnungswesen Berlin, 1995.

Senatsverwaltung für Wissenschaft, Forschung und Kultur. *Colloquium. Denkmal für die ermordeten Juden Europas. Dokumentation*. Berlin: Senatsverwaltung für Wissenschaft, Forschung und Kultur, 1997.

Settle Marc. "'Tree of Life' Planted for Peace." *BBC*, September 21, 2009. news.bbc.co.uk/2/hi/uk_news/8263288.stm.

Singer, Hartwig. "Antwort an einen Konservativen." *Nationalismus heute. Junge Kritik, Beiheft des Studenten-Anzeigers* 1 (1970).

Sozialdemokratische Partei Deutschlands. *Frieden mit der Natur, für eine umweltverträgliche Industriegesellschaft, beschlossen auf dem Bundesparteitag, Essen.* Bonn: SPD, 1984.

———. *Irsee Draft of New SPD Manifesto.* Bonn: SPD, 1986.

Spengler, Tilman. "Der Bauch als Avantgarde—Über den aufrechten Niedergang der Theorie." *Kursbuch* 65 (1981): 179–188.

Stender, Detlef. "Vom Leben der toten Dinge: Schränke zum Kühlen als historische Quelle." In *Alltagskultur, Subjektivität und Geschichte: Zur Theorie und Praxis von Alltagsgeschichte,* edited by Berliner Geschichtswerkstatt, 157–173. Münster: Westfälisches Dampfboot, 1994.

Stih, Renata, and Frieder Schnock. *Bus Stop,* translated by Steve Sokol. Berlin: Neue Gesellschaft für bildende Kunst, 1995.

———. "Under Goethe's Cool Gaze. Controversial Holocaust Memorial: Size at What Price?" *Der Tagesspiegel,* January 19, 1995, translated by Renata Stih and Frieder Schnock.

———. *Bus Stop Fahrplan, 1. Auflage,* edited by Leonie Baumann. Berlin: NGBK, 1995.

———. *Orte des Erinnerns: Places of Remembrance in Berlin.* Berlin: Stih und Schnock, 2009.

"Stolpersteine eines Künstlers." *Kölner Stadt-Anzeiger,* January 5, 1995.

"Stolpersteine im Bayerischen Viertel. Jüdische Geschichte in Berlin—ungewöhnlich dokumentiert." *Unabhängige Jüdische Stimme* 2, no. 3 (1993): 8–9.

Stölzl, Christoph, and Rosmarie Beier-de-Haan. *Deutsches Historisches Museum: Ideen, Kontroversen, Perspektiven.* Berlin: Propyläen, 1988.

"Stopping Stones." Accessed April 10, 2021. stoppingstones.org.

Strasser, Johano. "Weiterentwicklung der Doppelstrategie." *Juso, Zeitschrift der Jungsozialisten in der SPD* 3 / 4 (1973).

Stürmer, Michael. "Geschichte in geschichtslosem Land." *Frankfurter Allgemeine Zeitung,* April 25, 1986.

Swartzberg, Terry. "Aufhebung des Verbots von Stolpersteinen in München." Accessed April 10, 2021. www.change.org/p/aufhebung-des-verbots-von-stolpersteinen-in-m%C3%BCnchen-stolpersteine-m%C3%BCnchen.

Tenfelde, Klaus. "Schwierigkeiten mit dem Alltag." *Geschichte und Gesellschaft* 10, no. 3 (January 1984): 376–394.

Thompson, E. P. *The Making of the English Working Class.* New York: Pantheon Books, 1964.

———. "E. P. Thompson: Recovering the Libertarian Tradition." *Leveller* 22 (1978): 20–22.

Torgovnick May, Kate. "One Million Bones on the National Mall, All Countable in This Gigapixel Image," TED Blog, June 27, 2013. blog.ted.com/2013/06/27/one-million-bones-on-the-national-mall-all-countable-in-this-gigapixel-image.

Trüpel, Helga. "Plädoyer für eine 'kleine' Kulturpolitik." In *Zwischen Leuchtturmprogramm und Warnblinkanlage. Bündnisgrüne Kulturpolitik auf Bundesebene. Dokumentation des kulturpolitischen Ratschlags am 8. Juli 1995 in Bonn,* edited by Bündnis 90 / Die Grünen, Bundestagsfraktion and Bernd Wagner, 9–12. Bonn: Bündnis 90 / Die Grünen, 1995.

Tufró, Manuel, and Luis Sanjurjo. "Descentralizar la memoria. Dos lógicas de intervención sobre el espacio urbano en la ciudad de Buenos Aires." *Universitas Humanística (Bogotá)* 70 (2010): 119–132.

Verein für Volkskunde. *Österreichische Zeitschrift für Volkskunde, vol. 31–33.* Vienna: Verein für Volkskunde, 1926.

Vollmer, Antje. "Die Grünen brauchen eine Kulturrevolution. Die Grünen-Bundestagsabgeordnete Antje Vollmer über die Schwierigkeiten ihrer Partei." *Der Spiegel,* March 14, 1988.

Vollmer, Antje, ed. *Politik mit Kultur.* Berlin: Bündnis 90 / Die Grünen—Bundestagsfraktion, 2005.

von Plato, Alexander. *"Der Verlierer geht nicht leer aus." Betriebsräte geben zu Protokoll.* Berlin and Bonn: Dietz, 1984.

———. "Notizen zu einer 'Geschichte von unten' in Ost und West." *Geschichtswerkstatt* 24 (1990): 23–30.

Waffenschmidt, Horst. "'Schaufenster des Staates.' Aus der Ansprache zur Eröffnung der Ausstellung 'Der Bundespräsident.'" *Das Parlament* 44 (November 1984).

Wagner, Bernd. "Kulturpolitik und Politik des Kulturellen." In *Öko-Kunst? Zur Ästhetik der Grünen,* edited by Jost Hermand and Hubert Müller, 37–54. Hamburg: Argument-Verlag, 1989.

"Wahlprogramm—Kultur." In *Zum Thema: Kulturpolitik,* edited by Hajo Cornel et al., 37–48. Berlin: Die Alternative Liste Berlin, 1985.

Warnke, Martin. "Kunst unter Verweigerungspflicht." In *Skupturenboulevard Kurfürstendamm Tauentzien, Kunst im öffentlichen Raum,* edited by Barbara Straka, 25–29. Berlin: Neuer Berliner Kunstverein, 1987.

Wehler, Hans-Ulrich. "Geschichte—von unten gesehen." *Die Zeit,* May 3, 1985.

———. "Königsweg zu neuen Ufern oder Irrgarten der Illusionen? Die westdeutsche Alltagsgeschichte: Geschichte 'von innen' und 'von unten.'" In *Geschichte von unten—Geschichte von innen: Kontroversen um die Alltagsgeschichte,* edited by Franz-Josef Brüggemeier and Jürgen Kocka, 17–47. Hagen: Fernuniversität-Gesamthochschule Hagen, 1985.

———. "Im Gespräch. Geschichte ganz unten." *Bayerische Rundfunk* 3, Fernsehprogramm, July 16, 1987.

Weißler, Sabine. "Grüne Selbstverständlichkeiten: Zum Problem grün-alternativer Kulturprogramme." *Alternative Kommunalpolitik* 3 (1984): 23–24.

———. "Vom Umgang mit Geschichte." In *Zum Thema: Kulturpolitik,* edited by Hajo Cornel et al., 13–16. Berlin: Die Alternative Liste Berlin, 1985.

Weißmann, Karlheinz. "Die konservative Option. Vorschläge für eine andere Politik." *Criticón* 113 (1989): 129–133.

———. "Politik und Metapolitik." *Sezession* 57 (2013): 38–41.

Weizsäcker, Richard von. *A Voice from Germany: Speeches by Richard von Weizsäcker,* translated by Karin von Abrams. London: Weidenfeld and Nicholson, 1985.

Welsch, Wolfgang. *Unsere postmoderne Moderne.* Weinheim: VCH, 1987.

Werneburg, Brigitte. "Armes Berlin." *taz,* June 9, 2008.

"What Is the Witness Stones Project." Accessed April 10, 2021. witnessstonesproject.org/what-is-the-witness-stones-project.

"Wie ein riesiges Gefängnis. Die Entwürfe zum Historischen Museum sind jetzt ausgestellt." *Tagesspiegel,* June 1988, Feuilleton.

Wildt, Michael. "History Workshops in Germany: A Survey at the End of the German Post-War Era," translated by Lyndal Roper. In *History Workshop: A Collectanea, 1967–1991: Documents, Memoirs, Critique and Cumulative Index to History Workshop Journal,* edited by Raphael Samuel and History Workshop Centre for Social History, 54–64. Oxford: History Workshop, 1991.

———. "Droht Deutschland ein neues 1933?" *Die Zeit,* September 8, 2018. www.zeit.de/wissen/geschichte/2018-09/chemnitz-weimarer-republik-nazizeit-vergleich-rechtsextremismus.

Willinger, Markus. *Die identitäre Generation: Eine Kriegserklärung an die 68er.* London: Arktos Media, 2013.

World Commission on Environment and Development. *Our Common Future.* Oxford: Oxford University Press, 1987.

———. *Report of the World Commission on Environment and Development: Our Common Future* (1987). http://www.un-documents.net/wced-ocf.htm.

Ziehe, Thomas, und Herbert Stubenrauch. *Plädoyer für ungewöhnliches Lernen. Ideen zur Jugendsituation.* Reinbek bei Hamburg: Rowohlt, 1982.

Zieseke, Christiane. "Dezentrale Kultur—Stiefkind etablierter Kulturpolitik." In *Zum Thema: Kulturpolitik,* edited by Hajo Cornel et al., 17–18. Berlin: Die Alternative Liste Berlin, 1985.

Zimmermann, Olaf, and Theo Geißler, eds. *Kulturpolitik der Parteien: Visionen, Programmatic, Geschichte und Differenzen.* Berlin: Deutscher Kulturrat, 2008.

Acknowledgments

This book was conceived at a moment of optimism, when the mantra "Yes, we can!" was emblazoned on bumper stickers and T-shirts and echoed across news headlines and radio stations around the United States. On January 8, 2008, then Senator Barack Obama warned us that "the battle ahead will be long. But always remember that, no matter what obstacles stand in our way, nothing can stand in the way of the power of millions of voices calling for change." And many of us believed him. To study hope in this context made sense.

But the book was born at a moment of despair, when police brutality toward Black and Brown bodies grew increasingly brazen but also when the mantra "Black Lives Matter" somehow remained deeply controversial; when a devastating pandemic claimed millions of lives around the globe but the freedom not to wear a mask took precedence over protecting one's neighbors; when climate change ravaged some of the planet's most historic, stunning, and valuable landscapes and set up populations across the world for generations of immiseration; and when reason and research were cast aside by charges of "fake news." For a good portion of this book's development, hope seemed far away.

But that's the thing about hope: any time its fire might be extinguished, someone always manages to secret away an ember. However small, it still burns, ever ready to be stoked into something brighter when we are ready to do the work of kindling. I want to take a moment to recognize all those who saw the value in a study of how we hope, who celebrated the fire of optimism, and who reliably showed up with embers when the flame seemed to have gone out.

Above all, I owe a great debt of gratitude to Martin Jay, Stefan-Ludwig Hoffmann, Tom Laqueur, and Tony Kaes, who saw this project from start to finish. They have shared guidance, wisdom, inspiration, and patience in spades. For all that, a simple "thank you" will never be sufficient, but may it be a start.

A book, like a baby, takes a village, though, so I also want to thank Peggy Anderson, John Connelly, and Carla Hesse, who offered not only steadfast support but also powerful models of intellectual creativity and leadership. At Yale, Carolyn Dean, Fabian Drixler, Sam Moyn, and Marci Shore provided invaluable feedback at various (often multiple) stages of this project. Mike Printy at Sterling Memorial Library stood ever at the ready to help hunt down hard-to-find materials. And Naomi Lamoreaux, Katie Lofton, Alan Mikhail, and Amy Hungerford seemed never to tire of finding creative ways to support my work.

I have been floored by the generosity of those beyond my own institutions who have readily lent their time, energy, and knowledge. Paul Nolte has given above and beyond. Vielen herzlichen Dank! Warm thanks are also due to Frank Bösch, Frank Biess, Ute Frevert, Astrid Eckert, Geoff Eley, Stef Geroulanos, Peter Gordon, Peter Holquist, Brian Ladd, and Joes Segal, each of whom prompted me to see, think, and imagine the various elements of this history in new and exciting ways. I also remain so appreciative of the many workshops, working groups, and colloquia that have shared their insightful critiques of this book's various chapters. Der Kreis at UC Berkeley deserves special recognition for the intellectual nest it created for this work in its fledgling phase. I also want to thank the Contemporary History Colloquium at Freie Universität; the Center for the History of Emotions Colloquium at the Max-Planck-Institut für Bildungsforschung; the Modern Europe Workshop at Princeton; the International History Workshop at Columbia; the Centre for European, Russian, and Eurasian Studies at the Munk School of Global Affairs and Public Policy at the University of Toronto; the North Carolina German Studies Seminar; the Wende Museum; the GSA's New Narratives for the History of the Federal Republic Seminar; Yale's Memory Studies Working Group; and Yale's Program in European and Russian Studies. Portions of Chapter 6 and the conclusion were first published as "National Commemoration in an Age of Transnationalism," *Journal of Modern History* 91 (March 2019): 109–148. Chapter 1 builds on ideas first discussed in this article.

The research process is just as collaborative as writing and revision. The eyewitnesses and archivists who have answered questions and shared insights have played an immeasurable role in this book's formation. Special thanks are due to Antje Vollmer; Renata Stih; Frieder Schnock; Matthias Reichelt; Sonja Miltenberger at the archive of the Berliner Geschichtswerkstatt; Martin Düspohl at the Friedrichshain-Kreuzberg Museum; Robert Camp, Anne Vechtel, and Wiebke Winkler at the Archiv Grünes Gedächtnis; and Benita Piechaczek at Neue Gesellschaft für bildende Kunst.

No book materializes without external funding. I am grateful to the DAAD; the German department and the Institute for International Studies at UC Berkeley; the Center for German and European Studies at UC Berkeley's Institute for European Studies; UC San Diego's Institute for International, Comparative and Area Studies with support from the Thyssen Foundation; Yale's Whitney Humanities Center and the MacMillan Center's Council on European Studies; the Zentrum für Holocaust-Studien at the Institut für Zeitgeschichte in Munich; the Volkswagen Foundation and Mellon Foundation; and the American Academy in Berlin, each of which have provided crucial financial support for the development of this project at various stages. The Dahlem Humanities Center at the Freie Universität and the American Academy—with its warm and devoted staff—offered wonderful homes in which to finish this manuscript.

Then there are those who laid foundations without knowing they were doing so. Alon Confino and Michael J. Smith pushed me to think capaciously, to write clearly, to ask questions that crossed disciplines and that mattered (and mattered widely). Jimmy Wright and the amazing staff of the Jefferson Scholars Foundation encouraged me to find in my own interests ways to make an impact on the world. For this support, which never stopped after I left UVA, I offer my heartiest thanks. I reserve a special place of honor for Cora Schenberg and Peter Woods, who opened up the very possibility of this project in the first place. Had I more space, I would reproduce here some of Twain's delightful reflections on "The Awful German Language," which I generally share! For now, suffice it to say I am beyond grateful you have given me access to it.

Of course, books don't publish themselves. Kathleen McDermott at Harvard University Press deserves an award for her patience, understanding, and attentiveness. Helen Wheeler and Shana Jones have been instrumental in helping me put my best prose forward. Virginia Ling diligently crafted the book's index. I also thank my anonymous readers for their stimulating criticism.

Finally, there are those who have given of themselves in such multifaceted ways that a few lines of acknowledgment can be but a drop in an ocean. Still, I only hope that Alice Goff, Tehila Sasson, Elena Kempf, Sheer Ganor, Gloria Yu, Julia Wambach, Peggy O'Donnell, Chris Church, Gene Zubovich, and Katherine Zubovich see their influences reflected in these pages. Their ideas and inspiration are all over this book, and I wouldn't have survived writing it without their friendship. For his incredible ability to still the noise and provide grounding, I owe Baddr Shakhsheer a special thanks.

Daniel Porep's warmth, love, kindness, and intellect have helped me carry this book across the finish line, have kept me grounded while doing so, and have helped me to really see its arguments in motion in a place I somehow unwittingly made into my *Wahlheimat*.

Terry Renaud's many years of brilliance, incisiveness, caring, and patience repeatedly helped me to find the "there" there when I seemed to be hurtling toward an abyss. I cannot thank him enough.

Tori and Chris have never been particularly interested in my curious little academic orbit, but they always helped to remind me what lies beyond it and what really matters in the world.

Though my mother never got to see any of this materialize, she's the one who first taught me that art can do work in the world. It is to her that I dedicate this book.

Index

Page numbers in italics refer to illustrations.